The Road Taken

A MEMOIR

Patrick Leahy

Simon & Schuster

NEW YORK LONDON TORONTO SYDNEY NEW DELHI

Simon & Schuster
1230 Avenue of the Americas
New York, NY 10020

First Simon & Schuster hardcover edition August 2022

Interior design by Ruth Lee-Mui

Manufactured in the United States of America

1 3 5 7 9 10 8 6 4 2

Library of Congress Cataloging-in-Publication Data has been applied for.

ISBN 978-1-9821-5735-7
ISBN 978-1-9821-5738-8 (ebook)

IMAGE CREDITS

Interior:

Page 7: Official U.S. Senate photo; page 141: Patrick J Leahy; page 267: Courtesy of Barack Obama Presidential Library

Insert:

1, 2, 3, 4, 5, 6, 8, 10, 11, 12, 13, 15, 16, 18, 19, 20, 21, 23, 24, 26, 27, 28, 29, 30, 31, 32, 34, 35, 36, 37, 38, 39, 40, 41, 42, 43, 44, 45: Patrick J Leahy; 7: By Werner Wolff from Black Star; 9, 14, 22: Official U.S. Senate photo; 17: AP Photo by Ira Schwarz; 25: George Bush Presidential Library and Museum; 33: AP photo by Ron Edmunds

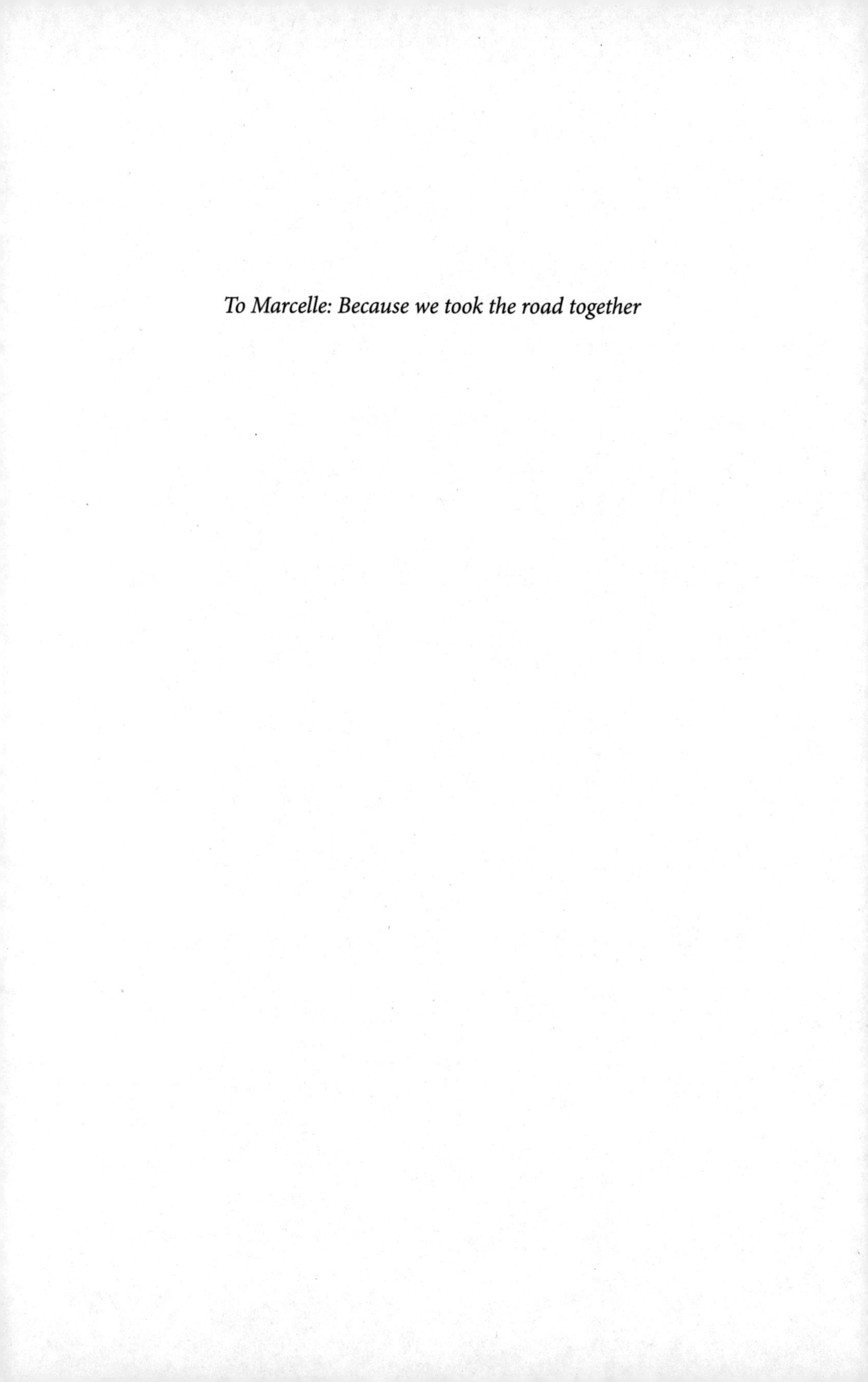

To Marcelle: Because we took the road together

CONTENTS

Introduction

In 1974, with my parents and my wife Marcelle's parents; our children, Kevin, Alicia, and Mark; and my sister, Mary, I stood in room 11 of the Vermont State House and announced my candidacy for the US Senate. I was a thirty-three-year-old four-term Chittenden County state's attorney, launching a campaign knowing that Vermont had never sent a Democrat to the US Senate.

I was running against a war in Southeast Asia that remained popular in Vermont, certainly with many editorial boards that shaped consensus. But more than any single issue, what propelled me was a belief that I understood the values of Vermont. Dublin-born parliamentarian Edmund Burke's speech to the Electors of Bristol was my North Star. I quoted him when he said, "Your representative owes you, not his industry only, but his judgment." Burke also said that a representative "ought not to sacrifice to you" his conscience.

I won, much to the shock of the political establishment in Vermont, which didn't see a thirty-three-year-old, a Catholic, or a Democrat on a fast track to the Senate. I was all three. And now I was a senator.

Within just a few months of taking office, and as the newest and most junior member of the Senate Armed Services Committee, we were asked to vote to reauthorize and continue the war in Vietnam. The authorization was defeated by one vote. I was proud to be that vote. My hope was

Vermonters would respect my judgment and my conscience, even if they disagreed with my vote to end the war. I trusted that judgment and hard work were exactly what Vermonters expect from their representatives.

The chairman of that committee was a Mississippian named John C. Stennis. He ruled the Armed Services Committee with an iron fist, and he was an ardent defender of the war under the fourth president who had allowed it to drag on. I worried whether he'd punish me for my vote of conscience. Instead, he took me under his wing: "Pat, you're not with me on this, and I'm not with you, but I do believe you did the wrong thing for the right reasons." That's the Senate and the politics that I came to love, and it became so much a part of my love of our country. The Senate where I arrived in 1974 for orientation wasn't just a collection of one hundred elected individuals—it wasn't just a "who," but a "what." That Senate was an idea—the idea that an institution doesn't belong to a single party or a single ideology, nor is it exhibited or embodied in a single issue. It was a wonderful amalgam of ideologies and accents and characters—boy, there were characters, and in this book, you'll meet them as I did, when I did, and learn from them all as I did—but more than that, the Senate was a concept, an outlook about how we might live or lead, learn or listen. It's about keeping your word. It's about caring for an institution and believing—really believing—that in the end, when institutions work, when common ground is fertile, something grows that belongs to all Americans and all of America wins.

I am not so naive as to assume that many—or even most—who pick up this book can remember a time when they looked at the Senate that way, not even remotely. I don't know that any of my recent colleagues can imagine their constituents thinking of the Senate as the nation's conscience.

But I can, and I miss those days.

I kept thinking about them as I wrote my remarks announcing my retirement. One word visited me again and again: "conscience." Thirty years ago, I visited a refugee camp. I brought my camera, as I do everywhere, so that I could show people back in Washington the human toll of an issue. Always on visits like this, I'd ask if it was okay to take someone's picture; to be a displaced person is to have endured enough without having someone invade your privacy. On this trip, a man encouraged me to take his picture. I looked at his worn and weary face through the range finder. We sat and talked afterward, and he said simply, "Don't forget people like me." The black-and-white photo has hung above my desk for thirty years since; every day I come to work, he's looking at me, saying, "You don't know my name, you don't speak my language, there's nothing I can do to help you—but what are you doing for people like me?" I refer to it as my "conscience photo." Conscience—that's what people are hungry for governments to stand for again.

This is the story not just of my political education, or even of the Senate's journey, but of America's journey—through the eyes of someone who entered public service in awe of what government can do and what the promise of America can mean, and can feel that awe still, even as it lives side by side, uncomfortably, with deep frustration.

It's the story of what I learned after I announced my candidacy for the Senate in 1974, before I returned to that very same room in the Vermont State House on November 15, 2021, and announced that I was not going to run for a ninth term in the institution that had done so much to build the America that I love.

But I promise you, this isn't a story that unfolds in one straight line downward from the pinnacle of 1975 to the hell of January 6, 2021.

Few journeys are that way in real life, because life isn't that way.

This is a story about the journey—America, its institutions, and the people, many heroic and all flawed, who make and break them—most of whom do their best, all of whom matter to this precious and fragile experiment in democracy.

I do not think all was perfect in the US Senate when I arrived as a thirty-four-year-old fresh-faced freshman Democrat. After eight years as a prosecutor, I'd like to think that I knew how to separate fact from hope, how to differentiate reality from a wish.

And there was much to question in the Senate to which I first became acquainted. Former segregationists still held powerful gavels as chairmen—in my own caucus. America was in a continuing struggle over civil rights, which had inspired me as a young college student—and yet the Senate was home to only one African American. The history books taught me that the Senate had gone from enabling segregation to joining with President Lyndon Johnson to end the era of Jim Crow, but to paraphrase Faulkner, around me I could see that the past wasn't dead. It wasn't even past. In a country where the sexual revolution and the fight for the Equal Rights Amendment marked a women's movement that would forever change the face of the United States, I joined a Senate where I would be sworn in to serve alongside ninety-nine other men.

Progress was a long way away.

But make no mistake: as a young man elected in the Watergate Class of 1974 determined to clean out the stables of Washington, I ended up finding much to preserve and protect in the world's most deliberative body—and learned from many imperfect people a code that I've tried to live by and live up to for forty-eight years since.

A Senate where members of a president's party could unite and tell him it was time to go and he had to resign. A Senate where Republicans and Democrats kept their word, valued the freedom of a six-year term, and worked—however imperfectly—toward what most of them believed was for the good of all the country.

I look back knowing that the values of the Senate—the vision of *that* Senate—have been eroded, and that the integrity and conscience the institution should stand for have been severely damaged.

The question for America is whether the damage is irreparable.

What is the answer a senator writing forty-five years from now will tell us?

I hope for my children, my grandchildren, and their children that a senator forty-five years from now can say, "*The conscience is back*."

But more than the wish, greater than the hope, it is because I know what the Senate can be that I have faith the Senate can be that way again. Why? Because it's the people, not the rules, who give the Senate its conscience.

All it takes is a determined group of Americans to make the Senate the Senate again. After forty-eight years, nine presidents, and more than four hundred Senate colleagues, most of them come and gone, certain words still ring true.

The first were the words of a folk singer and fighter who became my dear friend before we lost him far too young. Harry Chapin said simply, "When in doubt, do something."

The others were the words of Vermont poet laureate Robert Frost, which I first read in the library in Montpelier, just a boy with a library card and an imagination—words that reminded me that life is all about choices:

Two roads diverged in a wood, and I—
I took the one less traveled by,
And that has made all the difference.

To every reader and all the lives you touch: *It's up to you. Do something*—and make that *your* road taken.

Part I

Vice President Nelson Rockefeller ceremonially swearing me into office in 1975 with Marcelle, Mom, Dad, Kevin, and Alicia looking on.

— 1 —

Montpelier Mornings

"*Yessss?*" intoned a deep, disembodied, questioning voice.

I stared up at the biggest desk I'd ever seen in my four-year-old life, and soon a pair of eyes peered over its carved edge, looking down upon me behind wire-framed glasses. The tall man behind the desk had a pair of thin lips, closely cropped gray hair, and a three-piece suit that matched both his coloring and his demeanor. I was speechless. I'd just rode my tricycle straight through the open doors of this imposing figure's ornate office and, undeterred, had plowed straight ahead into the big desk.

All at once it dawned on me that I didn't belong here.

Too late.

I looked back at my friend from the neighborhood, each of us still glued to the seats of our tricycles.

One of us summoned the courage to break the awkward silence and brightly ask the question I feared we already knew the answer to: "*Are you the governor?*"

"*Yes, I am. Now get out!*"

As we turned our tricycles to make a hasty retreat, the man in the gray suit exhaled a hearty laugh. He reached into a glass jar on his desk and handed us each a piece of hard candy, a tribute to the audacity of our entrance or an inspired ploy for the votes of our parents.

His name was William H. Wills, the sixty-fifth governor of the state, from the town of Bennington, west of the Green Mountains. He'd been elected governor in 1940, the year I was born, following the landslide Senate election of Governor George Aiken, whom he'd dutifully served under as lieutenant governor.

Our brush with fear and fame was over.

We set out on our way, each push of the pedals fueled by fresh adrenaline and fading anxiety, the sound of our tires skidding along on the cold marble floors of the Vermont State House.

"*Did that really just happen?*"

It had. And it wasn't atypical. That was Montpelier in the days before metal detectors, security guards, or velvet ropes partitioned the places open to the governed from the places set aside for those who did the governing.

Late in the spring of 1944, the legislature was out on recess, and the glorious old building was virtually empty, just an expanse of marble between the small senate chamber at the east end and the governor's office on the west end, with the house chamber in the middle. Beneath the disapproving oil portraits of the ghosts of Vermont's past—pale, old Protestant men from Paine to Peck to Proctor, Chittenden to Coolidge to Crafts, Fairbanks to Fletcher—we explored an endless paradise for toddlers on tricycles.

Or at least we did until we got home, and I joined the rest of the family at our kitchen table and excitedly shared with my parents the tale of our adventure.

They did not share my enthusiasm.

There would be no more tricycle riding inside the capitol.

But there would be frequent visits there—the supervised variety.

Tucked along the Winooski River, Montpelier was the nation's smallest state capital, and that was just fine by Vermonters. The past century had transformed the capital, first when the railroad arrived and opened up markets for wool and its accompanying textiles and stone from the quarries. The factories along the river blossomed, and with them came a new demand for labor—men to power the mills, run the machinery, and haul the white stone off railway cars and into the factories, where artisans transformed it into crafts that were the envy of the nation, furnishing fireplaces and mantels from the estates of Newport to the finest residences in Manhattan.

It was in this time of transformation that the Leahys and our forebears arrived in Vermont with a willingness to work hard and a reverence for education.

My dad had no choice but to leave school at the age of thirteen when my grandfather Patrick Leahy died. But Dad was a self-taught historian who delighted in the memory of his first trip to Washington, DC, with the Knights of Columbus. A big Irish cop was hurrying the tourists through the Washington Monument. My dad was pausing to read every word etched into the marble, and the police officer was about to hurry him along when he spotted his K of C pin and asked where the group was from. "*Take as long as you need,*" the police officer said with a grin. It was the first time in my father's life that his religion moved him to the front of a line.

Dad also knew more about Vermont than most of the part-time governors who presided over the statehouse. We'd walk the halls, and Dad would point things out to us, as would a colorful, conservative Italian American legislator named Cornelius "Kio" Granai. He always went out of his way to talk with the grade-school kids and explain everything that was going on under that dome.

But the statehouse was just one improvised classroom and window onto the world. Diagonally across the street stood 136 State Street—the home Dad had bought for his mother and, later, the place my parents had started their printing business, the Leahy Press. The printing plant was connected to the back of our house.

In the early days, there wasn't a lot of extra money, and we rented out a spare room to legislators; it brought in a little income, and it gave me a chance to hear their stories.

I learned a lot in that house, some of it about politics, but even more about where we'd come from and what we valued. My mother was a first-generation Italian American born in South Ryegate, Vermont. My father's ancestors left Ireland during the potato famine for a new start, trading

Ireland's Emerald Isle for Vermont's Green Mountains. My dad was a kid when he became responsible for supporting his mother and his younger sister. He told us about the signs in Montpelier's storefront windows: NO IRISH NEED APPLY, or, if you could not understand what that meant, NO CATHOLIC NEED APPLY. Those memories were seared into him with a fierce sense of right and wrong. He made certain that my older brother, John, and I (and, when she was old enough, my younger sister, Mary) heard those stories and internalized them.

Vermont was changing. Immigration was remaking the state. But the anti-Papist Ku Klux Klan still had a presence in the state. On Sunday mornings, the Italian families in my grandparents' neighborhood gathered at their house, pulled down the shades, and celebrated Mass in a mixture of regional Italian dialects and accents from Sicilian to Friulian, proudly American, but equally inseparable from the countries and cultures they'd left behind.

Our family life and the family business were intertwined. The hum of the printing presses faintly echoed throughout the home, and the noise of our kitchen at suppertime signaled to Dad on the printing press floor that the end of the workday was approaching.

I was mesmerized by the presses, seeing the type set, learning to read upside down and backward. I developed an uncanny ability to spot typos, and because I was reading so early, I was able to get a library card for the Kellogg-Hubbard Library's Children's Room a year ahead of schedule.

Reading quickly became a passion. I was born almost entirely blind in one eye and never had the depth perception needed to play baseball or football. But I never felt like I faced a deficit. Instead, in the little library tucked in the basement of the main library, a wonderful librarian encouraged me to read. By the end of third grade, I'd read all of Charles Dickens, Robert Louis Stevenson, and Mark Twain, and the small school I went to decided I should skip ahead to the fifth grade.

Shortly after I arrived in the fifth grade, I came down with pneumonia, spending a month in the hospital and then months at home. I was terrified that I'd fall behind and be sent back to fourth grade. Under my quilt, bundled up with a barking cough, I tried to keep up with my schoolwork.

My mother picked up the assignments and brought them home. Somehow, even with the night and day operations of the family printing press and two other kids under our roof, my parents were always there. One of the worst nights of that battle against pneumonia, I woke up at three in the morning to see my mother a few feet away in the rocking chair, looking over me, her silhouette bathed in moonlight.

When I recovered, I convinced my parents to let me get a paper route, picking up my daily batch of newspapers for delivery at the *Montpelier Argus* office at 112 Main Street, and pulling my little wooden wagon through the neighborhoods. It was an afternoon paper. Thankfully, the only time I had to get up really early in the morning was when I took my turn at morning Mass as an altar boy at St. Augustine's.

One night a week, while either Mom or Dad worked late at the Leahy Press, the other would pack my brother, my sister, and me into the family car and head out to the grocery store. My sister and I would take turns as to which of us would sit in the grocery cart and pretend it was a freight train making its way down the tracks, weaving in and out of the aisles.

I always made sure to be out of the cart and on my two feet when we made it to the newspaper and magazine stands, where I could forage for the newest comic books, none more coveted than those starring the Caped Crusader himself. The luckiest nights of all were the ones when Marvel's or DC's latest issue made it into the shopping cart, and I became a voracious consumer of the Dark Knight comics, the dawn of a lifelong fandom. I'd take them home and read under the covers, flashlight in hand, a reward for sweeping the floors of the printing shop.

At home, my mother liked taking pictures with a couple of well-loved cameras still hanging around from the 1930s. I learned to use them; whether the gift for photography was genetic or not, I can't say, but I fast became a shutterbug. There was such a sense of adventure in putting a camera up to my eye and framing the view around me. Seeing my interest, my parents bought me a small Brownie and then a Hopalong Cassidy box camera with the movie hero's picture on it.

Mom clipped coupons from the Sunday paper and kept them organized in a rectangular vinyl coupon purse. She counted them out and handed them over in the grocery checkout line, and at the time I failed to process the occasional nervousness in her expression as she watched the numbers on the cash register account for each discount.

We were getting by, but my siblings and I could pick up in some of the whispered conversations at home that sometimes "*making it*" wasn't quite a given. There were lean years at the Leahy Press, our family business dependent upon the ups and downs of the overall local economy in Montpelier. There were also years when purchasing new equipment out of necessity no doubt put a dent in my parents' bank account; we were always one surprise expense away from worry.

But our parents never shared those anxieties with their children. At catechism we learned not to be greedy and not to overvalue material things. A swift strike of the yardstick or metal ruler from a strong nun put an exclamation point on those lessons. But at home we never were told that the Leahys were doing anything but living the best of the American dream in 1950s Vermont.

On the drive home from those grocery store outings, without explaining where we were going or why, Dad would often take an unspoken detour. "*Stay here, I'll be right back,*" he'd say.

The tallest of my siblings even then, I was usually in the shotgun seat, with the best view of the outside as I watched Dad—bathed in the glow of the car's headlights—button his topcoat, make his way to the trunk of the car, pull a big brown paper bag of our groceries out, and tuck it under his arm. I watched as he climbed the steps of the old tenement building—a two-decker, as they called it then—knocked on the door, and waited for someone to answer. His breath was punctuated by tiny clouds of cold air. The door slowly opened, and Dad smiled. He had a brief conversation with someone, handed over the groceries, and headed back to our car. He never explained himself or who the recipient was of our hard-earned provisions.

I stood over six feet tall before I was in high school, but because of my eye I couldn't put my height to use on the basketball court. Instead, I became the manager. Our coach and I would arrive ahead of the team at schools that we had not played before, and everyone would look me up and down, probably imagining my jump shot or my ability to occupy the paint.

They'd ask nervously, "*What position do you play?*"

"*Oh no, I'm the manager, I was too short to make the team.*" It created the requisite level of anxiety on the opposing team.

As those carefree days at St. Michael's High School wound down, I made a last-minute application to St. Michael's College. It seemed like a natural transition that after four years at one St. Michael's, I'd spend the next four years forty miles down the road at another St. Mike's.

I spent the summer before college working in South Hero, up in Grand Isle County, at a summer resort called Birchcliff, up bright and early every day, waiting tables three meals a day and bringing trays of sunset cocktails to the vacationers admiring the sailboats dotting Lake Champlain. It was a seven-days-a-week job, working primarily for tips, and you couldn't beat the view or the hours spent in the fresh air. I used some of my proceeds to buy my first "professional" camera, a Zeiss Ikon Contaflex Super B. It was a long way from Hopalong Cassidy.

The summer did come with one day off. My father picked me up and drove me back to Montpelier. On the way, he pulled onto a long dirt road. I can still hear the sound under the car's tires changing as we went from smooth asphalt to a rough and rocky road. But it was worth the diversion. We got out of the car, and Dad beamed as he showed me an old farmhouse with an unobstructed view of the mountains, no other houses in sight. It was five miles outside of Montpelier, but it might as well have been a hundred miles away: tranquil, isolated. Dad told me this would become our family's long-dreamed-of vacation spot. He couldn't have been prouder of the oasis he had struggled and saved to buy for our family.

— 2 —

The Bug

I was off to St. Michael's looking for a challenge after the ease of high school. I found a mentor in the history department. His name was Dr. Ed Pfeifer, and he was a Pied Piper. He too had grown up in Montpelier and had gone from St. Michael's Elementary School to St. Michael's High School in 1939, before he finished the hat trick, graduating from St. Michael's with a bachelor's degree in 1943 before World War II and a tour of duty aboard the destroyer USS *Albert W. Grant*. He was worldly. He'd come home from the war with a Bronze Star, a master's and PhD from Brown University thanks to the GI Bill, and an infectious love of learning. I was among several students whom he picked as protégés, thinking we had some promise, and to whom he assigned extra reading materials. He recruited us for seminars. He challenged us to think critically, test our ideas, and debate relentlessly. He made me push myself.

I was also beginning to catch the bug for politics—inspired by another Pied Piper for my generation. Massachusetts senator John F. Kennedy was running for president, and on our tiny Catholic campus, the interest level was rising. When I called home on the dormitory pay phone, I could hear both the excitement and the sense of resignation from my father, one of Montpelier's few long-suffering Democrats. He was thrilled by Kennedy, but he worried that an Irish Catholic could not win and that my friends and I would all feel devastated. A Democrat in Vermont, Dad was used to being in the minority, but this would have felt like an unusually pointed and personal rejection.

I knew from firsthand experience that Dad's anxiety was not unwarranted. In October, I volunteered to leaflet for Kennedy, and I'd head out, walking the neighborhoods, bundled up in my St. Michael's jacket. St. Michael's College was 100 percent male and 99 percent Catholic. Time and time again, after a pleasant conversation and a stranger gladly accepting my Kennedy leaflet, voters would confide in me that they did not like Nixon, but I had to understand that they could not vote for a Catholic. Here I was, standing there in the cold October air, with a very Irish name and wearing a St. Michael's jacket, and they never could've imagined that the Kennedy volunteer knocking on their door might actually be a Catholic. If I really wanted to shake them up, I could've told them that I was half Italian to boot.

A week later, I stood by the side of the road in Montpelier after visiting my parents, my thumb in the air, hoping to hitch a ride down Route 2 to either Burlington or Winooski, whichever way a generous driver was heading. A beautiful green Jaguar coupe pulled over, rolled down the window, and offered me a ride. Minutes later, the driver turned on the radio and tuned it to the evening's main attraction: the first Kennedy-Nixon debate. He asked me if I had a problem with that. Nervous to show my true colors and endure an hour-long lecture from a Yankee Republican, I thought it better to let him volunteer some sign of his political preferences.

Thankfully, it turned out he was actually a Kennedy supporter.

The two of us became more and more depressed as we drove along in the darkness, listening intently to the radio. Nixon was winning handily, it seemed. "*Well, at least there's another debate next week,*" the driver said with a sigh.

I climbed the stairs of my dorm dejected and ran into friends who also supported Kennedy. Surprisingly, they were jubilant.

"*Well, I just heard the entire debate, and Kennedy got his hat handed to him,*" I said, puzzled.

They replied without hesitation, "*No, they are going to show excerpts of it on the eleven o'clock news—you just watch.*"

I stayed up glued to the black-and-white television in the student recreation center. The difference between what I'd heard on the crackling car radio and what so many people had seen on television was astounding.

Nixon had lost too much weight. His loose suit seemed to devour him. There was something odd about his caked-on makeup barely covering a dark five o'clock shadow, and he perspired heavily.

The very tan, very young, very confident Kennedy stuck to his rote talking points but delivered them eloquently. He was cool, comfortable, and clear. He spoke directly to the camera, and though he might not have won the back-and-forth to the ears of two of his cheerleaders in a sports car on Route 2, he carried the night with the American people.

Kennedy finished the home stretch of the campaign on a seventeen-state barnstorm tour that must've been both exhausting and backbreaking for a candidate hobbled not just by a wartime injury but by a severe case of Addison's disease, hidden from the public. While Nixon headed to Hawaii and Alaska to keep with a gimmicky campaign pledge to visit all fifty states, Kennedy finished up his grueling pace, coming home to largely friendly turf in New England and visiting Vermont on November 7. He would then zip off to New Hampshire, Rhode Island, Maine, and a final rally at the Boston Garden, before he'd retire to Hyannis Port to await the results with his family.

Late afternoon on the seventh, I was packed into the big crowd at Burlington Airport, watching as Senator Kennedy's plane—the *Caroline*, named after his three-year-old daughter—touched down for a rally. We were ecstatic to see him. After losing two national elections in landslides to Eisenhower, the prospect of a Kennedy victory seemed tantalizingly within reach. For a candidate on the brink of completing an electoral marathon, Kennedy didn't give any hint of his fatigue. He gave a funny, rousing speech, standing behind the WJOY microphone, and shook hands and smiled for the flashbulbs, before he climbed the stairs of the airplane and gave a final wave, and just like that, he was off to Manchester, New Hampshire, where his campaign had effectively begun.

The next night, we all stayed up watching the returns, all of us packed in, encircling the same black-and-white television set. We booed when we learned before 11:00 that night that once again the Republicans had carried Vermont. But we cheered ecstatically as Walter Cronkite updated the vote tallies for Illinois. By the morning, it was clear John F. Kennedy was going to be the thirty-fifth president of the United States, no matter how Vermont had voted.

I was enthralled. When I was growing up, politics had been something that interested me. My father's devotion to Roosevelt was an early spark, and because Dad was the sacrificial Democrat bobbing above the waves in a sea of Republicans, perhaps I'd forged an early sense of identity about politics. When you're the outlier, you have to be comfortable defending your beliefs. It would've been easier, after all, to simply go with the crowd. Many of my early political values were shaped as well by life lived around me.

The Depression had hit Vermont hard. Mills and factories had been shuttered until they were repurposed for the war effort and reindustrialization. Those stories were still fresh in my parents' minds. Neighbors had gone hungry, and some still struggled. There were still "poorhouses" around the area, remnants of a period before the New Deal social safety net was created to ensure that people like my grandparents—men who had worked decades in factories until the arthritis or the back pain overcame them, widows of hardworking people like my grandfather, whose fighting heart struggled to keep up with his failing lungs impaired by the stone dust—wouldn't live out their final years in poverty. The idea that government could make such a difference wasn't theoretical. It was real.

Kennedy's campaign brought the history into the present for a young man just starting out. Kennedy was exciting—eloquent, breaking the mold of the older, grayer politicisms I'd grown up with in Vermont. He looked different. He even sounded different. He talked about doing things with "vigor"—pronounced *vigga*. At his inauguration, it was a Vermonter, Robert Frost, who that same year would become our state's first poet laureate, who rose, headed to the lectern, battled the sun, and recited "The Gift Outright" from memory, unable to read the poem he'd written for the occasion because of the blinding glare off the snow and the Capitol.

The words captured the sense of possibility of the Kennedy administration and his New Frontier:

To the land vaguely realizing westward,
But still unstoried, artless, unenhanced,
Such as she was, such as she would become.

I'd never felt so connected to an event in Washington as I did at that moment. But most of all, he had excited me and my friends with a call to make politics and public service bigger and bolder. It felt at once grand and intimate. And it didn't hurt that he too was an Irish Catholic.

Finally, a barrier had fallen in American politics—and with it, I'd officially caught the political bug myself.

— 3 —

The Spark

I was nineteen, the summer just after my sophomore year, and I leapt at an opportunity to improve my standing at school. My parents were attending a party at a summer camp belonging to a French-Canadian American family, the Pomerleaus. I heard Dr. Robert Spencer, head of the political science department, would be there, so I tagged along, hoping for a few minutes alone with the professor.

I didn't know the Pomerleau family well, but I knew that two of their three children would be there, one named René and one named Marcelle, a son and a daughter.

Judging by their names alone, I didn't even know which was the brother and which was the sister.

But when I arrived and took one look at Marcelle, the question was answered.

And with it, soon were answered most of the other questions in life.

I didn't say a word to Dr. Spencer that afternoon.

I was too busy flirting like mad with Marcelle.

She conveniently ignored me.

I heard her talking to her parents in French, but I could discern only every few words. Little did I know she had relayed complimentary impressions about the Leahy son she had met that night.

A week later, we had our first date. She was a nursing student and passionate about helping people. Marcelle asked me what I wanted to be when I was all grown up.

"Governor," I replied.

At nineteen, it seemed like the greatest job in the world, to serve in Montpelier in that statehouse I'd spent so much time in as a mischievous little boy. Imagine the idea of a *Leahy*—the grandson of immigrants—there among the oil portraits of the stodgy Brighams and Eatons and Holbrooks.

"Well, that's . . . *interesting*," Marcelle replied.

I think what she meant was closer to "Well, that's . . . *crazy*."

But sure enough, by that winter when she turned eighteen, we were already talking about getting married. Through my junior and senior year, we dated. I would hitchhike into Burlington from St. Michael's, and we would study together at the University of Vermont's library, because the student nurses were allowed to stay out late as long as they were studying. We were inseparable.

While I had won Marcelle's heart and, soon, I hoped, her hand in marriage, back on campus at St. Mike's, I wasn't faring as well on a different field of competition.

I'd joined the rifle team in high school, because I needed only one good eye for that, and I was rewarded with a small scholarship by being on the rifle team in college. I earned my letter and ended up outshooting most of the ROTC teams around the country. I hoped for an ROTC commission to go on to graduate school, but the recruiters rejected me because I was blind in one eye. It was infuriating. I challenged them to bring in their dozen best shooters anywhere in the military, and if I couldn't outshoot ten of them, and even all twelve of them, then they could turn me down.

They laughed and told me I was wasting their time.

I'd have to save my best shots for the courtroom.

That's where I knew I was headed: law school was where I had to go next, and that meant leaving Vermont.

One winter break at home in Montpelier, I shared the news with my parents. I look back now and wonder just how the news sunk in for both of them. I know they hoped that I would carry on the Leahy Press, and it would have been mine if I had wanted it. But they also had always, always backed me in all the things I wanted to do, and they encouraged me again. They were the kind of parents who always put their kids' dreams first.

I thought about going to Harvard, but I had visited Washington, DC, with my parents at the end of my sophomore year of college, and I loved it: the cherry blossoms in full bloom, the power of the imposing monuments along the National Mall, the buzz inside the Capitol Building.

I applied to Georgetown Law School and was accepted.

A classmate and I drove down there together, arriving around midnight. The law school at that time was in an old building, with a few dilapidated town houses next to it. I had rented a room in one of the town houses.

In the light of the streetlamps, I could see dozens of animals darting across the road. I had never seen this kind of wildlife in Vermont.

I found out they were rats.

We rang the buzzer outside until it awoke an annoyed student proctor who grudgingly let me into my new room. I stared at the cinder block walls, the pockmarked, dingy ceiling, and the mold stain on the thin mattress sitting atop an old wooden bed frame.

As I lay in bed, willing myself not to think too hard about the generations of germs that lay just beneath the thinnest bedsheet I'd ever seen, I thought that maybe in the morning I would call the other schools where I'd been accepted and find out if it wasn't too late to revive an acceptance.

I awoke to a beautiful early fall day and a bright blue sky. I walked all the way down the Mall to the Lincoln Memorial and back, looking up at the Capitol Building resplendent in the sunlight, and thought, *This is the only place I want to be.*

The only missing ingredient was Marcelle. She was finishing nursing school in Vermont—as she reminded me, one of us had to have an employable talent—and I dreaded the separation. When she was completing part of her training at Vermont State Hospital in Waterbury, I plotted a big surprise. That February, I drove home with my classmate in his old Volkswagen with a failing heater. Marcelle had the weekend off. We were able to be together at my parents' home. Then my classmate and I dropped her off in Waterbury and drove all night long to get back to Washington. The warmth of being with her was worth freezing in the car.

Surprisingly enough, later during the winter Marcelle's parents gave her permission to come to Washington for three days to visit. We went to the Uptown Theater in Cleveland Park and saw the movie *Breakfast at Tiffany's*. Henry Mancini's "Moon River" became our song from that moment forward.

We didn't want to be apart any longer than necessary. After Marcelle graduated, we were married.

We had a short honeymoon in Canada, taking a riverboat up the St. Lawrence and back, followed by a few days at the farm, where the Leahy Press had printed up signs that read MARCELLE'S ROOM, another that read PATRICK'S ROOM, and still others tacked to the doors between them announcing NO HUNTING OR TRESPASSING.

Waiting for us in Washington was a basement apartment I'd never seen—my classmates helped pick it out—which was furnished only with the mattress and box spring my parents had given us as a wedding present, delivered before we headed south. Marcelle and I rented a car and a trailer, emptied our parents' attics of old furniture, and headed down to start our new lives in our eighty-dollar-a-month one-bedroom English basement. We made the long drive down, arriving in the middle of the night and parking illegally around the corner since we were so exhausted.

The next morning, I woke up early to move the car, only to come face-to-face with a police officer halfway into the act of writing out a parking ticket. I talked with him and explained the circumstances, and he took pity on the young newlyweds from Vermont.

Marcelle worked at the Mount Alto VA Hospital, a rickety firetrap. It was a little over a mile from our apartment, and because we didn't have a car, I would meet her at one o'clock in the morning after a late-night shift or accompany her to work at midnight so she wouldn't have to walk alone.

We didn't have much, but we were happy, and soon we had a baby on the way. The sleep deprivation of life with a newborn in a tiny apartment was a wake-up call even to a law student seasoned in all-nighters. But adrenaline and coffee are powerful forces that kept me going through that final year of law school.

— 4 —

The Court

Georgetown Law Center meant incredible exposure to the people making history all around us in the nation's capital—constant reminders that the law was a living thing, designed, passed, implemented, and interpreted by real people.

Always a printer's son, I noticed immediately the heavy card stock and the raised calligraphy of the fancy stationery. It differentiated the piece of mail sticking out of the mail slot in our apartment door from the utility bills and advertising bulletins of everyday life.

The card inside invited Mr. Patrick J. Leahy to RSVP for a luncheon honoring the area's top performing law students—with the justices of the Supreme Court of the United States.

I'd visited to watch oral arguments in the court many times, occasionally indulging my imagination, picturing my much older self on the hot seat defending Vermont's position in front of the nine justices of the Warren court.

But never before had I thought of the justices as people I might meet or talk to up close and personal, rather than in the distance of oral arguments by osmosis.

I said to Marcelle, "We're going together."

Surely no one would think that our partners in life shouldn't be able to join us to attend one of the few festive, even elegant occasions interrupting what we all jokingly described as "*law school poverty*."

The luncheon was held not far from school. It was one of those impossibly perfect spring days in the nation's capital, the cherry blossoms, flowering shrubs, and daffodils by the Senate and the Supreme Court all in full bloom. The Washington weather had not yet turned from the warmth of spring to the sauna of summer, and the seasonal downpours had abated, for now.

As we walked in, it became evident that Marcelle and I were the only couple in the room, and she the only woman.

The gathering felt, to use a phrase popular at the time to describe too many of Washington's institutions, overwhelmingly "*Yale, pale, and male.*"

Chief Justice Earl Warren circulated, shaking hands, offering congratulations and brief introductions, evincing the glad-handing skills he'd acquired as governor of California. Nine round tables sitting twelve each were arranged throughout the room, and we picked up our table assignments at the reception table. One justice would be assigned to each table.

Marcelle and I sat down, met our student tablemates, and eagerly awaited a justice to join our table.

The nine men together were familiar to all of us from television. In addition to Warren, there was President Kennedy's recent pick and the 1937 Heisman Trophy runner-up Byron "Whizzer" White, along with the court's other New Frontiersman, Arthur Goldberg. Ike's second, third, fourth, and fifth justices entered: John Marshall Harlan II of Illinois, William Brennan of New Jersey, Charles Whittaker of Kansas, and Potter Stewart of Michigan. They were soon followed by President Truman's lone appointee, Tom Clark, and the one justice appointed during the FDR years and the oldest, seventy-seven-year-old Hugo Black. It was disorienting at first to see the justices not in their customary long black robes, but in gray and navy business suits, like seeing Babe Ruth or Ted Williams in street clothes rather than the uniforms inseparable from their public personas.

Black made his way slowly to our table, we all stood up to greet him, and he sat down creakily, feeling every mile of a journey that had taken him from Clay County, Alabama, to the Eighty-First Field Artillery during World War I to the US Senate, where he'd become a champion of the New Deal—and an ardent opponent of civil rights legislation.

I'd read a fair amount about Black before this first meeting.

I knew that he was the court's leading "textualist," a believer that within the confines of the articles and amendments inscribed in the Constitution there was room for interpretation, but that grand thoughts not written down on that primary parchment were not the purview of the federal judiciary.

I knew also that he had authored the court's tragic decision in *Korematsu v. United States*, upholding the internment of Japanese Americans during World War II.

But most of all, I was troubled by his abhorrent Senate record on the defining issue of our times: civil rights. Black had been an unabashed Senate segregationist and opponent of antilynching legislation. Depending on which accounts you believed, he was either an opportunistic former member of the Ku Klux Klan who had joined that shadowy hate group out of pragmatism, not zeal—seeking an opportunity to climb the political ranks of the Deep South—or a true believer who had delivered not just segregationist but full-throated anti-Catholic messages throughout his Senate campaigns. When his past affiliation with the Klan became public after his Senate confirmation, the blowback had been so strong that Black—rather than retreat into the confines of the court's apolitical chambers—had been forced to deliver an unprecedented national radio address defending his objectivity and separating himself from his past. President Roosevelt claimed the information was a revelation; Roosevelt had sought both regional representation for the South and a New Deal defender on a stodgy, conservative court. Interestingly, at this moment of controversy, Black's cause was publicly championed by the secretary of the NAACP, an old friend of his from Alabama.

I wasn't sure what to make of the justice, but I was interested to hear how his journey had led him to concur in the Warren court's unanimous ruling in *Brown v. Board of Education*.

I wasn't alone. As he picked at his salad, the courtly jurist asked the students to go around the table and summarize our biographies and raise any questions. All the students wanted to hear the inside story of the Warren court, which had ignited great social change and backlash for its rulings on civil rights. I wondered for a moment whether we'd all been on the wrong side of the luck of the draw, with the most liberal judges seated elsewhere.

But Hugo Black didn't disappoint. He described not a philosophy or a grand view of history, but an insight into how the court could work as an institution when the country needed it most.

Black explained that on the Vinson court, which had been resistant to sweeping changes on civil rights, he'd consistently sided with the majority, which believed that long-standing precedent needn't be overturned in this arena. Black had been a proponent of states' rights his entire career and didn't believe it was the job of the court to dictate for the states matters of right and wrong. But Black revealed that when President Eisenhower installed Earl Warren as chief justice, Warren sought out Black's counsel and confided in him that he believed the court could no longer avoid wrestling with the issues of discrimination in essential areas like housing and education.

Black signaled to Warren that *there was* a way to address those issues consistent with textualism, but it depended upon the specific cases the court might choose to hear and in the rationale for their deliberations. Black pointed to the Fourteenth Amendment.

It was the first of many quiet, private consultations he'd have with the new chief justice. Together, they came to the conclusion that the court couldn't dictate how states or individuals perceived the races, and that state and local legislative bodies had responsibility for issues like school funding. However, the Constitution's promise of "equal protection" under the law meant, in practice, that the standard of "separate but equal" set forth in the 1896 decision in *Plessy v. Ferguson* was an impossibility in the area of education. The California Republican and the longtime southern segregationist commiserated behind closed doors, and Warren deployed his tacit partnership with Black as a way to help move the entire court toward a landmark decision.

What Black said next stayed with me every day forward: on the eve of the court's ruling, the chief justice gathered all the justices together and made a final plea. The last months of consultation had all built toward this one moment: whatever they thought as individuals about the strength of any one legal argument, let alone the merits of civil rights, there were some constitutional questions on which the country needed to hear the court speak with one voice. "*We've been to war over this before,*" confided Warren, who had no illusions about the rancor the ruling would reveal in the country. He invoked the dangerous message a split decision would risk sending and argued the country, let alone the court, could ill afford it. The nine justices agreed.

The students were silent as we listened to Black. I could hear his fork scrape the china, his wrinkled pale hands trembling ever so slightly. We came from very different parts of the country, were raised on very different beliefs about freedom and equality. I wondered still whether his defense of his views on race—that he "*counted many friends who were Black*"—echoed a bit of the comments we Catholics had heard growing up in Montpelier among the Protestant aristocracy, a self-conscious and even condescending defense. But maybe that made the unanimity of *Brown v. Board of Education* all the more remarkable: a card-carrying Klansman had helped deal a staggering blow to Jim Crow.

But the bigger lesson sunk in: there were issues too big to be decided 5–4, and it was a skilled kind of politics—not purely law, not merely philosophy, but the practice of personal politics that had made the difference in how the court got where the country needed to arrive: 9–0. A great legal mind was to be respected; the ability to forge legal precepts into consensus was to be treasured.

Dessert was served, and then coffee.

Marcelle and I said goodbye and made our way up Constitution Avenue and could see the Supreme Court in the distance. It now seemed different, and more alive, than it had in my favorite class, Constitutional Law.

It wasn't an ivory tower or judicial monastery divorced from the rhythms and realities of the country. I thought for the first time that the figurative distance between the court and the adjacent Senate wasn't as far as it seemed: both were places where the art of politics was practiced, by imperfect people, and much hung in the balance.

— 5 —

Shattered Innocence

I kept in mind the practicality of Justice Black's anecdotes as I thought about what it might mean to one day practice law myself. I loved studying the law, jousting with my instructors, wrapping myself around the legal arguments frontward and backward, but I had a new appreciation for the fact that, ultimately, human nature was both a variable and a catalyst in the outcomes.

I was starting to think more and more about being a kind of public service lawyer, whether a public defender or, ultimately, as someone somewhere in government who might bridge those divides between theory and implementation.

Naturally, then, I was thrilled when one of those "pinch me" moments landed on my desk. I'd done well at Georgetown, and in the nation's capital, where the work of government was the chief industry, there were opportunities to see inside the machinery that I couldn't have imagined anywhere else. I was fascinated by the young—literally and figuratively—Kennedy administration, especially by the attorney general, who happened to be the president's younger brother. If President Kennedy seemed perfect in every way, each hair carefully in place and well over six feet tall, his younger brother Robert was comparably more relatable. He was short and wiry, hair askew, sleeves always rolled up, suits bought off the rack. He wasn't naturally eloquent. At times he seemed nervous. I'd watch him on *Meet the Press*, and if you peered closely, you could see a spot of perhaps baby formula on his lapel, the remnants of a morning routine in a household blessed with nine children and counting.

Imagine then my excitement when Attorney General Robert Kennedy invited a handful of law students from up and down the East Coast to come in and meet with him. We were all near the top of our classes, and he was recruiting the next generation to join the Department of Justice. His paneled office was dotted with crayon drawings authored by the brood of children he and Ethel were raising at Hickory Hill, a few miles away in McLean, Virginia. He was even smaller in person than I remembered him from television, wiry and compact. His enormous black dog, Brumus, a Newfoundland, lay near the fireplace, not bothering to raise its giant head as we paraded in and took our seats. He gave crisp and thoughtful answers to our questions. I had to tell him that Marcelle and I were so homesick that we wanted to get home, even as we respected the youth movement he'd brought to the department. He said that he knew Vermont well from skiing, that he could understand why I'd miss it.

I wondered whether our paths would ever cross again.

Less than a year later, I was standing in the Georgetown Law School library when someone came up to me and said something about the president having been shot. I thought he was laughing or giggling uncontrollably. I looked at him in confusion and disapproval.

"*That's not funny, that's not something you joke about—*" and at that moment I caught myself.

He wasn't laughing. He was trying to control his sobs even though he was a staunch Republican.

President Kennedy had been shot.

I ran outside and headed for the apartment.

On the way, I stopped at a pay phone to call Marcelle at the hospital, but then remembered she was home for the day. Marcelle's shift wasn't due to begin until the evening. I had to get home. I didn't wait for the D2 bus. I flagged a cab and headed northwest.

I saw the First Lady's stepfather, Hugh Auchincloss, trying desperately to hail a cab in the middle of Wisconsin Avenue. None were stopping. Usually, I'd see him being dropped off by his chauffeur in the morning.

It felt as if the world were at war.

The chaos. The pandemonium. I could see the projections of the market at the stockbroker's office. The tickers were dark. The stock market had suddenly been closed for the day.

The president was dead.

I got home, and Marcelle and I just stood together in the doorway holding each other, then sat on the couch and watched the television silently until I walked her to the hospital for the night shift. The walk back to our apartment felt lonelier than ever.

Days later, with the entire country shut down for a national day of mourning, Marcelle and I were frozen as we stood on the sidewalk, watching the president's funeral procession blocks from the White House. The only sounds for minutes on end were quiet weeping, fighter jets overhead, and the intermittent *click-click-click* of the automatic stoplights above, their metallic snap shifting from green to yellow to red, still doing their mechanical duty even with the avenue completely shut to traffic.

We watched the sad procession behind the casket, led by the riderless horse Black Jack from the Third US Infantry Regiment, President Kennedy's boots facing backward in the stirrups. The enormous, majestic animal had been part of more than one thousand military funerals, but never one quite like this.

The delegation made its way from the White House to the Capitol, where the fallen president would lie in state.

Back at our apartment in Glover Park, the next day Marcelle and I remained glued to the television, watching the funeral Mass at St. Matthew's Cathedral on Rhode Island Avenue and the sad final journey as the hearse brought the president's remains to Arlington National Cemetery.

We heard a powerful sound coming from overhead, and we felt the vibrations. We ran outside. In the gray November sky, Air Force One flew in a missing man formation over Georgetown, dipping its wing in salute over Arlington Cemetery—one final tribute from the crew that had brought the president home on that last, terrible flight from Texas.

We held on to each other and cried such heavy tears. I had admired President Kennedy so much: the barriers he'd broken, the romanticism of his story from hero of PT-109 to the White House in record time, the optimism of those years from the Peace Corps to the New Frontier. Even the language of his inaugural address had been about daring to do big things, with an optimism that yes, we could do big things, that the United States was on the brink of a newly revitalized era. I realized at this moment just how much those idealistic dreams had been shattered in Dallas, Texas. The volatile world was not on the brink of bending toward charisma and vision.

As I finished law school, I faced some decisions about my own future.

I was offered a Prettyman Fellowship, which in today's money would have paid over $100,000 toward a master's degree in criminal law, but we were homesick for Vermont, and I didn't see my future as a prosecutor anyway.

— 6 —

On the Job

I couldn't wait to practice law.

I also didn't have time to waste: we couldn't afford the rent for another month in the apartment. As soon as I finished my last exam, we packed up a rented car, squeezed our son in his baby bassinette behind us, and headed back to Vermont so I could start a six-month, sixty-five-dollars-a-week clerkship before taking the bar exam and, God willing, being admitted to practice.

We had an apartment in a third-floor walk-up in Burlington. Finally, there was a lot of room, and soon enough I was accredited as a full-fledged attorney. I thrived on the courtroom work, working a six- or seven-day week, and my courtroom performances—detail-oriented, careful, polite, prepared, and precise—got me noticed. Whether the case was mundane or complicated, I wanted to make a good impression. I would sit at the dining room table preparing my presentations and polish them in the morning while shaving in front of a steamed-up mirror.

But soon, without warning, a game of musical chairs changed my career trajectory overnight. A scandal forced two of the state's judges from the bench. The state's attorney announced he was returning to his law firm. One of his partners had been appointed by Governor Philip Hoff to fill the vacancy of one of the judges forced off the bench.

The governor called me to his home in Burlington on Friday. I'd seen him at the law office before but never had a real conversation before that evening. He was the first Democrat elected governor since 1853, a liberal crusader of the Kennedy generation with a big shock of blond hair to match. He was worried. The state's attorney's office had a huge backlog of cases that had not been tried and countless appeals that had not been argued, and he did not want a fiasco in the office while he was on the ballot for reelection that fall.

He was forty-one years old, one of the youngest governors in the nation, so maybe it didn't seem so surreal to him that he was about to make an audacious offer to a young man barely two years out of law school. He told me he wanted me to take over as state's attorney for Chittenden County on Monday.

"Just clean the whole mess up. Once I get past my election, if you want to come back, we'll make you a partner in our law firm, because I've heard how successful you've been in trying cases. Now go home this weekend and reread all of your criminal law books."

I did, remembering that Prettyman Fellowship I'd turned down.

I had been thrown into the deepest of deep ends, and I loved it. In no time, I was trying felony cases, including armed robbery and murder cases, running a one-man office.

I was on trial myself, in a way, but the pressure I put on myself didn't come from the outside. It wasn't that I had a chip on my shoulder. Quite the opposite. I felt I had an extraordinary inheritance, really: my father, the smartest man I'd known, would've given anything for the formal education I'd gained and the chance to prove myself in court at such a young age. There simply wasn't a chance that I wouldn't jump in with both feet. I was young and energy seemed renewable, sometimes with the help of a pot of black coffee or a plate of chocolate chip cookies, but one way or another I was going to test my endurance.

I tried cases during the day, hustled home to have dinner with the children, and then drove from Burlington to Montpelier. A friend of my parents was the state librarian, and he kindly loaned me a key to the state library so I could come in after hours and do my research. After a catnap at my parents' house, I would go there and write the briefs for my cases in the Vermont Supreme Court until about one or two o'clock in the morning. Then I would drive back to Burlington for a few hours' sleep, have breakfast with the family, try cases, have supper with the children, drive back to Montpelier, and repeat that cycle again and again over the next six months.

I ended up trying more cases than any law firm in the state, both at the trial court and at the Vermont Supreme Court, and was on call twenty-four hours a day. I was pushing myself hard. Opportunities—serendipitous ones—like this didn't come around often. I felt an obligation to make the most of the moment. I became an officer in the National District Attorneys Association, and I was soon in line to become president, called upon to help other prosecutors in other states.

At four o'clock in the morning one summer day, I was driving to Boston from Burlington, traversing an empty, lonely road beneath a big sky full of stars. The radio was blasting to keep me awake, and I was navigating through the static for anything that might come in clearly. In one of those acts of sky wave propagation common in Vermont in the summer months, a so-called atmospheric skip, a station broadcasting nine hundred miles away from Chicago came in crystal clear. The song filling my car and bringing tears to my eyes was Harry Chapin's "Cat's in the Cradle."

The words landed with a powerful resonance:

We'll get together then,
You know we'll have a good time then.

I thought of the children back home.

The demands of my office were stealing so many hours in the day, so much energy. I appreciated the time I could be with our kids.

I was supposed to spend the night after events and dinner in Boston, but I canceled the hotel room, drove back to Burlington, got home at two o'clock in the morning, and was there to wake up in my own bed and have breakfast with the children and take them to school. I noticed that while the children were surprised that I was home, since they'd expected me to be away, they weren't *too* surprised that I was there for early-morning Dad duty—and that was a very good thing.

It became the ritual with Marcelle and me: every single moment I could spend with the family was spent there, and I've never regretted the time.

As Chittenden County state's attorney, I did not get actively involved in politics, but 1968 was a year in which no one of conscience could sit on the sidelines. After Gene McCarthy stunned Lyndon Johnson in neighboring New Hampshire's presidential primary, and after the Tet Offensive, the debate over the war and the direction of the Democratic Party became personal. Governor Hoff backed Robert Kennedy for president, and I joined him. Hubert Humphrey had the backing of organized labor in our state, and I heard from many of the party leaders that whatever future I'd had in state politics had just gone out the window. To think, they said, I could've made it all the way to the Vermont Legislature, probably even become attorney general of the state, but now I was cooked, put out to political pasture at the ripe old age of twenty-eight.

But I believed in Kennedy. I'd met him. I believed he was genuine about the direction of the country. I also believed that Kennedy was the only person with a prayer of putting the country back together at a moment when we were so divided.

1968 was hard. There were riots in American cities. Tensions over civil rights were high. Martin Luther King Jr. was assassinated in Memphis, Tennessee. President Johnson had gotten off to a strong start domestically, passing Medicare and social spending, leveraging the collective grief over the Kennedy assassination to finally pass civil rights and voting rights legislation. But the war in Vietnam was devouring his presidency.

Forty thousand Americans were dead in the war, and escalation had been followed by escalation with no end in sight. Peace talks in Paris seemed bogged down. Vice President Humphrey, like it or not, was bound to Johnson's legacy on the war. Robert Kennedy, it seemed, was the one person left in public life with moral authority who could bring the country back together again, who could speak not just to those who opposed the war and to the college campuses, but to the working-class labor households, the struggling families, many of them Catholics who had believed in his brother's presidency. Kennedy had a gift for connecting with their aspirations too, even as he opposed a war in which so many of their sons were fighting and dying. He spoke equally passionately about civil rights as he did the importance of the rule of law and of order. I thought he just might be capable of stopping the return of the surly and cynical Republican his brother had vanquished in 1960, the newly reanointed once and future Republican nominee Richard Nixon.

On June 4, Marcelle and I stayed up late to hear the news that Kennedy had clinched the California primary and seemed to be on his way to the Democratic nomination. We went to bed smiling.

At three in the morning, I woke from a deep sleep to the sound of the special phone the state police had installed in our house, one we jokingly called the "bat phone." It was there for emergencies, which weren't uncommon; when the state police needed me at night, they'd reach out. I immediately recognized the voice of the state police dispatcher, but something was different this time.

"*They killed him! They killed him!*"

I was still groggy. "*Killed who?*"

"*Senator Kennedy!*"

"*What? Which one?*"

I was confused. There were two. Ted Kennedy was the senator from Massachusetts, and Robert Kennedy we'd just seen shaking hands in California.

She answered, "*Robert Kennedy.*"

I walked into our bedroom and told Marcelle. We turned on the television.

We never got back to sleep.

At breakfast, I was still in shock. I told Marcelle that I'd never be involved in politics again.

The next day, a letter arrived in the mail. It was marked KENNEDY CAMPAIGN HEADQUARTERS.

Inside was a thank-you note from Robert Kennedy, probably signed the last day he was alive in California. I imagined him going through mountains of paperwork to pass the time while waiting for the votes to come in, signing thank-you notes for volunteers in key states. Governor Hoff had told him about all the work I had been doing in Vermont, and the letter kindly asked if I would go talk to prosecutors in other states on his behalf.

I just sat there in silence.

That day I forgot my promise not to be involved in politics.

— 7 —

The County

In the meantime, the work of a state's attorney was not without its surprises.

One day, a complaint came into the office. An older woman was quite exercised about obscene crimes being committed, right in the heart of our state: young people—"hippies," she called them—were skinny-dipping near her house.

She *just knew*, and she wanted it *stopped.*

There was no protocol for such a situation that seemed at once to test New England's puritanical roots and Vermont's "live and let live" ethos.

I issued a memorandum to all law enforcement. I felt like Moses coming down from the mountaintop, so weighty was this pronouncement. The memo follows.

TO: ALL POLICE DEPARTMENTS
FROM: CHITTENDEN COUNTY STATE'S ATTORNEY, PATRICK J. LEAHY (BURLINGTON)
RE: UNCLOTHED PUBLIC OR SEMI-PUBLIC BATHING
DATE: JULY 7, 1971

A number of law-enforcement agencies have asked this office for advice in view of the revival of the time-honored practice of unclothed swimming known colloquially as "skinny-dipping." I was originally disinclined to slow the crime-fighting operation of the Chittenden County State's Attorney's Office long enough to issue a memorandum of such minuscule moment.

However, I have been reminded that in the past the plethora of Paper from this office has included such legal landmarks as my position on the use of sparklers on the Fourth of July (a position hedged with great patriotic fervor) and the validity of upside-down license plates (complete with instructions on how to determine the sobriety of the operator at the time he attached the plate).

With such powerful precedents in mind, I ensconced myself at my family's tree farm near Montpelier during the Fourth of July Weekend and researched the issue. I began by reviewing the old Norman Rockwell paintings, thoughtfully resurrected by the ACLU, showing such activities taking place allegedly in Vermont (along this line I was unable either to confirm or refute the persistent rumor that Vermont's number one politician, Calvin Coolidge, had also engaged in such activity within the borders of this State while subject to Vermont's laws).

I have also discussed—after grants of immunity—experiences of this nature enjoyed by some of Vermont's prosecutors, judges, law-enforcement officers and sailboat operators. After checking the Statute of Limitations, I have even reviewed past histories with some of my contemporaries during my teenage years in Montpelier. Also, each member of my office offered to investigate this matter in an undercover manner (so to speak).

It appears that most Vermonters I've talked to have engaged in such scandalous activity at some time in their life (with the exception of a couple I didn't believe who claimed to have done so in May in Vermont because of the possibility of frostbite). Times, however, do change. Today such things are apparently allowable in most movies, on Canadian Television, in the *National Geographic* and *Life* magazine, but by no means in the pristine rivers and streams of Vermont. Therefore, to guide any law-enforcement officer so lacking in other criminal matters to investigate, so as to have time to investigate this currently popular subject of skinny-dipping, I offer, in all seriousness, the following guidelines:

1. In public areas (e.g., North Beach in Burlington) and semi-public areas: Nude bathing is not acceptable. In such instances, the officer receiving the complaint should order the person to dress. Failure to stay clothed should result in a summons to Court.
2. On private land out of view of the public: The State has no legitimate interest and swimmers should be left alone.
3. In secluded areas sometimes publicly used (e.g., rivers, swimming holes, etc.): If no member of the public present is offended, no disorderly conduct has taken place. If members of the public (e.g., families wishing to use the swimming area) complain, then proceed as in No. 1 above.

My office dutifully sent out the fax and distributed the mimeographs of this all-important communication.

We didn't have a word for it in 1971, but it went "viral." The *Washington Evening Star*, the capital's conservative newspaper, questioned why federal law enforcement didn't have the common sense of a humble lawyer from Chittenden County.

I was scheduled to join my fellow district attorneys in Washington, DC, the next week.

One of our stops was to see J. Edgar Hoover, director of the FBI since 1924 and the first and only person to have held that position through eight presidencies.

Hoover seemed to tower above us all, sitting at the head of a long wooden table. I noticed something unusual. Hoover's chair was higher than ours. Our seats had much shorter legs. They had to have been trimmed.

It was the act of a person conscious both of his height and his ability to manipulate his environment to intimidate his guests.

Many in our group were especially concerned with the rise of the Mafia and organized crime.

Not Hoover.

He launched into a tirade about radical communists everywhere—from the civil rights movement to the anti-war movement.

I made a note to myself to ask our congressional delegation what unchecked powers an FBI director might unilaterally deploy against invisible domestic enemies.

But as the meeting wrapped, and we approached the director to shake his hand, he shot me a glare I will never forget.

"*I'm Patrick Leahy, Mr. Director . . .*"

"*I know who you are. I've read about you . . .* "

Time rushed by. I was pulled in so many wonderful directions, from the state's attorney's office to the children to time together with Marcelle as husband and wife. But politics was always somewhere in the background, sometimes the low hum of the television news, other times loud and unmistakable, like when I read the Sunday paper and voiced aloud my frustrations about what was happening in the country.

Richard Nixon had won one of the closest presidential races in history against Vice President Humphrey, despite the tailwinds of Vietnam and a divided Democratic Party. Nixon had campaigned on a "secret plan" to end the war in Vietnam, which he kept secret as president. The war went on; massive bombing campaigns even expanded its scope.

At home, there was still strife around civil rights, but the images on television and the messages were coded and complicated. The news covered rage-filled scenes from South Boston as court-ordered citywide busing as a remedy to segregation met fierce resistance. The images were just as disturbing as any I'd seen in the early 1960s in Birmingham, Alabama. But rather than try to heal those divisions, national politics exploited them. Nixon and his vice president, Spiro Agnew, were determined to magnify differences in the country in order to pull white working-class voters toward the Republican Party. Agnew was on the attack against hippies, as if some tiny fringe was the source of the country's deep angst over a war that would not go away.

Federally, the civil rights movement was moving to the back burner. Nixon saw an opportunity to make deep inroads in the formerly

Democratic Solid South. Nixon was quietly jettisoning the liberal Northeast Republican base of the old GOP. Code words like "states' rights" were becoming dog whistles, unlike the old George Wallace–style appeals to outright racism. Vermont's all-Republican federal delegates in Washington weren't restraining the slow-rolling revolution inside their political party.

I was feeling a responsibility to be vocal on issues beyond the scope of the state's attorney's office. I loved being a prosecutor, but I was starting to feel its limits: there were causes to advocate for beyond the courtroom. Moments were finding me.

On May 4, 1970, hundreds of students gathered for a vigil at Kent State University in Ohio to oppose President Nixon's expansion of the Vietnam War into Cambodia. The nightly news had brought into our homes the images of massive bombs being dropped from the bellies of American planes onto the Ho Chi Minh Trail below, leaving massive craters in the earth, holes that looked more like the moon than anything here on Earth. As on so many campuses, students at Kent State sang, marched, and carried signs. But above all, they were peaceful. The news bulletin was chilling. To my prosecutor's ears, it could have been considered manslaughter. Ohio National Guard troops emptied more than sixty-five rounds at unarmed students. Four were dead, nine more wounded. It was a massacre.

Protests sprung up on campuses nationwide. In Burlington, the students at the university announced they'd parade in protest. There was no way I could allow our protest to devolve into violence. The city's police chief announced he'd arrest the students because they were parading without a permit. I reminded him I was the chief law enforcement officer and there would be no arrests.

Instead, I arranged with Sergeant Bouvier in the Burlington Police Department to escort the students and divert traffic around them. I knew many in Burlington supported the war, and I didn't want someone to drive into the crowd of protesters. Sergeant Bouvier led them down the hill from the campus and then back up. After doing this a couple times—a steep hill on a warm day—they stopped marching and returned to campus to resume their vigil. I spent several days with them almost around the clock, each time underscoring the basic bargain: there would be no arrests unless they committed a violent act or destroyed property.

The feeling on campus and across the state was tense. It was compounded by images from outside Vermont of clashes between police, pro-war, and anti-war forces, a fog of confusion amid the tear gas. The attorney general of Vermont advised our Republican governor, Deane Davis, to call out the National Guard. Davis demurred; he said he respected my judgment and would call out the Guard only if I requested it.

I arranged a meeting between the leaders of the protest, the head of the Vermont National Guard (whom I asked to please wear civilian clothes), investigators in my office, and Burlington police officers, who knew their orders came from me. We emphasized our shared responsibility to maintain both order and freedom. I wanted everyone around that table to try to see themselves as Vermonters first.

But off campus, trouble was brewing. Another group of protesters took over the federal building housing the post office, the district court, the FBI office, and the US attorney's office. The US attorney panicked and said he was leaving for Rutland and would cede jurisdiction to me. I wasn't a seasoned seafaring man, but captains don't typically abandon their ships. I advised the office workers to keep their doors locked, and we turned off the power to the elevators. Around 10:00 at night, I climbed the stairs to the third floor where the protesters had gathered.

"I've been up for two days running, and that's my job. But I have three little kids at home, and I can't go home to my family until you leave," I shared, calmly but wearily. I also added that if they didn't leave, I'd have no choice but to arrest them.

The protesters huddled, came back to me, and relayed that I had been very fair to them and they'd leave.

On the way out, their leader said he knew I was bluffing and that I wouldn't really arrest them. As he stepped outside into the pitch-black night, the only lights were from the police cars lining the streets, and he couldn't help but notice that I had a prison wagon parked there and a waiting SWAT team. I said quietly, "*I never bluff.*"

After a night's restful sleep, I was back on campus. The protests remained orderly, although they were mushrooming by the hour. My pulse raced as a National Guard truck from Maine mistakenly drove through campus. It was an innocent mistake by an out-of-state driver who had gotten lost. The panic in the crowd was palpable. I gave the students my word that those troops were not there because of the protest, and we calmed what could've been an ugly moment.

Still, I couldn't help but feel as if these students who had helped keep the peace while voicing their conscience deserved something more. No elected leaders had come to stand in solidarity with them as they had in cities up and down the East Coast. The state's largest newspaper and most political leaders in Vermont still supported the war, or at least said little about stopping it. I felt compelled to be public about where I stood. On the final night of the demonstrations, I decided I'd walk with the protesters through the streets of Burlington.

A few blocks away, a group of men drinking at a local bar, hearing the march of the students outside, announced a little too loudly that they were taking baseball bats and crowbars to go teach the protesters a lesson. It was shaping up to be a classic confrontation between the long-haired sons and daughters of 1970 and their father's and grandfather's generations, for whom questioning a war was unthinkable. Two very large off-duty police officers—both pro–Vietnam War—happened to be a few barstools down from the men. They sternly told them that State's Attorney Leahy was marching, and they should go home. One officer pulled out his handcuffs, which underlined it all. Brawl averted, at least in Vermont.

— 8 —

The Leap

With the war close at heart, I thought of running for office, perhaps making the race for governor in 1972. It would've been a fitting decision if life were coming full circle from that very first date with Marcelle, when I confided my ambition to end up in Montpelier's corner office. But I realized I was far more passionate about the national issues—and besides, Marcelle and I both knew in our hearts that our family was too young. Harry Chapin's lyrics were still ringing in my ears.

Instead, we watched that year as national politics took a deeper plunge into a dark dichotomy that bothered me tremendously. Richard Nixon took his Southern Strategy to maximum effectiveness, building a political beachhead in the no-longer solidly Democratic South and across the libertarian-minded Goldwater West. His Democratic opponent, Senator George McGovern of South Dakota, a World War II combat veteran, son of a minister, married father of five, and mainstream prairie liberal, was somehow labeled as the candidate of "acid, amnesty, and abortion." The campaign's convention had been upended when McGovern tapped a popular senator from Missouri, Tom Eagleton, as his running mate, only to have Eagleton's medical records leaked by Nixon's dirty tricks operation, revealing past electroshock therapy. Eagleton stepped aside graciously, and Ted Kennedy's brother-in-law Sargent Shriver stepped in as second choice in the second spot on the ticket. Nixon was unstoppable. With his appeals to a “silent majority” and yet another promise to end the Vietnam War on America’s terms, Tricky Dick rolled to a forty-nine-state landslide. This time, it actually was “as goes Vermont, so goes the nation.” Only our neighbor to the south, Massachusetts, stuck with the Democratic nominee.

But there’s always another election, and 1974 was approaching.

An old Irish fable often repeated in the Leahy home growing up resonated with me: you throw your hat over the highest wall to force yourself to climb to the other side. There was no higher hedge in Vermont politics than the US Senate, especially when the man forever on the ballot was George Aiken. He was the dean of the Senate, elected the year I was born, and he’d run unopposed the last two times. He was an institution within an institution.

But Nixon was bombing Southeast Asia into oblivion, Congress wasn’t stopping him, and Aiken’s party wasn’t stopping the war.

I read the *Boston Globe* and the *New York Times*. I read stories about people like Tennessee’s senator Al Gore Sr., who was willing to lose his Senate seat over his opposition to the war, and people running in primaries in other northeastern states—Joe Duffey in Connecticut and Father Bob Drinan, the Jesuit priest in Massachusetts—willing to put their reputations on the line to defeat hawkish incumbents out of step with their constituents.

As a younger person, perhaps I felt the war more personally: the ages of the young people getting killed and coming home in body bags were closer to mine. I thought more than a few times that had I been born with two fully functioning eyes, I could have been among those statistics.

But at this point, it felt as if the seeming permanence of the war—every night on the news, every protest at the university, every young person who worried about the draft lottery—was the one immutable fixture of our lives, for too long and at too high of a price. President Nixon’s promises to bring us “peace with honor” had been little more than a slogan. The bombing had only escalated, the peace talks in Paris had stalled, and three years after the 1971 publication of the Pentagon Papers, the status quo seemed numbingly unsustainable. Why were Americans being asked to die in a war that had no end? This quagmire wasn’t going to end in parades down Main Street. There wouldn't be a V-day to mark victory in Vietnam. I believed—not just out of fatigue but frustration—that enough was enough.

So, as Marcelle and I sat and talked, it became clearer and clearer. She knew the answer before I did. If I wanted to run for office, and I was passionate about these issues, why not run for the office from Vermont that could most make the difference to the war's outcome?

A number of more prominent Democrats had already taken a pass on the race, and some had even endorsed Senator Aiken. I felt a tug of conscience to be in the race, however long the odds.

What's the worst that can happen, I thought—*that I lose?* There were many worse things that could happen to a young person than losing an election. I'd seen some of those miseries as a prosecutor, and I'd read about others happening thousands of miles away in Southeast Asia.

I was in.

I decided to announce my campaign for the US Senate.

At a sparsely attended press conference, flanked by Marcelle and our children and both of our parents, I talked about all the issues that animated me, not just the war but decent wages, the right to organize, affordable housing, good schools, and decent health care. In short, I laid out what I believed it meant to be a Democrat. But I closed with words that had stuck with me when I first read them in college and had come to define in my mind what public service was about. I had a special affection for the Irish, but it wasn't the origins of the phrase that stirred me, it was its meaning. The Dublin-bred statesman Edmund Burke had said two hundred years before that "your representative owes you, not his industry only, but his judgment." He had said that a public servant "ought not sacrifice to you" his conscience. Win or lose, that was what I believed I owed the state, but it was also part of an internal monologue. Longshot, underdog, or front-runner, I wanted to run a race that I could live with, win or lose, and that started with Burke's admonition.

Marcelle jumped into the campaign with me, enthusiastically. We didn't have much money. Though the state had provided me with a car with a police radio, lights, a siren, and a phone, we went ahead and just bought the car, so no one could accuse me of benefiting from my state position. On that investment, at least, no matter the outcome of the election, we got our money's worth: the car nearly fell apart driving around the state.

One morning, I drove out at the crack of dawn to the Vermont–New Hampshire border for breakfast with a former elected official who was traveling through the country at the behest of the Democratic National Committee to support our candidates in 1974. He had a wide grin and a thick head of hair. I sat down at a table at the Hanover Inn and could see the Dartmouth campus through the window, as I waited for my breakfast companion. "I'm Jimmy Carter," he said, reaching down for a handshake. No one in the restaurant recognized either of us, just two men meeting up over toast and coffee to talk about their hopes for a campaign now and perhaps one in the future. Carter radiated warmth, and optimism that the country was ready for a break from Nixonism.

Then something ground-shaking in the politics of Vermont happened.

On February 14, 1974, George Aiken announced he wouldn't run for reelection.

Aiken eventually endorsed forty-five-year-old Republican freshman congressman Richard Mallary. In a state that had never elected a Democrat to the Senate and had never elected anyone under the age of fifty, this coronation should have been enough on its own.

Of course, there was one other complicating factor—complicating, that was, for me. The Liberty Union Party, a democratic socialist party founded in 1970, fielded its own candidate, a Brooklyn-born transplant who had spent a couple of years working in Chicago for the Congress of Racial Equality. In 1968 he had settled in Strafford, Vermont, a town of fewer than one hundred, and was writing for the alternative weekly the *Vermont Freeman*. His name was Bernard Sanders.

I went to see Bernie to talk about the race. By then, I had a feeling that what had started out as a David versus Goliath contest had now become something different: Mallary was a strong candidate, but he was no Goliath.

There was another candidate on the ballot, growing in strength, and its name was Watergate. A scandal that had slowly metastasized over the last two years was getting fresh attention as the Watergate burglars moved through the court system and investigations by Congress into the president's reelection campaign dug deeper and found that the "third-rate burglary" had reached to the upper echelons of the White House. President Nixon was weighed down by the swirl of scandal. Vice President Agnew had resigned over unrelated scandals, and Nixon's new vice president, Gerry Ford, saw his Michigan House seat go to a Democrat in a special election. Maybe there really was something building in the country that was going to put House and Senate seats in play that had always been out of reach—not yet a wave crashing toward the shore, but certainly something swirling out there in the waters not far away from the horizon. But certainly, if it was going to happen here in Vermont, I needed every liberal vote in the Democratic column.

Sanders was endearingly rumpled, longish brown hair raked over the top of his head, wearing a corduroy blazer. He could've passed for a favorite English professor at the university.

I told him why I believed I could win, and I told him about the statewide grassroots field operation I was creating, the miles I'd traveled, and the momentum that I was building. I wasn't going anywhere—I was in this race to stay.

But it was clear he wasn't getting out of the race either. He had ideas he needed to communicate, and this race was the way he intended to do it, even though he knew he couldn't win.

Weeks later, Marcelle and I pulled into the parking lot for our next debate, the kids crammed into the back seat in their best clothes, which we asked them to keep clean at least until the debate had begun and the house lights went down.

Bernard Sanders was sitting on the hood of his car. We went over to greet him, and he looked up from a manila folder full of his notes. He seemed distracted. His four-year-old son, Levi, had fallen asleep in the car on the ride up from Strafford. A loving father, Sanders didn't want to wake the child from such a peaceful slumber only to leave him in the greenroom alone for the debate.

I looked at my family and had a moment of inspiration.

Why didn't our son Kevin stay with the young Sanders child and babysit him during the debate?

In the thick of a campaign, it was one of those rare genuine win-wins: competitors, never enemies; just two dads coming up with a solution that, coincidentally, would make the little ones in both families happier for avoiding having to fidget and sit through ninety minutes of politics.

As the race went on, I was learning on the job and improvising as I went along. I'd never run statewide before. I'd always, instead, been called upon to serve in some capacity, from managing the basketball team and captaining the rifle team at St. Michael's to being plucked from the law firm to become state's attorney. In all these roles, I'd proven myself and then some. But doing a job, loving a job, even excelling in a job representing the people in court, was different from going door-to-door asking the people of the state to give me a job. Marshaling a case in court was different from marketing myself.

I had to overcome my natural shyness, but I quickly found I had a secret weapon. Marcelle was a natural. If I paused at times before I walked up to a family at a diner and worried about interrupting their meal in order to ask for their vote or talk about my platform, Marcelle had a gift for putting me and everyone in the room at ease. She had a secret weapon of her own: she was always herself. She was nurturing and kind, the same person out and about with voters as she was when caring for patients as a nurse: genuine, caring, and a natural listener. We fell into an easy routine. If I was speaking or even debating or being asked questions by the press, I would glance over at her, and we had almost perfect sign language by expressions or hands. It might be a wink. It might be the way she smiled with her eyes, the warmth just washing over me. It might be the slightest of hand gestures. But from her reaction, I always knew what I was doing right or wrong—maybe to talk a little louder, maybe to stand a little straighter—and uncannily, she was always accurate. She knew how to bring out the best in me just by being herself. I wanted her by my side every minute she could spare.

The press, when they mentioned us at all, referred to our campaign as "*the children's crusade.*" And I suppose it was. They meant it somewhat dismissively, but I preferred to think of the romantic undertones. You bet we were a children's crusade, I thought—young, scrappy, idealistic. It was young people, after all, who had founded America, and young people who had led every movement for progressive change that kept the whole idea of America inching forward decade by decade. And of all the things to be in politics, "underestimated" is a pretty good one. Sure, I was thirty-three; sure, we relied on a cadre of volunteers and a skeletal staff. But beneath the surface, while Mallary lined up the chambers of commerce and the endorsements and the campaign cash, we were racking up names and addresses of new voters.

I drove that former law enforcement vehicle to every corner of the state. I'd have happily shown up to the opening of an envelope if there were people to talk with about Vermont. I was finding something everywhere I went: because Vermont hadn't ever elected a Democratic senator or even come close to doing so, many people in our state had never met a Senate candidate face-to-face. They'd never talked with a candidate, let alone had a candidate deign to come and ask them for their support. It struck me right away: People like to be asked what *they* think, what *they* want, what's going on in *their* lives. The unipolarity of our congressional delegation hadn't lent itself to that kind of engagement with voters.

And what I was hearing from people who had never voted for a Democrat in their lives, or had never voted at all, or didn't think that their vote had ever mattered much in a federal election, gave me hope. They didn't like anything they were hearing about Watergate. They didn't like what they were hearing about dairy prices or how far a Pell Grant really took their kid when the tuition bill came in, but more than anything, they didn't feel Washington was really listening to them when it came to any of those issues.

This became a subtle advantage. We couldn't just relate to a young middle-class family; we *were* a young middle-class family. Our memories of student loans were fresh. We were blessed to have our parents still with us, but we surely wondered what it would be like to take care of them if someone got sick and they got older. The cost of food or a gallon of milk? With three children at home, we were living the same hopes and anxieties they were.

And really, that became the spark of a campaign innovation. We were relying on a grassroots campaign. Fundraising was difficult, and I was husbanding our limited resources to advertise late in the campaign. But when we sat down to think about advertising in the closing weeks, necessity became opportunity. There's an old Yogi Berra saying: "*I came to a fork in the road, and I took it*." When you have only a little bit of money to spread around on advertising, you look for value. You look for impact. Mallary had quantity. He had all the money in the world to spend to saturate the airwaves with the kinds of professional commercials candidates in his position run. It was an enviable position in a traditional election. But our entire bet had been predicated on the hope that voters were open to something different. We learned that while buying many thirty- and sixty-second spots on television and running them often was expensive, much more affordable was buying one or two thirty-minute spots in the evening. Dorothy Tod, a young filmmaker about our age, relatively new to Vermont, had been collecting footage as we'd campaigned across the state. It was natural, organic, real. Why not put it on the air as almost a movie? I didn't think anyone had really done it before, certainly not in Vermont. The campaign cut a thirty-minute infomercial about us and ran it on television so that anyone who hadn't met us in person could feel as though they had. It was our fork in the road, and we took it.

Our campaign certainly felt different from anything Vermont had seen before. Whether that would change the traditional outcome was anyone's guess, and we certainly didn't have money to poll in the dog days of summer. One afternoon, though, an out-of-state visitor gave me an extra dose of optimism. The very small Vermont Democratic Party was having a fundraising event at a restaurant in Burlington. The keynote speaker, the big draw, was the thirty-one-year-old junior senator from the state of Delaware, Joseph Robinette Biden Jr.

I hadn't requested any out-of-state surrogates to come in for my campaign, because I wanted the race to be about Vermont and because I knew that, as an underdog, it was likely a fool's gambit to try to play that game. I'm not sure whether the Democratic National Committee or the Democratic Senatorial Campaign Committee had a hand in sending Biden to Vermont, but he was already by then one of the rising stars of the national party. Two years before, he'd come out of nowhere to defeat a popular two-term senator and former governor by the name of J. Caleb Boggs, winning by 1.4 points. Twenty-nine years old on election night, handsome, and Catholic, Biden was immediately anointed as future presidential timber, a breath of fresh air after the political heartbreak of 1972. But just weeks after winning, real heartbreak of a different magnitude touched the Biden family. Biden's wife and daughter were killed in a car crash, his two boys badly injured. I remembered reading about him then and wondering how anyone finds the strength to go on. Now, here he was in Vermont, back on his feet, very friendly, down-to-earth, and interested in my campaign.

He joked easily about our shared Irish heritage. "How you doing, old buddy?" he asked, as though we were longtime friends. He had an automatic ability to pull you in, lock eyes, and make you feel as if you were the only two people in a room. Of course, at the Vermont Democratic Party, that wasn't too far from being true.

Biden spoke to the small assembly, first recounting the many ways Vermont and Delaware were similar, from our farming communities to our Irish immigrant city strongholds to, yes, even our three Electoral College votes. He dutifully praised everyone running for office, including me, and he and his brother Jim departed for the drive to New Hampshire, where he was speaking the next day. The press reported on his speech, mentioned our new governor was there—the second Democrat to be elected governor in our history—and found time to speculate whether Biden could be a vice presidential hopeful in 1976 or a presidential candidate in 1980. Left out of the coverage was any mention of a thirty-three-year-old

Vermonter on the ballot that year who might follow in Biden's footsteps as an upset Senate winner.

I asked one of the reporters why and was told it had been in the story, but his editor cut it because I couldn't win.

But if I couldn't make it into the news that summer, one story couldn't be left out. Increasingly, there was only one story in America, it seemed. The Watergate investigation hearings dominated the evening news. Walter Cronkite, John Chancellor, Harry Reasoner, David Brinkley—the nightly news anchors brought Vermont the very latest from Washington, and it was ugly. For the first time, Americans were hearing about a president ordering dirty tricks against his opponents and knowing—and lying—about the origins of the break-in and botched burglary at Democratic headquarters. It was a stunning indictment of the person sitting in the Oval Office, and a sordid story about bags full of cash and alleged "White House plumbers" who sought to discredit reporters and smear political opponents. It had nothing to do with Richard Mallary or me. But it had everything to do with where our campaigns were coming from: one of us aiming to preserve a kind of clubbish continuity in Washington that Vermont had become accustomed to, the other trying to break up the club that had looked the other way when a president broke the law.

Just like that, after the Supreme Court ordered his White House to turn over Oval Office tapes that would reveal for all of America conversations about the Watergate burglary, the president retreated to the White House to deliberate. Impeachment and conviction seemed a foregone conclusion. On August 9, 1974, Richard Nixon resigned and climbed one last time up the steps of Marine One to head into exile in California, and with his departure, the country exhaled. But three weeks later, the bottom fell out for the Republican Party when now-President Gerald Ford pardoned Nixon on Labor Day weekend, just as the political season was heating up and voters were tuning in.

I admired Ford's instinct to try to heal the country. But I was deeply disturbed by an outcome that meant, ultimately, that a president really was above the law.

It didn't sit well with me as a law enforcement official and an officer of the courts. I'd sent people to prison for crimes they committed. What message did it send if the powerful could simply slink off, convicted only in the court of public opinion?

It didn't sit well with Vermont either. I could feel the crowds growing, feel a grassroots groundswell happening around the state. People in Chittenden County—the most populous in the state—were registering to vote in unprecedented numbers.

I just didn't believe that they were Mallary voters.

Five days before Election Day, my campaign manager, Paul Bruhn, and I woke up early and headed to the newsstand to be the first to see the headline on the lead story we had heard was coming: the preelection poll.

The headline was a punch to the gut: "Poll Dooms Leahy." I was told to prepare two speeches for election night: "One if you lose, and one if you lose badly."

People tell you that the only poll that matters is the one on Election Day. That's true. Or at least that's all well and good, except when it's five days before Election Day and you're the candidate looking at the wrong end of the poll that has you 35 points behind.

I tried to put it out of my mind.

If I'd listened to polls and pundits, I'd have never jumped into the race. Other bigger-name candidates would've run and I wouldn't have been the Democratic nominee.

I had run by a different set of rules throughout the race, and I was going to run right through the tape on Election Day that same way. I had faith in our campaign. We had developed an army of volunteers, especially of college students, and others who were impressed by the job I had done as a prosecutor. They were working for me all over the state.

Marcelle and her father went to the areas of Vermont where she had been born, which were heavily French Canadian and always voted Republican, and together they campaigned in fluent French.

My mother did interviews in Italian on the state's only Italian-language radio station.

Even the Republican doctor who had delivered me as a baby appeared in a TV ad, announcing why he thought I would make a good senator;

Norman Rockwell himself couldn't have conjured up a more reassuring, quintessentially Vermont character, all the more compelling because he was real.

These things the experts did not see, but we trusted that the people would see them.

They did.

Twenty-nine years after I rode my tricycle into the desk that George Aiken had once commanded in the statehouse, I was following him in the US Senate.

By a margin of 4,406 votes, in that year's closest Senate race, I became the first Democrat and the youngest person ever elected to the US Senate from Vermont.

5,901 votes went to Bernie Sanders.

Up in our hotel suite, I received a gracious concession call from Richard Mallary.

I was on pins and needles until that moment; now it felt real.

My campaign manager had talked to a friend inside the *Rutland Herald*: this time, the headline on the early edition would scream "Leahy Unexpectedly Wins."

As Marcelle and I got into a waiting elevator to head down to the Ramada ballroom to celebrate with a packed house of our volunteers, I turned to her with a kind of shocked look on my face.

"*You know Marcelle, this means I'm never going to be governor.*"

She smiled. "*That's okay, Patrick.*"

— 9 —

A New Life

The ethereal feeling of our victory quickly yielded to practical questions of how to rearrange the life we'd built in Burlington to accommodate part-time living five hundred miles away in Washington, DC.

Throughout the campaign, Marcelle had been my most fervent champion, always bucking me up when the odds seemed longest. She'd had just one constant, immutable position: "Just promise me that *when you win, we all go together*." Marcelle was unfazed by the long nights and prolonged absences of my service as a prosecutor, nor had she been discouraged by the 24-7 pace of the Senate race. But above all, she was unshakably committed to doing what was best for our family.

Now we were trying to make decisions as a young couple to give life and shape to that conviction.

A senator's salary in 1975 would be $44,600. It was a raise, but it wouldn't go far for a family of five that had to build a life in two states in very short order, with decisions to make about where to live and where to send kids to school.

We had no real savings. What extra we'd been able to hold on to, we had plowed back into the Senate race. We liked our duplex in Burlington, but there was no way to keep it and have a place to live in Washington big enough for all of us. Besides, while the duplex was a valuable investment, it paled in comparison to the sentimental investment of the property in Middlesex—the farm that had been my dad's dream and where we'd spent so many afternoons as a carefree couple falling in love and as young parents watching the children explore. If there was one place we always wanted to return to in Vermont, this was it. We decided the farm would always be our home base, and we flew down to Washington with the family to look around for places to rent.

We made a couple of trips back and forth and found a large enough town house for the family. It was all happening so quickly. We hired the movers, and Marcelle frantically packed up as I closed up my work at the state's attorney's office. That transition would be seamless: there was always work to do in Chittenden County, and besides, I needed every last paycheck.

The day before Christmas Eve, I was working late in the office when I saw several police cars go screaming by with their blue lights on. I called the station and learned that there had been a fatality on North Avenue. I'd already given everybody time off for Christmas. I asked them to just have one of the squad cars stop and give me a ride over. I arrived just as the coroner was doing his grim duty. I realized immediately that the deceased was the daughter of a friend of ours. I wanted to throw up. I turned to one of the police officers and said, "Take me back, I have to call somebody in my office."

I called Marcelle from my desk and went straight home afterward. Marcelle was up, shaken by what we'd experienced so unexpectedly.

On Christmas Eve morning, I had the police radio, the blue lights, and the rest of the equipment taken out of the car. I told the folks in my office that I'd been responding to these middle-of-the-night calls for eight years, seven days a week: that was my last one.

December 30, we packed up the children in the station wagon and drove to Washington—nine hours in the car, with a stop for lunch at a Howard Johnson's motor lodge in New Jersey.

The movers arrived on New Year's Eve. We were simultaneously taking things out of boxes—unwrapping pots and pans and plates—and preparing a meal for our family.

We asked the movers to join us for dinner.

We were all moved in when I was sworn in—days later—to a Senate of ninety-nine members because of a tie in New Hampshire: not quite the indignity of being the most junior of one hundred, I started out the most junior of ninety-nine, knowing that some poor rookie from the Granite State would soon take my place at the very bottom of the heap when a winner was declared.

Before school started for the children, we took a few days for sightseeing. The children loved the Smithsonian, but after three days, Mark turned to us and said innocently, "*When are we going back home?*"

We explained to him again that with Daddy's new job, we were staying there. He was not happy because all his friends were in Vermont. Only now did it register in his young mind that he wasn't going to see them every day anymore. The tears welled in his eyes, and he tried to process it all bravely. I was reminded how hard transitions are for children.

But on what should've been the third day of class at their new school, we all woke up to something that would change their perspective. The children were getting ready for school when the radio in the kitchen announced the news that made us all do a double take: "McLean schools—closed today."

The three children looked out the window, saw a dusting of snow on the ground, grass poking out through it, and asked if we were going to get a heavy snowstorm.

I said, "No, that's it, that's all they're expecting."

"They close school for an inch of snow?"

I said, "Well, this is Washington, not Vermont."

"Dad, we like it here—we'll never have to go to school!"

"*I'm sorry, this door is for senators only, you're welcome to wait over there,*" said the doorkeeper politely but firmly.

"*Senators-elect have the privilege to go on the Senate floor,*" said Senator Frank Church to the dutiful doorkeeper.

A blank stare. No response. I could hardly blame the clerk for mistaking me for a cub reporter or earnest young staffer. It was the freshman senatorial version of being carded outside a bar, only I didn't even have a fake ID.

"*This is the senator-elect from Vermont,*" Senator Church added, pointing in my direction.

Suddenly, a switch flipped to the "on" position: the young clerk pulled out his stack of papers from the appointment desk and thumbed his way down the list: *Ford, Culver, Bumpers, Hart* . . . Finally, he matched a name with a young face.

"*Well, hello, Senator Leahy!*"

He didn't wave me in, but it felt that way. Walking from the dull gray corridor by the elevator banks onto the Senate floor was like the moment in *The Wizard of Oz* when the film goes from black and white to stunning color.

It was the first time I'd been called "*Senator*."

I felt a little weak in the knees, but a voice inside urged me to act as if it were all natural and as if I were unflappable.

It wasn't, and I wasn't.

Stretched out before me, just a few feet away, were faces and figures I had mostly come to know only from national television and news accounts or from high above the Senate floor, just another spectator in the gallery as a Georgetown law student and glorified tourist taking a break to watch the debates.

Ted Kennedy. Barry Goldwater. Hubert Humphrey. All of them engaged in comfortable conversation.

Three months before, I'd been prosecuting cases in Chittenden County. Now I was standing on the Senate floor at the elbow of a senator who was championing the very ideals I'd dreamed of fighting for if ever I had a vote and a voice in a place like this. It was a long way from my tricycle-riding invasion of Governor Wills's office in Montpelier.

I had a surge of imposter syndrome, on the one hand struggling to believe I had made it here, while on the other doing my level best not to reveal my sense of awe so I'd be taken seriously. It was easy to get lost in the basement catacombs of the Senate office complex, and I found myself showing up to meetings early out of a disproportionate fear of being late.

Senator Church was indulging my earnest questions, each of us playing a role in a time-honored Senate ritual that married protocol and good old-fashioned, internecine politics. The first duty of senators-elect is to try to make their next six years easiest by winning a plum committee assignment or two. Senators-elect were expected to go around and talk to current senators on the "steering committee" and lobby for coveted committee slots. Agriculture, Appropriations, Armed Services, Judiciary—these were the places where meaningful policy was made and where senators proved their ability to bring home tangible benefits in the lives of the people they represented. Particularly coming from a small state like Vermont, it mattered much more to win committee seats where one could draw a straight line from his Senate service to the practical impact at home. The seasoned senior incumbents were to listen and good-naturedly humor our sometimes naive appeals, and then would be certain to share with us—the supplicants—their own hope that we might give consideration to a vote, position, or favor important to their agenda, in return for their indulgence.

On the one hand, it was a series of "pinch me" moments—the marble floors, the statues lining the walls, the grand Ohio Clock off the Senate floor. I remember the smell, the wafts of tobacco and cologne, and the cool, crisp air when a door opened from the outside. It was a rarefied air. On the other hand, it had the feel of fraternity rush season, and every rising freshman wanted to pledge the Alpha House: the Senate veterans were sizing us up, but they were doing so in a good-natured way, testing whether we were collegial and trustworthy, big brothers to aspiring little brothers.

Photographers' flashbulbs punctuated our walk from the halls of the Senate office building through the subterranean tunnels that lead to the Capitol. It reminded me that Senator Church was at the center of a political storm consuming Washington—one much bigger than the hopes of any senator-elect to land a plum committee assignment.

In December, the *New York Times*'s young investigative reporter Seymour Hersh—idiosyncratic, irascible, and already renowned for breaking the news of the My Lai Massacre four years before—had published a bombshell.

Hersh had reported on decades of hidden abuses by the Central Intelligence Agency, from attempted assassination plots overseas to abuses at home that hinted at spying on American citizens, from the civil rights movement to the anti-war movement. It was stunning to me, having been invested in an idealistic view of Washington and of the presidency itself: how jarring it was to think that even presidents I admired approved plots to spy on our heroes like Martin Luther King Jr. or assassinate adversaries like Fidel Castro. It was one thing for Richard Nixon to do extralegal damage to the Constitution, quite another to read that it had been part of a pattern for decades of Cold War intrigue. The implication that US senators had been caught up in a web of clandestine intelligence gathering grabbed the immediate attention of Congress; the implication that the mail of the American people itself had been surreptitiously surveilled struck a chord with the entire country. Coming in the aftermath of Watergate, and the entire reform movement that had ushered in a Democratic landslide for the ages. The demand for transparency and action were only growing.

Frank Church had a novel answer: he was proposing a special Senate Select Committee on Intelligence to investigate the CIA and pry open the hinges of secrecy that had rusted over in the decades since President Truman created the permanent intelligence community in 1947 by signing the National Security Act into law. Truman himself had worried about the challenge of balancing the need for civilian oversight of intelligence gathering with the urgent need to catch up to what the rest of the world, especially the Soviet Union, had already assembled: a vast, powerful spying and intelligence-gathering apparatus.

But the solution at the time had, in practice, failed to strike anything close to the right balance: only the chairman and ranking member of the Armed Services Committee were periodically briefed on the CIA's activities.

It was a poorly kept secret that the longtime archconservative chairman of the committee, Mississippi Democrat John C. Stennis, would interrupt his own intelligence briefing and warn, "*Well, I don't need to know that. Don't tell me too much.*" As a result, the CIA had become the plaything of presidents of both parties, with little oversight from Congress to keep it honest.

We just didn't know how badly it had gone astray.

But Hersh's reporting had given us a disturbing inkling, and now Frank Church was determined to bring it all to light.

I knew Church by reputation only. He was a Greatest Generation war veteran, like so many who entered public service in the 1950s and '60s, and Church had burst onto the scene as a thirty-two-year-old hard-charging, idealistic Boise lawyer, defeating an incumbent Republican. He'd quickly become a leader of the Senate's liberal wing, alongside Senator Humphrey, and was among the first to break with President Johnson over the Vietnam War. He was no stranger to David versus Goliath battles, but taking on the closely guarded secrecy of the CIA was a risky gambit even for Church, who many believed would be a strong candidate for president in 1976.

Church dutifully entertained my aspirations for a committee assignment that would best empower Vermont. But he didn't have to make a reciprocal request of me. I'd already volunteered to him my support for the creation of his investigative committee. The Democratic Class of 1974 had been elected to change Washington, to shake it up, not sit idly by—I was glad the Senate would assert not just its rights, but its responsibilities.

— 10 —

The Rookie

I still hadn't even been sworn in before the Americans for Democratic Action requested a meeting with me to talk about liberal priorities for the next session. On most of its agenda, I didn't need a sales pitch; where arms control legislation, civil rights protections, the reauthorization of the Voting Rights Act, and health insurance reform were all concerned, I was already on board. No convincing was necessary.

But on one issue I was unmoved. The ADA let me know that it expected the Class of 1974—a large class of reformers and outsiders—to upend the power structure of the old Senate. It had its first target: in its members' judgment, Louisiana's Russell Long was too conservative to serve any longer as chairman of the tax-writing Finance Committee.

Long was respected internally for his expertise on tax issues. I might not agree with all of Russell's positions, and certainly the electorate in Louisiana was very different from the electorate in Vermont. But you had to give the man credit; he knew the tax code inside and out, and with good reason: he'd written and rewritten most of it.

But I had another reason for hesitating to undo a Senate tradition. The Founders created the Senate based not on population, but on the idea that every state should be equally represented. For a small state like Vermont, that's almost an existential issue. We have one House district. California has dozens. Texas has dozens. Coming to the Senate and building expertise and clout on a committee is how a well-represented small state punches above its weight. So, I was reticent to dismantle the very seniority system that gave Vermont a chance to stand on its own two feet next to the big states and their overwhelming interests.

"*I won't be with you on that,*" I said simply. Better to be honest with an interest group than leave it investing hope in a lost cause. "*I'll vote to keep him chairman.*"

Word gets around quickly in the Senate.

A couple of days later, Russell Long came by my office. He had worked hard to tame a stutter many decades ago, but still it returned at times when he was tired or especially agitated.

I had never spoken to Russell about how I was going to vote on his chairmanship. He couldn't quite get his head around my approach to the issue.

"*B-b-b-b-but I never p-promised you or gave you anything.*"

I replied, "*Well, I believe in Senate procedure, and you didn't do anything wrong and seniority put you there.*"

He smiled. He had the big wide grin of his father, Louisiana's fabled Huey "Kingfish" Long.

"*My daddy always said, 'A promise to be fulfilled is worth ten promises already fulfilled.'*" Russell knew that people will stay around while they are waiting for you to come through with something, but after you deliver for them, many will forget. It wasn't my motivation, but without saying a word, I knew what Russell was thinking: he wouldn't forget.

The most intimidating visit of all during my orientation period was with the Democratic majority leader, Senator Mike Mansfield of Montana.

It was awe-inspiring enough to meet people I'd only read about in the pages of the *New York Times*. It was challenging enough to hire and recruit staff, navigate the hunt for office space, and think about how to rearrange our family life.

But a majority leader can decide whether your Senate experience will be positive or negative. He sets the tone. And Mike Mansfield was no ordinary majority leader.

Mansfield's reputation preceded him. Born in New York to Irish immigrants at the turn of the century, his mother died when he was just seven. One of his earliest memories was the two-thousand-mile-long train ride to Great Falls, Montana, to live with his aunt and uncle. He was miserable, running away from his adopted home so often that he ended up spending six months at the state children's home in Twin Bridges. At fourteen, he lied about his age in order to join the Navy and serve in World War I, but the Navy figured out the subterfuge and sent him home. Naturally, he joined the Army. When the Army figured out his deception and swiftly discharged him, he joined the Marines.

When he came home from the war, he went underground for a few years—literally. Working in Butte's copper mines deep beneath the earth shoveling rock and ore, he dreamed of a fresh start. With his wife's encouragement, he completed high school and college classes at night, and he went on to teach at the university, before entering the fray of politics. Quite a life.

For each and any of those chapters of his adventures, which reflect his resilience, Mansfield might've earned the nickname that would follow him as majority leader: "Iron Mike."

I couldn't tell you when that moniker first stuck to the man. All I knew for certain was that he was the one and truly immovable Senate majority leader.

By January 1975, Mansfield was comfortable and confident in his position. He'd held the post since 1961, taking the baton from no less of a master of the legislative machinery than Lyndon Johnson himself. But Mansfield was different from the man he'd followed. Johnson was inseparable from the famed "Johnson Treatment": cajoling, bullying, twisting arms, literally talking to his colleagues an inch from their face if that's what it took, imposing his sheer force of personality to secure an outcome.

Mansfield had an entirely different modus operandi. He set a quieter, humble example, finding ways to arrive at compromises.

No one could argue with the results.

Long before I had been elected, he'd shepherded both Kennedy's New Frontier and Johnson's even more ambitious Great Society agendas through the Senate—including the bitterly fought Civil Rights Act. Mansfield had quietly, humbly done more to pass more difficult legislation than possibly any leader before, dealing with a fractious Democratic caucus that tested his patience as well as his moral compass, but somehow, he made the process work. Budgets and appropriations bills were passed. Social legislation was ushered through. Never was his leadership challenged from within. He had presided masterfully over a Democratic caucus as ideologically heterogeneous as you could ever imagine, one that included liberals, moderates, and die-hard conservatives, and states and regions in transition.

I knew the legend of Mansfield before I arrived. Now I was about to have an audience with the man himself.

I sat nervously in the leader's anteroom. The decorations were spartan, reflecting Mansfield himself. I sat stiffly in an upright wooden chair, one of three in a row on the wall. There was no couch for lobbyists to luxuriate, waiting to see the leader. In fact, legend had it that the only non-Montanans whom Mansfield visited with at all were his Senate colleagues.

And he always made time for his colleagues.

But there was one colleague, I worried, whom he may have favored above all others, the man I'd replaced in the Senate. It was well known in Vermont that throughout their service together, Senator Aiken as Senate dean and Leader Mansfield began their day with breakfast together in the Senate dining room, just the two of them.

Not Mansfield's team of deputy whips.

Not the Republican minority leader Hugh Scott or his gravelly-voiced predecessor, Everett Dirksen of Illinois.

No, this ritual was saved for Mansfield and Aiken, and it became part and parcel of the legend of George Aiken, the ultimate voice of seniority, Vermont's quintessential "Mr. Republican."

I wondered whether Mansfield would hold it against me that my early announcement of my candidacy may have played a role in depriving him of his breakfast partner.

I wondered what Mansfield, a towering figure in an institution built on collegiality, had heard about me from Aiken. Did Mansfield peg me as an ambitious upstart, a likely problem child for him in a busy caucus full of big personalities?

The door to the leader's inner office opened, and Mansfield came out to greet me with a firm handshake. We walked into his private workspace, which was just as nondescript as the outer office. There were no photos covering the walls from ceiling to floor, as many senators seemed to assemble. No black-and-white portraits depicting the leader with the five presidents with whom he'd served. No framed awards or even his military decorations. Just a framed map of Montana, a picture of his wife and daughter on his desk, and an ashtray where his pipe rested.

Mansfield himself poured me a cup of coffee, and we sat down to talk.

I shared with him that I knew he had been good friends with Senator Aiken. His reply was matter-of-fact: "*Yes, I am*. I respected him."

But his reply wasn't cold.

"*And I look forward to working with you now,*" he said without any hesitation.

I felt a burst of relief.

Mansfield had two pieces of advice that he said he shared with every freshman.

The first was as simple as his office was unadorned: "*Work on what interests you.*" I paused and thought about it for a moment.

I'd been intimidated by the vastness of the institution since the moment I arrived in Washington. There's an iconic moment in the Robert Redford film *The Candidate*, which Marcelle and I had seen a couple of years before, in 1972. Newly and unexpectedly elected to the Senate, Redford's idealistic young lawyer character, Bill McKay, asks his campaign manager, "*What do we do now?*"

In Vermont, I was comfortable. It was home. I knew the job of state's attorney inside and out, despite being the youngest to ever hold the position. Here in Washington, it wasn't just that it was all new; it's that I was nagged by doubts.

Would I belong? Would I fit in? Would people accept me as a worthy replacement for someone who had served in the position as long as I had been alive?

Where would I fit in a freshman class that included the first American to orbit Earth, an Arkansas governor who had knocked off the legendary J. William Fulbright, and George McGovern's famous campaign manager who palled around with Warren Beatty?

I'd believed in my candidacy from the very start, but now I wondered whether everyone saw me as an accidental senator.

I was piling expectations and pressures on myself that no one could live up to, yet here was a majority leader who had seen and done it all saying, without saying much at all, none of it mattered.

"*Just work on what interests you.*"

But the second piece of advice made an even more enduring and reassuring impression.

"*Senators should always keep their word.*"

It struck me that across all those weighty debates, navigating the complicated and contradictory politics of a Senate and a Democratic caucus that included everything from social conservatives and segregationists to civil rights icons and prairie populists, Mansfield had succeeded because he understood the currency of the institution was actually trust, not ideology.

"*Senators should always keep their word.*"

It was a simple formula. If you knew what commitments colleagues had made to each other, you could count the votes. If you could count the votes, you could set the agenda. If you knew the agenda, you could set the schedule. If you could set the schedule, you could pass legislation and still send the senators home to be present in their states when it counted.

I thought, *This is actually pretty darn familiar to me. This is how it's done in Vermont, after all*—a place where so much was done based entirely on your word. As a lawyer, my office looked out over an alleyway, a stone's throw from another law firm. After hearing a shout from the neighboring office, I opened my window on a soft summer Friday to see the lawyer I was supposed to be having a trial against on Monday, calling my name from his window.

"*Hey, can we settle this thing? What do you want?*"

We haggled back and forth for a couple of minutes and agreed to settle the case.

He said, "*Look, I'll drop the papers on Monday, I want to go fishing this afternoon.*"

"*Fine—call the clerk and tell him we won't have the trial.*"

That was it.

It was inconceivable you'd break your word after a conversation like that, papers or no papers.

Once, some out-of-state lawyers had agreed to a settlement, but suddenly tried to back out. The judge took us all in chambers and asked them if we had in fact landed on a gentleman's agreement the night before. They said yes, they had, but they didn't have anything in writing and they'd changed their mind. The judge said, "*Well, I'm sure Attorney Leahy wouldn't mind calling the disciplinary board for your bar—do you happen to have the number right there?*"

They sheepishly asked for a ten-minute break, and after the color returned to their faces, they returned to what we'd agreed to the night before.

Keep your word. What a reminder of something I'd learned long before I had sworn an oath to the law or the Constitution. Back home at the Leahy Press, with our living quarters in the front of the house and the printing press in the back, I witnessed all of Dad's business dealings, and nothing was written down on paper. I went to the bank with him when he needed a loan to purchase a new piece of equipment. The banker asked him if he'd seen it. Dad replied, "Yes—I saw it at a printers' convention and it worked well." The banker asked how much it cost and how much Dad needed to pay for it. The money was in his account that week, and only later did he come back in and sign a note for it.

It turned out it wasn't just the Senate that operated on a person's word to another. In fact, everybody and everything I'd grown up around, and everything I'd experienced as a lawyer in private practice and working for the state, had operated that same way, and none of it had been chiseled in stone.

For the first time, I felt comfortable in the Senate. I thought, *Maybe I do belong here. Maybe the lessons I learned in Vermont were good guidance after all*—and my hunch was that Leader Mansfield himself had learned these same arch lessons about life and leadership not under the dome of the Capitol, but in Great Falls from his aunt and uncle, in uniform for his country, or in the mines of Butte as a mucker clawing his way toward a better life.

Maybe the Senate wasn't so different from the places and people I'd known after all.

Vermont's new senior senator, Bob Stafford, set out to help the state's new senator. Other than a tiny basement broom closet of a room, no real estate was dedicated to incoming freshmen. We had to wait until after we were sworn in to put our claim on the open offices. But Senator Stafford reached out and set aside part of his office for my use, ample space where I could have meetings or interview someone for a job. He deputized one of his administrative staff to type anything I needed typing with instructions that it was not to be shared with him, unless I specifically said otherwise.

In the Senate since 1971, a decorated veteran of two wars, Bob had been elected attorney general, lieutenant governor, governor, and congressman before arriving here. He really was Vermont's Mr. Republican, but he couldn't have been more kind to an upstart Democrat who had upset the state's political applecart. He didn't have to be that way. A different kind of person might've used the transition to assert his authority, to make it clear that he was no longer a junior anything. Instead, he said to me, "*Patrick, you're my Senate partner.*" It didn't have to be said out loud: Stafford had little patience for the "junior/senior" monikers that others might have needed to feel secure.

Every day felt like graduate school, except the professors were living legends of the Senate, the giants I'd watched from the visitors' gallery as a law student.

Some were people whose legends I approached skeptically.

Jim Oliver Eastland was the seventy-year-old Senate president pro tempore from Doddsville, Mississippi, and he looked as if he'd lived a life well beyond seventy. Every mile on the back roads of eastern Mississippi showed on his face, as did the Chivas Regal that he reserved for occasions including lunch, afternoon restoratives, dinner, after dinner, and late nights.

I had first read Eastland's name in law school. I identified him with his outspoken defense of segregation and participation in the southern caucus's filibusters against the civil rights legislation of the Johnson administration. When those legislative fights cooled, Eastland shaved off some of the rougher edges and reinvented himself as a pro-military conservative southerner more focused on bringing infrastructure and money home to rural Mississippi than on a public charge against racial progress. But I knew he represented a very different history of the Democratic Party than the one I celebrated.

It was a generational divide in many ways. I was part of a new cohort of senators inspired by the Kennedy administration's commitment to civil rights, the great dividing line in America. We believed in a Democratic Party animated by inclusion, that aimed to build a people-powered coalition of working people, organized labor, and young people committed to the environment, openness in government, and creating opportunity for all. The once Republican Northeast was trending Democratic with this coalition, while the conservative but formerly solidly Democratic South was going Republican in presidential elections, while largely reelecting again and again the old bulls of Democratic yesteryear.

In my first caucus meeting, there was little suspense in the election of Mike Mansfield's leadership team. But just as the caucus was about to unanimously reappoint Eastland as president pro tem, a voice called out, "*Let's have a recorded vote.*"

Senator Phil Hart of Michigan, a liberal some referred to as the "Conscience of the Senate," announced, with a big smile, "*Jim Eastland—you're my best friend here. But president pro tem is third in line for the presidency, and, Jim, you'd be a terrible president.*"

The laughs erupted in the room.

"*I suppose you're right, Phil,*" said Eastland in his exaggerated drawl. "*I suppose you're right.*"

Days later, I sat next to Ted Kennedy in the Judiciary Committee room in the Capitol as members waited for Chairman Eastland's arrival. It was another moment a young Irish kid from Vermont could have only dreamed of experiencing. I was about eight years Ted's junior, and he was still a year younger than his brother was when he'd become president. I expected Ted to run himself in 1976. I wondered: Would I have ever found the inspiration to make myself a candidate in Republican Vermont if it weren't for President Kennedy's inspiration? Starstruck and searching for an icebreaker to talk to the fallen president's brother, now my colleague, Ted spared me that decision by striking up a conversation and putting me at ease. "Ease"—that was the right word. Ted had an obvious gift of ease in the Senate; he was comfortable there and so he made you comfortable. "Welcome to the Judiciary Committee, old man Leahy!" he joked. All this from someone who himself had arrived in the Senate at age thirty. He offered me a tiny cigar from a silver holder engraved EMK.

I must've said something that indicated to Ted that I had noticed the strange, irreconcilable differences in a Democratic caucus that spanned ideological gulfs from Mississippi to Massachusetts.

"*You know, Eastland's an old-school person in more ways than, er, well, the, er, our issues.*"

With one sentence, Teddy had said much more: he'd acknowledged we were fellow travelers on the progressive civil rights journey, but that he was about to share some insight into Eastland that a skeptic might appreciate. Kennedy told me a story that stuck with me from that day forward. Years before, Kennedy had wanted to bring up a bill in the Judiciary Committee that Eastland opposed. Eastland told him that if he had enough support, he would put it on the agenda, but he, as chairman, would vote against it. Finally, Kennedy came to Eastland with a list of supporters who would vote for the bill.

Eastland reminded Ted, "*I'll vote against it, but I'll put it on the agenda.*" He put it on and called the roll, and Kennedy lost by one vote.

Chairman Eastland looked down the row of senators and asked a particular senator if he had not agreed to vote for Kennedy's amendment. He said that he had, but he had changed his mind.

Eastland grumbled, "*When you commit in this committee, you keep your word.*" He turned to the clerk and said, "*Change my vote to aye.*" The liberal bill passed out of committee, and as for the senator who had reneged on his promise to Kennedy, never again would he have another bill put on the agenda for breaking his word.

Teddy didn't try to explain away Eastland's racist record. In fact, he'd been pushing and prodding to move the party further and faster on civil rights and women's rights, particularly the Equal Rights Amendment, both areas desperately in need of repair in a Senate where the all-male caucus featured a single African American, the moderate Republican Ed Brooke from Massachusetts, and the last woman senator had retired in 1972. But Ted also had clearly found that within the Senate, there was something to be admired about a colleague who had institutionalist principles deep in his bones.

What I couldn't deny was the obvious: Eastland had clout.

As I made the rounds to meet my elders, a stop to see the president pro tempore was customary. I went to meet with him in his ceremonial office in the Capitol.

"*Boy, how old are you?*" he asked.

I didn't want to say thirty-four and a half, so I said, "*I'll be thirty-five soon, Mr. Chairman.*"

"*Has anybody ever told you that you are too young to be in the Senate?*"

"*Well, my opponent, for one.*"

Eastland let out a deep chuckle that turned into a phlegmy cough.

He had been appointed to the Senate in his thirties. "*Mississippi told me I was too young, and since then I've buried them all. Boy, want a drink?*"

It was 10:45 in the morning. "*Thanks, Mr. Chairman, but I must go to another meeting.*"

— 11 —

Finding My Way

There was something about the new license plate on the family car that made it feel more permanent. The official state-issued green license plate announced, simply, 2—the junior senator from Vermont.

I quickly learned the occupational hazards that came with driving such a car.

"How come your license plate says two?" asked a wise guy in the grocery store parking lot.

Putting on my best rural accent, I replied, "Well, we don't have that many *cahhs* up in Vermont." That quieted the critics.

On that chilly January day, I turned off Constitution Avenue and drove up to the steps of the Capitol.

My father, Howard, was the first to step out.

A tourist, having spotted the license plate, pointed to my father and instructed her husband, "*Take his picture! That's the senator from Vermont!*"

"*Well, who's that guy?*" the husband asked as I got out of the driver's seat.

"*Oh, that's his chauffeur. They all have one.*"

My dad, who had grown up in the minority for his liberal beliefs in the Republican city of Montpelier, would relish telling that story for years to come. His friends at Kiwanis would say, "*How's your chauffeur doing?*"

Moments later, I was back on the Senate floor to be sworn in as the first Democrat ever to represent Vermont in the Senate.

They swore us in alphabetically by state and ended on Vermont.

Under the eyes of my parents, Marcelle's parents, and two of our children, I was ready to take the walk with Senator Stafford down to the well of the Senate, where Vice President Rockefeller would deliver the oath.

"Senator, I really appreciate this," I said to Stafford.

"It's really about time to call me Bob," he replied.

Seconds later, I was face-to-face with Vice President Rockefeller, a tall, imposing figure with a big handshake and a broad smile. The former governor of New York and standard-bearer of the dying liberal wing of the Republican Party, I wondered whether Rockefeller had really known what he was in for when he accepted Gerald Ford's offer to serve as vice president. Rocky's Senate confirmation process had been bruising, and the conservative wing of the party, led by former California governor Ronald Reagan, was already contemplating a primary challenge to Ford for the 1976 campaign.

But today he was all smiles.

Moments later, with my hand on the Leahy family Bible, it was done. It was time to get to work: I was officially the forty-second person to serve Vermont in the Senate.

I took a secluded seat in the back row and watched my new colleagues parade one by one and two by two into S-207, the ornate room where Senate Democrats gathered for the weekly "caucus lunch." It would be my first, and as #99 in seniority, I thought it was most appropriate that I sit in the back.

Like much of the Capitol and much of official Washington, the architects had designed the room with intimidation in mind. The walls were covered in rich black walnut paneling, and the residue of Majority Leader Mansfield's omnipresent pipe smoke seemed to permanently hang in the air. I noticed the mantel surrounding the ornate fireplace—unmistakable Meadow White Vermont marble. What a journey for the grandson of Italian stone carvers who had come to the United States to turn the quarried stones of Vermont's hills and mountains into an export as beautiful as that from any state in the union. I thought of the grandfather who always reminded me, "*Patricio, you can be senator one day*," and I felt some tears welling in my eyes. No time for a waterfall.

I felt a large hand on my shoulder. Stuart Symington, the senior senator from Missouri, the first-ever secretary of the Air Force, and a protégé of President Truman, must've caught in my gaze the feeling of otherworldliness that was unmistakably on my mind.

"*Patrick—do you know what Harry Truman used to tell me? When he first came here, he'd look at his colleagues, pinch himself, and think,* How the hell did *I* get here?"

I chuckled. Now that was a story I could relate to at this very moment.

But Stuart wasn't done. "*Then six months went by—and Truman looked at his colleagues, and he thought,* How the hell did *they* get here?"

He laughed loudly. "*Trust me—you'll feel the same way!*"

If the Senate was a club, it was a welcoming one for me.

But three rows in front of me and Symington, a moment was unfolding that was something shy of friendly.

It turned out not everyone shared my enthusiasm for Frank Church's proposal to shine a spotlight of congressional oversight on the CIA.

Mississippi senator John Stennis was leaning in close to Frank Church, inches away from his face, jabbing his finger into Church's chest, giving him the treatment that I'd only heard stories about. I imagined Stennis's horn-rimmed glasses must've been fogged up from all the exertion.

It wasn't the Vermont way.

Church stood there defensively, not sure how to react at first. But he held his ground, arguing equally passionately why he was determined to open up the CIA to congressional scrutiny.

George Tames, the *New York Times* photographer, was lurking in the back row a few feet behind me. He stepped in with his battered Nikon and snapped the photo that would appear on the front page of the next day's *Times*: Stennis versus Church. I watched as Senator Stennis swatted the air as if to rid himself of an invisible insect and walked away from Church. He had said his piece, and he was off in search of other arms to twist.

The caucus meeting began, and just as it did the latecomers straggled in. Suddenly, I had Hubert Humphrey sitting on one side of me, Washington's hawkish Henry "Scoop" Jackson on the other.

Humphrey elbowed me. "*Boy, you learn fast!*"

"*What do you mean?*"

"*Tell him, Scoop!*"

Jackson leaned over conspiratorially. "*When you sit here in the back, you're near the door, and you can slip out without anybody seeing you when you get bored.*"

We laughed.

As the most junior member of the Senate, I wasn't about to slip out of anywhere until the leader told me I could.

Two days later, the full Senate voted 82–4 to pass Senator Church's resolution to investigate the CIA and create an eleven-member committee to bring to light the abuses that Senator Stennis didn't want to hear about in the first place.

The months ticked by as I found my footing. I brought my campaign manager, Paul Bruhn, to Washington as chief of staff. Our time together in the political trenches made him a rare person in Washington who could finish my sentences. We could speak in code and shorthand. I was going home on the weekends and working my way through dozens of meetings for constituency groups to get to know their new senator and plan the year ahead.

But one trip home to Vermont was different from the others.

The commercial flight to Burlington was smooth that day, a short Thursday afternoon passage over the Green Mountains, which, in mid-March, were still amply frosted white with a confection of snow and ice. Spring wouldn't arrive for a couple more months here, no matter what any groundhog might proclaim.

My weekly freshman anxiety about the risk of missing votes or missing the trip home was momentarily erased by the presence of one particular passenger, the person whose presence guaranteed there would be absolutely no risk of votes interrupting the trip. Leader Mike Mansfield was aboard the Eastern Airlines flight, headed to Vermont to deliver the inaugural speech of the Aiken Lecture Series at the University of Vermont, in honor of his longtime breakfast companion.

I was squeezed into the window seat, next to my senior colleague Bob Stafford. Attendance at this gathering—the latest celebration of Aiken's career—was a command performance for both of us, and particularly for me, the one who occupied Aiken's seat and was surely a top target for opposition in 1980.

Leader Mansfield puffed away on his pipe, his eyes focused on the binder containing his speech, a black pen moving backward and forward, slashing words here and there. I could see him tightening the speech, streamlining it, deleting grandiosity and replacing it with his direct, to-the-point expression of what he believed. After the wheels touched down, the leader turned to Bob and me: "*Well, boys, welcome home—let's go see what George has in store for us tonight.*" The more appropriate question might've been what Leader Mansfield had in store for Vermont that evening.

Mansfield rarely spoke on the Senate floor. He was a force to be felt, not heard, his best advice saved for quiet conversations in his office or in the cloakroom. The proof of his power was in the passage of legislation, not the flow of flowery rhetoric.

But this night, at 8:00 p.m., after a testimonial dinner in which Aiken was honored as the former dean of the Senate, Mansfield waxed poetic, philosophical, and political with a small p.

He opened with a heartfelt, almost romantic, tribute to Aiken and his wife, Lola, more emotive than anything I'd ever heard before from Mansfield.

He referred to Aiken as "*one of the nation's foremost authorities on wildflowers. Wildflowers and George Aiken go together, just as George Aiken and Lola Pierotti Aiken go together. Wildflowers grow in a quiet field, on a rocky ledge, in a garden, or in a wooded glen. That is how it is with George Aiken. He is at home and flourishes wherever he may find himself.*"

It was a beautiful sentiment, and Aiken and Lola seemed to bask in its glow. I took a morsel of pride in the way the leader had leaned into the pronunciation of Mrs. Aiken's Italian maiden name.

But soon the leader was on to the business that consumed his days and nights: "*A Senate in continual partisan conflict is an ineffectual Senate.*"

Aiken's comity and his reputation for bipartisanship were essential examples of how the Senate ought to be and of how senators might behave.

Mansfield had largely come to speak to Vermont about the war that would not go away—almost twenty years since Eisenhower first promised the United States would pick up where the French had left off, more than a decade and a half since Kennedy had deepened our commitment, and close to sixty thousand Americans dead since President Johnson upped the ante. Mansfield, the decorated veteran, no pacificist himself, branded Vietnam "*one of the most tragic wars in modern history*" and an "*outflow of devastation*" from our intervention. He described the aggregate contribution of our military-industrial complex as a negative force depleting our nation of resources, both economic and psychic. That while we remained mired in foreign wars, "*other nations are better at producing electronic equipment, pollution-free automobiles, and are buying our resources for manufacture and resale to the United States.*" His diagnosis was severe: "*the financial drain of these deployments is readily apparent*" and the end result was "*a severe shrinkage in the large margin for error which this nation possessed a quarter of a century ago.*" The crowd burst into applause, including the many rock-ribbed Republicans who regularly delivered Vermont into the hands of presidential candidates who had put us on the very course in Southeast Asia—"*waist deep in the big muddy,*" as Pete Seeger sang—that Mansfield had criticized. But he'd done it without mentioning a single president or invoking even one senator or blaming a political party.

Mike Mansfield had come all this way to tiny little Vermont, to this event in honor of his cherished former colleague, to decry a war that had consumed "*too much for too long at too great a cost,*" and clearly, he was calling on us to stop pouring billions of dollars and more lives into Vietnam, to "*make the hard choices between what is more important and what is less.*" It occurred to me: never once had a senator from Vermont actually voted to end the war in Vietnam.

After the speeches, the press swarmed around Mansfield and Aiken to solicit a comment before they headed off to file their hagiographic stories. Flashbulbs captured the two stars of the evening standing there warmly, arm in arm.

One reporter in the scrum invoked Senator Aiken's past statement that in Vietnam it was time to "*declare victory and withdraw*." The press believed that Senator Mansfield was encapsulating Senator Aiken's own position on the war. Perhaps in his heart, it even was.

But on the drive home that evening, I thought about the leader's peroration about "*hard choices*." Hard choices didn't strike me as aspirational positions or caveated arguments. My conviction remained: America needed to make a clean break with that war, which had gone on far too long.

There was no Leahy Lecture Series at the university. But I felt as if I'd been an audience of one for Mansfield's meaning; his words had reached me with clarity and conscience.

— 12 —

Conscience

The Church-Stennis showdown I'd witnessed from the back row of my first caucus meeting had been a preview that even in the clubbiest confines of the Senate, some issues can't be settled by compromise and accommodation. Some disputes are issues of conscience and conviction with no safe middle ground.

Soon it would be my turn in the barrel.

Perhaps because the senators knew I'd face a tough reelection fight in six years, I'd gotten one of my wishes from the Senate steering committee: a coveted seat on the Armed Services Committee.

But my first substantive vote in committee would be contentious. Be careful what you wish for, they say for a reason. In April, Chairman Stennis convened the Armed Services Committee to vote for further authorization for the war in Vietnam. Stennis was an institutionalist when it came to the Senate and to the Armed Services Committee, where he fought year in and year out for the sanctity of the defense budget. We couldn't have been more opposite on the great question of civil rights, he a son of the segregated South steeped in states' rights, and me a child of the civil rights movement inspired by President Kennedy.

But on the Armed Services Committee, Stennis put other differences aside to focus on the task at hand. He immediately spotted in me someone who was a workhorse, interested in the committee's work product, which could, in most ways and on most days, be technocratic and nonpartisan.

But never when the subject was Vietnam.

There were no elegant compromises to be had over America's longest war, particularly not at this point.

I had opposed the war for years. I was a Robert Kennedy supporter in 1968, and my belief that the war was a mistake hadn't softened in the intervening years.

As a candidate for the Senate, I pledged to vote against continued funding. I believed that step was critical to actually bringing the war to an end. Otherwise, we were just throwing words around. Congress's power really is the power of the purse. If you aren't willing to use it, you aren't serious in your position. I hadn't fought this hard to come to Washington just to join a debate society.

I was the newest and youngest member on the committee, from a state that still supported the administration's position. Not surprisingly, Stennis and the Ford administration wondered if I might be a weak link in the opposition to the war.

I could imagine their internal ruminations: maybe, just maybe, they wondered, a freshman senator like me, let alone an "accidental senator," would vote to reauthorize the war funding now and take a year to learn the Senate, to travel to Vietnam, to study the issue before I contributed to what they warned would be a "precipitous withdrawal." It was probably the argument I'd have made if I were them.

What they couldn't have known was how deeply I felt about the war. I wondered how the exit from any war fought so unsuccessfully first by the French and then by the Americans for twenty-five years could by any definition end "precipitously."

I girded myself for the expected onslaught of lobbying from the Ford administration, the calls from assistant secretaries and undersecretaries, and perhaps, I suspected, they'd whip up more phone calls from Vermont, the kind a person in my position might especially fear. Certainly, there would be editorials urging I vote to stand with the president and our troops.

But I didn't anticipate just how quickly the Ford administration would unleash a howitzer in its offensive aimed at Vermont's rookie senator. Marcelle and I were at home when the phone call came in from the White House. "*Please hold for President Ford.*"

There's something about a presidential phone call, including the theater of it all, that adds a sense of gravity to the moment and imbues the participants with a kind of self-seriousness. And this was my first.

President Ford sounded as if he expected I would be standing at attention for the president of the United States, ready to change my position. Little did he know that I was tugging at the phone cord to pull the phone into the alcove away from the hurly-burly of a home with three children late for bedtime.

"*Pat—I'm sure you know why I'm calling. Senator Stennis says you haven't made up your mind on the funding for South Vietnam—*"

"*Well, Mr. President, I've actually told the chairman . . . You know, I've opposed the war for a long time—*"

"*Senator, we can differ about the war. This is a question of our ally—our staying power—we have a government in Saigon that's trying to turn the page—everybody's watching what we do in Southeast Asia—all of Asia's watching.*"

Ford sounded wary. I wondered how many of these calls he was making tonight if he had made his way down to the committee's most junior member.

"*Well, Pat, I hope you'll meet with the administration. Secretary Kissinger is at a key moment in the diplomacy . . .*"

I agreed to meet with whomever the Ford administration deemed important to the debate.

Ford shifted to more personal topics. "*I used to love to ski in Vermont—*"

I couldn't help but think about how politics can be a strange funhouse mirror. Ford was a gifted college athlete, a football player. I wasn't surprised that he was a good skier. But a couple of accidental cartoonish moments in front of the cameras—a trip here, a fall there—and a young comedian named Chevy Chase had transformed him into a caricature on a new weekly television program called *Saturday Night Live*. I couldn't help but wonder whether Ford regretted leaving the company and camaraderie of the House of Representatives for a presidency in crisis.

Secretary of Defense Jim Schlesinger came by the Russell Senate Office Building to tell me how important the war effort was and to argue that we were moving closer than ever to succeeding in standing up a sustainable, resilient government in South Vietnam. Secretary of State Henry Kissinger visited me as well. He peered out at me behind his glasses and warned that if we "pulled out the rug" from under the regime in Saigon, it would disrupt an extraordinary piece of diplomacy and nation-building and the government would fall. I wondered just how secure a government could really be that feared its own population so much. My mind was unchanged.

Vermont's largest newspaper made it very clear that it supported the Vietnam War and editorialized that if I voted against it, I'd never be reelected.

But then again, it never thought I'd be elected in the first place. Marcelle and I decided that this was not a political vote. It was one of conscience, my first truly difficult vote in the Senate. I could not accept my own conscience if I didn't vote to stop the war. If that made me a one-term Senator, so be it.

We were both fine with that.

That day of reckoning arrived in mid-April. Stennis scheduled five votes in a row, with each vote losing by one vote. His theory was simple. He'd start with the bloated budget for Vietnam that he and the administration supported, and if it failed, he would next vote on a descending order of funding, until he reached the very bare minimum amount of funding he believed could sustain our troops' presence. In my mind every one of these votes was the same; everyone knew that the Pentagon had all kinds of tools at its disposal, including the alignment with the separate covert operations budget, to keep the war in business as long as it had one positive outcome in the Armed Services Committee. A senator might vote for a lesser amount and claim he'd downsized the war, but money was fungible, and there was no meaningful difference between the sums of money.

On each vote, they called the roll. "Mr. Leahy?" "No." Five times, I voted no.

I felt the heat on the back of my neck from the stares of the Stennis staff behind me. Stennis had reminded me that Vermont senators and House members had always voted to fund our presence in Vietnam, effectively voting for the war. But he soon realized that I was not going to change my mind.

He next turned to Virginia senator Harry Flood Byrd Jr., a very conservative independent who caucused with the Democrats and reliably supported the war.

"*Mr. Byrd, did you really intend to vote no?*"

Byrd looked at him and said unapologetically, sadly, "*I intended to vote no. They have lied to me for too long.*"

There was a gasp in the room.

Stennis looked at the tally sheet again, took off his glasses, and rubbed his eyes wearily. The weight of what had just happened sunk in.

"*You'll want to get the president on the phone for me. He'll want to know about this right away.*"

The United States was done funding a blank check in South Vietnam. For the first time, the Senate had voted to cut off funding—and we'd done it in a committee that had never before crossed the Pentagon.

I'd kept my word to Vermont and to my conscience, and I'd kept my word to my fellow senators. I couldn't imagine whether I'd just written my political obituary. But the feeling I most felt was one of liberation, and a thought: *This is what senators do.* The hearing room was as tense as any room I'd ever been in in my entire life, including courtrooms in murder cases, but at least I knew I'd done my duty.

— 13 —

The Cloakroom

The Senate cloakroom was a great place for a young senator to continue an education.

Senator Harry Byrd was the self-proclaimed "independent Democrat" from Virginia, the "independent" moniker originating with his decision to abandon the Democratic Party's endorsement in his 1970 reelection bid.

The reasons were simple: Byrd was the latest in a family line of the segregationist wing of the old southern Democrats. His family had long led the opposition to integration, and his father and namesake had been a signatory of the Southern Manifesto, opposing federal civil rights legislation. The same issues that had made me idealistic about public service were the very issues he had fought against with certainty and conviction.

But late at night in the cloakroom, in between roll call votes or filling the time during quorum calls, differences were not the topic of conversation. Byrd mixed and mingled easily with even the most progressive of senators, swapping stories of bygone eras.

Byrd regaled us with the tale of all-night weekend poker games with colleagues both Democrat and Republican at his family's antebellum home in Winchester, Virginia. The bourbon flowed liberally even if the family politics hewed conservative, and you could almost taste the thick clouds of cigar smoke in the retelling.

The cast of characters who religiously attended ranged from liberals like Washington's Warren Magnuson, known simply as "Maggie" to every colleague, quick with a joke and ever smiling, to archconservatives like Wisconsin senator Joe McCarthy.

McCarthy. The name had been both a paradox and an expletive in our house growing up. I could still hear the dinner table conversations in Montpelier, as my dad recounted the news from the Army-McCarthy hearings. There was something about being second- and third-generation Americans in Vermont that made us especially mindful of the feeling of being different, of being on the outside, that made us cherish the protections of the Constitution and the freedoms enshrined in that foundational document. The Constitution meant that even if you were in the minority, even if you were not one of the wealthy or powerful, you had rights that were protected, rights that included due process. We'd have thought that McCarthy would've appreciated that too.

McCarthy's family had come from Ireland, and as a Catholic he had to have known what it was like for his parents and grandparents to have faced prejudice and discrimination in the era of NO IRISH NEED APPLY. Yet this proudly Irish, overtly Catholic senator—this World War II Marine Corps veteran from Grand Chute, Wisconsin—built his national reputation on a witch hunt to out those he deemed disloyal to the United States, without proof or evidence. His warnings about an "*enemy within*" sounded an awful lot like the language nativists had wielded against the Irish just decades before. McCarthy was a demagogue, pure and simple. We took comfort in the fact that the Senate had, at last, taken the rare step of censuring a sitting colleague in 1954, voting 67–22 to condemn McCarthy for his witch hunt and putting an unceremonious end to the era of McCarthyism. But at the Byrd home in Winchester in the late 1940s, McCarthy was just one of the guys—until, abruptly, he was never invited back again.

McCarthy had started out well-liked by his colleagues. He was a good storyteller, and he became fast friends with Byrd and his father, Harry Flood Byrd Sr. When Byrd's daughter was married, she received a silver dish inscribed from honorary "uncles" Joe McCarthy and Warren "Maggie" Magnuson.

McCarthy was a young Turk in the Senate, a freshman at just thirty-eight years old, fresh off a stunning victory over the legendary Wisconsin progressive Bob La Follette Jr. But he was also a heavy drinker who would eat a stick of butter to coat his stomach, which permitted him to drink later and longer into the evenings.

At one of Byrd's endless poker sessions destined to bleed into morning, Byrd caught McCarthy cheating. He suspended the game immediately and sent a humiliated McCarthy home, putting him on the road alone for the hour and a half drive back to Washington to contemplate what he had done.

Three decades later, Byrd felt the moment as if it were yesterday: cheating was not only a violation of Senate protocol, but a transgression against a Virginia gentleman's way of playing cards. In a single, revealing gesture, McCarthy had violated the advice Mike Mansfield had given me about keeping your word to your colleagues.

For McCarthy, it was a sign of things to come and of the self-destructive ways that would put him in his grave before the age of fifty: the willingness to lie and to cheat, and the bonds he'd break so freely with his colleagues in the name of short-term victory.

In hearing Byrd tell the story, I understood for the first time why, despite his years of supporting the Vietnam War, he had made a break with the Ford administration at the same fateful committee hearing in which I'd voted against continued funding for the war. "*They have lied to me for too long,*" he said that day. This courtly gentleman's verbalized disgust with being lied to was universal—whether it applied to a guest in his home cheating at cards or official lies sanctioned at the highest levels of government.

"*Patrick, you should travel overseas. It's part of the job. Bring your wife,*" urged Fritz Hollings, the junior senator from South Carolina. "*We're going to NATO later this month. Come with us.*"

"*I'd love to—but those plane tickets are so expensive.*"

"*Plane tickets?*" Hubert Humphrey laughed. "*We're taking Gerry's plane.*"

"*Gerry?*"

"*The president. Gerry Ford. Have you ever heard of him?*" said Frank Church with a smile.

Three months into the job, I felt like the new kid at school trying to remember the number to my gym locker, hopefully getting the hang of it all. There was parliamentary procedure still to master, but more important, there was the unwritten rule book of how senators interacted with each other to make the "world's greatest deliberative body" live up to that standard on its best days.

The Constitution was very clear about our role in deciding how to spend America's most precious assets: our blood and our treasure. It gave Congress and Congress alone the power to declare war, and it also gave us the power of the purse to decide where America puts her taxpayer dollars to work.

It was no surprise, then, that the Senate's institutionalists encouraged new members to actually see the world, talk to our allies, and maybe understand our adversaries a little better before we voted on some of those irrevocable commitments.

Soon, I was receiving an orientation in a new vocabulary: "CODEL," the military's term for "congressional delegation."

We were set to depart for Europe Thursday morning.

On Wednesday night, the Senate completed action on a tax bill shortly before midnight, and I presided over the Senate for the last two hours of a relatively amiable session. The joys of seniority are such that the late shift in the chair as the Senate's presiding officer typically falls to freshman members. I got home around one o'clock in the morning, and Marcelle and I finished packing around three o'clock in the morning. We then proceeded to toss and turn for the next hour, nervous with anticipation, worrying that we'd sleep through the alarm to come.

An Army car and driver were at the house at six in the morning. Bleary-eyed but excited, we headed off to Andrews Air Force Base, where we met up with the other members of the delegation, led by Senator Humphrey, and included the Republican minority leader, Senator Hugh Scott from Pennsylvania; Virginia senator William Scott; another freshman,

Iowa senator John Culver, and his wife, Ann; North Carolina senator Robert Burren Morgan; and South Carolina senator Fritz Hollings and his wife, Peatsy.

Milling around the austere lounge at Andrews as military escorts loaded our bags for the trip, I was experiencing yet another one of those Harry Truman "how the hell did *I* get here" moments. I figured I was a long way away from what Stuart Symington had predicted would be the "how the hell did *they* get here" phase of my Senate service.

Out of the corner of my eye, I saw a phalanx of security enter the lounge, dwarfing a tiny figure whose reputation and power belied his small stature. Nicknamed the "Little Giant from Little Dixie," the Democratic Speaker of the House, Congressman Carl Albert, was one of the two or three most powerful people in Washington. Amid a brewing constitutional crisis at the height of Watergate, he'd come closer than anyone before of becoming the acting president of the United States, had Richard Nixon pulled the plug on his presidency before Gerald Ford was confirmed as vice president. Now, he was engulfed in his own scandal, accused of receiving illegal gifts from a South Korean agent. Albert was heading to Asia, probably eager for a reprieve from the tumult and turmoil of Washington. I shook his hand, but his warmest reception was reserved for his old friend Hubert Humphrey, who had a well-earned cult status among his peers.

Our delegation boarded what the veteran legislators called a "*flying submarine*," a virtually windowless 707. From the outside at a distance, to the naked eye it could've been a white cargo plane. But just before Marcelle and I stepped aboard from the jet bridge, I noticed the small American flag by the hatch, and I was reminded that when you travel this way, you're representing the United States of America. Our blue tourist passports were exchanged for maroon official passports, carried by the trip's military escorts to hasten our arrival and departure through the various bureaucratic stops along the way.

On board, we had the run of the plane, and the flight crew did everything possible to keep us comfortable. I felt slightly uncomfortable being attended to by these young officers in their dress blues, but Fritz Hollings, a Citadel graduate and World War II Army captain, assured me that in fact Navy officers competed for these assignments. Serving as a Senate Navy liaison was a prized post and could be a ticket to promotion as a rear admiral.

Although Marcelle and I wouldn't have minded dozing off after the long, restless night before, soon we were all gathered around Senator Humphrey, who held court with story after story of the Washington he remembered and his life at the center of the storm in national politics. He was a sixty-three-year-old father of four, but he'd seen it all.

Humphrey was the boy-wonder mayor of Minneapolis whose 1948 civil rights speech at the Democratic National Convention triggered the party's wake-up call and the walkout of the so-called southern Dixiecrats, led by then South Carolina governor Strom Thurmond, who was now Hollings's orange-haired senior senator. Humphrey had been elected to the Senate in 1948, serving as a leader of the liberal wing and Mike Mansfield's majority whip until Lyndon Johnson nabbed him for vice president in 1964. I'd been dedicated to Robert Kennedy's last crusade for the White House in 1968, but I still could remember feeling shattered watching the election returns that November as Humphrey lost to Richard Nixon by less than 1 percent of the popular vote.

Marcelle and I held hands listening to Humphrey expound on his experience as Lyndon Johnson's vice president: his hunting visits to the LBJ Ranch outside Austin, Texas; the agonizing internal debates over Vietnam and civil rights; and his sadness that his association with the Johnson administration and the war meant that he had difficulty appearing on college campuses where he'd once been a folk hero among liberals. *Oh, how different the world might've been if a handful of precincts in a handful of states had switched their votes in 1968,* I thought. There were so many "what could have beens," but none could erase *what was*, or quiet the lingering echo of Humphrey's graceful concession speech that night: "*I have done my best. I have lost; Mr. Nixon has won. The democratic process has worked its will.*"

But it was also a twist of irony that if Nixon hadn't prevailed against Hubert, there never would've been Watergate, and if there hadn't been

Watergate, there might not have been the tidal wave toward reform throughout the country and in the state of Vermont that had brought me to Washington in 1974. Who knows how one action can cast a ripple that affects another across the miles and through the years? What I knew was that here I was, and here he was, and while I never had the privilege to see Hubert Humphrey as president, I could at least learn from him as a senator. I was glad to know that after coming within inches of the presidency, someone of his stature thought so highly of the institution that he would ask his state to return him to service here.

As he wound up one particular stem-winder of an observation, Humphrey apologized for digressing. I'm not sure he appreciated what a captive audience he held in his grip: we were hanging on to each word. Senator Hollings announced that he didn't mind a bit: "*Lordy, Hubie, I'd be glad to buy a ticket for this!*"

Hubie. Fritz. Frank. Hugh.

I sat at the edge of this fraternity of friends, gradually easing my way into the circle.

Hollings in particular was a fast friend, once I learned to understand exactly what he was saying through his rich, Charlestonian, South Carolina low country baritone. Hollings was a face of a very different South from the one Humphrey had encountered at the convention in 1948.

If Strom Thurmond was the face of an angry, racist, defiant South, Fritz oozed charisma, with a big laugh and a sometimes biting wit.

In one Senate race, an opponent challenged him to take a drug test. "*I'm happy to, if you'll take an IQ test,*" Fritz replied, leaving the audience in laughter and the competition in tatters.

He saved his best barbs for a different target: himself. What was the secret to his enduring romance with his beloved Peatsy? "*We're both in love with the same man,*" he said, laughing.

But Hollings's sense of humor and easygoing nature belied a fierce ambition for his state and a confidence in how to best pull the levers of progress. He'd grown up in the segregated South, and he'd come into politics in support of that system that was anathema to what I'd been raised to believe. But Hollings, elected South Carolina's youngest governor at thirty-six, was also the chief executive to preside over the peaceful integration of the state's colleges and universities. His argument wasn't the same as Humphrey's moral clarity. It was a practical argument; Hollings appealed to the state's future, warning that neither federal investment nor good corporate jobs would be attracted to a state mired in segregation. He met the voters and the politicians where they were. He didn't start out making anyone feel guilty. He made them feel practical and self-interested. South Carolina's colleges were integrated without a single shot being fired.

But that's not to say that Fritz Hollings wasn't without a sense of moralism. Far from it. He didn't want to relitigate the South's past, but he had a very clear sense of where he wanted the state and the country to go. He'd brought Robert Kennedy to South Carolina to see the face of rural poverty, to meet people of every race who had never been inside a doctor's office, or a school, kids emaciated from chronic hunger. Hollings was the face of a new southern liberalism that didn't identify itself as liberalism, but it didn't sound that different from what I was talking about at home. This shouldn't have been so surprising, of course, because, as Fritz reminded me, rural Vermont and rural South Carolina probably had a lot in common, even if, he joked, we couldn't always decipher what the other was saying.

Our delegation landed in Brussels around eight o'clock at night in the pouring rain. Jet lag was kicking in. Brussels was embarking on a three-day Easter weekend, and I felt bad for our embassy team, who would be working extra hours because of our arrival. NATO was a plum assignment for the foreign service, but it came with frequent management of visiting delegations.

Hollings had been to this city many times over the years, but his formative introduction to Europe was as a young GI, when he had earned a Bronze Star in support of the campaign to liberate France. John Culver had been a marine during Korea, stationed in Europe. Each and every one of them was filled with awe to see the way in which Europe had been rebuilt over these decades from the rubble of war into a thriving network of modern economies and alliances, with Brussels at its hub. None of them took for granted just how precarious peace and order could be, because they'd seen its fragility firsthand.

My introduction to these issues was more grounded in policy, if not personal experience. The next day I had a series of meetings with NATO representatives. The conversations fascinated me, whether the topic was the potential of entering into cooperative agreements for the development of weapons that could serve NATO allies as a whole or how we might strengthen the relationship between the United States and Europe's common economic market. I'd heard and seen the many ways senators could be home-state boosters bordering on the parochial, whether protecting Louisiana catfish from competition or in defense of California avocados against Mexican alternatives. It was amusing to hear Europeans fervently defend the sanctity of words like "Brie" and "Champagne" against potential American intrusion and competition from our cheese and wine industries. I could only be thankful that they didn't dare lay some special claim to Vermont Cheddar. Politics is politics no matter the state or the language spoken.

Halfway through the first day, Marcelle came down with bronchitis, and the doctor on the trip, Colonel Robert Holmes, gave her a weeks-long prescription of antibiotics.

I joined the rest of the delegation for a mandatory reception and dinner hosted by Ambassador Leonard Firestone at the embassy. It began with a tour of the residence, which included many of the Firestones' Frederic Remington sculptures. It felt like a long journey from the more middle-class existences I and most of my colleagues had known, but our hosts did a good job putting us at ease.

The Soviet ambassador arrived at the cocktail reception in his usual understated uniform: his dark gray suit festooned with the World War II–era ribbons and medals of his glorious and meritorious service at the Siege of Leningrad, and a cartoonish black mustache that might've made even Stalin slightly jealous.

Senator Bill Scott, the junior Republican senator from Virginia who had broken the Democratic Party's post-Reconstruction stranglehold on the Commonwealth Senate seats, sidled up to him and sparked a conversation.

Five minutes later, there was an outburst in the corner. Scott was beet red, his cheeks flush with indignation, jabbing his finger into the Russian apparatchik's chest. "*I—I—I—I know what you are! You're a COMMUNIST!*"

"Of course I'm a communist. I couldn't be a Soviet ambassador if I was a capitalist."

Hubert Humphrey almost doubled over in mischievous laughter. American embassy officials scurried over to defuse Scott's explosive discovery and avoid an international incident. Hollings laughed and shared a story. "*Bill Scott was voted the dumbest senator, and he called a press conference to deny it. Imagine how flustered he was when the first question was 'So, Senator—who is the dumbest one of your colleagues?'*"

Hugh Scott wasn't so amused. "*This is my last CODEL with him—foreign leaders confuse me and him because we have the same last name.*"

Dinner was served.

My first time presiding over the US Senate was a late-night rite of passage that felt more like chaperoning a high school dance than it did a drill in *Robert's Rules of Order*. To a thirty-five-year-old from Montpelier, it was another "pinch me" moment, sitting in the same chair that Harry Truman and John Kennedy had sat in long before they'd been elected president, the well-worn ivory gavel close by to call for order, a cheat sheet of process points taped to the blotter in front of me as a reminder of the words it would be my duty to intone at key moments during the evening.

The real business of the Senate was happening off the floor, in the cloakroom and, I suspect, in the leader's back room. Amendments were being agreed to; others were being left on the cutting-room floor to get us out of there by the morning and on our way back home. Occasionally, I'd hear a burst of laughter from the cloakroom, and I'd cock my ear to listen carefully and divine whether the booming laugh belonged to Kennedy or to Hollings.

It wasn't just sounds that kept me alert while presiding over the Senate.

One evening, it was a distinct smell. Soon my nose confirmed its origins: the unmistakable scent of a cigar.

And not just anyone's cigar.

The parliamentarian was sitting a couple of feet away from the presiding officer's desk.

He smelled what I smelled.

"Senator—there's no smoking allowed on the Senate floor."

"You're right, that's absolutely against the rules."

"*And you're the presiding officer.*"

"*That's right.*"

"Senator, *I think that's Eastland who's smoking.*"

"*I believe it is Chairman Eastland.*" I paused a beat. "I don't see any cigar."

We both smiled. I wasn't about to pick up my gavel and intervene in this breach of protocol against the chairman of the Senate Judiciary Committee. The deference didn't need to be articulated.

"*You're going to do just fine here, Senator,*" the parliamentarian said, and chuckled.

Later that night, Hawaii's junior senator, "Sparky" Matsunaga, took my place in the chair just as a contentious vote was playing out on the floor. The clock ticked down, and Matsunaga's side was surprised that they appeared to be on the losing end, courtesy of a single unexpected absence. Sparky was talking to his compatriots about what had gone wrong, his microphone silenced. He was deep in strategy rather than announcing the tally and the vote's outcome.

The irritated junior senator from Greenwich, Connecticut, Lowell P. Weicker, stood at his desk, waving his arms, and bellowed to be recognized by the chair.

"*The chair recognizes the senator from Connecticut.*"

Weicker was flustered. As a junior Republican in a Senate led by sixty-seven Democrats, he must've felt the closest to victory he'd ever experienced in his six years of service.

"*Mr. President—the vote is closed. The vote is closed. Regular order, please, Mr. President, regular order must be observed!*"

Sparky, in his deepest dulcet tones, responded, "*Regular order is being observed. Perhaps a little slowly, but it is being observed.*"

The deputy majority whip emerged from the cloakroom with a prodigal Democratic senator in tow, who promptly raised his thumb aye.

"*The motion is agreed to,*" said Matsunaga, banging his gavel once and turning to the next item on the agenda.

Weicker, crestfallen, didn't know what had just hit him. The majority wasn't going to lose a vote to a technicality.

My political education continued.

— 14 —

The Rules

I was getting my sea legs in the Senate, no longer getting lost in the hallways or having those anxiety dreams kids have in college about waking up hours late for a final exam they'd never studied for. Gradually, I was gliding past those awkward "firsts" and simply getting into a routine. Every step of the way, people were simply gently steering me along.

One day after caucus, I was headed back to my office in the Russell Building when Hubert Humphrey called out: "Patrick—are you coming to lunch?" He gestured toward the senators' private dining room.

"Oh, Hubert, I'm new here. I—I—"

Humphrey laughed. "Pat, let me tell you, when I first came here, I saw who had lunch in that room every day. Jim Eastland, Richard Russell, all the southerners. And I thought, *I don't belong there.* Then Russell Long said to me, 'Why don't you ever eat with us?' And I explained to him I didn't want to make anyone feel uncomfortable. Do you know what Russell said? He told me, 'Hubert, it's the senators' dining room—and you're a senator. It would be uncomfortable if we didn't all eat together.'"

After that, I never hesitated to follow my colleagues into the dining room, just like Humphrey had suggested, and no one there looked at me like an interloper.

But there would be one invitation that would open an unexpected vista.

"Patrick, would you mind helping out tomorrow night?"

My ears perked up immediately.

For a freshman senator standing in the warm glow of the majority leader, the correct answer, almost regardless of the question, was yes.

I probably would've picked up Mike Mansfield's dry cleaning if he asked. But he didn't, and he wouldn't have. But I could tell from the twinkle in his eye that Mansfield had no routine assignment in mind as he chewed on the end of his pipe.

"We'll have votes late tomorrow on the defense bill."

The leader had my attention. Was there a legislative assignment he had in mind for me—votes that needed to be wrangled?

"We'll have a back room set up for the night. Would you be able to tend to the bar?"

#99 in seniority, I figured, brings with it more mundane responsibilities. Little did I know that it was also an opportunity to learn from one of the Senate greats and observe the quiet skill that had kept him at the helm of the institution for the last fifteen years without so much as a challenge or whisper of dissent.

This was no ordinary bar to pass the time between votes, no Senate speakeasy assembled to make the night go faster.

It reflected Mansfield's view of what made the Senate function, and creating this space for colleagues of both parties was silently embedded in the Mansfield code of what a majority leader owed both caucuses.

It was one of his subtle efforts to restrain the many forces arrayed against an effective Senate, from the lobbyists he banned from his spartan office to the layers of overly protective staff that he thought sometimes insulated senators from one another to the Senate's detriment.

Mansfield's back-room bar had no name or secret door knock, but the rules didn't have to be written down as they were unspoken and firm: *Senators only*.

Why? Mansfield didn't preach or lecture. It wasn't who he was. He knew how to count votes and twist arms, but he believed the job of majority leader was much bigger than that, and he was convinced that arm twisting was a form of energy that could be depleted if used too frequently.

A colleague had told me that on a chilly Friday in the fall of 1963, Mansfield had planned to deliver a Senate floor speech about the Senate itself, a rare moment in which the leader invited the public and his colleagues under the hood to hear from him about his thinking. Mansfield wasn't one for puffery or public philosophizing.

He penned the words carefully:

> I am what I am, and no title, political face-lifter, or image-maker can alter it. I believe that I am, as are most Senators, an ordinary American with a normal complement of vices and, I hope, virtues, of weaknesses and, I hope, strengths. As such, I do my best to be courteous, decent, and understanding of others, and sometimes fail at it. . . .
>
> [E]very member ought to be equal in fact, no less than in theory, that they have a primary responsibility to the people whom they represent to face the legislative issues of the nation. And to the extent that the Senate may be inadequate in this connection, the remedy lies not in the seeking of shortcuts, not in the cracking of nonexistent whips, not in wheeling and dealing, but in an honest facing of the situation and a resolution of it by the Senate itself, by accommodation, by respect for one another, by mutual restraint and, as necessary, adjustments in the procedures of this body.
>
> The constitutional authority and responsibility does not lie with the leadership. It lies with all of us individually, collectively, and equally. And in the last analysis, deviations from that principle must in the end act to the detriment of the institution. And, in the end, that principle cannot be made to prevail by rules. It can prevail only if there is a high degree of accommodation, mutual restraint, and a measure of courage—in spite of our weaknesses—in all of us. It can prevail only if we recognize that, in the end, it is not the Senators as individuals who are of fundamental importance. In the end, it is the institution of the Senate.

Mansfield never delivered the speech on the Senate floor.

As he put the finishing touches on the draft, the news ricocheted through the Capitol that President Kennedy had been shot in Dallas.

But twelve years later, Mansfield still stayed true to the lessons he'd been prepared to share with his colleagues, even as Washington changed and the challenge of holding the institution together grew more difficult. At its core, he thought of his job as the exercise of getting one hundred senators to know one another and invest above almost all else in their relationships with one another, so that consensus was the rule, not the exception.

I flashed back to my first conversation with him: "*Senators should always keep their word.*" It would no doubt be easier for senators to break their word to a colleague they didn't know well. Easier still to oppose the legislative priorities of someone a senator had never sat down and talked with about their state, their family, their personal journey.

Mike Mansfield had a lurking fear that centrifugal forces were pulling senators apart from one another. Campaigns were becoming more expensive. Senators were out spending more time fundraising. Television interviews were increasingly a cheap sugar high for those who jockeyed to give the snappiest sound bite or the most provocative take on events. Show horses were rewarded over workhorses.

Mansfield even quietly opposed the installation in the early 1970s of the Senate's electronic buzzers and clock system that let the senators know precisely how much time they had left in a fifteen-minute window to get to the Capitol and cast their vote. In Mansfield's judgment, the unintended consequence was clear: those buzzers empowered one hundred senators to spend more time in their offices, cloistered with staff or reporters or their fierce partisan supporters, and less time together on the Senate floor and in the cloakroom with their colleagues. Pop onto the Senate floor to vote with a minute left and retreat to your office—an opportunity to avoid meaningful contact with colleagues.

It made it easier for a senator to think more of herself or himself as an individual entity and to think less about the institution.

Mansfield didn't win the battle to keep out the gadgets and buzzers of modernity that intruded on the intimacy of the institution, but he waged an unspoken war to create cohesion nonetheless.

I wondered for a fleeting moment whether the leader's office could assign a staffer or one of the Senate dining room employees to tend bar instead of a fellow senator. Surely, it could've been a good night of tips for many of the young staffers who tended bar in the evenings anyway at the Hawk 'n' Dove or other Capitol Hill watering holes.

It sunk in. Mansfield was organizing an environment where senators of both parties could be alone with other senators for hours at a time with no risk of leaks, a place where the only people who knew what was said behind those closed doors were the senators themselves.

He had a deep and abiding faith that senators were custodians of the institution, "*no seniority or juniority*," as he often said, but one hundred of us sharing the responsibility to make the place work. But he needed to create an inviting location where those senators could know one another—Democrat, Republican, or independent.

No temptation to preen for the cameras. No risk of a photo of two opposing senators appearing too chummy for the sake of their politics. No staff trying to interrupt a conversation in an effort to prevent a senator from straying from political orthodoxy. No lobbyists with an agenda to peddle.

And in Mike Mansfield's back-room bar, this was one of the only times that happened anymore in Washington.

Leader Mansfield's back room was ordinarily missing one feature: the leader himself. He didn't spend too much time there. But he would pop in every now and then, stick his head in the side door and holler, "*You boys have everything you need?*"

Whether a senator was forty or pushing ninety, to Mansfield we were all his "boys."

When the leader did appear, he could usually be spotted in a corner with his Republican counterpart, Hugh Scott, the two quietly puffing away on their pipes, sometimes even playing cards.

At my post behind the bar, I learned quickly who preferred vodka, who drank Scotch with just a splash of water, and who the bourbon men were, but more important, I tried to take a mental note of the history recounted right under my nose. The "pinch me" moments arrived with great regularity as I observed a Senate in transition.

Barry Goldwater often shuffled in after a round of television interviews. He had his iconic horn-rimmed glasses perched above his nose—with no glass in them. I quickly realized the compromise he had made to accommodate the cameras: without the lenses there, they photographed better, and this way Goldwater kept his trademark intact. He traded the costume pair for the real thing inside his suit jacket pocket, and he eased back in a chair to talk with Senator Humphrey. Those two graying legends, both of whom knew the sensation of being introduced around the country as "the next president of the United States" only to come up short of their dream, agreed on little, but were always submerged deep in a friendly back-and-forth. They were a fraternity of two out of one hundred members: two who had been major party nominees, and with that came a healthy respect for political skill and experience.

One night, their conversation veered wistfully to memories of two very White House meetings. For Hubert, it was the reminiscence of the night President Ford had invited him down to the White House after the Carter victory just to have a small dinner with their wives, very much Gerry and Hubert rather than "President Ford and Vice President Humphrey."

Ford said, "You know, I regret only having had two or two and a half years here as president."

Hubert replied, "Gerry, do you know what I would have done just to have two and a half months as president?"

Little did I know then the illness growing inside of Humphrey as he sat swapping stories with Goldwater.

Goldwater was a very good storyteller in his own right and a prankster. For a man who had been caricatured in 1964 as an imminent danger if he had his finger on the nuclear button, victim of the brilliant Johnson

"Daisy" ad so incendiary it had to run only once on television to have its desired effect, he could laugh at himself and those around him with equal ease. He was a gifted mimic.

But this evening, his mind drifted back to one of the most difficult conversations he'd ever have in the White House. On August 7, 1974, as I was home in Vermont slugging it out as an underdog against Richard W. Mallary, House Minority Leader John Rhodes, Hugh Scott, and Barry Goldwater—"Mr. Conservative" himself—asked to see the president to tell him that the dam was breaking in the Senate. To avoid attention, they met in Nixon's "working office," in the Old Executive Office Building. The Watergate tapes had been simply devastating, but Nixon was holding on to hope that his staunch base in the Senate Republican caucus, combined with conservative southern Democrats, might give him a chance to hold on in a Senate trial even if House impeachment articles were a fait accompli. Rhodes told the president that House Republicans were not monolithic in their willingness to back the president, who just two years before had carried forty-nine states in a landslide. Scott, his pipe in his hand as always, gently told the president that the tide was turning in the Senate, sharing with him that Senator Sam Ervin, head of the Watergate investigation, had been very effective, and Nixon grew ever more fidgety as the conversation went along. At last, he turned to Goldwater.

Nixon rubbed his eyes wearily. "*Barry, do you share this assessment?*"

"*I do, Mr. President.*"

The meeting broke up. Goldwater was asked by the press whether he had pressed Nixon to resign. No, he told them. For someone often depicted as mean, it was a moment of great courtesy. Goldwater took no joy in this moment and believed at least that the three of them should leave Nixon the dignity of being able to say that his inevitable decision was his and his alone. If Nixon had lost Barry Goldwater, then the quiet part didn't have to be said out loud: the president couldn't be president any longer. Two days later, Nixon was gone.

Another rainy evening on the Senate floor, Mike Mansfield was huddled in a corner with Senator Phil Hart, figuring out the floor schedule, when he spotted a familiar figure—a tall senator with broad shoulders and a wavy head of hair with a distinctive part—his back to the room, closing his soaked umbrella.

"*Jack!*" Mansfield called out across the chamber.

As the man turned around, Mansfield's face went white.

Ted Kennedy had heard the leader call him by his brother's name.

It was such an innocent misfire of the neurons that connect our memory to our mouths. Mansfield had been elected to the House of Representatives in 1943. Jack Kennedy joined him there four years later. They were in the same class of freshman senators in 1953, and Mansfield had happily ascended to majority leader when Kennedy plucked Leader Johnson for vice president. The symmetry in their careers up the ranks had been uncanny, but more so was the personal connection between these two Irishmen.

Mansfield had seen Ted but thought Jack—the same way you do in that familiar déjà vu moment when you think you've seen the face of a long-lost family member in a crowd.

Ted looked stricken, but not as stricken as Mansfield, who rushed over to Teddy, reached out his arm, and said, "*Ted—I'm sorry—I looked up and—I just—I thought for a moment—the president—*"

Ted put his arm on Mansfield's shoulder. "*No, no,*" he said gently. "*I know you loved my brother, and he loved you.*"

Ted patted the leader on the shoulder again, as if to remind him that nothing else had to be said. Kennedy retired to a comfortable chair where he eased his aching back, and unburdened himself of the weighted legacy that came with being the final Kennedy brother left in the Senate.

— 15 —

An Unlikely Ally

I kept doing the spadework of being a good senator, tending to the home front of Vermont, where my committee assignment on the Armed Services Committee, however junior, was an opportunity to deliver. Union workers powered the factories and plants that made the goods and weapons upon which the US military depended.

One day at lunch in the senators' dining room, I received an unexpected offer that would only burnish that credential. "*I want to come to Vermont,*" announced Barry Goldwater, a longtime fixture on the Armed Services Committee.

He was Mr. Conservative and the first Republican presidential candidate ever to lose Vermont in a general election—but for Barry Goldwater, there was ideology on one hand and military hardware on the other. Barry wanted to see for himself the facility in Vermont where we were testing the Vulcan machine guns made by General Electric. It was a fearsome piece of machinery—multibarrel like a Gatling gun, because otherwise the rapid firing would've quickly melted the barrel of the gun.

We would surely be an odd couple, but I was thrilled by Barry's offer: the Armed Services Committee runs on bipartisanship, and with reelection on the horizon, it could only help me at home to showcase my position on the committee and my connection to a brand-name senior Republican.

I offered to see what flights would be available to get us up there on Friday morning, but Goldwater smiled and said, "*Don't worry about it, we're going out of Andrews.*"

We boarded a forerunner to the Gulfstream: four engines in the back with two on each side touching under the tail. Clearly the military wanted to stay on Barry's good side. The pre-positioned onboard reading material included a coffee table book on Arizona's scenic highways, and the cover on Goldwater's seat had two stars, because he was actually a major general in the Air Force Reserve. A Senate military liaison had done his homework about the powerful person aboard that morning; suffice to say, there was no ceremonial jug of maple syrup or glossy tribute to the byways of Chittenden County. I knew where I ranked.

It was a wintry day on the firing range. General Electric, to impress Goldwater, arranged to have an old tank on the end of the firing range about a kilometer away. The gun was enclosed in a bunker aimed at it.

The manager of the plant told Senator Goldwater to just press a button. He looked like a kid on Christmas morning as he happily obliged.

It was probably about a half-second burst, but it was like a laser with hundreds, even thousands of shells flying straight into the tank, hitting the tank, and ripping it apart. There was an explosion inside the tank, and the turret flew up in the air, spinning around and crashing down in the snow.

Senator Goldwater was standing behind the manager, a very serious person.

Goldwater gave me a wink and said, in a stage whisper, "*I'm going to hit the head. I'm not sold on the Vulcan. When I come back, I sure as hell want to try another one, Patrick.*"

He went to the restroom, and as soon as he was out of sight, the manager stammered to me, "But we don't have another one."

If it wasn't bitterly cold outside, he'd have been drenched in sweat.

I looked him in the eye and said, "*That's Barry Goldwater. He is the senior Republican on the Armed Services Committee. He could just snap his fingers and end this program.*"

The panic was palpable.

"Just go down to the National Guard, they have tanks down there. Get out your credit card and buy a used one, get it up here, and we will blow it up."

He stared at me, almost shaking.

"Now, you don't want to tell the president of GE that you said no to Barry Goldwater, do you?"

I was starting to feel bad for this earnest and intense manager.

He reached into his jacket pocket for his billfold and opened it to take inventory of his credit cards.

I could imagine him doing the mental calculations of credit limits and statement balances.

Little did he know that Barry was by then standing right behind him, doing his best to keep from doubling over in laughter.

At least two of us enjoyed the joke.

— 16 —

President from Plains

I was two years in the Senate when life took another turn that seemed like it could only have been forged in a Hollywood scriptwriters' room. The 1976 presidential race was playing out all around us. President Ford tapped Senator Bob Dole of Kansas as his running mate, a World War II hero who was also a fierce political combatant. The insurgent Democratic ticket was fortified by the junior senator from Minnesota, Walter Mondale, whom everybody called "Fritz." But it was the top of the ticket who seemed strangely familiar to me; the former governor from Georgia whom I'd sat down with for coffee at the Hanover Inn in 1974, two unknowns and underdogs meeting for the first time, was now on his way to the presidency with a brilliant, pioneering campaign. Everything about Jimmy Carter in 1976 seemed to speak to the political snapshot in time. His promise to "never lie" and always tell the American people the truth was a refreshing break from the Watergate era. His campaign posters with Mondale said it all: LEADERS, FOR A CHANGE. It worked; in a scarred, traumatized country still digging out from the twin traumas of Vietnam and Watergate, Carter-Mondale won by the slimmest of margins, but seemed to offer a second chance for so many exhausted Americans, whether they'd voted Democratic or not.

Some things, of course, didn't change. Even as vice president, Fritz Mondale considered the back room of Mike Mansfield's office a safe harbor. Maybe more so, even, a refuge away from the press and the White House, and it was certainly more welcoming. I think he longed for a chance to see familiar faces away from the ceremonial vice president's office on the Senate side of the Capitol.

One night I saw Fritz in the hallway. He surmised that I was headed to the Mansfield suite to tend the bar for the evening. Fritz said he could use some "holy water" after a long day.

"Is there anybody back there yet?"

I said yes.

"I'll be there in a minute, Pat—cover for me."

I had barely made it behind the bar when Mondale strolled into the room, puffed out his chest, and yelled, "*What's wrong with you people? Stand up, it's the vice president of the United States!*"

A shower of cookies and crumpled-up cocktail napkins flew in the direction of Mondale, who loved every second of it.

I took our son Mark to the summer congressional picnic at the White House. He was six years old and fascinated by politics. The warmth of Hubert Humphrey had hooked him quickly on the idea that maybe Washington, DC, wasn't such a terrible place after all.

And now he was about to experience the closest thing to a political version of meeting Santa Claus at the department store: he was face-to-face with President Carter himself.

He and the president went off walking hand in hand.

A little while later, Mark came back with a plate brimming with lobster.

I asked him where he had gotten such a feast—very different from the hot dogs and burgers everyone else was snacking on contentedly.

Mark said, "*President Carter had asked if I like lobster, and I told him yes, and he showed me where the lobster was.*"

Three days later, I went back to the White House for a meeting and thanked the president for his kindness to my boy the other day.

Carter smiled knowingly. I mentioned the lobster, and the commander in chief asked if I had heard the whole story. The president had asked Mark what he liked eating, and Mark had confided that "lobster's my *favoritest* food."

He probably had eaten it once in his life.

Carter said, "Well, they have lobster over there, Mark, if you want some."

"Well, Dad told me not to pig out, Mr. President."

"You go get all the lobster you want and tell him the president told you to do so."

Mark exclaimed, "Okay, thanks!" And boom, he was off.

I just sat there and laughed and thought, *Oh God*, and Carter said, "You know, it's nice to be a child again."

I liked President Carter, instinctively. I think many of my Senate colleagues from previous generations weren't quite sure what to make of him or his administration. There were mixed signals at times. On the one hand, probably at Fritz Mondale's urging, the Carter administration had tapped the beloved Mansfield for an ambassadorship, a sophisticated gesture that landed well. On the other hand, Carter represented a new kind of southern Democratic politician that didn't quite sit well in either faction of our caucus. Carter had always been progressive on civil rights, and he had a thinly disguised discomfort with those like Stennis and Eastland, who seemed like a musty reminder of the South he was working to usher into quiet memory. But Carter was a southerner, manifestly evangelical and religious, and more economically moderate than those on the left in our caucus, including Ted Kennedy, with whom he seemed destined to clash. I could relate, in different ways, to all of them.

I was from a small state where bringing home investments and earmarks could lift people out of poverty and affect real lives, something I had in common with the old bulls. But I'd been elected as an outsider, something I had in common with Carter and Gary Hart and the newer generation. And of course, I'd been inspired by the Kennedys and loved that I had a chance to serve with Ted. I was able to work in all three of these very different worlds, to move in, out, and between quite comfortably, while always being myself. Carter didn't seem as at ease with the concentric circles of the party, but here was the rub: his administration needed all their votes to enact an agenda.

My relationship with President Carter was always strong, and the rapport was always warm. Maybe it was because we'd known each other since 1973 when both of us were longshots. Maybe it was because we shared humble roots, or because we shared an understanding of rural America.

But there were moments when I could relate to the eye rolls and side glances so many of my colleagues evinced when the subject of the White House came up in our caucus.

Carter's 1976 presidential campaign was a brilliant stroke of a person not just meeting the moment, but understanding it intuitively. Carter really did tap into something deep in the electorate: a desire for an outsider, someone honest to clean out the post-Watergate Washington stables, someone with decency and character. Gerry Ford was as decent as they come, himself not that different from Carter. But America didn't want an insider that year, and that was the genius of Carter's campaign.

But an outsider couldn't govern by remaining aloof from Congress.

Carter had a strong moral compass and an unwavering sense that the United States had to stand for certain principles in the world, that we really were held to a different standard and measured harshly when we didn't "*walk the walk*."

I agreed with him. It was why I'd so admired Frank Church's crusade to hold the abuses of the intelligence community up to the light of public transparency. We weren't just any country; we weren't the Soviet Union or the People's Republic of China; we were the United States, and the world counted on us to live by our professed values.

And so I wasn't at all surprised when President Carter asked Leader Robert C. Byrd to push ratification of the Panama Canal Treaty through the US Senate. Carter knew that as long as the United States maintained sovereignty over the canal, it would be a lasting symbol and lingering stain of the colonial era in the hemisphere, one that the Soviets wielded against us for propaganda value in the struggle to win "*hearts and minds*."

But just because you're *right* about an issue doesn't exempt you from working the politics to bring unlikely potential allies to your side. The Carter White House didn't seem to grasp that, inevitably, grassroots conservatives would churn their direct-mail fundraising apparatus to turn the word "treaty" into a dirty word. The canary in the coal mine was the public opposition of the former governor of California, conservative icon and likely Republican presidential aspirant Ronald Reagan.

Reagan was telegenic, smooth, and charming—and the perspective for which he was speaking had a foot soldier in the Senate who spied an opportunity to make political hay, the senior senator from North Carolina, Jesse Helms.

One day, on a flight home to Vermont, I was flipping through *Life* magazine and happened upon an interview with the Duke himself, John Wayne. I found Wayne's movie characters as irresistible as the next guy; I'd whiled away hours in the movie theater in Montpelier watching everything from *Sands of Iwo Jima* to *True Grit*. I knew that Wayne's personal politics were somewhere to the right of the John Birch Society, so I was surprised to read that, because he had a vacation home in Panama and knew so many locals, Wayne of all people supported the treaty. He believed that patriotic, hardworking Panamanians who should love the United States instead resented us because—in their mind—so long as we held on to the canal, we were denying Panama the chance to become economically self-sufficient.

I felt as if I'd discovered gold in the hills of John Wayne's Orange County conservatism. As soon as I landed, I called the White House with a suggestion: invite John Wayne over for cocktails, and invite the undecided Republicans and any wavering Democrats to hear from John Wayne himself about the merits of the treaty. Imagine how valuable it would be to a conservative Republican or a Democrat from a conservative state to have a photo in his local newspaper standing next to Rooster Cogburn himself.

The response from the White House staff was condescending: "*John Wayne's a Republican movie actor—what does he know about the Panama Canal Treaty?*"

I argued my case. A legislative liaison from the Carter team replied, "Well, thanks, Senator, we'll run this up the chain."

I knew what that meant.

A week later, I ran into Fritz Mondale in the gym. I pressed him to consider it. He agreed it would be helpful.

Days later, I asked Fritz whether it was under consideration. He shrugged. He had the look of a frustrated vice president who was constantly having to defend the commonsense politics he'd practiced for twenty years to a group of Georgia political operatives who thought they knew best. But I admired Mondale's loyalty to a president who had given him the opportunity of a lifetime; Mondale wouldn't criticize anyone, but his silence spoke volumes.

— 17 —

Farewell, My Friend

Approaching three years—the halfway mark—of my first Senate term, the passage of time seemed like such an oxymoron. On the one hand, those first days in the Senate were memories I could recite for my parents with perfect clarity, as if they'd occurred that afternoon. On the other hand, I felt far removed from that neophyte just trying to make his way. The guidance of extraordinary mentors, hard work, and the pressure to deliver day by day, week by week, made the time fly by.

Marcelle and I brought our children home for Christmas knowing that 1979 would be an even busier year, and we all deserved a peaceful Vermont Christmas.

The snow was falling softly that evening in Middlesex, but I couldn't enjoy it. Christmas recess after a long and tiring session should have been a welcome respite, a magical time with the children up in Vermont, but an inner-ear infection and the accompanying vertigo had almost put me in the hospital. Every time I stood up, the room started spinning. The doctors had ruled out the worst causes of vertigo—and prescribed me strong medication to ride out the infection—but it was a miserable feeling nonetheless. The Capitol physician had actually loaned me a wheelchair for the time being. I had gone upstairs to bed just to stretch out so the floor would stop moving around me.

The phone rang in the hallway. My eyes were closed in the dark room to try to regain my sense of equilibrium, but I heard the door creak open. It must have been important. Marcelle walked in, quietly holding the phone trailed by a long extension line.

"*It's Hubert*" was all she said, and she put the phone down on the nightstand.

It was an unspoken but understood fact that Hubert's cancer was back with a vengeance. The year before, we'd voted to create a new position in the leadership: deputy president pro tem, giving Hubert Humphrey a car and driver, as he navigated an array of experimental treatments at Bethesda Naval Hospital. He looked very thin. He was mostly now convalescing in Waverly, Minnesota, but his staff had installed a toll-free line, ostensibly for his official duties, but really so that he could keep in touch with his friends around the country.

"*Patrick! I heard you were having a rough go,*" he boomed. "*I hope you got home safely and you're listening to Nurse Marcelle!*"

I smiled and thanked him for calling, but something pushed me to ask the pregnant question.

"Hubert, how are you doing?"

The pause was palpable, and the weight of waiting for a heavy, if expected, answer sat on my chest as I stared up at the spinning merry-go-round of a ceiling.

"They've *given me a short time left, Patrick. But I wanted to call and tell you and Marcelle and your children how much I love you all.*"

My eyes burned as I held back the pressure.

"*Patrick, I love you, and please, if we never talk again, remember I love you.*"

"*God bless, Hubert—we feel the same—*"

"*Well, I'll let you go, Patrick—get back on your feet soon.*"

Twenty days later, he was gone.

Hubert Humphrey's death jolted me. I hadn't lost someone that close to me since I was a teenager and my grandmother and grandfather passed away. But there was something harder to process with Humphrey's death: he was only sixty-six years old, full of life, and he'd lived such a remarkable career that felt cut short so unfairly. I could never explain why he'd taken me under his wing, or why he and Muriel had been so kind to Marcelle and our children. Having a mentor had meant so much in those earliest days, when I felt most unmoored, but the way Hubert did it was so exceptionally understated. He never said, "Kid, I'm going to help you out here." He just did it. He just showed up. He never asked for anything in return, not that I could've repaid the favor. He just did what was right.

Kids process death in their own way. One night, I found our son Kevin in the living room, where he'd lined up all the political pins and memorabilia Hubert had given to him through three years of visits to "Uncle Hubert's" office in the Russell Building. Now he was lovingly organizing them and preparing to pack them safely away in a shoebox for posterity. "He was my friend," said Kevin.

"We were lucky," I replied, and tousled his hair.

The Irish are especially good at staying busy when there's a death in the family. There's always a task at hand to take the mind off the loss: a wake, a grand funeral, a home visitation filled with food and drink and laughter.

After Humphrey died, I threw myself into being for his replacement in the Senate what Hubert had so kindly been for me: a gentle guide, not that she needed it, because, after all, her name was *Muriel Humphrey*.

Shortly after Hubert's passing, Minnesota's governor, Rudy Perpich, asked Muriel to serve until the general election, as her husband would have wanted. They'd been partners in everything for forty-two years of marriage, from the mayorship in Minneapolis to the White House and his post–vice presidential service in the Senate. Now, Muriel had become the first woman to represent Minnesota in Congress and the first Second Lady to serve in the Senate.

She knew everyone by name, but greeting them for the first time as colleagues, she seemed worried. After Vice President Mondale swore her in—a beautiful and bittersweet moment, given how much Fritz's own path had been intertwined with the Humphrey family—we all gave her big hugs.

A week later, she delivered her first speech on the floor during an evening session, on affordable childcare, an issue that mattered to her and to Hubert. Afterward, she sat quietly at her desk, the memories hanging thick in the air around her.

I went over to her and said, "Muriel, I think some of the people are gathered in the back room, you have to come back and join us."

"Oh, Patrick, Hubert told me about that room and that you all get together there and tell jokes—I don't know—do you suppose they would mind?"

"Of course they won't mind, Muriel, everybody loves you, and besides, you're a senator."

I told her the story about Senator Humphrey telling me why I should eat in the senators' dining room despite my young age: "We're all senators." I was quickly choked up.

"Patrick, let me do the crying."

We both laughed—and we marched off to the back room, smiling for the first time in weeks.

Mansfield's back room was full of unwritten rules: *You don't leak. What happens here stays here. Senators above all respect their fellow senators.* But one rule stood out above all others: *No one sits in Jim Eastland's favorite chair except Jim Eastland.*

I mean, nobody would even think of sitting there.

Vice President Mondale would pop in for a Scotch, and Eastland would sort of just growl a greeting. He certainly wouldn't get up. But when I walked through that door with Muriel, Eastland came alive like a hunting dog that had heard a rifle shot: he jumped to his feet and hollered, "There's a lady here, stand up! Mrs. Humphrey, why don't you sit right here."

Eastland led her to his chair, which was right next to a couch. Another senator started to sit down on the couch next to Muriel. Eastland hip checked him and sat beside Muriel.

He turned to me and said, "Boy, get the senator a drink."

I knew what to do in a moment like that. I fixed her a drink right away, and I thought of my friend the civil rights legislator whose beloved wife was now being feted by his adversary on the other side of the defining issue of our lives.

Only in the Senate. I think Hubert would have smiled.

— 18 —

Home Front

I was in law school the first time I heard Bob Dylan's "Subterranean Homesick Blues," and the words stuck with me for their prescience about politics:

> *You don't need a weatherman*
> *To know which way the wind blows.*

Well, you don't need focus groups in Vermont. You just need a reliable car, a half a tank of gas, and a couple of dollars to invest in the day's newspaper. You can feel which way the winds are blowing without putting your finger to the air.

As my first reelection loomed, my plate was full, and I felt pulled in different directions. Marcelle and I had absolutely made the right decision to listen to Mrs. Stafford's advice and keep our children and the family in Washington during the week. It sometimes meant them staying up later or coming to the Capitol to be with me, but we almost always had dinner as a family. We had grown closer. My weekend routine up and back to Vermont had been tiring, and I hated being away from our family for those weekend nights, and I missed the children's sports games on the weekends. But it was working overall for our family, just as my political education in the Senate was working during the week. I don't think my idealism had dulled one bit, even as I'd come to appreciate that my assumptions about the Senate and about my colleagues had changed as I'd gotten to know them as people rather than caricatures. I soaked it all up as I had in law school, enjoying the chance to learn from the veteran senators for as long as I had them around.

Still, always lurking in the back of my mind was the fact that I knew many senators probably wondered how long I'd be around. Marcelle and I had made the decision early on to approach my six-year term without weighing every vote and every decision against the odds of reelection. But I knew I had a target on my back. I'd seen people like Orrin Hatch win in 1976 by making incumbency a disadvantage, and I'd watched younger Democratic incumbents go down in defeat in 1978, like my friend Dick Clark from Iowa, so I figured in 1980 I'd have the worst of both worlds: enough of a record for an opponent to try to label me "part of the problem," but also young and unestablished enough that I couldn't point to a long record of accomplishments to insulate me from these attacks. I had to make do with the hand I had been dealt and with the brand I'd built in the time I'd had to build it. There was a daily awakening I struggled with; it seemed that just as I was acquiring a practiced fluency in a Senate job I loved, I had to go out and fight to keep it. I'd treated the privilege to serve as a once-in-a-lifetime six years, but I so very deeply wanted the ride to continue.

In 1980, I'd have my work cut out for me. Ted Kennedy and President Carter were facing off in a demoralizing and divisive fight for the Democratic nomination for president. Teddy was beloved in our caucus and Carter much more aloof from the Democrats in Congress, but everyone was torn about whether Ted made the right decision to take on Carter in a primary. It was uncomfortable in the Senate, but it was absolutely complicating for the national party: instead of focusing on winning in 1980 and reelecting Democratic senators, the party's best operatives were scrambling to either defeat Carter or defend him.

At home, I faced an opponent, with significant financial resources, and I knew as well that any vulnerable Democrat would also face a barrage of independent advertising from the Republicans, as they'd done quite effectively in the 1978 midterms around the country. I was saving our hard-raised dollars for the final sprint of the campaign, rather than for polling.

Votes ran late on Thursday evening, so I took the first flight home on Friday morning, a short flight into Albany, and I was in the car by 9:30 for the drive across the border to Burlington. It was going to be a hot day up north, but I was happy to be out of the sauna of Washington, DC, and back with our family, which had dispatched for the summer at the farm the first day after the school year ended. I'd be home with Marcelle and the children by the early afternoon—but first I had my favorite kind of opinion research to complete on the drive.

We didn't have 7-Elevens in Vermont, or Walmarts, or the endlessly homogeneous strip-mall, roadside sprawl that had infected so much of New England and simultaneously erased the unique local character of small-town life.

Instead, from the Northeast Kingdom to the Eastern Vermont Gateway, you'd find tiny stores blending into the roadside neighborhoods and thoroughfares.

Here, it wasn't Kmart or Giant, it was Aldrich's or Foote's, and many of the stores had formal names that no one used because each store was inseparable from the family that ran it. You weren't buying from a franchise; you were stopping in to see a neighbor.

The stores were often old, converted clapboard homes, well run and well loved by families who had lived in Vermont for generations. Many, just as I had growing up connected to the Leahy Press, lived up above the store or in a few rooms behind it. Inside each store you could find a potpourri of provisions, from bait and tackle to coffee and perhaps a fresh batch of homemade doughnuts protected by a plastic dome.

Forty-five minutes into my trek, I pulled off the road and stopped in at my first country store of the morning to pick up a piping-hot cup of coffee and a copy of the *Free Press*.

The clerk behind the counter looked me over with an expression of familiarity, that slight flicker of recognition. A woodstove that would be roaring with heat months from now resided in the center of the store, a temporary resting place for a pile of hand towels for sale, marked eighty-nine cents each.

"Good morning," I said with a smile, as I made my way to the coffeepot.

His eyes followed me as I poured a cup of Maxwell House into a Styrofoam cup.

"It's going to be a hot one," I said, referring to the weather, not the coffee in the bottom of the glass carafe, striving at best to be lukewarm.

"*Are you—are you—*" The clerk was working his way toward a risky question for any politician.

I remembered the story a Republican colleague from Wyoming, Alan Simpson, had told me.

"*Hey, you—you look just like that Simpson guy we sent down to Washington!*"

"*I get that all the time,*" Alan had replied, feeling witty.

"*Kinda makes you mad, don't it?*" Alan's constituent shot back.

Fortunately, this interaction would be smoother.

"*Senator . . . Leahy?*"

I stuck out my right hand in greeting as my left hand pulled a couple of one-dollar bills from my pocket. "*Good to see you again. How are you doing?*"

It was a hard and reliable rule I'd learned in the 1974 campaign: when you're a candidate in Vermont, you never say "*good to meet you,*" because there's a solid chance that somewhere along the journey you really already have met them. No politician needs to risk inviting the inevitable complaint when he leaves the room: "*That so-and-so's gone Washington—he forgot he met me at the American Legion in '77!*"

"*How's business these days?*" I asked.

The fellow behind the counter sighed and shrugged, and declared hopefully that "*things will pick up with the out-of-towners.*"

He made the sign of the cross, but he didn't have to invoke divine intervention: even in these economic times, you could count on the summer visitors from Massachusetts and New York to blow in with an endless supply of disposable tourist dollars on their vacations to the lakes, and for the pace of out-of-staters to continue through mid-November with the leaf peepers, as we called the foliage tourists.

Another customer walked up to the cash register and joined our conversation. "*I put in seven dollars at the pump,*" he said to the clerk, as he laid out a sweaty five-dollar bill and eight quarters. "*Prices are up again.*"

"*The Arabs,*" said the clerk. "*At least it's not a shortage again—yet.*"

"*How much does it cost you these days to fill up your truck?*" I asked.

"*Senator, I couldn't tell you.*"

"*Well—ballpark—how much—fifteen dollars?*"

"*Senator, I really mean it. I can't afford to fill up my truck.*"

"*Heating oil will be way up again,*" said another customer, as a small crowd gathered two rows deep around me.

"*Senator Stafford and I are working on the heating oil program now—before winter comes, so everyone can warm their homes,*" I said. "*That's what we were doing this week in Washington.*"

Heads nodded.

A man in a work shirt asked me about a broken stoplight down the street. I took down his phone number and the intersection on a piece of paper and promised to call my office with the details.

"*Well, I need to get home—our children will be asking! Good to see you all today.*"

As I stepped onto the sidewalk, a young man from the local newspaper had just arrived. I'd be surprised if he was twenty years old. He caught his breath. "*Senator Leahy, we heard you were here—they sent me over from the newsroom . . .*" I answered a couple of questions from the cub reporter, he snapped a photo—apparently his beat included not just writing the stories but taking the photos, and I'm guessing that next he'd put on his editor hat before working on the layout and turning on the presses—and soon I was back in the car and off on my way.

Twenty-five minutes later, I stopped at another little country store—this time for gas.

The same scene repeated itself.

A few older couples were gathered on the sidewalk outside the Coca-Cola vending machine.

"*We voted for you,*" said an older woman with a kind, weathered face.

"*Don't let Washington change you,*" urged another.

"*What was your position on giving away the Panama Canal?*" asked a big, burly figure whose perspiration was matched only by the droplets of condensation on his ice-cold bottle of Coke.

"*Oh, I voted the right way on that one,*" I replied.

"*Keep the government's hands off my Medicare,*" said another.

"*How is that beautiful wife and family?*" asked another.

"*I hope I can earn your vote again,*" I replied.

"*Do you remember me?*" asked an older gentleman. These could be famous last words.

I paused.

"*You sent me to jail in '73!*"

I did a double take and started to make a mental note of just how many steps it would take to get to my car without making a scene.

"*Oh, I was pretty mad at you. But I was guilty,*" he said matter-of-factly. "*But in jail, my cellmate was even madder at you! You'd sent him away too. And that son of a bitch was a businessman!*"

"*Well, I—*"

The man cut me off. "*And then I thought,* Hell, if he does the same thing to rich guys as he does to people like me, well, we could do worse in Washington."

I don't know if I breathed an exaggerated sigh of relief or if it was just my pulse returning to normal—but I felt better right away.

Crisis avoided.

"*Well, thank you! If I can ever be of help—we have the offices in Montpelier and Burlington . . .*"

I was soon back behind the wheel until my next stop.

By the time I pulled up the gravel driveway at Drawbridge Farm, on the car seat next to me were a stack of four identical newspapers—each picked up at my store stop-offs—and five empty paper cups of gas station coffee. For the price of a quarter tank of gas, two dollars in coffee, and the duplicate newspapers, I'd been rewarded with the equivalent of five local focus groups and built-in local earned media opportunities. Who needed consultants when you could multitask on a commute?

I was reminded that my secret from 1974 remained truer. I didn't have to hear it from Tip O'Neill's mouth to know that "all politics is local." It's also about listening. Just as voters can sniff out who really is on their side and who is reading talking points, a politician better have a good ear to listen to what people are really saying at home. In 1974, those conversations gave me great confidence that people were making a mistake assuming Vermont would remain reflexively Republican. But listening again five and six years later, just talking to people, their message this time gave me a reason to worry more and dig into the campaign. People felt anxious about the economy and disconnected from Washington. If they happened to know the good work we were doing, they didn't yet realize who was making those changes on their behalf. Of course, that's what campaigns were about: defining those differences in ways people could digest them, meeting them on their terms. But nonetheless, the political tea leaves were unambiguous: people were hurting, and 1980 was going to be another difficult election campaign.

— 19 —

By My Fingertips

I knew reelection would be tough. What I couldn't have predicted was just what a national undertow I'd face, and how strong that current was moving to catch anyone sleeping in the final stretch of the campaign.

All the newspapers' and party's polls had found me ahead, sometimes comfortably. But none of that was consistent with what I was hearing as I campaigned all over Vermont. Leader Byrd was urging our caucus to run on the fruits of their seniority and of the productivity of Washington. I was sensing something very different: whether it was the cumulative effects of years of inflation, the long gas lines at the pump, or the Iran hostage crisis, which brought back memories of the loss in Vietnam, people felt a hopelessness born out of their government's seeming helplessness. They were still angry at Washington, as they had been in 1974 and '76, turning away from trusting the government at the very same time we were being urged to run toward it.

I asked my pollster, Peter Hart, to take a survey. My instincts were right: heading into the final ten days, with just one debate left to alter the dynamic, I was trailing.

I was angry that the race had gotten this tight, and mad at myself for forgetting how I'd been elected in the first place. There was a Leahy playbook that I'd waited too long to rely on, but I refused to believe it was too late. The debate—broadcast on all three networks and on Vermont public television—would be seen statewide. People actually tuned in. Folks leaned in and listened by late October.

Marcelle took me aside the weekend before. She was distressed from watching the campaign unfold so much of the year on autopilot. It felt to her like an out-of-body experience: as if the campaign were adjacent to us.

"Patrick, stop with these people telling you to act senatorial, like you're above everything. You are a trial lawyer. A good, tough trial lawyer. People know you as the former prosecutor. Be yourself. Prosecute the case."

She was right.

I threw away the briefing book the team and I had drilled on for a week. I watched a weekend of television ads and thought, *If I were a voter, I'd vote against that senator from inside Washington too.*

I came in to the debate ready to go right at my opponent.

He began with a polished opening, reading the talking points he got from the Republican National Committee. They were the same talking points deployed in Indiana and South Dakota; just replace the name "Leahy" with the name "Bayh" or "McGovern."

I interrupted him. "You know those points aren't right. You know that distorts my record. The positions you're taking are not Vermont positions, they're from the national Republican Party, and they are total distortions."

I then laid out in rapid *rat-a-tat-tat* fire what I'd done and what I stood for.

The camera was on my opponent and caught him looking at the papers, which said "Republican Senate Campaign Committee."

Four days before the election, I got a call from Senator Dale Bumpers of Arkansas. He'd been a former governor, elected the same year I had been, and he had started off his reelection campaign 30 or 40 points ahead in the polls. He called me and told me he was slipping in the polls, and each day they dropped further, although he thought he could pull it off. He said he'd called John Durkin, who was in our class and who most likely would win reelection in New Hampshire. He told John, "*I cannot spend all the money I have here, can I send you some?*"

John replied, "*No, I'm going to win here, I don't need it.*"

Dale asked me if I could use the money.

I'd never heard of anyone in American politics having a hard time handing out money to win reelection.

Of course I would be grateful for the contribution—because I knew that I was trailing.

But I was worried by what Dale had relayed.

I'd been campaigning along the Vermont–New Hampshire border and had talked to people from both states.

I thought both John Durkin and I were behind.

I called John and urged him not to trust the positive polls. He thanked me, but he had trust in the numbers.

Instead, I trusted what I *wasn't* hearing from voters. I stood in the cold to shake hands with union workers at the shift change outside a plant in Rutland, Vermont. They had always supported me, and I would come there even in nonelection years just to stand outside and say hi as everyone went in. Now, I stood there saying, "I need your vote," and in return I received a stony response: "*Well, we intend to vote.*" This race was coming down to the wire.

Election Day in America is a remarkable event. This was my second time as a statewide candidate. All the months of campaigning came down to this day when the candidate can only do so much: sure, there are a handful of radio and television interviews to help goose the vote in critical towns or areas of the state, but for the most part you've laid your cards on the table to be counted. You've run your race. The waiting is the hardest part.

Marcelle and our parents were huddled in our hotel room, as we had six years before, only this time I was the incumbent, and the news was not good for Democratic incumbents. Our contacts at the Democratic National Committee said that the early exit polls were showing catastrophic defections from President Carter among labor households up and down the East Coast, including Pennsylvania and New Jersey. If the Carter-Mondale ticket was losing there, we would all be in trouble.

By the middle of the evening, the news was worse. We were hemorrhaging Senate seats. The national media was swept up in the hoopla over the defeat of Birch Bayh and George McGovern, national figures from conservative states. I was just as stunned by the reports of the race next door. In 1974, my Georgetown classmate John Durkin had prevailed in the country's closest Senate race, winning by two votes after a re-vote. Tonight, there'd be no nail-biter; even as the results from Manchester's Democratic wards came in, Durkin was behind by double digits, and New Hampshire would have a new Republican senator in Warren Rudman.

I was pacing the room as our results trickled in. It was a seesaw night, back and forth. Ronald Reagan was running ahead of President Carter, and that was little surprise in Republican Vermont. I knew all along that I'd have to outpace the Democratic ticket to get reelected. But an independent presidential candidate, former Republican congressman John Anderson, was doing well, and it appeared for much of the night as though Carter might be kept under 40 percent of the vote. It was ominous.

But as Chittenden County's numbers came in, I seemed to be holding steady by the slimmest of margins—everywhere from a high-water mark of four thousand votes to a thousand and change, tight enough to keep me on my feet, unable to sit still.

It felt like 1974, only the stakes were more personal: now I was the known quantity, and I couldn't help but feel like this was a referendum on me, a verdict on whether this Irish Catholic kid was, as the newspapers loved to imply, an "*accidental senator*."

Dad looked up at me from a comfortable chair. "*Sit down, Patrick, have something to eat.*"

"*I can't, Dad, I have to see the numbers. Why is it always so close?*"

"*Better to win by a handful of votes than lose by a landslide, I always say,*" my father said with a grin. He was right, of course. Dad always was.

The Democratic ticket was on its way to a national thrashing, losing forty-four states to Ronald Reagan.

But in Vermont, our tiny margins held up. I couldn't help but think that my weaknesses had become my strengths. Because I had never known some great advantage of incumbency, I had never taken anything for granted, and I had run as myself, not as some Washington version of me. I had stayed much closer to my state's grass roots and sensibilities than colleagues who bought into the playbook that urged them to nationalize the race and run on their majority.

I'd been the first Democrat ever elected to the Senate from Vermont; I was now the first Democrat ever reelected: I was going back to Washington for a second six-year term.

It was a miserable lame-duck session.

On November 13, just nine days after the landslide loss to President-elect Reagan, President Carter appointed Stephen Breyer to the First Circuit bench.

It was an extraordinarily generous gesture by a defeated president to nominate a gifted legal thinker who happened to work for his political adversary Ted Kennedy. Carter could've sulked. He could've wallowed. He certainly could've held a grudge against any Kennedy loyalist. But he didn't. Instead, he saw a newly created seat on the First Circuit, and he acted to try to install the very best person on it.

I wondered if Fritz Mondale had influenced the decision, a Senate institutionalist trying to score one last win for the world's greatest deliberative body by picking not just a Senate insider, but one who could be confirmed during a lame-duck session because even Senator Thurmond and his staff had come to like Breyer.

It was the right thing to do, but it was also the smart thing to do.

But Breyer had one ironic hurdle to overcome: political payback.

Lame-duck Democratic senator Robert Morgan launched a filibuster against Breyer as the clock ticked down on Carter's presidency. Morgan was bitter about Breyer's role in exposing a judicial nominee from North Carolina's alleged improprieties.

Jesse Helms had won his scalp in the Senate race: appearing in a television commercial in which he'd urged a vote for John East over Morgan because North Carolina needed "*a real Christian in the Senate*," Helms had gone all in to elect another Republican senator. East had defeated Morgan by just 10,401 votes, almost all of them attributed to his vote for the Carter administration's Panama Canal Treaty. Morgan had cast a vote of conscience on the treaty, without any hand-wringing or horse-trading. He had lost his seat for a virtuous cause.

Now, Morgan's anger over his previous clash with Breyer would consume his last days in Washington.

Ironically, party politics didn't prevail. Senator Thurmond organized a handful of Republicans to break the Morgan-led filibuster of Breyer. Thurmond didn't agree with Breyer on anything, nor was he friendly with his boss, Ted Kennedy. But Thurmond believed that Breyer had always operated in good faith. He wouldn't tolerate Breyer becoming a casualty of a renegade Democrat for having exposed the truth.

On December 9, we confirmed Steve Breyer to the First Circuit by an 80–10 vote.

Our paths would cross again.

— 20 —

Among the Ruins

There was deep bitterness in the Democratic caucus about the way the Carter White House had cost us our majority. For the first time since the New Deal, Senate Democrats would be in the minority. Not a single Democratic senator had lived even one day out of power. But for twelve of our ranks, it was a permanent rather than a temporary exile.

There was anger at the White House and bitterness toward Majority Leader Byrd.

I had felt the Reagan wave coming, but even I did not think it was going to be a tsunami. It was a blessing and a curse that I was running scared back home in Vermont. It meant that I felt the bad news coming ahead of time, but it also meant that I had time to guard against it. For me, it meant doubling down on localizing the race—on forcing voters to think about Patrick Leahy of Chittenden County, rather than the caricature of a Washington liberal in Jimmy Carter's cardigan into which Republicans' cartoonish attack aimed to transform me. It was the only kind of politics I'd ever known, and the brand of campaigning I'd depended upon to get to the Senate in the first place.

I resembled Yogi Berra's old quip: "I came to a fork in the road, and I took it." For me, there had only really ever been one way to run. But, ironically, my more seasoned colleagues didn't have such a singular instinct to fall back on; they knew too much, or thought they did, and they invested in the Robert Byrd approach to reelection: the Washington way. In a different year, it might've worked. They hadn't been back home campaigning, but instead were working hard, coming back to Washington to take care of things on their legislative agenda. Bob Byrd wanted to keep us in there as long as he could to prove the advantage of incumbency and delivering from Washington. But all the country wasn't West Virginia. People expected to see us. They expected us to speak directly to them.

In a different year, the chairman of the Appropriations Committee, who put through a bill in a couple of days' time for well over $1 billion in aid to his state after Mount Saint Helens erupted, would have been rewarded by voters. But this was no ordinary year, as I reminded myself watching Chairman Magnuson wheeled through the halls of the Dirksen Building, diabetic and broken, his feet swollen by gout. His political carcass had been left among the rubble, along with the chairmen of the Agriculture, Judiciary, Foreign Relations, Environment and Public Works, and Health Committees.

They'd all lost, and I faced a recount.

Frank Church was especially bitter. For four years, he'd been there for the president despite his state's increasingly right-wing bent. As the Foreign Relations Committee chairman, he'd been the principal driver of the Panama Canal Treaty, which had inspired a John Birch Society–type "ABC—Anybody but Church" political action committee to spend hundreds of thousands of dollars in attack ads committed to Church's defeat. But the coup de grâce came on election night: with national media predicting a blowout victory for Reagan, Church begged the White House not to concede until the polls closed in the mountain states and on the West Coast. Moderate, lunch-bucket Democrats in the Idaho panhandle might come out and vote to reelect Church if they didn't believe all was lost. These were the blue-collar voters who had stuck by Church for four terms. President Carter didn't wait. He conceded early. Frank Church lost by four thousand votes out of nearly half a million cast.

It didn't feel like Christmas in Washington. Vice President Mondale didn't hold the traditional holiday parties at the Naval Observatory. But he did invite all the senators who ran that year and their spouses to join him for dinner.

My pangs of survivor's guilt were especially active as Marcelle and I sat down at that banquet table. Other than Gary and Lee Hart, we were the only couple to have come out of reelection in one piece, because we had both been new enough to Washington to trust our own instincts in states where we had never been "part of the club."

After we had a few cocktails, Fritz Mondale stood up and kicked off the evening with a sober toast. His glass in hand, he announced, "*You all are some ungrateful SOBs. None of you have proposed a toast to thank Jimmy and I for the wonderful job we did on your reelections.*"

There was a stunned silence, after which the room erupted into a collective roar of "*HahahagotohellFritzhaha.*" We started picking up dinner rolls and throwing them, and Mondale just kept on speaking as if he were giving a serious talk and nobody else was there. It was brilliant.

It was the first time I'd seen Frank Church or Birch Bayh laugh since November. The sliding pocket doors to the dining room opened up, and a Secret Service agent stuck his head in, just as a dinner roll bounced off the vice president's head. Mondale winked at him to leave. The Secret Service agent looked over to me, and I just mouthed over my shoulder, "*It's all good—don't worry!*" I noticed that the agent left the door open just a crack—just in case.

Within an hour, we were all hugging and laughing, feeling better about the world, and the bond between all of us was restored. Political careers had been shattered. Realities had been disrupted. But life and laughter went on.

When the laughter ended, the realization hit hardest, both the good and the bad.

After the election wave of 1980, the Senate I'd entered was gone: a kind of political Brigadoon, a remarkable memory that suddenly, without sufficient warning, had vanished. The number of senators who remembered the extraordinary era of legislating during Eisenhower, the New Frontier, or the Great Society was cut down to a handful. Even the number of senators who remembered the fights over reform at the heart of Watergate, those who remembered the battles to implement oversight of a runaway executive branch and why it mattered—gone. Both party caucuses were starting to trend more homogeneous, but more than that, we had lost so much institutional memory in a six-year span—to retirement, to appointment, and to defeat.

But I was still here.

Before the bodies were even cold across the political landscape, I knew that I'd had the second-closest Senate election in the entire United States. Twenty-seven hundred votes separated me and Stewart Ledbetter.

My sense of gratitude was deep, and the feeling of relief and rejuvenation deeper than I'd anticipated. I'd never seen myself as an accidental senator. But now, for a second time, voters had reaffirmed that I was their choice to serve in Washington.

I felt emboldened, no matter how close the margin. My integrity was far more important than the political reaction to a vote. I read and reread Edmund Burke's speech to the Electors of Bristol, which I had quoted when I first announced for the Senate in 1974. Burke spoke of his enlightened conscience, which "*he ought not to sacrifice to you, to any man, or to any set of men living. . . . Your representative owes you, not his industry only, but his judgment; and he betrays, instead of serving you, if he sacrifices it to your opinion.*"

Marcelle and I pledged to not think about reelection again until the year before I'd be on the ballot. We had five years now to be confident and comfortable in our place here. We'd save the worry for later and just live—and do our best to help govern.

Not everyone was as quick to understand the message. I was speaking to a community group in December, outlining my priorities for the new Congress—health care, housing, jobs, and the environment. I wasn't bending from my convictions.

A man raised his hand after I was done speaking. He sneered, "*Look at how close your reelection was, did it teach you nothing?*"

I quipped that I wasn't smart enough to divine the lessons of that race on my own, so I called the senator who had the closest reelection in America and asked him whether he was going to heed the lesson and trim his sails in the new Congress.

The questioner arched his eyebrows.

"*That senator's name is Barry Goldwater, I'm pretty sure you've heard of him.*" The audience applauded.

Back in the Russell Building hallway, I told Barry the story. He laughed. "*We're not going to change our stripes. But we need to change our luck. Let's mix something up.*"

I was intrigued.

"*So, listen, you liberal Democrat from New England, Abe Ribicoff is retiring, and he's got an office I've had my eye on for a long time, and I'm moving in there. You ought to move into mine.*"

I told Barry that I did not have the seniority to move. He swatted at the air as if to rid himself of an invisible insect. "*Don't worry about that, Patrick. Republicans are in charge now; you can move next Friday.*"

I did.

We had to patch all the holes in the walls where Goldwater had hung his ham radio equipment to talk to the troops, along with a menagerie of taxidermic hunting trophies he'd brought back from the Arizona desert.

But a change in scenery would do us all some good.

Part II

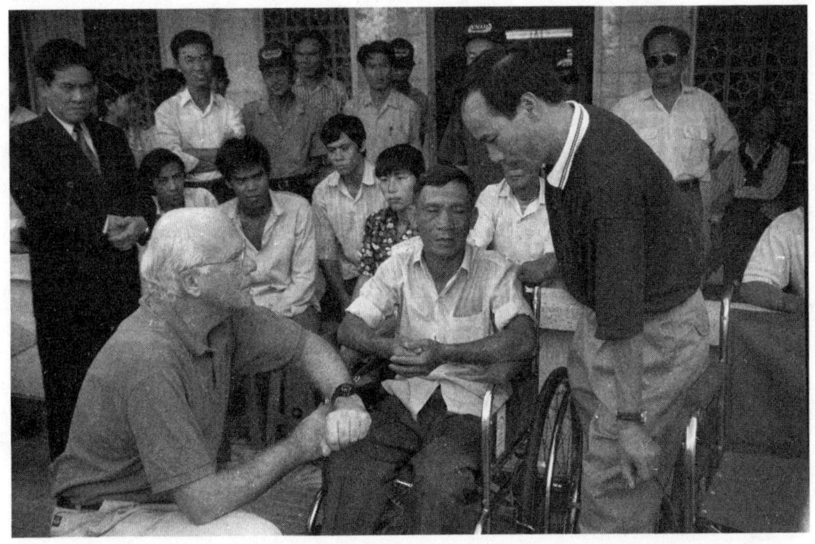

Marcelle took this picture of me and our friend Ca Van Tran in 1996, chatting with a Vietnamese land mine victim in his new wheelchair funded by an AID program that became known as the Leahy War Victims Fund.

— 21 —

A New Lease

The temperature lingered in the mid-fifties as Inauguration Day approached, unseasonably warm, a defiant contrast to the political chill in the air for Democrats still reeling from the landslide loss.

The Senate's lame-duck session had been a bittersweet parade of farewell speeches from men I'd grown up knowing as big, boldfaced names in our body politic and many of whom I'd learned from these last six years. My Senate Class of 1974 seatmates Bob Morgan and John Durkin—swept away.

But the biggest bodies left behind on the political battlefield had helped write the history of much of the second half of the twentieth century.

Warren Magnuson—author of pioneering consumer protections. Seared into me was my first memory of the man they called "Maggie" as chairman. I wanted to get a small line-item appropriation for Vermont, and I kept trying to get recognized as the most junior member and finally wore the chairman down. Squinting through the thick black plastic glasses always sliding down his nose, stubby cigar in his even stubbier fingers, Maggie asked, "*What do you want?*"

I said, "*I have this amendment, it involves Vermont.*"

"*What's the amendment?*"

"*Well, it's fifty—*"

"Well, aren't you too junior to be asking for a $50 million line item?"

I said, *"No, no, Mr. Chairman, it's fifty thousand dollars."*

"Oh, for God sakes, don't bother us with that, just tell the staff and they'll just write it in."

I needed no further introduction to the chairman, and now he'd been defeated.

George McGovern—the Greatest Generation son of a minister turned World War II bomber pilot who went on to lead the fight against the Vietnam War.

John Culver—the Harvard fullback who played college football alongside Ted Kennedy and could light up a room with the power of his oratory.

Birch Bayh—author of not just one but two successful amendments to the Constitution, the legislator who succeeded in rewriting our foundational document to give eighteen-year-olds the right to vote.

Gaylord Nelson—the founder of Earth Day.

Frank Church—the indefatigable investigator who had brought oversight to the intelligence community.

It was not an understatement to say that the post–World War II American story could not have been written without them. And now? All of them gone.

I walked around the Russell Building trying not to dwell on the departures and all the upheaval.

At the other end of Pennsylvania Avenue, the pain was just as real, blunted perhaps by the frenetic way President Carter was furiously negotiating into the twilight hours of his days in office to bring the American hostages home from Tehran.

The weekend before the inauguration, I picked up the newspaper and thought, *My God, finally President Carter is catching a break.* Sunday's headline blared that an agreement was close, at least in principle, to release them, and that the president might soon head to Germany to meet the hostages upon arrival. He intended to do this and be back in time for President-elect Reagan's inaugural at noon on Tuesday. From the White House briefing room, President Carter announced at four o'clock Monday morning that the breakthrough had been achieved.

I had a meeting with President Carter scheduled for 9:15 that morning, the last time, I thought, that I'd be seeing him in person before he headed home to Plains, Georgia, and the last time, I imagined, that I'd be seeing the inside of the Oval Office for a long time.

I assumed the meeting might be called off, that the president might soon be wheels up from Andrews Air Force Base to greet the released Americans.

I called my office. There had been no call with news of cancellation from the White House, so I buttoned my shirt, put on a tie, and headed downstairs to say goodbye to Marcelle and make the drive to 1600 Pennsylvania Avenue. At the kitchen table, fully dressed, his hair neatly parted, sat our oldest child, Kevin, with a look on his face that indicated he had something to ask me. *Could he come to the White House one last time?*

Soon enough, we were on our way. Washington was awash in decorations, with freshly hung signage indicating everything from the parade route to parking restrictions. Maintenance crews were inspecting freshly painted lampposts, and workers were assembling the parade viewing stands, which would be occupied by the triumphant Republicans.

We arrived at the White House's northwest gate, where the guard sheepishly explained that as the invitation was only for me, Kevin would have to wait in the car. I said no, that was quite all right, that I had been told by a legislative liaison that he could come into the lobby. Showing the infallible nature of the security system, the guard said, "*Oh, that's okay, Senator, bring him on in.*"

Kevin asked, "*Who told you that you could do that, Dad?*"

"*Don't ask, son,*" I said, and off we went to the lobby, where we were met by someone from the Senate liaison office, who said they were delighted to see Kevin, although they had not expected him. We chatted for a while and then headed on down to the area outside the president's office. Kevin was going to wait outside for me.

When we arrived, Fritz Mondale was standing there to arrange an appointment to see the president. He looked exhausted, his hair askew and his tie loosened.

I volunteered that naturally, I would stand aside and wait for him to go in, and that he could use my appointment time. Fritz said no, he'd wait for me.

"No, I insist," I replied.

We went through this Alphonse and Gaston routine for a bit, until he said, "*Well, look, I got defeated for reelection, and you're in there for six years. I know my place. You go ahead first.*"

I chuckled at the gallows humor.

"*Besides,*" he said, "*all I want to do is tell Jimmy to get those hostages back so we can all go back home to bed.*"

I reminded Fritz that among the hostages was a Vermonter—six-foot-nine Bill Keough, a former superintendent of schools from Burlington who had endured those 442 days so far in captivity with the other fifty-one American hostages. I had written to him several times while he was there and brought a new letter I hoped Vice President Mondale might bring with him when they went over to greet the hostages.

When a receptionist came out and asked me to go into the Oval Office, he was accompanied by the president's Senate liaison, Dan Tate, who asked Kevin to come in too for a minute.

The president put on a tired but big smile for Kevin, shaking his hand and sharing that he would miss their visits together. The *click-click-click* of the flashbulbs went quickly, and soon Kevin melted out of the room along with Tate, leaving President Carter and me by ourselves.

We sat in the wingback chairs facing each other seven feet away from the Resolute Desk. On the ground along the walls, painstakingly protected in bubble wrap, rested the framed personal photos that President Carter had decorated the walls with over these last four years. A painting by his teenage daughter, Amy, was leaned against a couch, next to be packed away.

In a sense, it was not that different from the way the abandoned halls of the Russell Building looked at this very moment, with departing senators clearing the way for their successors. The room had an empty, melancholy feeling, not unlike the last day of college, when the dorm rooms are emptied and the mementos packed, the finality of it all hanging in the air. But the president seemed determined to finish this half-marathon by running through the tape and finishing the tragic business that had devoured his presidency.

I shared with him how badly I felt about his defeat, but congratulated him on how he had worked out the hostage negotiations. It was a long, hard journey, from the scenes of our blindfolded diplomats being paraded in front of the cameras, to the failed rescue mission and the helicopter crash in the desert, to these last complicated diplomatic and financial arrangements to finally bring them home. Only because of his strong personal involvement and urging, alongside the expertise of Deputy Secretary of State Warren Christopher, Treasury Secretary Bill Miller, and others, was it possible to make it work in these dwindling hours.

Phil Wise, the president's appointments secretary, came in and handed him a note about a phone call. I could see the note in his hand indicated that President-elect Reagan was on the phone for him.

Wise immediately left the room, and the president went over to pick up the phone. I whispered hoarsely, "*Mr. President, I'll be happy to step outside*," and started to get up from my chair.

"*No, just go ahead and stay there. That's quite all right*."

President Carter cradled the phone between his ear and his shoulder as he flipped through the papers on his desk. The White House operator had difficulty making the connection between Washington and California, but in a few more seconds, Reagan was on the phone.

The president listened to him for a few moments and then thanked him for what he had said. President Carter added that his people had been keeping the Reagan transition team posted on the hostage transfer and that he knew that they had been keeping Al Haig, the incoming secretary of state, posted as well.

I couldn't help but wonder what might be going on in Carter's mind. He had been working sometimes literally around the clock on this crisis, while the president-elect seemed unfazed by the details, content to hear the updates periodically through his aides or through the throngs of reporters greeting him as he stepped into his waiting limousine. President Carter shared with Reagan that after he received the final word at two or three o'clock that morning, he'd thought of calling former governor

Reagan to tell him, but then decided he wouldn't wake him up at that time. I'm not sure what Reagan said in reply, but President Carter said, "*Well, I'll be happy to call you if something further comes up tonight.*"

Then President-elect Reagan made an interesting comment. President Carter had said that he did want to go over to Germany to meet the hostages, but he did not intend to do it if it would interfere with President-elect Reagan's inaugural or if he could not be back in time to hand over the presidency at the appointed hour tomorrow. President-elect Reagan told him that he knew how important this whole matter was to the president, how much he'd agonized over it, and that whether the final return of the hostages was before or after the inaugural, President-elect Reagan wanted President Carter to go meet them and to use Air Force One for that purpose. Moreover, he said that if it was after the inaugural, President Carter should feel free to go as President Reagan's personal representative.

President Carter's face brightened and his eyes glistened. After a short pause, he thanked Reagan for a "*very generous comment*" and then said, "*Well, Ronnie, have a good day.*" Carter paused. "*In fact,*" he said with a little bit of a chuckle, "*have a good day tomorrow too. I'm sure you will. Thank you, Ronnie.*"

He hung up.

We talked about what he planned to do now. He was at peace with himself. For the first time in years, he was not going to be in active, public life, with no public duties to perform or offices to run for ever again. The president and Rosalynn could go back home to Plains, have time for themselves, live as human beings, and think about new ways to serve. He had the advantage of being one of the youngest former presidents in history and the youngest former president living, and both he and Rosalynn wanted to write books. For once in his life, he did not have to worry about financial matters. The book would itself create a certain amount of wealth, but with the modest needs that he had, he could be perfectly satisfied and happy, he said.

I told him how much I appreciated his comments in his farewell address, especially on two points: the growing danger of partisan, single-issue groups and his emphasis on arms control and the curtailment of nuclear weapons. He said the latter was the sort of thing that needs bipartisan support, and while it was an enormous disappointment to him not getting a nuclear proliferation treaty ratified, he held out hopes that the new administration would follow such a treaty's guidelines until it could put its own stamp on another one. He said he would certainly not criticize the administration for changes it might make, as long as they were all aiming toward the final goal.

I was skeptical of anything the Reagan administration might be willing to do with the Soviets on that issue, after all of Reagan's talk in the campaign about ending the appeasement of the Soviets. The president replied with something I could tell he meant with great conviction: "Patrick, the presidency can change people. It can widen your perspective."

I told the president I'd miss him. I'd always considered him a friend, and despite the White House's reputation for aloofness from Capitol Hill, this president was a person I could call when I needed to, irrespective of whether we happened to agree or disagree on a particular issue.

I told the president that I knew how busy he was and started to get up to leave. He took me by the arm and said that he remembered how much he enjoyed meeting me that first time at a breakfast at Dartmouth College. It felt like yesterday but also a lifetime ago: in the span of those seven years, a Chittenden County state's attorney had won two terms in the Senate and that former governor from Georgia had stunned my well-funded, well-known Senate colleagues to capture the presidency and rewrite the laws of electoral gravity before his political fortunes changed so precipitously.

I reached out for a handshake. He put his arms around me and embraced me, and I embraced him in return and told him that I was proud of him and, by mistake, called him by his first name.

I don't think that he appeared to mind.

He smiled wearily. "*Good luck, Patrick.*"

Outside the Oval, I put my arm around Kevin, bid farewell to the staff, and looked back one last time to see the solitary president, hand placed on his aching back, taking in a last moment or two of reflection, staring out the big window into the Rose Garden where he'd marked so many triumphs and even more turmoil.

— 22 —

Gone Too Soon

"*Senator, I'm very, very sorry that I have to be the one to tell you this,*" mumbled the Senate page as he handed me a teletype printout pulled from the AP wire.

I assumed that it was probably a story in which I was quoted as saying something I wished I hadn't. If only the story documented such a minor moment in the course of life.

My face turned hot and my eyes lost focus. At age thirty-eight, my friend Harry Chapin had been killed in a fiery crash on the Long Island Expressway.

Just weeks before, as I flew back to Washington from a CODEL, I'd plugged in the earphones on the Concorde and the first thing I'd heard was an announcer's voice: "On channel four, 'Story of a Life,' written and sung by Harry Chapin." I'd made a note to myself to call Harry shortly after getting back, which I did and still could hear his words: "*Patrick, we have so much to do this year!*" He was already planning a series of concerts to benefit the cause of ending hunger in America, the cause that had animated him and brought us together as friends in the first place.

Now, on his way to one of those free benefit concerts at Eisenhower Park, his tiny Volkswagen Rabbit had been destroyed by a semi-trailer truck, and Harry had succumbed to internal injuries hours later. I was sickened. I felt myself starting to shut down, as if some emotional bottom had fallen out.

I went back to the Russell Building, but I couldn't think, and I couldn't seem to react to anything at that point. Our son Kevin called me from a pay phone on the Mall, not far from where he had been playing softball on the Ellipse. News had spread among his friends after they heard the story on someone's radio.

He was in tears.

"*Kevin, come to the office. Let's be together.*"

It felt like a death in the family. Long before he'd become a close family friend, let alone a fellow activist, and years before we'd ever had a reason to meet, Harry had provided the soundtrack of my life.

"Cat's in the Cradle" had spoken to me as a young father and an over-scheduled prosecutor driving to Boston—a reminder to turn that car around after the workday ended and get home to Marcelle and the children. *That song* at *that particular moment*, playing as an atmospheric skip from a radio station in the Midwest at 4:00 in the morning, had been the bolt from the blue reminding me that our children would follow my example, not my advice.

I thought about the years after Marcelle and I had come to really know Harry and his wife, Sandy. They came to visit us at our tree farm in Middlesex. We had other friends visiting us there with their daughter, who was the same age as Alicia, and by candlelight, Harry sang us one of his unpublished songs. Sandy had written the words and he wrote the music. "Tangled Up Puppet" was about a young girl who just wanted to be herself except when she wanted to be with her parents. He sang that, and we parents looked at our two almost-teenage daughters and soon were in tears.

I remembered Harry staying with us when he had a performance in Georgetown. I had a vote in the Senate scheduled, and so Marcelle drove Harry to the concert. Together, they were navigating around seemingly endless road construction, and the detours forced her to change direction through the rain, with terrible visibility. She was petrified she'd make

Harry late. He finally turned to her and said, "*Marcelle—don't worry, I'm the star. They can't start until I get there.*"

That became our inside joke, any time since then if we were running late to an event at which I'd be speaking. Marcelle would say to me, "*Relax, Patrick—remember Harry Chapin. They can't start until you get there.*"

I remembered a night when Mark was not feeling well and received a phone call. The gruff voice on the other end asked if Mark Patrick Leahy was there.

"*You mean Senator Leahy?*" Mark replied.

"*No, I mean you, Mark!*"

"*Who is this?*"

The voice burst into a familiar song and was instantly recognizable.

"*Harry! I've had a bad cold, I've been home.*"

Harry said that's why he was calling.

They talked for about ten minutes before Harry had to begin his concert an ocean away in Australia. He'd just wanted to see how Mark was doing.

What a friend. What a light extinguished from the world without rhyme or reason. Just a horrible, inexplicable accident.

Marcelle came by the office and brought Kevin home. I wanted to go with them. But it was an evening in which we had a very late-night session, and it seemed to go on forever.

Back on the Senate floor, Michigan senator Don Riegle and Bob Dole spent some time visiting and comforting me. They'd both been part of Harry's meetings when he came to the Senate to talk about hunger. He'd been a Pied Piper to liberals and conservatives alike, who all knew that Harry was sincere about an issue that knew no partisan demarcations; no matter ideology, everyone needed to be able to feed their kids.

I got back to our home in McLean and went into Mark's bedroom. He had cried himself to sleep. He used to sleep every night in a long Harry Chapin concert shirt, almost like a nightshirt—the material soft as can be, thin from years of use and hundreds of cycles of laundry.

He *wasn't* wearing it tonight. He lay quietly in a different shirt, wrapped in the sheets and blankets as he had tossed and turned until finally surrendering to sleep.

Marcelle explained that when he had arrived home, Mark took the Harry Chapin shirt, folded it, and put it in the dresser drawer, never to be worn again.

The tears rushed to my eyes again. The lyrics from "I Wonder What Would Happen to This World" suddenly had a tragic new clarity:

What one man's life could be worth

I was shaken by the realization that it can all just end, without warning, for any of us, but especially for Harry. After all, we were almost the same age. I'd just turned forty. I'd worked so closely with three people on the hunger issue: Hubert Humphrey, George McGovern, and Harry. Now two were dead, one was defeated, and I was in the minority while someone who believed that fighting hunger was a frivolous liberal cause—Jesse Helms—chaired the Agriculture Committee. It was a low moment.

I said to a close friend, "Don't think about what you'll do ten years from now, think about ten minutes from now . . . Don't make grand plans . . ."

I decided to start working and taking my positions like there might be no tomorrow, because it was now suddenly clear that was always a dark possibility.

— 23 —

Loyal Opposition

The heady, early days of the Reagan administration unfolded in ways that were predictable. It's never especially hard to cut taxes in Washington, and Reagan's sunny pledges to slash rates on the wealthy and let the benefits "trickle down" were landing well with congressional audiences. Even those of us who opposed his plans from the start knew that it would likely take some time before most Americans realized that it wasn't *their* taxes being cut, and it was their health care, their roads, and their schools being gutted in the budget to pay for *someone else's* tax cut. But there was a lingering bit of political anxiety on our side of the aisle about a permanent change Reagan would have the opportunity to make, with far-reaching consequences for all: the Supreme Court.

Barry Goldwater sat down next to me on the Senate subway headed to the Capitol for votes. He had something on his mind that he wanted to share.

"Pat, I've been talking to the White House about Potter Stewart's seat."

Stewart had announced his retirement at age sixty-six, taking many by surprise. He was in good health, and he wanted to enjoy those years before infirmity struck. Stewart had cut a towering figure as an associate justice, both for his intellect and his wit. We all chuckled reading his words in the court's ruling on the definition of pornography: "*I know it when I see it*." But more than that, he was, like other Eisenhower appointees, a quintessential swing vote and a hard jurist to pigeonhole on the ideological spectrum. On the one hand, he dissented in the rulings that enshrined the entire concept of Miranda rights in the legal lexicon and found no "right to privacy" in the *Griswold v. Connecticut* case, even as he warned, in his dissent, against legislatures passing "silly" laws affecting what people did in the privacy of their bedrooms. He wrote a concurring opinion in *Roe v. Wade*, even as he rejected that inherent "right to privacy" upon which it was based. But Stewart, for all the complexity of his legal views, expressed a thought about the court itself that always resonated with me when we sat down to consider a nominee. He'd said he thought of himself "primarily as a lawyer," and that when you read a ruling, you should "*not know whether it was written by a Jew or a Gentile, Democrat or Republican, you just know it's written by a good judge.*"

Now many of us in the Senate were worried that Ronald Reagan—whom many had naively dismissed just a couple of years before as an unelectable, archconservative Hollywood actor—would choose an ideologue, not one of Potter Stewart's "*good judges*," to remake the highest court in the land.

Enter Barry Goldwater.

"*Pat—I'm recommending Sandra Day O'Connor's appointment. She was a friend and classmate of Bill Rehnquist's, and she's from Arizona. If Reagan goes for it—and I think he might—a lot of people are going to say that because I'm recommending her, she must be extremely conservative.*"

I listened.

"*She's no nut, Pat. She's a conservative, not an ideologue. She'd treat the law right; she's open to debate.*"

I told Barry I'd always keep an open mind. I trust he was worried about the danger of senators stampeding toward a party-line vote in the Judiciary Committee if the nominee was seen simply as a proxy for Reaganism, and even more worried about a liberal revolt on the committee led by Ted Kennedy.

Barry, of course, had been doing more than talking to the Reagan White House. He was mounting a full-fledged campaign for O'Connor, an Arizona judge who spoke to his Sunbelt libertarian instincts.

As word leaked out about her likely nomination, it was conservatives who first grumbled. Steve Symms, who had defeated Senator Church and best epitomized what it meant to be among a handful of Reagan revolution "*accidental senators*," rushed to the microphones to warn Reagan that O'Connor was not sufficiently pro-life. Her social conservative bona fides were not in good standing with the right-wing interest groups. Make no mistake: no one could find any evidence that O'Connor was secretly pro-choice. But the Moral Majority had been clamoring for the Gipper to choose someone slightly to the right of Phyllis Schlafly for the court, a full-throated ideologue and card-carrying conservative movement firebrand. The Reverend Jerry Falwell led the drumbeat against O'Connor.

Reagan didn't seem bothered by the grumbling from his party's right flank. He made the O'Connor nomination official.

I met with O'Connor one-on-one. She was confident but never arrogant. She talked about the mentor Barry Goldwater had been in her rise in Arizona, her friendship with Rehnquist dating back to Stanford Law School, and her years as a prosecutor out west. She had opened her own tiny law firm in the desert, not because she was inherently entrepreneurial, but because the law firms refused to hire women on the supposition that they'd abandon the profession as soon as they had kids. She had been a successful legislator in her own right and an elected judge in the state's largest county. I bonded with her almost immediately about the work of a county prosecutor. It struck me that the court would benefit from having a perspective beyond the old judicial monastery—someone who had lived experiences beyond the bench—let alone the first woman to serve. My mind drifted back to that luncheon with Hugo Black and eight other gray- and white-haired justices: how nice it would be to have a justice who knew what it was like to be a woman in the United States.

I assured O'Connor I'd keep an open mind and let the hearings and our private discussion inform my vote.

Days later, at the kickoff of the confirmation hearings, my staffer and I stepped into the elevator in the basement of the Dirksen Building—and there already inside was the nominee herself, her husband, and a US marshal.

"*I think we are all going to the same place,*" she quipped.

A few seconds later, the elevator started up and came to a shuddering halt between floors. The marshal was on his two-way radio, trying to see what we could do.

O'Connor turned to me and quietly said, "*If this won't be used against me in my hearing, I have been in an elevator like this when something like this has happened before, and there is a way out of it.*"

"*So, what's that, Judge?*"

She said we all jump on the count of three.

"*Works for me.*"

The security guy wore a nervous expression and started to question her advice. "Oh, what the hell, let's try."

One, two, three—and we jumped. The elevator car shook, rattled, and continued on up to the floor we were supposed to go to.

O'Connor did a good job in the hearings, refusing to be pinned down on her specific public policy views in order to preserve her space and freedom of action on issues she might be called upon to address as an associate justice. She talked openly about her experience and her philosophy, but she wasn't going to be anyone's—on the left or right—check-the-box ideologue.

I was comfortable with her answers.

The Judiciary Committee voted 17–0 to send her nomination to the floor.

Senator Jeremiah Denton was the lone holdout. He voted "present." It was confusing to me how a person of such undeniable, awe-inspiring physical courage—Jeremiah had been held as a prisoner of war in Vietnam for almost eight excruciating years, a towering figure who had blinked the word "torture" in Morse code when his captors paraded him in front of television cameras—could struggle to find the courage to stand up to the social conservatives and openly support his president's nominee for the court.

I checked with the Senate parliamentarian to learn whether Denton could repeat that stunt on the Senate floor. I had every intention of challenging his vote. The rules allowed a senator to vote "present" only if one had a conflict of interest or, without a conflict of interest, with unanimous consent of the Senate. I was going to require him to ask for unanimous consent to vote "present," and I was going to object, unless he could describe a legitimate conflict of interest.

I was growing tired of people trying to play both sides against the middle. There's no question in my mind that if Sandra O'Connor had been appointed by President Carter that Denton and an awful lot of other conservative Republicans would have voted against her, but now they were caught between the voters and their president.

"*It's chickenshit,*" said Barry Goldwater, ever Sandra O'Connor's advocate inside the Senate. "*They're all afraid of Jerry Falwell and that whole blow-dried bunch of Bible thumpers.*"

I watched as Goldwater stood down by the desk guarding the well. Any senator who was going to slight O'Connor had to walk by Mr. Conservative to do it.

This time, Denton voted aye.

She was confirmed 99–0.

I saw her a few weeks later on the street between the Dirksen Building and the court.

"*Justice O'Connor! One, two, three—*"

"*Jump!*" she replied.

— 24 —

Independence

As a student of history, I had always worried about the power of any single interest group creating a kind of herd mentality. In my own life, I'd heard one of our greatest World War II generals turned president warn America about the power of a "military-industrial complex." I'd seen the power of the McCarthy movement to create a hysteria that intimidated senators for a long time. I came into public life with a conviction about all of that; it was only the good-faith commitment of public servants to do their homework and follow facts that prevented powerful messengers and messages from leading people off a political cliff. It was part of why Edmund Burke's words resonated so much with me. I didn't like the interest group game, and I knew that there were too many senators driven by it, whether it was the Americans for Democratic Action on the left or the Chamber of Commerce on the right. I vowed quietly never to be that way.

I entered the conference room and greeted my friends from Vermont's American Israel Public Affairs Committee (AIPAC) chapter, who had come down to lobby against President Reagan's planned sale of airborne warning and control systems (AWACS) to Saudi Arabia. The staff alerted me that there would be an "ask": the group wanted me to add my signature to a letter to the White House objecting to it.

I had been wrestling with the issue and studying it first from the perspective of the Armed Services Committee and, more recently, as a member of the Foreign Operations Subcommittee on Appropriations. I'd seen the many unintended consequences of arms transfers to foreign countries, let alone to insurgents engaged in Cold War skirmishes. Too often, I worried, a regime we might be arming today out of convenience could tomorrow be on the other side of a conflict, or weapons or even defensive installations marked MADE IN AMERICA might be used in ways we'd never imagine allowing ourselves to do.

I didn't come to this debate as a cheerleader for sending AWACS to any country where we wouldn't have sole control over them. We were also just months removed from Israeli prime minister Menachem Begin's Operation Opera, the Israeli attack on an Iraqi nuclear facility.

The mission had completely blindsided President Reagan and undermined our partner Egyptian president Anwar Sadat, who just two days earlier had been engaged in an Egypt-Israel summit and was suddenly accused of collusion. Sadat was facing enough regional suspicion already for having made peace with Israel under the Carter administration. The Reagan administration hoped to see more of Israel's Arab neighbors follow Cairo's lead and normalize relations with Israel. It was outraged by Begin's failure to consider the collateral damage he was doing to Sadat, whom Jordan and others were watching closely for proof of concept about whether peace was worth the risk.

But the Reagan team was equally outraged that Begin hadn't bothered to speak with them before sending American-made F-15s undetected through Jordanian and Saudi airspace to drop twelve tons of American-made bombs on a secret nuclear site southwest of Baghdad. The American fighter jets evaded detection by the American-made AWACS temporarily stationed in Saudi Arabia; for a mission on which America was not consulted, America's military-industrial fingerprints were all over the forensic aftermath.

The Arab world had erupted in protest. Now, President Reagan was determined to transfer to the Saudis the next generation of AWACS in a sign of friendship with an aggrieved partner upon whom we relied for intelligence cooperation, among other interests.

To my friends gathered in the conference room, I mentioned that I had my own reservations about the sale of AWACS into a volatile region, but also that I was sympathetic toward the Reagan administration's well-intended efforts to calm a difficult situation after Begin's brash move.

"*Well, we aren't very happy with our prime minister these days,*" one of my constituents replied.

My mind immediately flashed back to Abe Ribicoff's words of caution in a closed session of the Senate just three years before. Abe had since retired, and Barry Goldwater now occupied his office down the hall, but the Connecticut senator's warnings still resonated.

"*Respectfully, he's not our prime minister, he's Israel's prime minister. We have a president. We may or may not agree with him all the time, but we have a president. We will provide for our commitments around the world, whether it's to Ireland or Italy or anywhere else, and I care personally about every one of those countries, and I believe in the state of Israel, but first and foremost, we should ask if it's in the best interests of the United States.*"

I wouldn't sign the letter. I didn't know whether I could support the president's request, and I suspected that in the final analysis I couldn't and wouldn't, but I was determined for it to be my decision, after my own careful analysis, right or wrong. I owed that much to my conscience and to the institution, whether I'd been reelected by 2,700 votes or 207,000 votes. I wanted to be measured on how and why I came to a position, not just what the position might be. I wanted to be proud of how and why I voted the way I did.

— 25 —

Veep

"*Pat, do you still have that town house in McLean?*"

I smiled, impressed and more than a little surprised. The vice president hadn't expected to see me in the Capitol today, but we'd bumped into each other in the senators' dining room. He was there to commune with Senator Paul Laxalt and the new administration's closest allies on the Hill.

His knowledge of Leahy trivia came from a good memory, not a good briefing. "*You remembered, Mr. Vice President. No wonder you made a good CIA director.*"

"*Well, a really good CIA director would probably know what you were doing inside that house,*" cracked George Herbert Walker Bush, now the third vice president of the United States I'd encountered as a senator.

Indeed, after he'd arrived in Langley after a yearlong diplomatic stint in Beijing, we had chatted about the fact that I had a town house not too far from the CIA headquarters. Now we had both navigated an eventful few years: President Ford's defeat, Bush's failed presidential primary campaign against Reagan, his luck earning a spot on the GOP ticket, and my first reelection, as the Reagan-Bush ticket provided the cresting political wave that washed away my friends and colleagues and nearly lifted my Senate opponent to victory. Even that rising tide couldn't lift all Republican yachts, but it had forever changed the face of the Senate; of the fourteen Senate seats targeted, only Gary Hart and I hung on in that election cycle.

I liked Bush immediately. He had an easy smile and a firm handshake, and his penchant for the personal was disarming. Some people seem smaller in real life than they do on television. Bush was the opposite. Reagan had a big physical presence and an ability as a public performer that Bush couldn't rival. This Texas transplant by way of Greenwich, Connecticut, could never fill up the television screen or the convention hall with charisma the way Reagan could, but he was earnest, and he appeared to really listen. If Reagan excelled at the big public gestures, Bush, by contrast, was a master of the private, personal touch, all the more endearing because it was genuine.

I wasn't sure that Bush would ever enjoy the close relationship with President Reagan that Mondale did with Carter, but he was clearly trying hard and, ironically, would regularly be deployed to the Senate to whip up votes for the Reagan budget, which, as a candidate, Bush had decried as "*voodoo economics.*"

I buttonholed the vice president for a moment about regulatory reform. I knew that it was a priority of the new administration, but I argued it didn't have to be a divisive, partisan issue. I told him that the administration could build support for a bill similar to the one John Culver, Paul Laxalt, Orrin Hatch, and I had passed through our subcommittee on the Judiciary Committee the previous year.

"*Well, a bill has to be considered at least bipartisan with the diversity of those cosponsors attached to it,*" Bush commented.

"*Yes, Mr. Vice President, either we had a darn good bill or at least two of us didn't understand what was in it.*"

Bush laughed.

He shared with me that Delaware's junior senator, Bill Roth, had claimed that Senator Laxalt had actually stolen his issue on regulatory reform.

"*Oh, don't worry, there are no prima donnas in the Senate and no one will worry about who gets credit for it,*" I replied with a wink.

He cackled.

I had to head off, along with his friend and former opponent Texas senator Lloyd Bentsen, to a meeting called by Senator Byrd.

"You're going there to plot against the Republicans, Pat?"

"Well, Mr. Vice President, to paraphrase Daniel Webster, it is a small minority, but there are those of us who love it."

President Reagan's first major speech to Congress brought a hard dose of reality to Democrats that we really were buried deep in the minority and Reagan really was president.

There's nothing quite like that setting to underscore who holds power and who doesn't. Speaker Tip O'Neill sat behind Reagan, a reminder to all that no matter what, Democrats still had the House of Representatives. But Reagan's cheering section among southern House Democrats underscored that he had a very good hand to play; those Democrats wanted to stay in Congress, and they knew that the D after their names had become a big liability in Dixie. This was now a Republican town in many ways, at least for now. President Carter had brought Gregg Allman and Willie Nelson and Johnny Cash to Washington; Reagan had his own group of celebrities and artists from his Hollywood days, including Frank Sinatra. It was suddenly Democrats who were the party out of power and allegedly out of ideas. Reagan's election was being described as a "revolution," and the press didn't use that word lightly.

But if we were out in the cold political wilderness, this presidential address also brought a warm surprise from Vermont. Bill Keough surprised me in my office—the Reagans had invited the hostages held by the Iranians to visit the president and First Lady.

Bill had spent a good deal of time in captivity harassing his captors probably more than they did him.

I had written to him several times while he was there, and sent a letter with President Carter and Vice President Mondale when they went over to greet the hostages.

I asked him if he'd received it, and he laughed when he said he had. Apparently, when he saw President Carter, he was so excited, he put his arms around him and gave him a big bear hug. Carter literally was lifted off the ground. Then this six-foot-nine giant of a man turned to Mondale, who had watched the whole thing. He said Mondale had a look of apprehension on his face and immediately whipped out the letter from me and said, "*Wait a minute, wait a minute! I've got a letter here from Pat Leahy!*"

Bill laughed and said he thought Mondale was showing such alacrity because he didn't want to get picked up in the same way.

Marcelle came down to hear the president's speech. We walked around outdoors. It was a lovely evening, and the temperature was mild. There was a nearly full moon rising over the Capitol, and it was absolutely beautiful. I hummed "Moon River" as we walked.

The combination of the weather and having Marcelle there made me enjoy the job the most that I had in years—majority or no majority. I felt myself finally putting the election behind me—and enjoying being in the Senate again. The partisanship of the past two years had taken a lot of the joy out of being in office. The lack of privacy, the time away from my family, and the lack of time to think, write, and work had worn me down more than I'd realized.

But walking around that Wednesday night, I had to admit that I really still felt a sense of awe looking up at the Capitol Building. I was part of this extraordinary experiment called the US Senate, and that was a gift—no matter how hard-fought.

I wanted to believe that now, with six years ahead, I could accomplish something for my country; there can only be one hundred of us in the US Senate, and as I looked around at some of the new members, maybe it was most important that at least some of us who had a sense of history and a sense of the meaning of the office continued to be there. No, I couldn't pass major legislation from the minority as a still relatively junior member, but I could dig in and bring money home for Vermont and I could hold Washington to account. I could even use the prize of a six-year term to keep scratching my itch to understand foreign policy in greater depth.

The joint session of Congress only reinforced this realization.

A number of the Republican congressmen were strategically placed throughout the chamber with instructions to clap and cheer at appropriate times, which they did with great fervor.

President Reagan, who had become a better actor than he was on the screen, registered what seemed to be genuine surprise each time they cheered, but apparently was willing to accept the accolades nonetheless.

One time, the cheering and clapping was so blatantly staged that several of us started chuckling. We had a row made up of Pat Moynihan, Ted Kennedy, Russell Long, myself, and Dale Bumpers sitting directly behind the Joint Chiefs of Staff, and we were a little bit like schoolkids as we passed remarks back and forth about the blatant stage effect.

I finally leaned over to Ted Kennedy as the cheering started one more time and said, "*Don't worry, Ted. If you had been elected, we would have done the same for you.*"

Ted cracked up, and when Ted cracked up, it was never an understated laugh. The members of the Joint Chiefs who overheard us were doing their best to keep straight faces.

— 26 —

Danger Ahead

One of the greatest concerns I had about the Reagan administration was that the president's bellicosity as a candidate could lure us back into a dangerous, unchecked military adventurism. I'd come to Washington to help dig the United States out of the deep hole we'd mistakenly dug in Vietnam; I was not about to allow another administration to dig a new hole somewhere else.

But it felt like that's exactly what the Reagan administration wanted to do.

"*In America's backyard, we will draw the line and go right to the source, if need be.*"

Here we go, I thought, as I heard the secretary of state trot out the inflammatory claims from the 1980 campaign about the communist threat in Central America. The Reaganites saw Reds under every bed and Stalinists under every sombrero.

Secretary of State Al Haig never lacked in confidence—or in rhetoric, I was finding out rather quickly. His military record was as impressive as his academic background, having studied at Notre Dame, West Point, Columbia, and Georgetown, and having come home from Vietnam as a battalion commander with a Silver Star, Distinguished Service Cross, and Purple Heart. He'd remained in the Nixon White House through the darkest of days before the president's resignation.

But now he was America's top diplomat, and what he was really saying to our committee about weapons and proxy wars and paramilitary threats in our hemisphere scared the devil out of me.

"*Mr. Secretary—about your answer—this business about 'going to the source.' Are you suggesting that weapons are coming from both Cuba and the Soviet Union and we're going to match them?*"

Haig sputtered that he didn't want anybody putting words in his mouth to portray him as a sword rattler. But I wasn't putting words in his mouth—they were *his* words—and I was just trying to give him a chance to explain them before they appeared in print the next day.

Some former high-ranking military brass aren't used to having somebody actually argue back at them.

Haig reverted to clichés. He referred to the "*criticality of the situation,*" whatever that meant. I worried that the administration didn't know what it was doing, now that the campaign rhetoric had to be reconciled with governing, and I feared that its default assumption was that by saber-rattling, it would push the Soviets to back off. I hoped that it didn't think our adversaries could be that naive. But I also hoped that it wasn't willing to blunder its way into a quagmire without a plan, or a meaningful debate.

After the unsatisfactory discussion, I shook the secretary's hand. "*You always have a good tan,*" I said jealously.

"*Well, if your blood pressure was as high as mine was, you'd be red too,*" Haig replied, I hoped jokingly.

After Haig left, John Stennis stretched back in his chair, wearily removed his thick glasses, and rubbed his eyes.

"*I hope we are being more careful than it appears,*" said the Senate's leading Democratic hawk and ardent cold warrior. "*After all, we didn't do all that well in Vietnam.*"

Remembering what Stennis had said in the Armed Services Committee about abandoning South Vietnam just six years before, it was a strong statement from an unlikely voice indeed.

Reagan was popular, just as Johnson had been when he embarked on a quagmire in Southeast Asia and just as Nixon had been when he refused to pull us out of it. It was our job to ensure that we didn't go right back into the barrel because we were afraid to question a popular president. I feared we were in for a long four years, trying to provide some measure of oversight to the ideologues in the White House.

— 27 —

Shots Fired

March 30, 1981, was just another afternoon in the Senate. After the caucus lunches, senators were milling around the floor waiting for the two leaders to work out the vote schedule for the day. There were a number of Reagan administration nominees to confirm, and hopefully we'd be able to voice vote most of them.

Then I heard something disturbing. As I had in 1963, I thought someone was repeating a bad joke.

The whispers whipped around the Senate floor, a rumor that the president of the United States had been shot.

But as I looked up at the press gallery and saw no movement there, I thought the rumor simply had to be wrong.

Maybe a shot had been fired outside the president's event. In Washington, DC, the random violence was becoming a hallmark of life.

But I saw the sudden parade of senators into the cloakroom and followed quickly behind. Senator Gary Hart held the remote control, changing the TV from channel to channel, as we realized that it was true indeed.

Sixty-nine days in office, and President Reagan was headed to George Washington University Hospital badly wounded, his amiable press secretary, Jim Brady, suffering a gunshot wound to the head. Immediate reports suggested Brady was killed.

The cloakroom felt completely different. No laughter. No conversation.

No booming voices. The only sounds were the hum of the AP wire ticker in the hallway behind the Senate chamber and the ever-increasing volume of the televisions as hard of hearing senators turned up the volume to be alone in the news.

Ted Kennedy walked out, pale and distracted, and headed to the solitary refuge of his desk on the floor. I did not have to guess too hard to imagine the memories that were flooding back for him from Dallas and Los Angeles less than twenty years before. He sat alone, left, and returned thirty minutes later to deliver an emotional appeal to the country for unity and a prayer for the president. Ted returned to the cloakroom and collapsed into a chair as if he were coming home at the end of a long, long day of work. His eyes were fixed on the television news.

I walked over, patted him on the shoulder, and, with tears in my eyes, let him know that his words had been needed for all to hear, but also to let him know that this moment must come with particularly painful meaning for him.

He looked up and said simply, "*Thanks, Pat, I know what you mean.*"

The Senate went home that evening with a slew of unanswered questions. We didn't know how on earth a gunman had gotten so close to the president of the United States and his senior staff on a street in downtown Washington. But more important, we still didn't know whether the president would survive or whether he might be disabled. We thought we knew enough not to take at face value the tidbits the White House press office was leaking to the media, including the brilliant one-liner of Reagan saying to the emergency surgeon, "*I hope you're a Republican.*" Even amid tragedy, Deputy Chief of Staff Michael Deaver and the California mafia were expert at stagecraft.

Less savvy about communication was a very shaken Secretary of State Alexander Haig, who appeared on television and announced that he "*was in charge.*" Vice President Bush was out of town, and Air Force Two was bogged down with radio issues, and the White House had been unable to reach the vice president and temporarily transfer powers to him while Reagan headed for surgery. Haig had handled the moment impulsively.

The next day at a caucus, we were told by Senator Dan Inouye that a leadership meeting was held with the vice president at the White House, to bring them up to date on the president's condition. Apparently, at that meeting, the secretary of the Treasury reported on the activity of the Secret Service, the secretary of defense reported on a low-level alert sent out to our military and the easing of tensions, and the attorney general reported on the plans for prosecution of the man arrested. The director of the CIA William Casey, the counselor to the president Ed Meese, and the chief of staff Jim Baker were also there.

Al Haig was not—and neither was there anyone in attendance from the State Department. At that point, across the table from me, Gary Hart pantomimed a guillotine-type gesture. Al Haig's moment in the sun apparently may have been a costly one.

But we were all relieved by the news that the president seemed to have pulled through surgery well despite losing a great deal of blood. As a former prosecutor who had been to more crime scenes and reviewed more autopsies than I cared to remember, I knew too well the ravaging destruction a bullet could inflict on the human body. I appreciated just how much a difference of millimeters might have made in the president's fate.

As the president recovered, our depleted Senate Democratic caucus had a recovery of its own to make.

We weren't just in the minority for the first time since 1952. The psychic impact was so much worse.

President Reagan was wildly popular, and the aftermath of the assassination attempt had rightfully rallied the country around him. It had also highlighted his unique skills that our caucus was largely bereft of: Reagan's big smile as he waved out his hospital window, his practiced quips, and his command of sound bites, which masterfully camouflaged a policy agenda that was wildly out of step with the realities of the good people who had voted him into office. But he had that rare ability to make the whole country feel good while doing something very bad for it.

Meanwhile, our caucus, having been comfortably cocooned in the majority for decades, was shell-shocked.

In a rare moment of levity at our caucus lunch, Leader Byrd proclaimed that the Almighty must wonder what to do these days when the leading proponent of the Reagan budget—Bill Roth—goes home at night, takes off his wig, puts it on the stand beside his bed, and kneels down to pray. According to Byrd, Roth prays that the president will let him fight hard for Reaganomics, but in the end for God to make sure it doesn't pass because it would be an economic disaster. On the other hand, Byrd said that *he* goes home and prays that he has the strength to fight strongly against the budget, but in the end tells God he wouldn't be entirely unhappy if it were to pass, if the Republicans would get the blame for the economic disaster that would be sure to follow. We were caught between the reality of Reagan's hold on the country's imagination and the artificiality of what he was proposing.

That evening, Reagan made his triumphant return to Capitol Hill for his address to the joint session of the House and Senate.

The president looked much better, although thinner after the assassination attempt.

Reagan's rhetoric throughout his speech was good, as usual, and details were minimal. He told us everything that he disliked about the straw men of liberal alternatives to his agenda, but was very short on specifics about his own. I'd decided that this was by design, not a defect. I had that same thought just a few days ago, following his first press conference since the shooting.

Certainly, his responses to press questions seemed like he was trying to wing them. I couldn't help but think that he had very limited background information to support his positions. But this was the Reagan approach—the big vision, not the green eyeshade presentations of the Carter years. He was to play the happy warrior, and it was working.

But clearly Reagan was willing to have others wield the stilettos on his behalf. My town hall meetings were becoming populated by angry constituents who read aloud from mailings they'd received or repeated advertising they'd heard on the radio. It felt as it had in 1980. Whoever this Leahy guy was—raising everyone's taxes, growing government, and refusing to work with the deified president—well, I'd sure have liked to give *that* senator a piece of my mind!

I wasn't alone. The mailings sent from the Republican National

Committee into the districts of key senators and congressmen were peak campaign-style vitriol. Republicans were really playing hardball and letting everyone know that they would campaign against those who fought them on this budget.

One attack group working out of the White House was disbanded once Reagan's senior team started receiving criticism for it. But it quickly reconstituted itself elsewhere, under the auspices of none other than Senator Jesse Helms. It was the start of the permanent campaign, the playbook that had earned Republicans their majority starting with the onslaughts in the elections of 1978 and 1980.

That it was gleefully sanctioned by a sitting senator against his colleagues was a breach within the institution; a million miles away in Tokyo, Mike Mansfield would've been coughing on his pipe if he knew what had become routine in the place he'd presided over for sixteen years. Mansfield had been known to tell freshman senators to remember that every one of the one hundred senators here was someone in whom their state had found something good inside. Six years later, I was coming up empty searching for that quality in the senior senator from North Carolina.

It was against that backdrop that President Reagan was going to smile, greet people, shake hands with them, and play the above-the-fray citizen servant: "*Ah, shucks. I just want to do what is best for the country and get it back in tow.*"

Then he would leave it to his hatchet men to go out and get their way.

We were caught in an external and an internal struggle with the Reagan White House.

Externally, we didn't have a megaphone big enough to compete with Reagan—or an equally telegenic speaker for our side.

Internally, we were torn over tactics. Leader Byrd was scheming of any way to stop the Reagan White House from using an arcane Senate procedure known as "*budget reconciliation*" to force the entire Reagan agenda through Congress with a simple fifty-one-vote majority.

Byrd the institutionalist argued that at almost all costs, we should save the committee system, because the new budget reconciliation procedure, if followed regularly into the future, would make the Budget Committee the only one with any clout at all. It would diminish the importance of each individual senator. I agreed with Byrd that what set the Senate apart was the right of one senator to have an impact on every given issue. When abused, it was catastrophic, as it had been on civil rights for decades, but at its core it was the principle that separated us from the House of Representatives.

The committee system, it turned out, could be another one of these hidden virtues of the institution. John Stennis stood on his weak failing legs, leaned forward, and reminded us of a time in history when he believed the committee system itself pulled the United States back from a precipice.

President Truman had fired General Douglas MacArthur in the waning days of the Korean War. MacArthur had been welcomed home with ticker-tape parades. He was an even bigger celebrity than he'd been before, an avatar for extreme right-wing positions. Some of these were positions Stennis himself might've embraced. But Stennis saw a danger in a uniformed military man disobeying the commander in chief. The mail stacked up to the ceiling, calling on the Senate to impeach Harry Truman.

Finally, to defuse things, the Armed Services Committee began hearings on the MacArthur sacking. The hearings dragged on and on, and recessed periodically, and then, after a while, nobody ever went back to them.

Stennis's growl turned into a laugh: "*To this date, a report has not been filed on the MacArthur hearings, and no matter what he said about old soldiers, MacArthur faded away.*"

Truman had done the right thing, and the public wasn't quite ready to accept it yet. But at least the emotions were defused by the Senate committee process. It was at moments like this when I learned an awful lot from the old bulls, even as I worked to retire some of their anachronistic social beliefs and bigotry to the history books—next to MacArthur. But it hit me that the system—whether found in the Constitution in the rules the Founders set or in the norms and traditions the Senate can create for itself—all the little safety valves that protect the country—is an extraordinary machine. Well into my second term, I wanted to understand it even better.

— 28 —

Old Meets News

Change was coming to the Senate: C-SPAN was about to install television cameras in the Senate gallery, in accordance with a long-deferred agreement that had been piloted in the House and that had apparently encouraged a new generation of Republican backbenchers to give regular speeches to an empty House, their audience back home and on the hustings rather than their colleagues.

Now, the cameras were heading to the Senate, and there was no value in fighting it, at this point, but it didn't stop the caucuses' veteran lawmakers from warning those of us who supported the cameras of the unintended consequences to come.

Russell Long was at his best.

"*C-c-can't you see the d-d-debate on social welfare benefits if we had television? No cameras—everybody would v-vote to extend the benefits and put most of their speeches in the record. The whole business'd be over in an hour. But if we had television coverage, we'd all be down there and everybody would have to make a speech. 'Momma, Poppa, I'm here! I'm just fighting for you. I'm going to fight for you till hell freezes over, and when hell freezes over, I'll fight for you on the ice.'*"

He was right, of course. Everyone would speak, and relatively little would get done. Long warned that it would be hard for the Senate to exercise its responsibilities under the glare of television lights. "*We aren't the House—those boys are running every two years. Th-th-they need the cameras.*"

We were, after all, supposed to be the conscience of the nation, and with a group of new senators who seemed far more interested in getting a minute or two on television than in showing any sense of history, responsibility, or ability to really plan for the future, television might just be one of the last straws to change the Senate into a more complicated version of the House.

John Stennis had heard enough.

"*Can't you see television covering us all milling around down at the desk when a vote comes up or checking to see just what the vote's about?*" He said we might as well hold up a great big banner that says LOOK AT US. WE'RE ALL DOWN HERE BECAUSE WE DON'T KNOW WHAT THE HELL WE'RE DOING.

But there was little the senator could do to persuade his colleagues to resist, and he clearly was growing fatigued by it all.

I sat next to him that night in the cloakroom. I could sense that something was on his mind.

"Son, this is a special place."

He told me about the night in 1973 when he'd been shot outside his home in Cleveland Park. He'd gone in, sat on the couch, apologized to his wife, "Ms. Stennis," about getting blood all over the couch, and gently said, "I think you best call an ambulance."

The paramedics took him out to Walter Reed hospital a few minutes' ambulance ride from his home. He'd lost a great deal of blood and was rushed into surgery. While Stennis was in the operating room, phone calls started coming in from literally all over the world from news services, friends, and family.

There were only a couple of receptionists on duty at the switchboard, and they were swamped. A man came in during the middle of the evening, said that he knew how to operate a switchboard, and asked if he might be able to help. They were glad to have the volunteer. He sat there and manned the switchboard with them from around nine or ten o'clock at night until breakfast time the next morning. By then a new shift had come in, so the man said that he would leave.

They asked, "*By the way, who are you?*"

"*My name is Mark, and I'm a friend of John's.*"

That man never shared with the receptionists that in fact he was one of Stennis's Senate colleagues. Stennis shared that memory with reverence, not just for what his colleague had done, but for the self-effacing way in which he had done it.

"*That's what we need more of, not tee-vee cameras, Pat. People who do what's right when nobody's looking.*"

Stennis had aged about ten years in the last year, and he was clearly aware that, in the Senate he'd grown up in and in his own life, suddenly there was less runway in front of him than behind him.

I touched his forearm and gave it a squeeze.

— 29 —

Full Circle

"*Let us pray.*" The Senate chaplain quieted the chamber.

A new Senate always underscored the passage of time and the fleeting privilege of being a US senator. The last year had been difficult, and not just because of the 1984 political cycle. Dad had declined rapidly at age eighty-four. I'd cherished our time together, knowing something neither of us wanted to admit, which was that it was dwindling. Even as slowed down as he was by an ailing heart, his passion for history could revive his energy levels. He delighted in visiting the private collections at the Smithsonian, examining the original signatures of Abraham Lincoln on the yellowed pages of legislation, hearing from the docent how Lincoln would start signing the bills in the early evening in the president's room at the Capitol with a strong, bold "*Abraham Lincoln*," and finish signing late at night with an almost indecipherable "*A L*" as his hand grew tired. There were no autopens back in the 1860s, clearly. The historians at the Library of Congress loved Dad and often asked when he could come back, because he sometimes knew more about a subject matter than they did, especially if it drew on his encyclopedic knowledge of Vermont.

I arranged to have a private tour for Dad of the Washington Monument. I wanted him to see that view one more time. We pulled up in my car, and a park ranger was standing by to greet us. The walk to the monument wasn't easy for Dad, and the park ranger advised him to go slowly.

"*Take as long as you want, Mr. Leahy,*" he said calmly.

I remembered the story of my father as a young man visiting this very spot with the Knights of Columbus, and the police officer with the Irish brogue who had spotted his fellow Catholics and whose mantra had switched from "move along" to "take as long as you want."

Now, I wished this day could last forever.

It didn't. Dad was soon gone, peacefully. At his wake, hundreds lined up in Montpelier to say goodbye. Men and women my parents' age came up to me and shared secrets, awakening in me memories long past.

"*I was out of work—your father just showed up at my door—he brought me groceries.*"

And another: "*He sent me home from the Leahy Press with a bag of canned goods. He knew my sister's kids had moved in with us.*"

And another: "*Senator, your dad heard we were on hard times, he gave me fifty dollars to get us through. He never let us pay him back.*"

Even as he lay in peace, my father was still teaching me and my siblings to do the right thing, even when no one was looking.

Ten years in the Senate had flown by. I still believed in everything I believed in when I arrived here, but I was confident in how to actually advance those issues and ideals in ways my thirty-four-year-old self wouldn't have imagined. I'd never been prone to big speeches or stem-winders, but even more so right now, I realized you could get so much more done by working with people and understanding them first before running to the cameras or holding a press conference.

Back in the Senate, the generational change was coming.

I couldn't help but look around at my colleagues to see the newest senators, fresh-faced and awestricken, walk down the aisle with their senior colleagues to take the oath and be seated in the new Congress.

The decision of Senate Majority Leader Howard Baker to join the Reagan administration had left a vacancy in Tennessee, and his replacement was none other than a new old face: thirty-six-year-old Al Gore Jr., whose father, the first Senator Gore, had been defeated for the very same seat fourteen years beforehand.

West Virginia had sent another famous last name to the Senate as well: Governor Jay Rockefeller was an interesting story. He'd grown up in New York, scion of the iconic family, and after college followed the call of President Johnson's War on Poverty and the anti-poverty program Volunteers in Service to America (VISTA) to West Virginia, where he fell in love with the Mountain State. He'd made it his home, served in the legislature, and become a successful governor. Now he was sharing a spotlight that had long belonged almost entirely to Robert C. Byrd. Rockefeller noticed my Senate pin and said, "*Boy, that's the trouble with you guys. Some of you just flaunt your wealth.*" His sense of humor was disarming.

Paul Tsongas, the junior senator from Massachusetts, had resigned days before to give the state's newly elected freshman a leg up on seniority and to let Tsongas tend to an urgent matter on the home front: at just age forty-three, he had declined to run for reelection to battle full-time the non-Hodgkin's lymphoma that threatened his life. Arm in arm, Ted Kennedy walked the new senator, John Forbes Kerry, down the aisle, a grin on Ted's face, joking that he was giving away "*the bride.*"

Forty-two-year-old Mitch McConnell was the first Republican sent to the Senate by Kentucky since Reconstruction, a polio survivor who had run an insurgent upset campaign against the Democratic incumbent Dee Huddleston, eking out a 5,100-vote victory propelled by tenacity and the Reagan coattails. He was escorted by the ever-courtly Wendell Ford.

I watched the new senators' faces and relived what it had felt like for me in 1975, and the feeling of relief in 1981, that incomparable feeling of "*I made it.*"

The Senate was changing, and here we were, still standing.

Strom Thurmond had, in the span of the last year, become an old man, with hair color changes almost daily, various shades of orange desperately trying to cover the gray. I wondered if his young wife dyed it for him at the kitchen sink. Whatever the reason, he had grown surlier, his hearing starting to fade.

Barry Goldwater, a little bit younger than Thurmond, had become a lot more mellow by contrast, sharp as always, but without his famous edge. He was conservative without being cantankerous.

I looked over as well at a man who was still holding on—raging, like

Dylan Thomas had written, "against the dying of the light." John Stennis had rushed back to the Senate floor after having his leg amputated during the Christmas recess. The cancer had been contained, the doctors told him, and the old bull was back with a clean bill of health.

Stennis watched in rapt attention as each senator was being sworn in and applauded each one. But when the chaplain stood for the prayer, John Stennis also tried to stand, his shoulders trembling as he lifted himself from his wheelchair and leaned against his desk, his head bowed in prayer, perspiring from the exertion.

I thought, *There is a SENATOR*! We had spent the better part of ten years canceling out each other's votes. We agreed on little when it came to policy, other than to proudly deliver for people back home, the code of the Appropriations Committee. But the institution was our bond. Like a pair of mismatched bookends, we could stand, me on the left, John on the far right, so many colleagues in between us, both of us believers that this was no ordinary place. It was also no ordinary time of year. It was time for my third presidential inauguration in Washington.

Four years before, Mark and I had explored the Brigadoon-like ornamentation that seemed to spring overnight in Washington to mark the transfer of power. This time, there would be no transition. Ronald Reagan had carried forty-nine states, sparing Fritz Mondale just his home state of Minnesota. We'd sensed the loss was coming, and miraculously, despite the upset in Kentucky, we'd actually gained two Senate seats, starting to dig our way out from the deep hole that 1980 had left us in, painfully enough. The mood was more of resignation to Reagan's grip on the public rather than shock, as it had been in 1980.

But this time again, Marcelle and I took Mark down to the eastern front of the Capitol to show him the platform where the president would be inaugurated and deliver his address. The Secret Service was eyeing us, and one started to come over to give us a warning, but was stopped by the Capitol Police, who reminded them that this was one part of the city where senators actually outranked Secret Service.

We went to Bob Dole's offices—the former offices held by Howard Baker and now named the Howard Baker Rooms. Baker always said that the view down the Mall was the second-best view in the city. It didn't take much imagination to know that 1600 Pennsylvania Avenue was what he thought was the best one, and there's no question in my mind that Bob Dole was also looking at that address, even as he prepared to take the reins as leader.

Scaffolding erected to facilitate repairs to the western front of the Capitol marred Dole's view of the Washington Monument. "Scaffolding will probably last longer here than I will," cracked Dole. The dry, typically self-effacing humor was Dole's weapon of choice, most often self-directed.

A cold snap had hit Washington, the opposite of the balmy January four years before.

The inaugural was changed to indoors at the last minute, which created unexpected problems for me.

I'd been asked to do some photography for *U.S. News and World Report* and had spent some time the day before scanning the best angle and the best light for the inaugural platform. Suddenly we were placed inside.

But I still made an effort to navigate a clear view of the president's podium. At the very last second, several late-arriving House members were crowded into a hitherto open area, and my view was effectively blocked. During the proceedings, I had to stand on tiptoe and, at one time, even hold the camera upside down to get an extra half inch or so of clearance. I feared the worst but still submitted the photographs.

The following week, when the magazine hit the newsstands, two photographs headed its inaugural coverage—one of the president taking the oath and the other of him giving his speech—and both bore the credit "Patrick Leahy."

"*What are the odds that my favorite photo was taken by a Democrat?*" joked the president, when I asked him to sign a blown-up copy for my office. It was classic Reagan, not so different from the quick wit he'd displayed in the hospital after being shot, looking up at his surgeon and quipping, "I hope you're a Republican."

And it was a big part of why we'd have to contend with a Reagan administration for four more years.

— 30 —

To Stop a War

The president was hell-bent on using his second term to draw us deeper into ideological confrontations overseas. The civil war in Nicaragua was exhibit A. All my instincts told me that it remained a quagmire waiting to happen, and the contras were another classic case of the kind of client we couldn't afford in our own neighborhood, where our past support of every strongman from Fulgencio Batista to Augusto Pinochet continued to haunt us. I was all too aware that we might "win" with the contras and lose hearts and minds for the long term.

But it didn't stop the president from trying.

The CIA director was a much-maligned figure in the Senate. Bill Casey had been a longtime political supporter of President Reagan, even serving as his 1980 campaign manager and brokering the forced marriage of Reagan and Bush to form a winning ticket. He could've served almost anywhere in a Reagan administration. Someone who knew Casey had been an OSS recruit during World War II persuaded him that it would be a fitting coda to his long career to return to his roots and manage the Agency.

As director, he too often forgot that impartiality about the intelligence, rather than loyalty to the president, is the coin of the realm. Even the conservative Barry Goldwater chafed hearing from Casey about the contras.

One day, Barry asked me if I remembered how Admiral Bobby Inman used to sit next to Casey in the Intelligence Committee briefings and constantly tug at his socks. I nodded.

"I finally told him that a four-star admiral ought to be able to afford some new socks," Goldwater recalled. "Inman said that it was a nervous habit he got into, and every time he saw Casey start lying to the committee, he'd start tugging at his socks."

Goldwater sighed. "*Now, when I see him tugging at his socks, I start questioning Casey more.*"

It appeared that not nearly enough questions were being asked over at the White House—either of the CIA or of the ideologues determined to arm the Nicaraguan opposition no matter how much Congress opposed it.

The president invited a number of us from the Intelligence Committee down to the White House to talk about it. Reagan was in salesman mode, which I found disappointing.

I believed that the best conversations between the White House and Capitol Hill were candid and conversational, trusted asides where a president or vice president could get out of the presidential bubble and seek outside perspectives. Sometimes the advice falls on deaf ears, like it did with the Carter administration on the Panama Canal Treaty. But other times, a White House can use Congress as an early-warning system. Vice President Bush was especially good at this.

But this wasn't going to be that kind of meeting. President Reagan announced that he remained determined to help the "freedom fighters of Nicaragua," and I had to give him credit for always knowing the magic words to use to frame any argument. He insisted that he wouldn't stand by silently; the United States simply had to do something to stand with freedom-loving people in Central America. I broke into the conversation.

"Mr. President, you can't call it nothing—we are doing some things that could be productive . . ."

Reagan looked at me as if I'd been speaking Japanese.

"We can't do anything because of Congress. You have held us back," said Reagan, referring to the Boland Amendment to limit US government assistance to the contras. But I referred the president to another covert action we presently had ongoing in Nicaragua. He said there weren't any such actions because Congress stood in the way.

Robert "Bud" McFarlane interrupted and said that perhaps we shouldn't discuss the matter there. I pointed out to McFarlane that we were in the Oval Office with the national security advisor, the president of the United States, the vice president of the United States, and several senators from the Intelligence Committee. I said that I assumed that this was a secure area and that the president was cleared to have this information since it came from his own directive.

At about this point, the president got the hint and said, "Oh, you mean *that* item," as he looked over at George Bush, who was nodding his head rapidly.

The president of the United States seemed completely unaware of activities happening in his name. I told the president that they ought to make some effort to seek a bipartisan consensus. I went back to the Senate, and a number of us met in Leader Byrd's office about seeking some kind of consensus.

We called the president back, reaching him in the family quarters, to tell him that a number of us would be willing to work on it over the weekend if he had some people who could work on it with us. He said that was a good idea, and we agreed to get back together over the next several days.

We got back that night and found that we would be meeting with the president over the weekend. The president asked us to put off the meeting until Sunday morning, which we did. The next day, Bob Byrd, Chris Dodd, Dan Inouye, John Kerry, Bennett Johnston, David Boren, and I met first with Republican senators Bob Dole, Paul Laxalt, Ted Stevens, David Durenberger, Malcolm Wallop, and Jesse Helms. The president was there, along with Vice President Bush, Deputy Secretary of State Ken Dam, Treasury Secretary Donald Regan, Bud McFarlane, and Pat Buchanan, the new presidential speechwriter.

I told the president that I felt he could get fifty-one Republican votes to pass his contras aid package on Tuesday in the Senate, but that I thought it would be much better to work out something where he might have a whole lot more votes and show the countries of Central America, especially Nicaragua, that there was a uniformity of opinion. I told him this was a chance to have all of us together, and we might have something we could all agree on.

Bennett Johnston said, "Mr. President, we're making you an offer you can't refuse."

We worked throughout the day, using the chief of staff's office, and went back and forth to meetings with other senators and White House officials.

We weren't getting too far; Bob Dole pointed out that we'd been there for four hours and had not yet reached any kind of agreement.

"That's quite a complaint from somebody who wants to spend four years here," I replied.

We finally came back, having given the administration a position that would have brought economic pressure on the Sandinistas, hopefully a cease-fire, and the beginning of some negotiations.

I should have realized just what the Republican plan was all along. It was to attack us as soft, never to find a compromise. I turned on the *Today* show to see the House Republican whip, Dick Cheney, accusing the Democrats of trying to turn the contras into a partisan issue.

My blood boiled knowing that we had invested an entire weekend negotiating in good faith, while the White House merely played rope-a-dope against us and prepared a partisan attack for television. Still, as senators we wanted to find a consensus.

Senator Durenberger, the chairman of the Intelligence Committee, and Senator Boren both told me they'd been told by Secretary of State George Shultz that he was going to share with me the contents of a letter the president was sending to bolster his resolution. That resolution, of course, said that the president would be allowed to pursue any military or paramilitary means he deemed advisable in Nicaragua. Shultz never showed it to me or anybody else, nor to my knowledge did he have any intention of doing so.

I became convinced that administration officials were content to lose the vote in the House, knowing they could win with Republicans in the Senate and then blame it on the Democratic-controlled House, picking up a foreign policy issue for the 1986 midterms.

It was pure political theater, and a terrible, even dangerous way to conduct foreign policy. If only I'd known then that some in the White House had a different plan to get money and arms to the contras, one that bypassed Congress entirely.

— 31 —

Up Close

I wanted to see the reality of the Nicaraguan civil war for myself.

The little boy's hair was soaked and shiny with sweat as he hobbled along the dusty courtyard outside the primitive Rus Rus field hospital five miles from the Nicaraguan border. His bony shoulder blades poked through his tattered but otherwise immaculate T-shirt. He leaned on his crudely fashioned homemade wooden crutch and made his way with great but practiced effort toward the little patch of shade provided by the hospital roof's overhang, a minuscule refuge from the Honduran summer sky. The stump where his right leg had once been was carefully covered with the pinned back and tightly knotted pants leg of his dungarees.

The little boy's face was aged beyond what I guessed were the ten long years he'd spent on this earth. His features were weathered even, if that's a word that can be applied appropriately to someone so young but whose features revealed he'd lived life's hardest lessons in a short amount of time. His right hand was callused from the repetitive motion of bearing the weight of his right side on the crude crutch.

"*Is the boy a patient here?*" I asked one of the USAID workers, who then turned to a Honduran doctor and repeated the question in Spanish.

The answer was short.

"*No, Senator, he lives here now.*"

I was puzzled by the response and it must've showed.

There was a pause and then a longer exchange in Spanish.

"*Senator, he grew up in a village a few miles away. A couple years ago, he was playing in the forest and he stepped on a land mine.*"

The USAID worker's interest was piqued as well. He asked the doctor another question. He wanted to know which side had planted the landmine, the Sandinistas or the contras. They asked the boy.

"*Senator Leahy, he doesn't know which side put the land mine there.*"

"*What happened to his family?*" I asked.

The doctor shook his head sadly as he explained.

I could make out a couple of words but waited for the translation.

"*They're Miskito Indians—all subsistence farmers. They couldn't take care of him and he couldn't work the land,*" the young American shared with me. "*So, they let him stay here.*"

The words were translated into English, but I was still having a hard time processing their meaning.

"*This is his home now.*"

The little boy worked odd jobs at the hospital, sweeping the porch, helping to empty the lighter wastebaskets, and in return he slept in a spare bed if there was one. Otherwise, there might be a cot or a pallet of older blankets.

All because an unexpecting innocent footstep triggered an explosive just sixty millimeters in diameter, an ordnance resting on the forest floor, hidden beneath a blanket of decaying banana leaves.

I was sick to my stomach and could feel my face growing flush with emotion.

The little boy was probably my son Kevin's age, but he had seen horrors no one should ever live through, and they had steeled him to the cruelty of the world. I wanted to hug him as I would've our children, but I was a tall, imposing stranger and I didn't want to scare him.

I walked over beneath the overhang, reached out, and tousled the boy's hair. He smiled and looked up at the doctor, searching for a familiar face to reassure him that these interlopers meant him no harm.

"Es un buen chico, nos mantiene a todos en línea!" the doctor said with a smile.

The little boy's mood brightened momentarily. His dark brown eyes showed the first recognizable twinkle.

The aid worker, realizing the limits of my Spanish, whispered, "*The doc said he's a very good boy—he keeps them all in line!*"

I bent down and said to him, "*I have sons about your age. You look like a fine boy.*"

He smiled.

Soon, we were back in the helicopter and headed a few more miles up the Coco River corridor to reach a landing strip where a military plane would return us to Tegucigalpa for the flight home.

It was a short flight, and my mind kept drifting back to the lonely little boy at the Rus Rus hospital. I turned to my control officer from the embassy and asked him, "Are land mines common here?"

They were, he said. Both sides used them.

"*From the Soviets?*" I asked.

"*From everywhere, Senator. It's a global arms bazaar down here. Anything can be found on the black market. RPGs, Kalashnikovs, helicopters—and a lot of land mines. There's a price for anything.*"

There was a price, I thought, and that little boy at the hospital was the one paying it.

I pictured him wide-eyed at age seven, running between the banana trees, lost in a world of imagination before one fateful step and . . . it was gone. All of it. I imagined him waking up in the hospital, the pain, the first time he looked down the tangled bedsheets and saw that his leg was gone. Did he know then that he'd never go home? Did his mother wake up in the middle of the night crying for her little boy?

I'd come on this delegation trip to reevaluate my position on the civil war tearing apart Nicaragua, the seemingly endless bloody conflict rippling through the hemisphere. But it all seemed futile. The words of the USAID worker echoed in my ears: "*He doesn't know which side put the land mine there.*" And if he did, I wondered, *would it matter*? It couldn't bring his leg back. It couldn't reunite him with his family.

I didn't like President Daniel Ortega, and I didn't fall for his Marxist propaganda. And I didn't like the contras much either. They struck me as mercenaries, not freedom fighters. The people of Nicaragua could have benefited from many things from the United States, but more armaments and munitions didn't seem like the answers any of them were seeking.

I told the control officer the story of the little boy. "*Can't the embassy do anything for him?*" I asked.

"*We're funding hospitals to save lives and get people bandaged up and back to their lives. We're building schools. But we don't have the money for rehabilitation.*"

"*Or prosthetics?*"

The control officer shook his head. "*It's just not in the budget, Senator.*"

Someone had finally spoken six words that day that a US senator could actually *do something* about changing. The young diplomat probably didn't realize that in his resigned explanation a senior member of the Foreign Operations Appropriations Subcommittee heard a challenge, and maybe an opportunity.

— 32 —

Third Time's the Charm

At forty-five, no longer the new kid, I was starting to feel like a guardian of the institutional order myself.

Three terms—what once had sounded like an eternity away—might now be within my grasp, if only I could win reelection in 1986.

I was determined to run my strongest campaign yet for reelection. After the heart-stopping finishes in 1974 and '80, my plan had been to use the privilege of a six-year term to legislate—to be a senator, to leverage the seniority I was starting to accrue, and to really engage in the minutiae of the job, which I couldn't do as the top target of Republican challengers in 1980. I'd turn to reelection about a year and a half before Election Day.

There's something liberating about winning not just one but two races as closely as I had. It brings with it a kind of serenity: I was not rattled any longer by a two- or three-point swing in the polls. I'd defeated two different but difficult opponents. I'd had the wind at my back one time, when the national tide favored Democrats, and had the wind in my face another time, when it couldn't have been worse for the party. Through it all, I was still here—still a senator—and it made me start to feel quietly confident. In two very different election cycles, people in Vermont had still found a reason to give me a chance—twice. It was emboldening. But it also made me realize how quickly everything in the Senate could change in a nanosecond. I'd seen giants fall, I'd seen upstarts elected, and I'd seen many wear out their welcome. I was at ease with all those possibilities, and I believed that the country of 1986 wasn't all that different from that of 1974; people wanted to know that even if their government couldn't fix their lives, it was at least listening.

But reelection to a third term and a Democratic majority could make me something else: a chairman, with an ability to really make a difference for people.

I would keep my eye on the prize. I was comfortable with my political instincts, my barometer having been tested twice before. I'd built a good statewide organization, with a very strong staff, and I'd been home signaling my accomplishments without being showy. People understood it mattered to have a senator on the Appropriations Committee when it came time to repair a road or bridge, or to have a senator on the Agriculture Committee when it was time to defend the Northeast Interstate Dairy Compact, which protected New England's farmers from being swallowed up by the midwestern advances.

The Senate Democrats were spending the weekend down in West Virginia for a strategy session. I wished I could have been with them, but I couldn't be in two places at once and knew that the reason I was reelected in 1980, when many other Democrats were defeated, was that I focused on taking care of Vermont first.

I'd be back in Burlington for the Aiken Lecture Series, where this year former secretary of defense James Schlesinger was the keynote speaker.

It had been a decade of twists and turns since the first Aiken Lecture. We'd first convened as the Vietnam War sputtered along, and Schlesinger's assignment then was to persuade the new junior senator from Vermont to keep it on life support. I still remembered Leader Mansfield's remarkable speech in favor of ending the war and making America strong at home again.

This was the first Aiken Lecture since its namesake's passing in 1984. The Vietnam War had ended, South Vietnam had quickly fallen, and now, at last, there was a memorial, a black granite V, in Washington, a tribute to the more than fifty-eight thousand Americans who had died in a war that had seemed endless.

Schlesinger endured. After his tours of duty with Nixon and Ford, he'd served as America's first-ever secretary of energy under President Carter and was now writing and speaking on the lecture circuit.

He opened his address at the university with a surprising statement: Vermont, he celebrated, had revered the independence and integrity of George Aiken, and if it wanted to continue that tradition, it should "take the advice of a conservative Republican and reelect Pat Leahy." The line received the biggest applause of the evening. I somehow knew the look my father would have on his face up in heaven.

In a period of a couple of months, I'd done more to prepare for the upcoming election than I had for either of my other elections. Republicans were pinning their hopes on former governor Richard Snelling to be my opponent. He had grown a beard, had bought an expensive French yacht, and was sailing somewhere off the coast of France. While some interpreted this as a signal that he had no intention of running, I knew that in a Republican state he could still turn around and come back from yachting, announce that he's going to run, have an organization in place within a few days, and quickly raise an enormous amount of money.

I wanted everyone to know that I was preparing for a titanic race no matter who the Republican nominee would be.

I spent a long morning meeting at the White House with Secretary Shultz, Defense Secretary Cap Weinberger, Deputy Director John McMahon from the CIA, along with Intelligence Committee chairman Senator Dave Durenberger.

That night, the president told a joke about an older couple where the husband is asked by the wife to go out and get her an ice-cream sundae, but to please write it down because he'll forget. The husband insists, "Of course I won't forget." The wife says, "You always forget, write it down, I want vanilla ice cream." He says, "Don't worry, I'll remember. Vanilla ice cream." She says, "But write down that I want hot chocolate sauce." He says, "Don't worry, I'll remember hot chocolate sauce." But she says, "You should write it down, because I will also want a cherry on the top, write it down so you won't forget it." He says, "I don't have to write it down, I'll remember it: vanilla ice cream with hot chocolate sauce and a cherry." She says, "And I also want whipped cream." He says, "I'll remember that too. Vanilla, hot chocolate fudge, cherry, whipped cream." Off he goes. Half an hour later he comes back with a bag and says, "I got what you wanted." He opens the bag and pulls out a ham and cheese sandwich. She looks at him in disgust and says, "I told you to write it down or you'd forget something. You forgot the mustard."

This was Ronald Reagan at his most charming.

As he laughed with me and encouraged me to share a yarn or two, I wondered whether it dawned on him that just hours before he had helped recruit my opponent into the race as a matter of national urgency. Something told me that Ronald Reagan's future happiness did not rise or fall with the Senate fate of Dick Snelling.

Back in the Capitol, Bob Dole assured me that when he went to Vermont to campaign for Dick Snelling, he would campaign *for* Snelling and not against me. There would be no personal attacks. It was interesting. Dole was the consummate hard-hitting partisan, and former Republican leader Howard Baker was the person who built bridges between Republicans and Democrats. Both were likely contenders for president in 1988. But it was Dole in Vermont who spoke highly of me as a senator and merely pointed out that he wanted Dick Snelling elected because he wanted to keep a Republican majority. I found nothing wrong in that kind of campaigning, especially as the majority leader had a responsibility to his party to do so. But for Bob Dole the institutionalist, there were lines that senators didn't cross when campaigning against a fellow senator.

The White House, however, reveled in the partisanship. I made it down to the White House for a signing ceremony for the Farm Bill. I was the senior Democrat in Agriculture in attendance, and the protocol would normally suggest that I would be positioned up front with the president. Not only was I carefully brought through a back way, where I had to go through metal detectors and so forth, but by the time I got there, I found that with the Reagan White House, when it has a signing, it does the ceremony with various people's names marked on the floor where they are to stand.

I was put literally as far away from the president as I could possibly be.

I watched all the way through the president's speech, tucked away in the back where nobody could see me. I realized that he had to walk from where he had given the speech to a small table where the bill actually was for him to sign.

I could see his notes from the back, and when he was almost at the end I started moving.

To the great glee of the press corps and the chagrin of the White House political people, I was standing by the president's chair as he arrived, and I held the chair for him.

Reagan gave me a funny look, as if to say, "*What the hell are you doing here, Leahy?*"

But he sat down to sign the bill, and the picture that showed up everywhere showed me standing next to him. Leahy 1, Snelling 0.

Late that night, I drove home to Marcelle in my Dodge Aspen, ninety thousand miles on the odometer. It probably didn't fit the image that the political cartoonists portray of politicians being chauffeured back and forth in a limousine. I saw two fast cars coming in my rearview mirror, and the first one that zipped by was a red Firebird with the license plate USS-1 from Colorado, obviously Gary Hart. The other was an old Pontiac convertible with the license plate USS-1 from Massachusetts. That was Ted Kennedy.

I wondered, as I watched them pass by, if this race down the George Washington Parkway was a precursor to what we might see in the next presidential race.

But for me, I was happy going my own pace in my old car, and my eyes were firmly fixed on winning in 1986.

Even as I ran against the White House's chosen Senate recruit, I tried my best to stay engaged with the administration on Central America.

Aid to the contras was the issue that seemed to never go away.

Meeting at the White House again, the discussion devolved into contradictory talking points.

National Security Advisor Bud McFarlane reassured the visiting senators that the contras were concerned about the people in Nicaragua and they wouldn't ever take any action to hurt them.

Almost in the next breath, Ronald Reagan said the contras had been very successful in that they had brought the country to its knees—that because of the contras, the Sandinista regime couldn't feed the people, and that meant the regime now had no choice but to pay attention to us.

I don't think the two men were even listening to each other. It was kind of a frightening thing to go to the White House and see how completely immune to the details the president could be, and how much he liked to rely on his cue cards and a few well-memorized lines. The presentation was always engaging, but we were trying to shape policy, not merely personalities.

John Glenn, Russell Long, John Stennis, and I sat across from Reagan. He started to riff about why we had to support him insofar as we're all Republicans "*in this together*." He went on that way until Howard Baker finally got the chance to break in and point out to him that some of us were Democrats. The veneer was wearing thin.

Shortly before Election Day, it was publicly revealed that an elaborate scheme funneled the proceeds of secret arms sales to arm the contras, in direct contravention of the law.

It would be known as the Iran-Contra Affair.

We were headed for a constitutional crisis, and the main question was whether President Reagan was really in the driver's seat of his own foreign policy.

— 33 —

Howard Leahy's Landslide

Election night, November 4, wasn't anything like the two before.

I wasn't pacing the floor with worry.

We had rented the usual hotel ballroom in Burlington for our victory celebration, but I was able to come downstairs and accept those results well before 10:00 p.m. The results were staggering: a margin of 56,325 votes.

My campaign director, Bill Gray, introduced me at the podium, but not before he raised a glass and nearly robbed me of my ability to speak.

"*Tonight,*" he said, "*let's all raise a glass to Howard Leahy—he finally got his landslide.*"

The tears flowed. Dad had been such a part of each and every one of these campaigns. But I felt his presence looking down upon all of us.

Across the country, the news was just as encouraging as it was up north. Democrats won eight Senate seats and succeeded in erasing some of the Republican gains Reagan had swept in six years before—from Alabama to Florida, South Dakota to Washington, many of the Reagan freshmen who had vanquished my Senate mentors had now been defeated themselves.

We were back in the majority.

The next morning, the family and I headed home to the farm in Middlesex.

As I walked down the road from the farm at dusk to pick up the mail, I couldn't help but think how beautiful it was here on a cold, clear autumn evening with a lovely sunset over the mountain range, quiet and peaceful as I looked out over the fields and thought about the year I had just been through.

It hardly seemed possible that I had just completed the most strenuous campaign that anyone had seen in Vermont. It was a campaign that started almost two years earlier with constant fundraising and in many ways set a new standard for the state. It was an election that I eventually won because of the commitment of thousands of volunteers throughout Vermont. No amount of money raised, ads run, or anything else could have brought about that kind of commitment. People were responding to the issues that I had spoken about, both in foreign and domestic policy. Most people knew that they could count on me to speak out and that I had no illusions that I would always be right.

I couldn't help but think that here I was, at the age of forty-six, about to start a third term in the Senate. It would feel so different leaving the peacefulness of the farm in Middlesex to go back to the hurly-burly of Washington.

I'd be returning to a Washington in crisis. I was confident that the Iran-Contra issue would be a difficult test for the country and the administration as the whole affair unraveled and more information was made public.

I was also faced with the responsibility of putting together an Agriculture Committee that could try to address the absurdity that the most productive agricultural country in the world was importing food, and seemed unable to maintain our farm families in a way that made it possible for them to earn a living running a family farm.

In some ways it would have been nice to simply stay in Vermont and enjoy the peace and tranquility. But I would know that I'd wasted the advantage of being in the Senate. After all, there are only a hundred of us. It's the only parliamentary body in the world where an incumbent has the ability to stand on the floor of the Senate and say anything he or she wants, where one can be involved in everything from social policy to foreign policy, from taxation to establishing budgets, from planning for the future to protecting the past.

Any one of us willing to sit back and not take advantage of that is cheating themselves. And if the past few weeks had been any example, I wouldn't cheat anybody—or myself—when it came to that experience.

The contrast of old and new in the Senate seemed particularly acute in the days after the election. The lame-duck session would be short. Dole called a Saturday session to allow for tributes to so many retiring and defeated colleagues. It was an occasion that never ceased to remind me just how lucky we were to serve here.

Tom Eagleton was retiring after nineteen years, a respected colleague. He'd been a mentor to many young senators, and his acts of generosity were celebrated. Shortly after Tom announced his intention to retire, he'd given his subcommittee seats to freshman members so that they could advance in seniority. The words flowed easily in honor of Eagleton. But the most profound expression of his esteem wasn't words at all. From my desk, I watched as Senator Stennis gripped the bar on his desk and pulled himself from his wheelchair to stand on his one leg, to deliver his remarks about his colleague.

By the time Stennis was finished, his shirt was soaked through in sweat. His body was betraying him. His speech was labored. We came from completely different places in time and geography and ideology, but my eyes misted over as I watched this simple of most difficult gestures: John Stennis was determined to keep faith with those he considered "Senators"—with a capital S.

— 34 —

Mr. Chairman

I was forty-seven years old, a father of three, and now the father of three successful campaigns for the Senate, the very last one by a comfortable margin, thanks to my chief of staff, Ellen Lovell, and campaign maestro Mary Beth Cahill. Yet it turned out I was still capable of the occasional "pinch me" moments I'd experienced so frequently as a freshman senator.

The funny thing is, those moments aren't typically the ones you read about in books, or those you might expect. They aren't the moments when an aide passes you a note that "*the president is on the phone for you*," although those can yield some pretty good stories. There are still moments that give you goose bumps—"Pomp and Circumstance" being played by a Marine band, the image of Marine One taking off from the White House lawn—but more often it's the moment it dawns on you that the passage of time has given you an opportunity to do something that your mentors did long before.

For me, as 1987 began in earnest, becoming chairman of the Senate Agriculture Committee was that "*how the hell did* I *get here?*" moment.

Politics was trending increasingly partisan. Television sound bites, talk radio, and the cameras all around were too often cheap sugar highs for the loudest voices. Money was becoming more important in politics, and Senate races were becoming far too expensive. The committee was my oasis away from all that unpleasantness. Some very partisan people had served on the committee over the years, but it had always been the place where I most frequently saw all of them at their most nonpartisan, because on this topic, really, there was nothing to be partisan about. Politics really did stop at the edge of fields and farms and forests. When I'd arrived in 1975, the committee was the stomping grounds of three very different Greatest Generation heartland legislators: George McGovern, Bob Dole, and Hubert Humphrey. I was closest to Humphrey from the start. His stories about growing up in a tiny prairie town named Doland, South Dakota, living over his father's one-man pharmacy, sounded an awful lot like the Vermont of my youth. He joined his dad on excursions to sell the Humphrey family's homemade cures for livestock to the farmers in the community. He remembered the blinding dust storms that ravaged the region in the days before federal incentives for sustainable agriculture. But he remembered something else that he shared in common with Dole and McGovern.

Hubert couldn't forget the family encounters with hardworking farmers who would stare at the crates of homeopathic veterinary medicines his father, Hubert Sr., was selling, look down at the ground to do the calculations in their mind, and then mumble something softly about "*Well, maybe I will buy it next time you pass through*," or "*Maybe I'll come see you after the harvest*." He remembered the children staring out from behind the farmhouse's drafty windows, mesmerized by the Humphrey Pharmacy truck loaded up with goods to sell along their route, as though his father were Santa Claus and the truck were his sleigh.

The Humphreys weren't well-off. But unspoken in these exchanges was just how hard some people could work to wring a living out of the fields—whether it was wheat, corn, or soybeans—only to be left holding the short end of the stick. Humphrey's dad didn't write the debts and credits down in his ledger. He lent out whatever was needed to fill the gaps between farming's good years and bad years. Hubert remembered the smoked hams or chickens that showed up on his family's porch at Christmas from the farming families, another unspoken token of appreciation, another prairie ritual. No one ever said, "*We're broke, Mr. Humphrey*." No one ever said, "*We're hungry*." No one ever had to ask, "*Can I pay you back later?*" No one had to. Every unspoken word could've filled a financial ledger.

Dole's experience on the plains of Russell, Kansas, was ripped from the very same pages of Humphrey's book. McGovern's childhood in Mitchell, South Dakota, in the shadows of the Corn Palace, was marked by the Great Depression's grasshopper plagues and the seemingly endless dust bowls that felt like the coming apocalypse. For the son of a Methodist minister who tended to a congregation where even the most taciturn farmers might break down crying as the family farm went belly-up, a congregation where kids' clothes were in tatters and rib cages were often just a bit too pronounced, where suicides were whispered about but never confirmed, always just referred to as an accident in the barn; these were searing years that forever defined McGovern's sense of right and wrong when it came to the plight of farm families.

Dole, McGovern, and Humphrey had all looked into the same eyes, and they were determined to do something about it when they had a chance.

All three had run for or served as vice president, had run for or was going to run for the presidency, and they could each give as good as he could get, but this area of American policy, to them, was set aside from politics. No one should be hungry. No farmer should live and die with the fluctuations in commodity prices. No farm family should be wiped out under a mountain of debt because of a hailstorm or a drought. And so they worked closely together across party lines to help people throughout the country who did not have food and to build a school lunch program, which bought America's surplus crops and used them to help ensure kids didn't come to school hungry and unable to learn. McGovern and Dole together even passed legislation, which I supported, to create food stamp programs for impoverished parts of Africa and other countries where girls were expected not to go to school but to instead stay home and help out the family. But when families found out they could be fed in school, and that was one less meal for the family to provide, the girls were allowed to go to school. Children, both boys and girls, were healthier and they also had an education, and American farmers had a federal purchaser who made it all happen.

For me, I never told Dole, McGovern, or Humphrey my story, about what I'd witnessed peeking from the passenger seat of my family's car: those unscheduled, unexplained stops on the way home from the grocery store, when Mom or Dad would take a couple of bags of food from the trunk of the car and bring them up the stairs to a tenement or row house. I thought my story paled in comparison to what they'd all lived in the 1930s in the farm belt. But the lifelong lesson was the same, whether you were from Montpelier or Mitchell, Russell or Doland; you didn't have to wax nostalgic about it, you didn't need to put it into a long speech, because you'd lived it and it forever changed you.

Now, I had moved all the way from the most junior member on the committee to the most senior, all in the span of a dozen years, and I wanted to use my gavel as chairman to restore that sense of common ground and collaboration, not by lecture but by example.

The committee had become a different place under Chairman Jesse Helms; somewhere along the line, someone had renamed it "Agriculture and Forestry," dropping the word "Nutrition" from its name. I hoped it would be more than a symbolic act of renewal to restore hunger and health's undeniable place at the heart of farm and food policy by renaming it the "Agriculture, Nutrition, and Forestry Committee." To my joy, every Republican and Democrat on the committee voted for it. It underscored a commonality so obvious it was often overlooked.

But that was just the start. Greater inspiration came from an overheard conversation in the cloakroom. *I was driving in the middle of nowhere when President Reagan called me,* I heard one of my quick-talking, more urbane colleagues saying a bit too loudly from the phone booth, the doors left wide open and his long legs stretched out.

The middle of nowhere, I thought with a little chuckle. *Well, if you're from there, you know it's always the middle of somewhere.* It was the first lightning spark of a brainstorm. All these years, I'd been traveling when Senate recesses allowed to try to understand the world a little better, to build some relationships with leaders from other countries, allies and adversaries alike. And from that very first CODEL onward, I'd found that almost without fail, when senators travel together, their partisan differences dull and their shared perspective grows. You see a country and you see each other through the other person's eyes, just as much as you do your own.

But I'd never heard of a CODEL at home, to help senators understand that rural Indiana and rural Vermont had a lot in common, to make it clear that everywhere was somewhere and nowhere was just a place on the map that you hadn't experienced—yet.

I had a wonderful staff—led by John Podesta, Janet Breslin, Ed Barron, and Chuck Reimenschneider—who could tell me where the gaps in food, nutrition, hunger, and farming policy were, but I could make those changes a reality only if the committee was rowing in the same direction. I went to Dick Lugar on the floor. Quickly, we hatched a plan to commence weekend field hearings the very next month. Between my perch on Foreign Operations and Dick's long service on the Foreign Relations Committee, one thing we knew how to do was wrangle permission to use a military aircraft for official business. We secured an Air Force airplane and plotted a schedule to travel to a number of states that were heavily agricultural. We invited both Republicans and Democrats on the committee. We'd go to a Republican state and then we'd alternate; next time we'd go to a Democratic state, and back and forth. We decided to bed down at farmers' homes and hear from them the night before a field hearing. I would yield leadership if it was a state that a Republican senator was from so he could lead the discussion. Around and around we went, from South Dakota, where a former Hill staffer turned Democratic freshman senator named Tom Daschle had reclaimed the seat long held by George McGovern, to the Mississippi Delta, where Republican Thad Cochran was serving in the seat where the former president pro tempore Jim Eastland had resided for four decades. From Louisiana to Delaware, it was so clear: hunger was a problem. We grew different crops, we had different accents, but everywhere, everywhere, whether it was the grape growers and the United Farm Workers of California or the dairy farmers of Vermont, people felt invisible. We were at least showing up. There was no "nowhere" on our committee.

Most of all, these field hearings actually galvanized the kind of bipartisan cooperation that made it possible to pass legislation. We were learning issues together. We were taking notes on good ideas that came out of the field hearings, from witnesses in each state who were all telling different versions of the same story. It's a lot harder to vote against someone else's priority when you've sat next to them on a flight for four hours, or stayed overnight on a farm with them in their home state and shared your first sip of coffee in the morning or maybe that glass of single-malt holy water at night before you retired for the evening. Their issues become your issues. When you've invested the time with your colleagues over a weekend away from your state and your family, the last thing you do is allow a legislative period to evaporate with nothing to show on the issue. You want the committee to succeed and you become invested in your colleagues' success. It creates a self-fulfilling momentum: no time for show horses or speeches when there's work to be done and something in it for everyone.

The camaraderie of the Agriculture Committee insulated all of us from the bitterness of what was happening in the political world beyond the Senate. National politics was there for anyone who wanted to participate, and some did—for Ted Kennedy, it came with the territory. For freshman senator Al Gore, as we approached 1988, it seemed like destiny to run for president and try to reach the highest office in the land. The 1988 campaign was a tough one. Democrats sensed an opportunity to take back the White House after eight years in the wilderness. Republicans were determined to hold on at all costs. The earnest governor of Massachusetts, Mike Dukakis, became our nominee and, sadly, a candidate for the political meat grinder. Vice President Bush became the Republican nominee and showed a side to his competitiveness that seemed far afield from what I'd seen as he worked both sides of the senators' dining room. He stood back and allowed his political party to cut Dukakis to shreds and turn him into a murderer-furloughing liberal who opposed prayer in schools and didn't think students should recite the Pledge of Allegiance. It was a stunningly effective exercise in caricature, and it worked. George H. W. Bush became the forty-first president of the United States, and an unlikely heir to the Reagan legacy.

But for me, while this was a dispiriting turn of events, I had work to do inside our Senate majority. Early on, I latched on to something I was hearing more and more about around the living rooms of farm families in Vermont. We're a small state. We've never even tried to be the biggest at anything. But we've excelled by being the best, in a quiet kind of "show, don't tell" sort of way. We took that quiet pride in everything from our maple syrup to our granite and marble to our Cheddar cheese. If it had the word "Vermont" in front of it, it meant something about quality and craftmanship. Now, more and more, I was hearing from farmers that there was a whole new market ready to be defined in organic farming. It was a natural outgrowth of the artisan culture we didn't feel compelled to call a culture, it was simply who we were, living out traditions that had been passed down from parents to children for generations.

But there were also new traditions being forged in Vermont in a blend of imports from out-of-state and longtime Vermonters. People who had tired of big cities had moved to Vermont to live closer to nature. They were natural environmentalists. They wanted to make their own food and care for the land in ways that were simpler and closer to what was happening in New England hundreds of years ago. Naturally, they gravitated toward eating cleaner and healthier and started to seek out products they could trust. Word spread. I was hearing more and more from farmers, including multigeneration farming families, who wanted to pioneer a whole new type of farming, with no pesticides, no growth hormones, and no chemicals. They believed it was the right thing to do and they were passionate about it, but they also thought it was an economic opportunity to change agriculture.

But it all came with a price, they told me. Growing organic required a lot of work and came at a premium for price. Yet in the best proof that these farmers were onto something special, big factory farms that used every kind of pesticide were getting away with deceptive labeling and marketing, from "all natural" to even "organic," when in fact they were dumping every chemical you could find on their crops. I decided to go back and fight for organic standards.

It wasn't going to be easy. In a way that only he could, the previous chairman of the Agriculture Committee, Jesse Helms, didn't just strongly oppose organic standards, he laughed at them. They used to call Jesse "Senator No." He was a champion of the big factory farms and seemed to be the only person left by the late 1980s who still regularly used the words "hippie" and "beatnik." To Helms, organic farming sounded like part of the counterculture he'd spent thirty years railing against, a horrifying amalgam of tractors, sitar music, and marijuana smoke. I suspect he would have found great company with the busybody who had implored my office to seek out and arrest any alleged skinny-dippers, and he remained leery of the Senate's leading Grateful Dead fan.

Fortunately, Republican ranking member Dick Lugar had a whole different outlook. We sat down and decided to work on it quietly, and to have our staffs collaborate on language that could give a level playing field to this nascent industry. "*Let's get this done through the committee,*" Dick suggested. No loud bill introductions, no rallies for legislation, no "*call your senator and demand organic standards.*" I agreed completely. *The first rule of bears is don't poke them,* I remembered. We didn't need a big fight with Helms and the industry; we just needed an outcome. Dick and I saw the process the same way. Sunlight, not limelight, was what grew crops, in farming and in legislating on agriculture.

Of course, lo and behold, we put our legislative language together, drafted by Katheleen Merrigan, just as a self-anointed expert started making the rounds, urging me to mount a big public campaign for organic farming. He proclaimed to be not just an expert on the industry and the policy, but on marketing and branding. We asked him to demur. No one liked an interloper, and his plan wasn't just to poke the bear but to shine a flashlight in its eyes. "*Let us legislate our way, if you don't mind,*" I suggested.

Our legislation passed uneventfully in the Senate committee and made its way unimpeded through the Senate as part of the larger Farm

Bill reauthorization. The Senate was deferential to a bill that had passed out of committee unanimously, even if we knew the organic standard buried deep inside would face a fight ahead at some point. In the *Schoolhouse Rock!* version of making farm policy, we were merely inches away from completing the long journey upstream from "*I'm just a bill, sitting here on Capitol Hill*" to the president's desk.

I'd imagine that to an outside observer, a conference committee is a little bit like watching rugby or curling once every four years at the Olympics; if you don't follow the sport religiously, if you haven't mastered its ins and outs, at best you're able to absorb about a tenth of what you're seeing unfold in front of you. It takes a practiced ear to listen for and appreciate a language all its own. Late one afternoon, we met in the big hearing room in the Russell Building to bring together all the Senate and House conferees to go through a heaping pile of differences between the Senate and House legislation. We had to vote one by one on whether to include any point on which the two bills varied. We were working to produce a master bill, unamendable, for each body—Senate and House—to vote on in final form and send to President Bush.

The early session was widely attended by staff for all the conferees and outside interest groups: labor unions, big corporations, trade associations representing every imaginable product from pesticides to chicken coops, and even foreign interests like the embassy of France, which was on hand to monitor whether any legislative tweaks by Congress could impinge on its treasured rights to words like "Champagne" and "Brie."

I knew that when we arrived at the discussion of the organic provisions on the Senate side, we would have some pushback from House members from districts where the big corporate farming entities were omnipresent. Dick Lugar and I brought up the entire organics bill that had passed in the Senate committee. The House members criticized it. I could see the representatives of the bigger agribusiness interests taking copious notes, likely to report back to their home offices that the House members they'd cultivated relationships with had indeed come through and defended the status quo. The vote was called, and the conferees voted not to allow our provisions in their entirety into the conference report.

Out of the corner of my eye, I could see the know-it-all lobbyist fidgeting in his seat, his face bright red, agitated, no doubt ready to run to the phone and call his contacts on Capitol Hill, none of whom was in the conference committee, to raise hell and tell them what a terrible development he'd just witnessed in this process.

Around 6:30, we announced a short dinner break, and as soon as I walked away from the dais, I was buttonholed by the activist. He was practically adorned in sackcloth and ashes, crestfallen about what had just happened to "his" bill. Funny, I didn't recall seeing his name on the legislation, but I wasn't going to correct him. He was going to organize a press conference for the morning with all the liberal interest groups that stood in favor of organics, to urge a series of calls to reluctant members of Congress. "We have a different plan, I really hope you'll keep your powder dry," I advised him. "*Why don't you go get some dinner and come back for the later session?*"

The later sessions of the conference committee tested anyone and everyone's ability to sit and sit and sit some more. As the hours ticked by and the list of potential amendments diminished, the room cleared out. The lobbyists were long gone. Around one o'clock in the morning, all but the chairman and ranking member of the House had left, their rank-and-file members handing them their proxy votes.

At this point, I brought up the multipage piece of legislation with a few technical corrections here and there regarding various forms of farming and a number of definitions with respect to labeling. The chairman on the other side looked at me, gave me a smile, and said, "We have no objection," and, hearing none, the committee conference accepted organic farming.

An hour later, we gaveled out the conference committee and went home. As I walked down the hallway, the forlorn activist ran after me. "*Senator, what's the plan? I thought you had a plan?*"

I looked at him and smiled. "*Were you there when I offered the technical corrections to those subsections and paragraphs?*"

"*Yes.*"

"*That was the plan. We won. Please don't tell anyone. Go back to your hotel and sleep.*"

He looked at me, puzzled.

"*And cancel your press conference, please.*"

The next day, the massive bill was passed by voice vote in the House and Senate, with all that language we needed to protect the nascent organic farming and food industry from its artificial imitators. Shortly thereafter, I was invited down to the Old Executive Office Building for the bill signing with President Bush. The bill was on the table, an enormous heap of thick paper with one page set aside for the president to sign. As chairman, I had a terrific spot reserved for me over the president's shoulder. Gone were the days of being the Reagan administration's electoral target lined up in Siberia for the photo op.

President Bush looked back at me and said, "Pat, did you read this whole bill?"

I replied, "Mr. President, you're the one signing it. I've read about as much of it as you have."

We were all laughing, and the guffaws were contagious up and down the row of legislators. On the way out after the photo spray, the reporters shouted, "Mr. President! Mr. President! What was the joke?" Bush pretended not to hear them.

I walked up behind him to see him around the corner. The press yelled, "Mr. Chairman! Mr. Chairman! What was the joke?" I said I was so excited to be there I forgot what the joke was.

President Bush put his arm around me and asked what time I was leaving work. I said, "It was a long week, so probably about six thirty."

He said, "Why don't you stop in and we can have a drink together."

I was looking forward to the drink and the company of the person I'd first met in 1975 as a nominee to lead the CIA, just as much as I was looking forward to seeing what the organic farming bill would do for Vermont and the country.

— 35 —

Peace At Last

"*Senator, you can make a big difference if you get involved.*"

How do you make peace when so many are still living the war?

This was a question the silver-haired man in the wheelchair was determined to answer through his own example. His name was Bobby Muller, and he was a warrior's warrior.

Bobby's a marine. In his case, I say "is," not "was," because the commitment to mission that motivated him as a twenty-three-year-old lieutenant leading his infantry platoon in battle wasn't dulled one bit by the bullet that severed his spinal cord. The injury put Bobby in a wheelchair for life, paralyzed from the waist down, but it awoke in him a powerful sense of activism and responsibility that burned with unrivaled intensity. His steely blue eyes radiated passion, and his clipped Great Neck, Long Island, accent punctuated his words, which were direct and to the point.

"*I have two asks for you, Senator Leahy. One—we need to clean up the mess we left behind in Vietnam. We're twenty years on, and people are still dying because of it. Two—we need to ban land mines so this never happens again.*"

"*I'm in.*"

Bobby waited for the caveat, but none was forthcoming. He'd touched a nerve, and he probably didn't anticipate that he had me at hello. I'd opposed the war when I first ran in 1974. It had never been lost on me that were it not for my one blind eye, I would've served in Vietnam and could've been among the 109 Vermonters who never came home. I'd felt a responsibility to stick to my convictions and became the first senator from our state to actually vote against funding America's longest war, to stand up and say what everyone knew by then: that we didn't belong there and we shouldn't stay. But years later, I wasn't any less haunted by the legacy of what we'd left behind, the tremendous damage done not only to our military and to men like Bobby, who would never walk again, but to the civilian populations in Southeast Asia. It was a seemingly endless parade of horrors: Agent Orange, land mines, bombings, atrocities, and thousands of Vietnamese children fathered by American GIs—tragically called "*children of the dust*"—abandoned in orphanages.

It was fourteen years after the last helicopters took off from the roof of our embassy and Saigon became Ho Chi Minh City, but the war was still with us.

Bobby Muller was talking about making peace. Finally.

"*I think I know how we start,*" I added.

After my trip to Central America four years before, I had succeeded in securing funding on the Foreign Ops Subcommittee, side by side with Senator McConnell from Kentucky, for a war victims fund. We were helping people like the young boy I'd met at the Rus Rus field hospital near the Nicaraguan border get help to make their lives easier. Wheelchairs, canes, prosthetics—whatever was possible.

But we could only do it where we had a partnership with a foreign government. We didn't even talk to Vietnam. The postwar embargo remained in place. We had no embassy. No listening posts. I wondered: Could using our war victims fund become a way of creating an opening to Vietnam?

I called the State Department. Dick Armitage was a Boston-bred Republican, a deputy assistant secretary of state for Asia, who cursed like a sailor—because he was one. He'd served three tours of duty in Vietnam after graduating from the Naval Academy in Annapolis. He was sympathetic but said it would be impossible to do. "*There's a lot of opposition, Senator,*" he said.

I set out to confront the opposition. The easiest action in the federal government is to do nothing. There's a built-in risk aversion in the bureaucratic culture: if you never shake things up by taking a chance, you'll never fail. But Washington's version of "*not failing*" was little comfort to the broken people we'd left behind in Southeast Asia.

Two months later, I was meeting with President Bush about his agenda in the Middle East—and the cooperation it required from the Appropriations Committee. Our relationship was cordial, connected by dozens of handwritten notes sent back and forth dating back to his days patrolling the DMZ of the bipartisan senators' dining room as President Reagan's trusted lieutenant.

George Plunkitt of Tammany Hall once wrote of politics, "*I seen my opportunity and I took it.*" A lull in the conversation and my surmisal that Bush wasn't especially looking forward to his next meeting converged in opportunity.

"Mr. President—can we talk about Vietnam?"

I laid out my idea.

The president's secretary of state, James Baker, jumped in: he thought it sounded like a good idea. I pointed out that someone in the State Department had slow-rolled the discussion.

"Jimmy—get him on the phone." Only Baker's boss and tennis partner of thirty years would call him "Jimmy."

Secretary Baker got on the speakerphone.

"*Well, Senator Leahy is always pushing for that all the time, but it is not the greatest of ideas,*" said the disembodied voice from Foggy Bottom.

"*Well, I've got somebody here who thinks it is a very good idea. Mr. President . . .*"

President Bush got on the phone. You could almost hear the tires screeching as the man at the State Department did a full U-turn, knowing the president was on board.

We agreed that the easiest way to turn the idea into action was to have the War Victims Fund make a large grant to the Vietnam Veterans of America Foundation (VVAF) to start charitable work on the ground in

Vietnam. We could not do a full government-to-government partnership, but who better to begin the hard process of reconciliation than America's veterans themselves? And who could question their patriotism? After all, who could look in the eyes of the VVAF's leader and tell him that he couldn't go help rebuild the lives of the people who had once shot at him across rice paddies and triple-canopy jungles?

My first call back in the office was to Bobby Muller: "*So, Lieutenant—are you ready for another tour of duty in Vietnam?*"

"*For twenty-one years, I never knew that those words could put a smile on this old face,*" Bobby replied.

Months later, I brought four senators and their spouses with me to Vietnam—the first CODEL there in several years.

We visited a makeshift workshop and rehabilitation center outside Ho Chi Minh City where VVAF's work was making progress. Word was spreading about its presence on the ground.

People who had lost their legs stepping on land mines—either as combatants or as civilians—were now coming here in anticipation of finally getting their first wheelchairs. The wheelchairs were very well made, but the canvas for the seating was magenta colored because that's all they had available; there was something incongruous about the imposing steel-and-rubber wheelchairs with these bright pink seats.

Several people were lined up to get their wheelchairs, men and women who had been crawling on the ground for years, some begging for food scraps in the marketplace or hopping along on little stools in place of their long-lost legs.

The local Vietnamese Communist bureaucrat delivered a long speech on a very hot day. The only words I could understand periodically was "Patrick Leahy." One legless man stared at me throughout all the speeches. I had the feeling I'd known before as a candidate and a public figure: watch out for that person in the crowd who stares just a little too long, whose attention is fixed so clearly on you.

I thought, *While this tiny, weather-beaten man might be getting a wheelchair today, he must hate me as an American. He must think of us every time he looks down at the place where his two strong legs once belonged, the legs that would've pedaled his bicycle in the busy streets or stood resolutely in his fishing junk as he made his way down the Mekong Delta in search of the day's catch of shrimp.*

The speeches concluded; the local Communist functionaries led all the visiting dignitaries to stand among the real guests of honor—the amputees—as the moment arrived for each to receive his or her new wheelchair.

I was face-to-face with the unusually focused man who had watched me so closely through the program. Without warning, someone asked me to pick him up and put him in his wheelchair. I became nervous.

Marcelle, always and ever a nurse, whispered to me quickly the best way to pick him up so that I wouldn't risk breaking his bones.

With no legs and a slight figure, the man probably weighed sixty pounds.

He just stared straight ahead. I thought again, *How must he feel about this six-foot-three, two-hundred-pound American bending down to touch him?*

He must think, I hate you.

I picked him up and gently put him in his wheelchair.

As I started to get up, he grabbed my shirt, and he pulled me down and kissed me on my cheek. His broad betel-nut smile was warmly genuine; his hands, callused from dragging himself along on the ground all this time, were held up to my face in an unspoken expression of friendship.

I was stunned.

Four feet away, the scene repeated itself: Senator John Glenn, helping another person into a wheelchair, found himself enveloped in a sobbing, smiling bear hug.

The sweat and the tears ran together down our faces.

A half hour later, after we boarded a bus to take us onward toward our next stop, John Glenn commandeered the microphone for the PA system and announced, "After what we've seen today, if anybody complains about anything, you can walk back to Hanoi and fly home yourself."

We all understood. Each of us had been moved by the unexpected reaction, by the ability of people to forgive and, through it all, to love their fellow human beings.

When we got back to Washington, I told the story to President Bush and thanked him for his partnership. He became visibly emotional, patted my arm, and said simply, "*Patrick, we are on the right road. Stay on the right road.*"

— 36 —

The Natural

"*Governor, I think you should come to Burlington in late September.*"

For all my years in the Senate, Jim Aloysius Farley's old quip had remained hopelessly prescient in presidential elections: "*As goes Maine, so goes Vermont.*"

Ford.

Reagan.

Reagan again.

George H. W. Bush in 1988.

Every one of these Republican presidents was each and all a person I'd worked with constructively, and disagreed with at times vigorously but politely, but not a single Democratic partner in the White House had carried Vermont.

I looked back on my freshman senatorial experience with President Carter and, especially, the day-to-day presence of Vice President Fritz Mondale, and I wished I were able to tell my thirty-six-year-old self to savor it more. I wished I were able to grab my younger self by the shoulders and let him know that eighteen years would go by before I'd even have a real hope of working with a president of my own party, in the majority.

But here we were, as the heart of summer started to break, and this Labor Day weekend, something had me feeling especially optimistic. This time, finally, I believed we had a chance in 1992.

"Vermont's changing—if you swing through, you'll get a national story about competing for states Democrats haven't won since—"

The hoarse voice at the other end of the line interrupted me, excitedly.

"Since LBJ in '64. You know, Pat, ahh remember watching the results that election night . . . and when I saw Vermont went Democratic for the first time, well, they didn't vote for Kennedy, they didn't vote even once for FDR . . . if Vermont's going for Johnson, I thought this is going to be the landslide of all landslides . . ."

I paused and ran the math in my head. *"Governor, in 1964—were you even old enough to vote?"*

"Ha, no, Pat—you know, I was a Kennedy volunteer like you in '68, and I didn't get to vote until Humphrey, and I know you served with Senator Humphrey . . ."

I chuckled.

Bill Clinton did his homework. About Vermont. About politics. About me.

His knowledge of political history was encyclopedic, and he liked to share it the way the most committed baseball fans love sharing the statistics on the back of old baseball cards.

"So, Bill—Burlington in late September. You're coming through Boston for fundraising, I'm sure. Come up to Vermont in the afternoon. We'll get a big crowd on the water, right on Perkins Pier. It's a beautiful photo."

"Late September? Pat, I thought you'd say you wanted to do this in late October like Jack Kennedy did."

I thought of that late afternoon in 1960, watching Jack Kennedy at the airport, as he dutifully performed a weary last-minute addition to his schedule as he worked his way home to Boston and to Cape Cod for election night. How interesting that something in the New Frontier candidacy had simultaneously enthralled both a young college kid in Montpelier and an even younger Arkansan who had just entered high school in Hot Springs.

"Well, Bill, Vermont's three electoral votes. If you were coming in late October, I'd say we had a real problem."

Clinton laughed. He had a deep laugh that reminded me of the last southern governor I'd met running for president, Jimmy Carter.

Clinton's wife, Hillary, had already campaigned in Vermont, and she had drawn a good crowd. Her encyclopedic knowledge about health care and education struck a chord with a crowd of professional women and mothers who turned out to see this brilliant lawyer who had worked for years on policy in Arkansas and at the Children's Defense Fund.

"*We should do this, Pat. I need to get to Maine too. Perot's doing well there, and it's Bush's adopted state. That'll send a brushback pitch in Kennebunkport.*"

"*Well, you know what they say, Bill. As goes Vermont—*"

"*So goes Maine!*"

We were already finishing each other's sentences.

I was running for my fourth term, and the polls were widening against my opponent, the Vermont secretary of state Jim Douglas, a traditional Republican who was now transforming himself into a fire-breathing populist to appeal to the state's Perot voters, twisting himself into a pretzel over issues like term limits. In a year of dissatisfaction with the Republican in the White House for being out of touch on the economy, I liked where I found myself in my campaign, even if habit and instinct had conditioned me to work down to the wire.

"*I think you can compete in Vermont, Bill, and besides, I have a good feeling about the incumbent senator on the Democratic ticket, and I think he can put together a good crowd for you.*"

Clinton laughed.

Three weeks later, on a beautiful Indian summer afternoon at Perkins Pier marina on Lake Champlain, I stood on a stage next to our governor, Howard Dean, as he warmed up the crowd.

I watched the procession of cars and flashing lights marking Governor Clinton's motorcade pull up the avenue toward the event, and an anticipatory murmur rippled through the crowd.

Burlington had never seen a rally so large. The motorcade stopped short of the ramps that would've led the governor and his entourage to the security of the backstage speaker's area.

A gaggle of photographers and reporters leaped from a bus trailing behind the governor's white sedan, and they raced ahead, huffing and puffing. Secret Service agents positioned themselves for what by now must've been a familiar exercise: the presidential candidate opened his car door, stretched tall on the car's running board on his tiptoes, waving to all who had turned around to see him, and then plunged into the crowd along the rope line marked by Jersey barricades surrounding the rally perimeter. Bill Clinton was the first candidate I'd ever seen shake hands through the crowd on his way into a rally, not after it.

I felt a tinge of sympathy for our governor, whose speech was now drowned out by the crowd excitedly reaching out to touch the person they hoped might become the forty-second president of the United States.

Howard Dean built to his crescendo, and then it was my turn to speak and introduce the candidate—as Clinton was barely a third of his way through the foaming crowd.

"*We have thirty-eighty days to go before Bill Clinton and Al Gore will lead the United States of America!*"

The crowd cheered.

"*Thirty-eight days before it's time for us in Vermont to say no to gridlock in Washington, no to trickle-down economics on Wall Street, no to the deadlock on dairy prices!*"

More cheers. I could see the top of Governor Clinton's head as he continued his way hand by hand, hug by hug.

"*Thirty-eight days until we can have a Supreme Court that's there for all of us!*"

Big, booming applause.

I was feeding off the energy myself.

"*I watched the Republican convention in Houston.*"

Boos erupted. The Republican nominating convention that summer had left a lasting impression on all of us, a residue not easily wiped away. For four nights, Republicans had subjected the prime-time audience to a divisive lineup of Clinton-bashing right-wingers, with a particularly ugly speech by Pat Buchanan, the anti-gay, anti-immigrant, anti-woman populist who had challenged President Bush's reelection. Now it was clear which wing of the Republican Party was in the driver's seat, and suffice to say they didn't reside up north in Kennebunkport.

"*We saw what their convention stood for. They want us to fight each other. To hate each other. To be divided. We need a nation for all of us. We heard their ugly words, and we knew their meaning. Well, they left out one four-letter word at their convention: 'hope.' Let me introduce to you—the top of the ticket that can give us back our hope . . .*"

Out of the corner of my eye, I spotted Clinton jogging, finally, toward the stage, and he bounded up the steps as the crowd cheered.

"*Governor Bill Clinton!*"

We embraced in a big bear hug.

Clinton began his remarks and proceeded conversationally, referencing some comments Howard Dean and I had made earlier in our speeches, back when he was fully enveloped in the crowd.

I wondered how he had even heard the speeches, let alone been able to digest and internalize them while shaking all those hands and posing for all those pictures. It reminded me of the better high school basketball players I'd known at St. Michael's: those who were able to keep a picture in their minds of what was happening on the court behind them, even as they drove the basketball forward toward the hoop.

Clinton saw the whole playing field and made it look not just effortless but natural, as if he'd just walked in and joined a familiar conversation among friends.

He drawled, "*Ahh saw the latest poll in your newspaper . . .*"

The applause grew.

"*And I thought,* That can't be right, Vermont never votes for a Democrat . . ."

The laughter kicked in.

"*But then I saw this lovely crowd and I knew: we are on the move in Vermont!*"

The rally erupted.

Clinton was in his element. He casually mentioned "*what we all understand, coming from small, rural states,*" implicitly linking Vermont and Arkansas, making the Republican attacks on his governorship a referendum on places like Vermont.

He spoke eloquently about the "*power of the presidency to help the people,*" and to those who knew anyone leery of turning Republican Vermont blue, he exhorted them to tell their families, "*You're not voting for a Democrat for president, you're voting for your future . . . you're voting for change so we're gonna be one country again.*"

Twenty minutes after his motorcade had stopped all of Burlington in its tracks, Governor Clinton was back in his car, waving, smiling, headed off to his next stop—after the biggest rally in Vermont's history.

This wasn't my first political event, but even for me, it felt that afternoon that we might just be on the brink of something new, something different, not just an end to twelve years of Republican dominance in presidential races and twenty-four years of their victories in Vermont, but the start of a new time in Washington. We were going to have a young Democratic president again, I thought, one with Kennedy's charisma and Carter's accent and ability to reach beyond blue states. Finally, for the first time since Reagan wiped out our party in 1980, I thought politics in America might be moving leftward again.

I felt refreshed. I was seasoned enough now to appreciate what I didn't fully in 1976: that these moments are fleeting.

On election night, I didn't need to wait up too late to know that I'd been reelected by an almost 11-point margin. We celebrated in the ballroom to the tune of the Grateful Dead's "Truckin'," which had become an anthem for the Senate's leading, long-established Deadhead, a caucus of one.

An hour or so later, it also became clear that with 46 percent of the vote, Governor Clinton would do what only Lyndon Johnson had before him. The mercurial independent candidate, the self-financed billionaire Ross Perot, drained the incumbent president's support, leaving President Bush in second place with 30 percent, a Green Mountain State low-water mark for the party of Lincoln.

Marcelle and I would have to stay up later to learn that this time, finally, as Vermont went, so would the nation: with unexpected gains in rural areas in the West, the South, and the heartland, and buoyed by the defection of some Republicans to Perot's campaign, Bill Clinton was closing in on an Electoral College landslide with a plurality of the popular vote.

Vermont had returned me to Washington, to a capital city that was in for a change.

In Houston, the scene was sedate as the networks broke away from the regular election-night programming. The presidential seal had been placed on the podium at the Westin Galleria hotel. The person I had known and respected in so many different incarnations—CIA director, vice president, and for these four years as a friend on Vietnam while he'd been president—waited in the wings as James Baker introduced him. President Bush made the longest short walk imaginable to a podium to concede the presidency.

The years, the presidency, and the campaign had hardened his already angular features, and it wasn't hard to see the weight he had placed on his shoulders to speak not just for his campaign, but to the country. "*The people have spoken,*" he said, "*and we respect the majesty of the democratic system.*" He said he wanted "*the country to know*" that his team would work with the president-elect, "*because America must always come first.*"

The president folded his speech and slid it back into his suit jacket pocket, just like the list he kept years ago of requests and reminders when he roamed the senators' dining room as vice president, and he waved goodbye to the crowd, and just like that, as the lounge band played "Deep in the Heart of Texas," the forty-first president walked off into retirement. He was a gentleman in defeat as he had been in victory.

As the clock approached midnight, in front of the Old State House in Little Rock, to the tune of a slightly less hallucinogenic seventies anthem, Fleetwood Mac's "Don't Stop," Bill Clinton declared victory.

I squeezed Marcelle's hand. "*Something tells me we're going to be busy.*"

A House majority, fifty-six Democratic senators, and, now, the White House; the stage seemed set for a great era of progressive legislating.

Before we went to bed, the first disappointing news of the evening was confirmed. I'd learned by now that even in an institution like the Senate, change is part of the process. John Glenn used to call Article I of the Constitution the "HR office" of a democracy. Good people aren't always reelected. The country seesaws back and forth between majorities, midterms of first-term presidents go the other direction more often than not, and so often big forces out of our control can decide our fate. That's what was happening on election night.

Terry Sanford from North Carolina and Wyche Fowler of Georgia were respected colleagues and faces of what many had referred to as the "new South," Democrats who had always been progressive on civil rights. Unlike Stennis's generation, they'd never protected Jim Crow. They gave hope to the idea that Lyndon Johnson had been overly pessimistic when he declared that signing the Civil Rights Act of 1964 was the right thing to do, but it would set in motion the gradual shift of the once Democratic Solid South to the Republican Party. But the news flashed on CNN: Sanford had been defeated, and Fowler's race was headed to a run-off in which he'd be an underdog.

If we were shedding southern Senate seats with a Democratic ticket led by two southerners, following a recession for which the Republican incumbent was held responsible by the public, would our Senate majority be durable?

It was a legitimate question. The Senate I had joined in 1975 had two Democrats from Mississippi. By the dawn of the Clinton administration, retirements had turned those seats over to the Republicans and they weren't coming back. If this was the unending trend below the Mason-Dixon Line, we'd be in trouble.

But what I was sure of was that, regardless of the political challenge for 1994 and beyond, we had work to do and little time to do it. Whatever might come, we had the House of Representatives, we had the Senate, and we had a new president with ideas to turn the economy around. I remembered those short golden years of my first term and knew these moments didn't come around often enough; they didn't come with an expiration date, but neither were they self-executing. I'd been around long enough to know it, as had Bob Byrd and the Republican Senate leader Bob Dole. Over in the House, the seventy-year-old congenial Republican minority leader Bob Michel knew it too, as did his ambitious, scheming minority whip Newt Gingrich. Washington can be a combustible place at moments like this, and I could feel the crucible starting to bubble.

— 37 —

Change

The Clinton presidency did bring with it something else: a Senate that took an overdue step—maybe a baby step, but a step nonetheless—toward looking more like America. It had felt strange to me, and especially to Marcelle, when I came to the Senate as one of one hundred in an all-male body. As a young lawyer, I'd met Senator Margaret Chase Smith and had been impressed by her, but she was the rare woman to have been elected, and she was gone by the time I arrived on the scene. Muriel Humphrey had been beloved in her brief time serving out Hubert's term, but it was really Nancy Landon Kassebaum who had come to the Senate to stay.

As late as 1985, she was joined by only one other woman, a senator from Florida whose stay was brief. The only racial diversity represented in our ranks came in the form of Ed Brooke of Massachusetts, an African American Republican defeated in 1978, and Dan Inouye, a Japanese American from Hawaii, later joined by Senator Sparky Matsunaga and, briefly, Senator S. I. Hayakawa from California. Barbara Mikulski arrived on the scene in 1987. Other than that, it really was, literally and figuratively, an old boys' club.

1992 started to change that, finally. Patty Murray from Washington, Dianne Feinstein and Barbara Boxer from California, and Carol Moseley Braun from Illinois were all elected in their own right.

Carol was the first African American woman ever elected to the

Senate. I first met her at an event in Washington. Marcelle and I had come up in our aging car and found a parking space a block or so away. A Lincoln Town Car pulled up with Carol in the back seat. I joked to her that you can see the difference between being a senator from a big state and being one from rural Vermont. She laughed and continued up the stairs.

In that moment, I wondered how it must've felt to be "the first," let alone the "only one" out of one hundred. I had almost tried to hide in my first caucus meeting in 1975, struggling with a kind of imposter syndrome, wondering if the old Senate bulls would ever find me worthy. But other than that moment before I was sworn in, when the clerk by the door assumed I was an aide or intern to Senator Church and momentarily delayed my arrival on the floor, no one had ever looked at me and, based only on surface appearances, wondered whether I belonged here. As a white man of a certain age, I'd always be able to blend in. Carol would never have that luxury. There's an occasional comfort in a certain kind of anonymity, especially when you're learning the ropes. Carol would never enjoy that freedom to melt into a crowd. In fact, none of the women senators did the way we men did. Stories were written about aides carrying their purses, or aides bringing step stools to their press conferences so they could see over podiums that had been built for senators over six feet tall. No one ever wrote about the aides who attended to male senators, carrying their briefcases, driving them home, or doing much more than that—even though, at one point in Strom Thurmond's dotage, his chief of staff was known to everyone as the "101st senator." The women had a harder challenge in that respect, reminding me of the old Ginger Rogers line that she had done everything Fred Astaire did, except backward and in high heels. The same words applied to the changing Senate and to those women who helped force that change.

Not long after Carol Moseley Braun arrived, a story rattled around the Senate. She'd been in an elevator with Senator Helms. It was said that he whistled the tune "Dixie." Whether it was a dog whistle or an innocent whistle or simply Senate folklore, I couldn't say for sure. But I knew Helms had said a lot of ugly things over the years, and having been in hundreds of elevator rides with him, I knew he'd never once whistled "Dixie" around me; in fact I'd never heard Jesse whistle at all. It wasn't hard to imagine what had changed. I wondered if racism, America's original sin, was a force we could ever really conquer entirely, subtle or unsubtle. But I also wondered whether Eastland and Stennis and Russell Long, southern men of a very different era who had taken me under their wing so generously, would have gone out of their way to share those same courtesies and wisdom with someone who looked so very different from how they did, someone whom they would have had to seek out, instead of just exercising next to them in the Senate gym. I'd never know for sure. But I knew that I'd probably already benefited from a form of senatorial affirmative action for so many years when, in a homogeneous body, despite my youth, people said I "looked the part." Now I was glad the Senate was inching closer toward at least looking like a place where most anyone could belong from the first moment, not just our sons but someone like our daughter and later our grandchildren.

The first years of the Clinton presidency reminded me just how quickly political fates can turn, particularly when a political opposition with remarkable discipline sets out to undo a presidency.

So many things that had gone right for Bill Clinton in his campaign suddenly started to unravel. If his gift had been an ability to connect with average Americans and to connect to their lives, a small mistake here and there started to chip away at the image he'd built as a candidate. One story that whipped its way through the Senate suggested that Clinton had stopped outgoing flights at Los Angeles International Airport so that he could receive a $200 haircut on Air Force One from a hairstylist named simply Cristophe. My colleagues laughed about it. "I don't have enough hair to need Cristophe's services," I joked. But the damage was done; Rush Limbaugh and conservative radio blasted the story for days as evidence that the president was out of touch. It had all the ingredients of a powerful piece of propaganda: Hollywood, elitism, regular folks paying the burden of someone else's privilege. Of course, the story wasn't actually true—other than the cost of the haircut.

But far more cutting was the Republican blockade of all Clinton initiatives. As long as I'd been a US senator, infrastructure had been a bipartisan issue. We had all believed in bringing money back to our states and districts for schools, libraries, bridges, and waterways. Senator Byrd told the president that if he attempted a similar gambit with a federal investment stimulus package, it could pass with bipartisan support. Instead, Dole and the Republicans lured the White House into a long negotiating session that dragged on for weeks and weeks. All the while, Clinton was under daily fire for allegedly governing too far from the left and for trying to keep campaign promises like allowing gay Americans to serve in the military. It was an ugly kind of homophobia, most embodied by Senator Jesse Helms, who acted as if this were the entirety of the Clinton agenda. What struck me about the cynicism of it all was the narrative the Republicans were creating. They were arguing that Clinton was focused on gays in the military instead of bipartisan issues like the economy, while they held his economic stimulus package hostage on Capitol Hill as Clinton tried to negotiate a bipartisan bill.

Then the Republicans focused on a single issue: the deficit. Never mind that through the Reagan and Bush years, all they'd done was grow the deficit. Now, they were laser focused, they said, on reducing its size.

Finally, the president realized his only shot at passing an economic program and actually cutting the deficit depended on lining up every Democratic vote he could find to pass an investment package and raise taxes on the wealthy. Without a single Republican vote, we passed it. Our reward? With incredible discipline, the Republicans went out on television and radio and day after day labeled it the "biggest tax increase in history." Their ability to tout a single message left Clinton and all of us dispirited. What upset me so much as an institutionalist was the raw cynicism of their strategy: yes, it was good politics, but when one political party divorces itself from any responsibility to govern, the country is perched atop one very slippery slope.

Soon, the verdict of the midterm elections was bearing down on all of us like a death sentence.

"*Teddy's fine, but I hear Sasser is going to lose badly,*" warned Chris Dodd.

I suppose I should've been surprised, but I wasn't surprised.

I'd lived through a political massacre like this one before. 1980—the very election in which Chris had first come to the Senate, succeeding Abe Ribicoff—I'd witnessed the defeat of so many Democratic stalwarts.

Now, the coming political apocalypse of 1994 felt eerily like 1980 all over again.

Ted Kennedy was facing the toughest reelection campaign of his lifetime, which is to say, for a Kennedy in Massachusetts, the first tough reelection campaign he'd ever experienced. Mitt Romney, a self-financing multimillionaire business whiz and son of a Michigan governor—Republican royalty—had given Teddy quite a scare, even narrowly leading Kennedy in a handful of pre–Labor Day polls. But just as water finds its level, Ted had climbed back into the race with a couple of strong debate performances.

But in states that were less reliably Democratic, something else was happening.

Senate Democratic incumbents and candidates all found themselves attached, sutured, and otherwise firmly glued to a running mate whose name didn't appear on the ballot: President Clinton. "*Radical*" Clinton. "*Liberal*" Clinton. "*Out-of-touch*" Clinton. When they weren't stuck trying to remind voters that they were on the ballot, not Bill Clinton, they had to contend with their other running mate: "*Washington*," and I don't mean General George. The Republican candidates were, down the line, fiercely disciplined, running a nationalized campaign against Clinton and Washington, and I could hear echoes of the word "*Carter*" from fourteen years before. "*Washington*," they argued, was badly broken by out-of-touch elites; what they forgot to acknowledge was how their obstructionist blockade of all of Clinton's policies was exactly what had broken the city and caused such reason for cynicism and disgust.

"*Imagine that*," said Dodd, shrugging his shoulders. "*Jim Sasser's inches away from being Senate majority leader, and his state's throwing all that clout away.*"

Even if I'd seen it before, it did defy logic, I had to admit. Tennessee, like many rural states including Vermont, had benefited from having a delegation in Washington with seniority and experience. The state knew what it meant to have friends in high places. During the FDR years, the Tennessee Valley Authority had changed rural life and living circumstances, bringing electricity and jobs and revolutionary investment to the state and region. With Howard Baker as majority leader, Tennessee had seen more than its share of federal funds. And now, for the first time in history, Tennessee was on the brink of having a second majority leader from its state in the span of just ten years, along with a Tennessean in the White House as vice president.

But it wasn't meant to be.

Marcelle and I turned off the television early that night, as the results pouring in were even worse than expected.

Tennessee ousted not just Sasser, but turned Al Gore's old Senate seat over to the Republicans. It was the first time in history an entire Senate delegation flipped to the other party in a single night.

Majority Leader George Mitchell's open Senate seat went Republican, along with five other open seats. Moderate and sometimes conservative Democrat David Boren, always intellectual, had retired to become president of the University of Oklahoma. His handpicked successor in the moderate mode of Oklahoma Democrats was drubbed on election night by a House Republican, Jim Inhofe, who promised to fight the "*gestapo tactics*" of federal regulators.

"*Cut their pay and send them home*" had been a rallying cry of the Republican insurgents, an homage to anti-Washington campaigning and the populist appeal of term limits. This was one election night even more than others when you really didn't want to be a "*their*" or "*them*."

Republicans won the House of Representatives for the first time since 1954 and ended eight years of our Senate majority.

The next afternoon, my friend on the Appropriations Committee, Dick Shelby, the last of the conservative southern Democrats, announced he was switching parties. Dick was a workhorse who lived delivering for Alabama. He had seen the writing on the wall, the long-in-coming change in states like his where seniority and experience no longer seemed to count, as they had for decades, if the candidate had a D after his name.

"*In Newt we trust*" was the mantra of the ascendant Republicans in the Senate and House: Newt Gingrich, the next Speaker of the House of Representatives. I had known of Gingrich largely as a foil to the last Republican House leader, Bob Michel of Ohio. Michel was a gentleman, a seemingly permanent fixture during the Reagan and Bush years as "*Mr. Republican*," a reliable, midwestern man of the institution. Bob had allowed Gingrich, a Georgia firebrand, to become his second-in-command in a bow to the changing reality of his party. Gingrich, a congressman who had left his first wife while she battled cancer, saw no conflict between his private circumstances and his public positioning; he happily organized conservative Christians to sweep races across the South and Midwest, promising to turn a conservative religious agenda into law, even as he lived quite differently. Michel, by contrast, was decent, courtly, and committed to comity. Gingrich was brash and committed to one thing only: winning. His gripe with Bob Michel, fundamentally, had to do with Gingrich's winner-take-all mentality: Newt didn't think being a respected, even revered "*minority leader*" was any prize at all, if you could instead burn your way through the scorched earth of politics to become Speaker. It turned out an awful lot of Republicans agreed with him.

What surprised me was not that the House could flip so quickly after nearly a half century or that the Senate could turn over again; after all, I'd lived through the latter once before. What stunned me was just how much, unlike even 1980, the new senators saw the Senate as little more than a smaller version of the House of Representatives. I had been elected as a Watergate Baby, pledging to change Washington, to shake up the system. I wasn't allergic to reformers or outsiders; in fact, I'd been one, and often I felt still like an outsider in the more wealthy and comfortable dens of Georgetown. But I'd always believed that the Senate was supposed to be a different kind of institution, a place where each senator's prerogative was bigger than party caucus—otherwise, why have a Senate at all? The struggle ahead was not just about Democrats and Republicans, it was between institutionalists and those who had little patience for the institution, builders versus destroyers.

In our first Agriculture Committee meeting since the change in majority, the organizing resolutions and a number of procedural bills and nominations were pushed through quickly. It felt barely as if the committee had changed, only that the seats on the dais had been rearranged in recognition of the new majority. Chairman Lugar, my counterpart in the committee's leadership of the last eight years, had, as always, communicated well in advance the agenda. There were never surprises between us, and it made for a reliably efficient, even businesslike atmosphere.

But today, before the new chairman gaveled down the business meeting, he paused.

"*I have a further item for the agenda, but I have not discussed it with Senator Leahy, and I request that he not even vote,*" Lugar announced.

My jaw clenched and my brow furrowed. What a strange comment coming from my friend.

I looked down the dais at the knowing smiles.

Lugar made a motion to have an arcane Senate rule waived. It turned out that unlike in the House, Senate protocol precluded the committee room displaying a portrait of a former chairman if that person was still serving in the Senate.

Lugar's motion upended the rules: he wanted my portrait hanging there in what was now his committee. I was the first sitting senator to have such a portrait in the Agriculture Committee.

Usually a low-key, soft-spoken, calm midwesterner, Lugar's voice suddenly sounded like an auctioneer forcing through a sale: "All those in favor say aye, no nays, it's passed."

Everyone started applauding. Dick had obviously talked to the other senators and told them he wanted this to be a surprise.

Maybe the Senate was still the Senate.

But later that week, I extended my hand on the Senate floor to introduce myself to the new senator from Pennsylvania, Rick Santorum. Santorum had defeated Harris Wofford, a decent, well-liked son of the civil rights movement who had been appointed to the Senate after John Heinz's death in a plane crash. But Santorum's politics were different from those of the moderate Pennsylvania Republicans who had come before—a lineage that stretched from Hugh Scott to John Heinz and Arlen Specter.

"*It's nice to have another Italian American in the Senate,*" I said to Rick with a wink.

He looked me up and down, perhaps wondering how a "*Leahy*" had ended up in America by way of Italy.

"*I'm not sure we're the same kind of Italian Americans,*" said Santorum with a smile that always left you with the impression that he'd smelled something foul.

Santorum was ambitious. He told colleagues he hoped to become either the first "*real*" Catholic majority leader or the first "*real*" Catholic president of the United States. I could only imagine what George Mitchell or Ted Kennedy thought when they heard that one. But the audacious ambition fit the Gingrich mold, and indeed Santorum had been a Gingrich acolyte in the House, someone who boldly shared that he had learned how to campaign for his former Pittsburgh House seat by driving the district listening to a Gingrich cassette tape mailed out to ambitious GOP candidates. And so, Rick wasn't just "*pro-life.*" Instead, he was fighting in a "*war on Catholicism.*" Publicly, at least, he didn't have opponents, he had enemies. How, I wondered, would he ever govern in an institution built on finding a bipartisan path?

We soon had our answer.

The Senate debated a long-lingering GOP hobbyhorse: a balanced budget amendment to the Constitution.

On policy grounds, I thought it was a grave mistake to force the Congress to balance the federal budget every year. Remembering what my parents shared about the Great Depression, I knew the difference it made to Vermont and to the country to be able to come to the rescue of working people when economic devastation hit. The notion that a future Congress wouldn't be able to do that because Congress in 1995 had sacrificed a lifeline on the altar of ideology and fiscal austerity repulsed me. I knew a balanced budget amendment was a great sound bite. But the reality of the damage it would do to governing in tough times wasn't worth the benefit of a snappy press release. Besides—and this really burned me up—I hated the idea that Congress, especially the Senate, would sacrifice its own prerogatives in perpetuity. Did we really believe we were so reckless that we couldn't trust ourselves with the power the Constitution invested in us—the power of the purse? In my estimation, we already had a balanced budget amendment: it was called the Constitution of the United States. It gave us the power to tax and the authority to spend the taxpayers' money. If you believed in a balanced budget, then by all means make choices about how to spend money or set taxes in keeping with those values. We didn't need an amendment to mandate we do so. In my mind, this was yet another situation where I had to ask myself: *Who are the real conservatives?* Those who wanted to change the Constitution for the first time in decades when there were other obvious alternatives, or those voting to protect it? The hypocrisy especially struck a nerve: not a single Republican senator two years before had been willing to vote in favor of President Clinton's first budget that cut the deficit in half.

The balanced budget amendment soared through the Gingrich House. But in the Senate, by a one-vote margin, the Republican chair of the Appropriations Committee, Mark Hatfield, proved to be the real conservative, the one who stood against giving away the Senate's rights and traditions to fight some phantom menace.

There are many moments when Senate life and family life collide. How many times growing up had our children had to come to the Senate and have family dinner in my office, because Daddy would be enduring a late-night vote-a-rama? How many times had I sped to a school event coming from a vote, just to make sure I got there, even if a few minutes late? But there are also beautiful and happy moments that come from the unplanned collision of your personal life and your work in the Senate.

I'd always been fascinated by the entertainment industry and the ways in which creative people brought riveting stories to the big screen. As it so happened, as a member of the Judiciary Committee, which weighs in on issues from copyright protection and intellectual property to the rights of artists and musicians, you sometimes get to know people from the industry.

Once, I was meeting with the executives from Warner Bros., which was sometimes jokingly referred to as "the house that Batman built." We somehow got on the subject of my love for those Batman comics and for the movie franchise. I mentioned that I'd gotten our children hooked early, and that our son Mark, after service in the Marines, was now in California working as an actor. Would we want to have a father-son cameo in the upcoming Batman movie starring Val Kilmer? they asked.

Unlikely as it was, soon I found myself on a movie set with a small part in a ballroom scene in which Jim Carrey, as the Riddler, would look at me with a suspicious stare as if to say, "*Don't I know you?*"

It was a "pinch me" moment more surreal than anything I'd experienced even as a freshman senator.

On the set, Tommy Lee Jones walked by me, fully made up to play Harvey Two-Face, a villain of villains.

Mark and I studied the script together. A young aide assigned to putting me through my paces made small talk. He explained that in my scene, I'd be dancing a waltz with a woman before the Riddler threw the room into chaos. "By the way," the young man explained, "you might be interested to know that your dance partner was a former Miss Vermont."

"That won't make Mom jealous," Mark said.

We laughed. No worries there.

I didn't recognize the former Miss Vermont's name at all. I thought maybe if I talked with her, then I could place her.

As we took our places on the dance floor, we made conversation. She said she and the other Miss America contestants had all gone to Washington for a reception in the Rose Garden with the president of the United States. I was trying to figure out what the date must've been. I asked how the president was, and she replied that they all thought President Eisenhower was very nice. President Eisenhower!

I imagined Marcelle somewhere off to the side laughing uncontrollably. After all, she too had watched the Eisenhower inauguration—on a black-and-white television set in school, in the fourth grade.

I stood on the shore of Lake Champlain, my hands in my pockets, leaning in and listening to the folks from the Vermont Fish and Wildlife Department. They directed my attention to a picnic table, where a neatly displayed pile of otherwise undistinguished crustaceans set the stage for a worrisome conversation. In front of us were something they called "zebra mussels," for the subtle stripes that glistened black and white under the bright blue sky; I suppose they were about as evocative of those majestic sub-Saharan animals as an ugly bivalve can be. But these were no ordinary shellfish. They were an extremely harmful invasive species that spread uncontrollably, clogging fuel pipes of boats, killing off fresh water's good bacteria, changing the chemistry of the crystal-clear lake itself, and covering every rock below with razor-sharp shells.

The state officials explained that these mussels had been polluting the Great Lakes of the upper midwestern peninsula for fifteen years and had now found their way eastward, to our big, beautiful lake shared with New York and Canada. I thought of my summer job during college ferrying trays of sunset cocktails to all the people enjoying their summer vacation on that remarkable lake. I remembered the rally with Governor Clinton on the marina just five years before as finally we turned Vermont blue. But most of all, my mind flashed back to the family picnics with Marcelle and our children those summers in the 1970s, when Washington emptied out for a congressional recess and we drove home for the splendor of a Vermont summer. Lake Champlain was as extraordinary as any body of water I'd ever seen in any of the states or countries I'd traveled to as a senator, and now it was imperiled by a glorified mussel, for heaven's sake. I asked the officials what other states were doing to combat this infestation, and they alerted me that Lakes Michigan, Ontario, Superior, Huron, and Erie—the five so-called Great Lakes—were receiving hundreds of millions in federal research dollars to help solve their predicament and rid themselves of this invasive species, which endangered a huge source of tourism and hospitality revenue. I scribbled a note to myself for follow-up, and afterward, from the car, I called the office in Washington. I was neither a marine biologist nor an expert in bacteria, but a Senate seat can be an able substitute for any such deficit.

I quickly learned that in fact just south of $300 million over five years was set aside in the budget for research and technology to help states and municipalities address crises like this one afflicting their lakes. Solving the problem was becoming a boon for research universities in areas touching the Great Lakes and ocean communities. It was called the Sea Grant program.

There was only one problem. While any state on the Atlantic or Pacific coastline could avail itself of the federal dollars, those of us inland were shut out, unless we represented a Great Lake state, even if our majestic lakes shared the exact same malady as Ontario or Michigan. It was absurd.

But there was a solution. It took just seven words. As the Commerce Committee readied a reauthorization of the Sea Grant program, Susanne Fleek and J. P. Dowd on my staff drafted a simple phrase to be added to the bill: "The term 'Great Lakes' includes Lake Champlain." Lake Champlain was created by the same tectonic plates as the Great Lakes, so it seemed only fair that Vermont too should be eligible for federal assistance just as the other states were. No one said a word in opposition.

From my perspective, this was just good old-fashioned problem-solving. It reminded me of the way in which, when we passed a Farm Bill, I could expect to see an amendment from Ted Kennedy and John Kerry to include New England's cod fishermen in farm programs designed to benefit farmers who, because of drought or pestilence, were no longer able to grow their crops. In these New Englanders' eyes, the fishing families of Gloucester were no different; their harvest was from the sea, and the codfish were long gone. It hurt no one to modify the language. In fact, as a legislator, I always appreciated steps that were inclusive; the more senators were invested in the passage of a piece of legislation, the easier it was to shepherd its way to passage and onto the president's desk for signature.

And that's exactly what we'd smoothly engineered with a slight modification to the technical language of the Sea Grant program; the matter was solved quietly and efficiently—until all hell broke loose shortly after the ink dried.

Perhaps a legislative aide for a midwestern senator who hadn't paid attention earlier suddenly woke up to what had been accomplished, and they feared that in a budget free-for-all, a little more money for Vermont must've meant less money for their state. Even as an appropriator, I'd rarely thought of the process in such zero-sum terms; victory was something you wanted more colleagues to share in together.

But the press, helped by some careful leaks and snarky anonymous quotes, seized on the issue. Overnight, it became a sensation: Great Lake–gate.

The histrionics of some senators and their home-state newspapers were incredible. Some worried publicly that one senator from Vermont had effectively put at risk America's encyclopedias and atlases, which would now have to be rewritten to accommodate not five, but six Great Lakes.

Vermonters grinned from ear to ear; in other states, especially in the beer belt, not so much. Senator Russ Feingold from Wisconsin sidled up to me on the floor on a Tuesday morning. He'd been back home over the weekend and had kindly clipped an editorial cartoon from the *Green Bay Press-Gazette*. It caricatured me standing next to a map of the "sixth Great Lake," and depicted me as "the fourth Stooge." We laughed. "Pat, you're famous in Cheesehead territory," he said.

But still, the midwesterners, even Feingold, were determined to band together and take back what they argued was rightfully theirs, even if they privately conceded they'd have done what I did if they were in my shoes.

Pressure grew to change the language back, but that was not so easy, especially if I objected. I said I'd be happy to change it back so long as we were including the funding for Vermont. In fact, I offered up, with these darned zebra mussels multiplying everywhere, we should boost the overall funding for everyone. What a balm for any wound a little extra money coming home would provide.

The issue was addressed, and the crisis averted; no library would have to throw out its atlases, and no young person from Ohio would gaze upon Lake Erie and feel less special than their parents and grandparents who had come before them.

With a quick motion accepted by the chairman, all was resolved; a Leahy amendment had put Champlain in a hallowed category, and a month later another Leahy amendment took it away, in return for a handsome ransom to help preserve Vermont's favorite lake and protect it against environmental destruction.

"*We have agreed to call Lake Champlain a cousin instead of a little brother to those larger lakes in the Midwest, while accomplishing our goal of improving the ecology of our lake,*" I told the press with a big smile. Bottom line, Vermont got the money.

Somebody asked Tom Brokaw of NBC News if he knew me and how could a senator do anything so silly. Brokaw replied that throughout the fracas, his network had run so many stories about the controversy, each of them showing these stunningly beautiful pictures of Lake Champlain, that I was delivering tens of millions of dollars in free advertising for Vermont. The news anchor approved; "*I suspect the chamber of commerce is ready to erect a statue in Pat's honor,*" he observed wryly.

A couple of months later, I woke up early to catch the sunrise on the lake. Stretching out on the little boat, I dipped a fisherman's hat over my eyes, and, waiting for my cue on the walkie-talkie, I let the fresh air and the gentle waves rock me to sleep. A well-deserved catnap. "*Senator Leahy, we're ready for you,*" said a voice a few feet away, waking me up, interrupting the moment. A video camera on a ramp was moving in closer. I cleared my throat and prepared my line, as the klieg light turned on and the light on the video camera blinked red for "recording."

"*You know, I still think it's a great lake,*" I said direct to camera with a smile. The first ad of the 1998 Leahy reelection campaign was complete, and this time it would be the only one I'd really need, if I needed any at all.

1974, 1980, 1986, and 1992 had been varying degrees of difficulty in my Senate races; the first two, of course, were nail-biters, and the third had been a race against a former governor recruited by the Reagan White House, even if I won comfortably at the end. 1992 had been easier still, even if I had to navigate populist waters against an opponent who was well funded and positioned as an outsider to capture the spirit of the prevailing political winds. But this year, 1998, was shaping up to be something entirely different.

An extremely wealthy man had moved from Massachusetts to Vermont, and by virtue of a second home, a ski chalet, he was able to claim Vermont residency in order to come up and run against me.

I was thinking about all the things I could do to highlight an obvious difference between us, including not being the least bit shy to mention the term "native Vermonter" or mention exactly when the Leahys had come to Vermont in the 1800s. Our roots were deep; his seed had barely been planted. But I did worry that this man from Massachusetts had one advantage: he promised to spend whatever it took to win a Senate seat. I started planning accordingly.

Then a funny thing happened. An hour before the time expired to announce for office and file the necessary petitions to qualify for the ballot, a farmer came into the secretary of state's office with his thousand signatures. He wasn't just any farmer; he was a neighbor of a filmmaker named John O'Brien, who had captured his folksy wisdom in two films already, earning him a cult following of sorts in Vermont. His name was Fred Tuttle.

Fred announced that he would spend only $251, a dollar per town, or, as he pronounced it, *tieon*. Fred's primary opponent, Jack McMullen, was outraged that someone dared to interrupt his carpetbagging foray into Republican politics in Vermont. The first big mistake McMullen made was to challenge Fred's signatures and claim there were eight signatures that were probably incorrect for the towns they were supposed to be from. McMullen filed a complaint to kick Fred off the ballot. He and his lawyers did not realize that if you do make a mistake in your petition, you're allowed fifteen days to correct it. The farmer understood that there were eight signatures gone, so before the time was up, he walked back in with eight hundred more signatures and a phalanx of television cameras covering it.

Fred and Jack faced off in a primary debate. Jack probably knew every single piece of legislation from the last ten years and could robotically answer any policy question, but Fred had a secret weapon: he was actually from Vermont. Fred started questioning Jack by handing him a list of ten towns. He asked Jack to read it aloud. The towns all had idiosyncratic names; we don't say *Calais* we say *Callis* and so on. Jack got eight of the ten wrong, and Fred said, "*Well, you got most of them wrong, and those are really nice towns and are probably hurt by the fact. You should go by and apologize.*"

McMullen was now in a deep hole of his own digging. He agreed to another debate. Fred came prepared again, as only a Vermonter could.

"How many teats are on a Holstein and how many on a Jersey?" It is spelled "teats," but it is pronounced *tits*. I'm sure his opponent probably knew to the decimal point just how much milk was produced in Vermont and so forth, but he had never milked a cow in his life. He stammered, saying there were probably four teats on a Holstein and six on a Jersey, at which point Fred explained that all cows, pronouncing it *caows*, have four teats, "that's all they've ever needed and all God gave them and that's pretty much it." McMullen was vaporized.

Fred was invited to be on *The Tonight Show with Jay Leno*. Leno called me and said that to be fair they should offer me equal time. I said, "*Jay, I don't need to go. This guy is wonderful, he's a very nice man, and just take care of him.*"

Fred called me when he came back from Burbank, California, and he said, "*Pat, by Jeezum, those airplanes are a lot different than the tube planes we flew in WWII. You know, they don't even charge you for a drink on it!*" He flew first class. Then he said, "They picked me up in one of them great big *lemonzenes*! You ever ridden in one of them *lemonzenes*?" I knew he meant "limousine," so I said I had, and Fred said, "By Jeezum, they are just too big!"

Fred had become an overnight sensation. We saw him marching in a parade just before the primary. Jack McMullen was glumly walking down the street with several people all dressed the same, carrying his banner, encountering dead silence from the bystanders. Now in parades in the summer in Vermont, you can have the local undertaker go by and people will applaud, but here there was dead silence for the out-of-towner.

Fred rolled by in an old car with a rumble seat and someone else driving to just enormous applause. He saw us and said, "Pat! Marcelle! Come *heah*!" He grabbed our hands and said, "*Ya know, I ain't gonna do nothin' to hurt ya. I'm gonna vote for ya.*"

I said, "Fred, I really appreciate that, but I think you are going to win the primary."

The press crowded in, and I told them, "I've been to hundreds of parades in Vermont, and back then, everyone received applause. This was the first time there was dead silence. Fred Tuttle is going to win."

Of course he did. The national press was at his house the next day. He came out wearing his baseball cap, which said FRED on it, and they said, "How are you going to run against Senator Leahy?"

He said, "Run against Senator Leahy!? The boy's doing a good job, I'm going to vote for him, Dottie's going to vote for him, thank you very much."

On the *Today* show, they asked Fred, "We know you're going to support Senator Leahy, but what if he has a heart attack?"

Fred replied, "I'd have a heart attack too!"

After that, I would pick Fred up for our debates, which were mainly held in high school auditoriums. The schools were used as voting sites for the election, and we'd announce that any kid who went to vote with their parents could come to class an hour late. Fred told all the students his biggest piece of advice was to stay in school—his regret was that he hadn't. Together, we would present the school with a flag flown over the Capitol.

On election night, Fred called me. He said, "Pat, I had a nightmare!"

I said, "What was your nightmare?"

He said, "I dreamed I won!"

I said, "What were you going to do, Fred?"

He said, "I'd hide in the barn, they weren't never gonna find me!"

I had punched my ticket for another six years in the Senate with 72 percent of the vote, but just as important, I'd earned the vote of my opponent, never my enemy, a quintessential Vermonter and, along with it, a friend for life.

— 38 —

Pinch Me Moments, Still

I'd served through five presidencies. I'd seen political competitors come and go. But in front of me unfolded a scene that underscored how much we all had in common, if we were willing to look for it.

As I stood in the anteroom with my camera, the symmetry on the other end of the lens became clear.

Jimmy Carter defeated Gerald Ford in 1976.

The Reagan-Bush ticket defeated President Carter.

Governor Bill Clinton defeated Bush to become the forty-second president of the United States.

And every one of those campaigns had been hard-fought, the defeats as bitter as any in memory.

And yet here they were—every president I'd served with except for Ronald Reagan, who was in seclusion battling Alzheimer's—united on a trip to Amman, Jordan, for a state funeral, to pay America's respects to King Hussein for decades of partnership.

Every one of these American presidents was now good friends with the others. President Ford was well into his eighties and had trekked all the way from California to Andrews Air Force Base, and then Air Force One flew all night to Jordan. He had hurt his foot and his ankle, and his difficulty maneuvering was clear to anyone watching.

A White House steward sent an advance person off to bring the former president a cane, but Ford was adamant that he did not want to be seen using a cane, even though we were going to have to walk some distance in the march of mourners streaming behind King Hussein's casket.

I suggested gently that, as the senator there, I was supposed to be up near the front. I said, "*Why don't I walk with you? You take my arm. We can be talking during the procession, and if you have any trouble walking, just lean on my arm. We are about the same size, so nobody's going to notice.*"

Ford nodded gratefully and chuckled when I told him Egypt's president, Hosni Mubarak, had complained, "*Are they gonna make us walk all the way to Sharm el-Sheikh?*"

As we marched, President Clinton seemed to take point, looking ahead for photojournalistic snipers on the horizon: "Hey, guys, there are cameras up ahead."

Our heads snapped back to a somber position.

I wanted to snap a photo, which Mubarak noticed, and the gregarious autocrat exclaimed, "*Bill, Gerry! Pat wants to take your picture!*"

The two American presidents turned around, and Mubarak jumped into the shot in an exaggerated pose, wagging his finger at the Americans: "Another thing I want to tell you guys!"

Mubarak was in on the joke: always well versed in the divide between how the United States was perceived on the streets of his country and the easygoing and comfortable relationship he enjoyed with every American president since he had taken power following Anwar Sadat's assassination.

After the sweltering walk, we were back in yet another "hold room," waiting to greet Queen Rania and the heir to the Hashemite Kingdom, Abdullah.

I asked President Ford if I could get him a chair. He said no, he didn't want to be the only one sitting.

"Hell, I'm tired. I would get two chairs. We can sit together."

He grinned. "I know what you're doing—and thank you."

We flew most of the night back to Washington, arriving in the wee hours of the morning as the sun rose above the Capitol.

Ford would head immediately home to California.

"With all due respect, Mr. President, at your age you could have just declined coming and nobody would've felt that was inappropriate."

"Patrick," he replied in his fatherly way, "sometimes you do things just because it's the right thing to do."

— 39 —

The Distraction

"We'll get through all of this—but don't try and justify the unjustifiable."

President Clinton sighed at the other end of the line—not quite a sigh of resignation, not quite a sigh of relief.

But he knew he could trust he was talking to a friend.

Three days before, he had gone on national television and angrily admitted what the news media had already reported: what he had denied for seven months had been true all along—he'd shared an inappropriate sexual relationship with a young White House intern named Monica Lewinsky.

Now he had gone into seclusion for a summer vacation on Martha's Vineyard, and the Secret Service had alerted him to my phone call while he was trying to escape into his own world, taking a solitary walk on the beach along the home he and the First Lady had rented.

"Hold for the president," an aide had announced after the president told the Secret Service that he'd jog up through the dunes to take the call.

The sense of urgency on the other end of the line was confirmation enough of what my former and President Clinton's current chief of staff, John Podesta, had told me earlier in the afternoon: the president felt isolated, tortured by the silence, staring at a phone that wasn't ringing.

I'd volunteered to give him a call.

"Pat—Pat—they've been merciless on me—"

I'd cut off the presidential pity party midstream: I was his friend, and I'd be his friend come hell or high water through the process still to come, but no one had much stomach for the president to seek our sympathy.

Besides—what was the president going to do? Fire me? Twenty-three years in the Senate and two razor-thin election victories had earned me my independence, and I knew the president would appreciate my candor, if not my bluntness.

After all, he knew I was his friend.

We talked for another half hour. Mostly, he talked—and I listened.

He understood that after almost six years of the Gingrich-led GOP trying to manufacture scandals—from investigating the firing of White House Travel Office personnel to the shameful insinuations made about the suicide of the Clinton family friend Vince Foster—at long last the Republicans had found something salacious to sink their teeth into, and they wouldn't give it up without extracting the retribution they'd long sought.

A storm was on its way, and it would consume all of us and test the Senate.

The House under the Republicans wasted little time in passing articles of impeachment against President Clinton. They had run a spectacle of a process, all of it produced for the television cameras and for rabid partisan consumption.

I hoped that the Senate would behave more like the Senate of old and meet its responsibilities to be a deliberative and serious body, actually delivering a process and a trial that people could look back on and declare was fair and worthy of the Senate, whether they agreed with the outcome or not. We weren't the House, and we didn't need to behave like the House.

I spoke with Senator Daschle, our minority leader, about an idea. Why not convene the two caucuses in the Old Senate Chamber, together, and have the Senate organize itself for the impeachment trial without television cameras and the bright lights? Why not do it that way, with everyone together, Republicans and Democrats, instead of having everyone separated by party from the get-go, even if we were likely to end up on opposite sides in the end?

Daschle loved the idea. He gestured over to the majority leader, Senator Trent Lott, to come over and join our huddle. Majority Leader Lott was someone I always felt like I could do business with; he was a partisan and he was a conservative, but he kept his word. Lott had joined the Senate from the House, inheriting John Stennis's seat in a transition that brought the South full circle. For the first time since Reconstruction, Mississippi was represented by two Republican senators. But Lott had instincts that were more senatorial; he thought of himself as a caretaker of the institution. Both leaders liked the idea that the Senate would show that our process would be dignified and thoughtful. But they worried that the White House would object, because the Clinton team was counting on Clinton's public popularity to put pressure on Democratic senators, and House Republicans were counting on the exact same theory. They both worried that camera-happy members of either caucus would quietly stew that they'd been denied their oratorical moment in the sun if the cameras went away. "Why don't you two just go up to the gallery and announce it together so no one has a chance to react?" They did, and the arrangement landed well with the impeachment-wary editorial boards, who worried America's impeachment saga was becoming little more than reality television.

More important, when all one hundred senators went into the Old Senate Chamber, something changed in all of us. It could have been 1975. Senators Kennedy and Hatch presented the history and protocols of trials in the Senate. Others asked questions of the parliamentarian. No one ran out to the cameras afterward. It was a moment for what Stennis might have called " 'Senators' with a capital S."

I was assigned, along with Ohio Republican Mike DeWine, to take some of the depositions of witnesses. My old prosecutorial instincts resurfaced. I was in love with being a lawyer again. It was funny how natural it felt, even though I hadn't been inside a courtroom as a litigator in close to twenty-five years. At the Madison hotel, we deposed Monica Lewinsky. I'd known her only from the news coverage. Coming face-to-face with her, I thought, *My God, this could be anyone's daughter*. The spectacle and humiliation she had been exposed to would have left anyone shaken. I wondered how she would ever put it all behind her.

During the trial, I watched very closely and took hundreds of pages of handwritten notes, even though we had the Congressional Record for the actual wording. Former senator Dale Bumpers from Arkansas led President Clinton's defense and delivered the best speech of the entire process, all from a yellow legal pad on which he'd written a few notes.

And just like that, after a trial that lasted one month and two days, six years of investigation had finally met their logical and foreseeable end. President Clinton was acquitted, as senators always suspected he would be. A few in our caucus suggested a censure motion to follow so there was some kind of formal accountability. But the idea of spending one more minute on this sordid, stupid mess seemed beneath the Senate. History could make its own judgments about how everyone involved would stand up to scrutiny, but I was confident at least that the Senate had done its duty with appropriate decorum.

— 40 —

Havana Dreaming

Perhaps more than anything else, I felt that the gift of another term in the Senate was an opportunity to try to make progress on difficult issues overseas, within the limits of what a senator could do. There were so many frozen conflicts globally that benefited no one, none more so than the relationship between the United States and Cuba. I wondered whether there was any way to perhaps start a dialogue that might set the stage for an administration to explore a new path in our hemisphere. With Marcelle, of course, I headed to Havana during a Senate recess.

"*I'll talk with you instead, Senora Marcelle. You're a nurse and a humanitarian.*"

A visibly perturbed and theatrically practiced Fidel Castro, an arched eyebrow aimed in my direction, turned to address Marcelle, ignoring the pointed question I'd asked about his restrictive policies on what President Kennedy had once called an "imprisoned island."

Castro's aides and apparatchiks were slightly ashen. I guess I'd committed the apparently unexpected offense of interrupting Castro with an impertinent question, just about ten minutes into what I expected would have been one of his famously long monologues, speeches that had by then become inseparable from the image of an outsized historical figure who to this day holds the record for the second-longest speech in the history of the United Nations: a whopping four hours and twenty-nine minutes in 1960. Even Strom Thurmond had to tip his cap to Castro's unparalleled capacity for filibuster. My eye had been on the clock: the Cubans had invited Marcelle and me and our traveling companions—Senator Jack Reed of Rhode Island, my foreign policy advisor Tim Rieser, and my chief of staff, Luke Albee—to join Castro at the Palacio de la Revolución for a ten o'clock dinner after a long day, with the proviso that El Comandante had booked a subsequent midnight dinner following ours. Time was short, and my interruption had been strategic: the passage of time hadn't made Castro any more succinct, and I wanted to break through the barriers and actually dare to have a candid, constructive conversation. We hadn't negotiated for months with bureaucrats in Washington and Havana to travel to Cuba only to be subjected to an in-person lecture the likes of which I could've just as easily read printed on the pages of *Granma*.

Castro was soon right back to talking with me. He actually seemed to enjoy someone challenging the implicit rules of his idiosyncratic and equally autocratic brand of hospitality: *no one* interrupted Castro. We talked about agriculture in Vermont, especially dairy, and products that our farmers hoped could someday be available for export to the island if the long-standing embargo ever ended.

But most of our conversation focused on the strained history between our two countries, something I'd lived through vicariously as a young man.

As a nineteen-year-old college student at St. Michael's, I followed the news reports of the 1959 Cuban Revolution and the overthrow of America's corrupt and feckless ally Fulgencio Batista. I remember the grainy televised black-and-white images of the triumphant fatigues-clad Castro brothers and Che Guevara; with some initial romanticism, stories of their guerrilla revolution launched from high atop the Sierra Maestra mountains had quickly reached our tiny college campus nestled under Vermont's Green Mountains along the shores of Lake Champlain. But it wasn't long before I was horrified by the news bulletins coming out of Old Havana: thousands of families fleeing Cuba for the shores of Florida, their property seized; entire industries nationalized; and Castro-organized kangaroo courts and firing squads executing hundreds of veterans of the Batista regime with the chilling order "*To the wall!*"

I was in law school at Georgetown two years later as the nation's capital was paralyzed by the Cuban Missile Crisis. Marcelle and I were living happily as young newlyweds in a one-bedroom Glover Park apartment, close to the veterans' hospital where she was a nurse, when our tranquil life was interrupted by warning sirens piercing the silence. It felt as if Washington was in the crosshairs. Instructions in class taught us to look for the nearest bomb shelters. My wise professors suppressed their reasoning and common sense, dutifully doing as instructed and reminding us that if we heard the air-raid siren go off, we were to immediately duck under our desks—as if a Formica desktop would provide any defense against a Soviet missile launched from Cuba. My parents mailed us $100 to stock up on canned goods in the event of panicked shortages. Thirteen days later, it was over: diplomacy prevailed, Nikita Khrushchev removed the Soviet missiles from Cuba, and life went back to normal. The only evidence that we'd come to the brink of nuclear annihilation littered the shag carpeting of our apartment: Marcelle and I hosted a party late into the night for my classmates celebrating the end of the crisis. Our record player came in handy: we all danced to Little Eva's "The Loco-Motion," "Sherry" by the Four Seasons, and, after everyone left, one last, long slow dance for Marcelle and me to Andy Williams's "Moon River." By the time the night ended, it looked as if doomsday really had arrived after all. We woke early that October morning to clean the apartment and hide the evidence of the night before—broken beer bottles and crunched cans of Heurich's Old Georgetown ale—in case Marcelle's parents arrived at our doorstep for a visit to check in on the young couple.

Decades had passed since Castro's revolution, Che Guevara was long dead and dismembered, and eight presidents had come and gone promising to end the Castro regime but failing to make the words "Cuba libre" stand for anything more than a mix of lime juice, rum, and Coca-Cola. All these years later, Castro was still there, reveling in his resistance to outside American pressure.

I wondered whether we could ever break the impasse that kept our two countries from talking to each other, and kept our two peoples from really even knowing each other, with the possible exception of a Cuban who had won the hearts of all New Englanders: Luis Tiant, El Tiante, who, alongside a kid catcher from Bellows Falls, Vermont, named Carlton Fisk, had brought the Red Sox to game seven of the 1975 World Series.

Baseball, of course, was one of the ties between our two countries that did seem to bridge the 228 miles between Miami and Havana, and baseball was part of what had brought us to Havana that sweltering day in the first place. The Baltimore Orioles and the Cuban national baseball team were playing a historic exhibition series, first in Havana and then in Baltimore a little more than a month later. Castro himself was enjoying center stage playing host to the Americans. I'd watched the game from the stands and paid attention as Castro strolled onto the field to a huge roar of applause and adulation from the Cubans, shaking hands with each member of the American team and then each member of the Cuban team, again to great applause and shouts of "Fidel, Fidel!" Still in the iconic fatigues for which he had become famous, older and his scruffy beard grayer than when I'd first read about him, Castro still filled out his uniform and stood ramrod straight at attention, as both the American and Cuban national anthems were played. I wondered then whether this was the only time any of these Cubans had ever heard a live rendition of our national anthem, and thought again just how anachronistic it was that we could compete on the same baseball diamond but our leaders spoke never a word to each other.

This dinner was my chance to probe whether there was any chance to change any of that, to find any common ground. I can't say that there were any breakthroughs, but I did break the ice of formality. I asked Jack Reed, a West Point graduate who stood five feet seven inches on a good day, to tell Castro exactly who we were and how important I was. Jack smiled and indulged a long-running joke that embodied our *Mutt and Jeff* vaudeville routine when we traveled together. In fluent Spanish, he told Castro, "*The big guy feels he is the important one, so be nice to him, but I'm the go-to guy, and if you need something, see me.*"

Castro's eyes widened. "*Senator Leahy, do you know what he said about you?*"

I replied, "*Oh yeah, I've gotten used to it, this has been a running joke with us.*"

The conversation grew warmer after that, and Castro signed baseballs commemorating the occasion for all of us.

For dessert, and with characteristic humility and understatement, Castro announced he had arranged to serve us the best ice cream in the world. Cuban ice cream—Coppelia—is all it's billed as being. I said, "*I have to disagree, because I come from Vermont, where we have Ben and Jerry's. I'd be happy to send you some.*"

Castro responded dismissively: "*I don't care.*"

A few moments later, he was back on the subject of national pride and added, "*Chairman Leahy, even you have to admit we have the best cigars in the world.*"

I replied, "*Yes, and I've had some.*"

"*But not in the United States! It's illegal under your unlawful blockade!*"

"*I have.*"

He said, "*How do you explain that?*"

I replied, "*I told people that I was burning Castro's crops, that Communist!*"

Castro let out a full belly laugh. His staff, which had at first appeared shocked, now felt permission to laugh as well. "*So, you're the terrorist we've been looking for,*" Castro said with a chuckle.

I thought maybe Jack Reed now had some competition when it came to an Abbott and Costello, Statler and Waldorf one-liner routine. Fidel Castro was butting into our act.

On the way out, as if to take her into his confidence about a top secret matter of national security, Castro took Marcelle by the arm and said, "*If your husband sends the ice cream, be sure to pack it in dry ice.*"

The next morning, Luke Albee and I went for a walk in Old Havana along the Malecón, along with our translator. Stashed in my camera bag were a few brand-new, clean white baseballs, knowing the odds were high that we would happen upon kids out in the streets playing pickup games of baseball.

In Cuba, the kids played with pure love of the game, energy, and improvised, handmade bats and balls; yesterday's broom handle could be today's homemade Louisville Slugger, and a misshapen mix of rubber bands, yarn, and borrowed stuffing could be miraculously smooshed and sewn to be reborn as an adequate baseball.

Luke and I spotted two teenagers playing, using the wall of an old building as a backstop, one whirling a great mix of fastballs, sliders, and a biting curveball, the other in the batter's box, fighting off each pitch to keep his turn at bat alive. I said to the translator, "*If the pitcher strikes him out, I'll give the pitcher this baseball. But if he gets a solid hit, then he gets the ball.*"

The batter launched a sharp line drive off his bat and far into the park that faced the Atlantic Ocean. I threw him the brand-new baseball. His face lit up. It might as well have been a game-winning, bases-clearing home run that he'd just hit. The pitcher, though disappointed, congratulated his friend on his reward. I reached into my camera bag, and I said, "*Oh, I just found another ball!*" and tossed that to him. I couldn't remember the last time I had seen such big smiles. How ironic it was that I had to journey to Communist Cuba to discover such pure joy for America's national pastime.

As we boarded our US government plane to head home, we were treated to the almost comical spectacle of state control: a reminder from a Cuban government minder that whatever we did, no matter what, we absolutely must not take any photos while inside Cuban airspace. As the plane began its slow climb, naturally, the very first thing I did was train my lens on the countryside below—and clicked away, snapping photos of the beautifully developed area the Soviets had established for themselves back in the day, marked by what looked like a former country club replete with putting green and areas to sunbathe. So much for the simple life of the proletariat. Abandoned radar dishes had fallen over, like old Soviet tumbleweeds, on the deserted installation. Maybe it had been an officers' club before the Berlin Wall fell, a plum assignment for an up-and-coming KGB officer in the shadows of the Hotel Nacional and the old casinos, where the likes of American Mafia chieftains had once enjoyed their own personal paradise in cahoots with Batista. Like the Mafia bosses of the fifties, the Soviets assigned there must've hoped like hell the good old days wouldn't end and that the Cold War would continue in perpetuity so they could stay. Havana's a lot nicer than Siberia.

As the sun set and the cabin lights dimmed, I wondered whether I'd built a foundation for a fresh start in Cuba or whether Washington and Havana were hopelessly frozen in perpetual animosity. For all of Castro's bombast, and for all the asinine consequences of our frozen Cuban policy at home, I hoped that the smiles on the faces of those kids playing baseball gave us something in which to invest our hopes.

A few weeks after my return to the United States, I was back in Baltimore for the completion of the exhibition series between the Orioles and the Cuban national team. After a long and bureaucratic go-round with my exasperated but supportive friend, Secretary of State Madeleine Albright, we had found some diplomatic loophole around the embargo that allowed me to send Fidel Castro a sample of each flavor of Vermont's sugary, addictive bounty, Ben & Jerry's. After the game, as the logistics teams for the Cuban side were packing up and preparing to head back to the airport, Luke Albee and I brought them three heavy coolers (packed with dry ice at the urging of Cuba's biggest ice-cream connoisseur) that we knew could survive the flight without the ice cream melting. We explained the situation to one of the Cuban diplomats on hand, and then we watched with big smiles as he explained to the aircrew, in rapid-fire Spanish, that this was no ordinary *helado*, this was a gift from the US Senate intended for El Comandante himself. To emphasize that point, the diplomat pantomimed tugging on a beard. The men scurried around, treating the coolers like the boxes of treasure they were; I imagine no one wanted to risk being *that guy* bringing Castro a melted mess of Chunky Monkey. Fortunately for them, they must've done a good job preserving our well-packaged delicacies. A month later, I received a homemade carved wooden box filled with every kind of rum made in Cuba, with a hand-scribbled note from Castro saying, "*The product of your state was good, now try a product of mine.*" We were no longer debating who had the better ice cream, but I wondered whether this was the start or the end of our communication, and whether we were getting anywhere.

— 41 —

Elián

My back channel with Fidel Castro turned out to be much more valuable sooner than I'd ever bargained.

In November, fishermen just three miles off the coast of Florida discovered a dehydrated and delirious five-year-old boy clinging to an inner tube. His mother had been among fourteen refugees killed in a storm trying to escape Castro's Cuba. The Coast Guard assured the fishermen that they'd take him to Florida for medical treatment, rather than return him to Cuba under our anachronistic "wet foot/dry foot" policy that incentivized Cubans to risk life and limb trying, usually in vain, to cross the Atlantic, knowing that if only they could put one foot on dry land, they'd win refugee status. The boy gained a cult following in Little Havana after a judge initially granted custodial status to a great-uncle he'd never met who was living in the area. The *Miami Herald* ran sensational stories suggesting the boy had been saved by a pod of dolphins, which had protected him against sharks and spirited him to safety.

His name was Elián González.

There was only one problem with this seemingly only-in-America refugee story that was tugging at Florida's heartstrings: the boy had a father back in Cuba who loved and missed him deeply, and whom Elián loved desperately. Fidel Castro delivered a clear and uncompromising ultimatum that enraged Miami and unsettled politics in the United States:

he demanded that our attorney general return Elián to his father within seventy-two hours.

A custody battle in America's courts was about to become a front-page international crisis smack dab in the middle of a presidential election year in America in which Florida's twenty-five electoral votes might make the difference.

The custody fight quickly wound its way through our court system, with judge upon judge siding with Elián's father, who had come to the United States to fight for his son. My friend Greg Craig, a brilliant lawyer, a former Ted Kennedy staffer, and a Vermonter turned Washingtonian, signed on to represent the father in court, as the distant relatives with whom Elián was living refused to reunite the boy with his father. For me, it was a matter of the rule of law. I'd been an officer of the court. I was the ranking Democrat on the Judiciary Committee. The law had to mean something. Court orders had to mean something. Greg Craig called Elián's Miami relatives to try to reason with them, to find out if perhaps there was some compromise they'd entertain that, for the good of the boy, would allow Elián, who had already lost his mother, to be reunited with his dad but have some ongoing relationship with his extended family in Florida. Greg wanted Elián's father, Juan Miguel, to hear his son's voice. I couldn't imagine the heartache I would feel if I'd been separated from any of our children. As soon as they heard that the boy's father was on the line, they hung up.

There would be no Solomonic solution.

I believed the only right outcome was for the boy to go home with his father to Cuba. But I also knew that the Clinton administration would be in a world of hurt, our political system would be thrown into disarray, and only Miami's hardliners would benefit if Castro greeted a returning Elián and his father with parades and pomp and circumstance—another victory for the revolutionaries over the vanquished Yankees. I got word to Fidel Castro that I was willing to advocate to my president that the boy should go home with his father, but there would be no raucous celebrations in Cuba if President Clinton sided with us in this dispute.

The response came back swiftly to me: "Understood."

Castro let me know that the father would get a better job and a better apartment, but that would be it. There would be no splashy propaganda campaign.

President Clinton knew what the right thing to do would be in this case, even as he coveted Florida's electoral votes for his chosen successor in November. The Republican candidate for president, Governor George W. Bush, was quick to take the position that González should be given citizenship and remain with his relatives here at home. The Democratic candidate, and my former Senate colleague from Tennessee, Vice President Al Gore, his eyes on Florida, broke with the position of his own administration and sided with Bush.

Attorney General Janet Reno faced a decision that was as unenviable as it was uncomfortable: whether to intervene and send law enforcement to forcibly reunite Elián with his father.

In the early-morning hours on the Saturday of Easter weekend, after days of negotiations had made no progress, she sent officers in riot gear to the great-uncle's apartment in Little Havana. I felt badly for the attorney general. The Clinton administration had been attacked for losing federal agents at Ruby Ridge and hurt later by accusations of an overreach and overreaction at the extremist Branch Davidian compound in Waco, where dozens, including children, died when the cultists set fire to their own compound rather than surrender.

There was no "winning" in this Elián González crisis for the Clinton administration.

If it chose to send officers in undermanned and poorly armed and they'd been wounded, or if the situation had spiraled out of control, the administration would have paid a price no responsible administration could bear.

But the cost it chose to bear instead was politically painful: a photograph really is worth a thousand words.

The photos, taken by Elián's Miami relatives, ran immediately on CNN and in the tabloids, and provided a deceptive snapshot. I knew too well that photography is all about perspective. Who stands behind the lens? What do they want you to see?

The family, which had refused every opportunity to allow a five-year-old boy to see the father he loved, wanted America to see that young boy cowering before federal agents with semiautomatic rifles. They wanted America to see a steel ram used to break down their door.

They didn't want America to know that those officers had pleaded for minutes with the family to open the door and come outside to arrange an orderly custody transfer. They didn't want America to know that the little boy was terrified of the noise and the shouting and the crying, much of it in a language that wasn't his own and in a situation he couldn't understand.

They certainly didn't want America to know that the five-year-old boy had climbed into the officer's arms afterward and left without a tear, heading to a private flight to be reunited with his father at Andrews Air Force Base.

But America deserved to see the truth, objectively.

Greg Craig suggested that I join him and the boy's father at Andrews to meet Elián's flight from Miami. He knew I'd been with them in this journey, despite the political risk. He also knew that I'd bring my camera. But something gave me pause. I didn't like the way the family in Florida had taken advantage of the difficult separation in Miami to make a political statement, turning photography into propaganda for one side. I thought that since our argument all along had been about the rule of law and about a father's love for his son, this chapter of the story shouldn't end on a political note. I arranged for the Pulitzer Prize–winning photojournalist David Burnett of *Time* magazine to be there as a neutral observer when Elián saw his father for the first time. Whatever happened, good or bad, happy or sad, it would be recorded for history to judge, the camera in the hands of someone who let the photos do the talking, not the politicians.

On Easter morning, I was getting ready to debate Senator Orrin Hatch—my Republican counterpart on the Judiciary Committee—on *Meet the Press* over the González issue, when a fax came across my desk. It was from David Burnett: a copy of his photograph of Elián reunited with his papa at Andrews Air Force Base.

Elián wasn't scared. Elián wasn't crying. There were no guns, no body armor, no battering ram. Just a little boy beaming, reaching his hands up to put a snowflake, playfully, on his father's face. I folded it and put it in my suit jacket pocket as a reminder of what this fight had been about all along.

An hour later, I was in Tim Russert's studio being attacked for not protecting the family values of America by ripping a boy from the bosom of his family to send him back to Cuba and into the arms of a murderous Communist. Orrin Hatch served with me in the Senate, but he could be a sanctimonious pain in the neck when he's deep into Republican talking points, wailing away via satellite from Salt Lake City.

I listened to Orrin's screed with an eye on the studio clock. I felt a little like a point guard watching the shot clock, as I knew that when he was finished, there was time for Tim to throw it back to me for one last comment. I whispered to the producer nearby that I had something the camera should zoom in to see.

As Tim Russert turned to me, I held up that photograph that had been taken just hours before. The camera zoomed in. I said, "*Orrin Hatch and I are both people of faith, and this Easter morning we feel that deeply. I believe in family values. What could be more of a family value than a son who had seen his mother die, had a father who loved him, and was now being reunited with his father?*"

"*We'll have to leave it there. Senator Hatch, Senator Leahy—to be continued,*" said the inimitable Tim Russert. "*And remember, if it's Sunday, it's* Meet the Press."

The camera lights went off and the studio went dark. Everything gets quiet after the hustle and bustle of a live show. Tim loosened his tie and smiled. From one Jesuit-educated kid to another, he winked and said, "*Patrick Leahy—you must've been one hell of a tiger in the courtroom.*" We laughed.

It felt good to know we'd helped the country see the truth even when it wasn't easy. *Especially* when it wasn't easy. And Fidel Castro kept his word. There was no parade for Elián along the embarcadero in Old Havana.

The next months were marked by a presidential campaign that seemed destined to go down to the wire. Vice President Al Gore and Governor

George W. Bush were opposites in every way, with the exception of the fact that they both came from seasoned political royal lineages. Bush was outgoing and glib, the rebellious son in a family that counted a president and senator in the past two generations and two governors in the current one. Gore was stiff and serious, the dutiful son of a senator who always wanted to be right on the issues and wanted to avoid the kind of political defeat that had ended his father's career in the Senate. The country was deadlocked in many ways. People liked Clinton's economy; they didn't like the seeming nonstop drama of his presidency. It was strange in a way; Gore and Bush were both running to be the "un-Clinton," even as they both tried to emulate, unevenly, the things Clinton had done that had resonated with the country in the first place. The race was fifty-fifty headed into October. I didn't agree with Al Gore's position on the Elián González case, but the politics of his decision were likely vindicated: Florida was the decisive beachhead in the 2000 election.

Marcelle and I were miserable watching election night turn into election week—and the next two weeks afterward, as a furious Florida recount wound its way through the courts. I walked across the street from the Russell Building to sit in the audience at the Supreme Court, as lawyers for Bush and Gore argued their case. I was heartbroken as the court issued a decision that it obviously had so little confidence in that Chief Justice Rehnquist noted it was to apply to this one situation only, rather than becoming precedent.

Al Gore had won the popular vote. The case was strong that if all the votes in Florida were counted, odds were that he'd carried the Electoral College as well. But instead, the court's pronouncement ended it all. Gore gave a graceful concession speech. He believed in the sanctity of our peaceful transfer of power. George W. Bush was going to become the forty-third president of the United States.

Part III

Conferring with President Obama and Vice President Biden in the Oval Office.

— 42 —

The Fraying

If President Bush knew deep inside that he was a president who had been effectively selected by the Supreme Court, if he was uncomfortable with the scenes out of Florida, he never let on. His father had a gift for humility; W, on the other hand, had the gift of self-assuredness, even swagger. He set out to make good on a big political agenda. Like Reagan before him, Bush found it was easy to get Congress to cut taxes. But he soon ran into a surprising roadblock in a Senate split 50–50.

Jim Jeffords had replaced Senator Stafford in 1989 after a long run as attorney general and our lone congressman. Jim was a pretty traditional Northeast Republican. His passion was education—and he salivated at the way the fates seemed to be lining up in 2001: he was chairman of the Education Committee, with a president of his party who had promised to fully fund education for the disabled.

What Jim didn't anticipate was how much the White House saw their political fates differently; their goal was to pass the largest tax break possible and kick the can down the road about funding education for the disabled. Jeffords worked to pass President Bush's signature education initiative, No Child Left Behind, only for Bush to leave the money behind. Jim felt terribly burned.

The Democratic whip, Senator Harry Reid of Nevada, had worked well with Jeffords and started to believe that Jeffords was unhappy enough in his caucus that he might actually switch parties. Harry got Leader Daschle's permission to negotiate with Jeffords, offering him seniority on committees and anything else if he would switch. The quiet discussions went on for months.

I was stunned just how much the George W. Bush White House misunderstood the Senate, an unforced error for the son of a former vice president who had mastered that part of the job.

The National Teacher of the Year in 2001 happened to be from Vermont. When she was honored at the White House, Jeffords didn't make the guest list. It was a slap in the face to an Education Committee chairman from Vermont.

The White House claimed afterward that it didn't have enough room because it would have had to invite the whole delegation from Vermont. Our whole delegation was three members. Years before, when the teacher of the year was from California, thirty or forty members of the California congressional delegation were invited. Jeffords was headed closer to leaving the party he'd reveled in for decades.

But it was a painful decision-making process for Jim. I sat down next to him in the back of the Old Senate Chamber. I shared with him that I wasn't going to press him either way, and that I hoped he knew that whatever decision he made, we'd always work together for Vermont.

Days later, Jim Jeffords announced he was done with the Republican Party and would caucus with the Democrats. President Bush's first year was suddenly in tatters.

I stopped by to see Bob Stafford at home where he'd retired, in Rutland, Vermont. He was Mr. Republican in the state, still. Stafford told me George H. W. Bush called him about Jeffords, a conversation that had begun not as "Mr. President and Senator Stafford," but as "George and Bob."

Bush asked, "Are you close to Senator Jeffords?"

Stafford said, "I am, George."

Bush asked, "Bob, is it true that he's rumored to switch parties?"

Bob said, "Yes, George, he came in to see me a couple days ago about it."

Bush asked what he told him. Stafford didn't hesitate. "I told him I think he'd be much happier as a Democrat than he is in the Republican Party."

There was a long pause. "Oh, I see. Well, thank you, Senator."

"You're welcome, Mr. President."

— 43 —

Attacked at Home

"*Senator, you may want to pay attention to this.*"

We were just about to make the turn onto the Fourteenth Street bridge, and the traffic had been my biggest worry that morning. But it was 8:50, and we were making good time as we headed toward the Capitol. I was on my way to speak to the Judicial Conference at the Supreme Court, a command performance for the chairman of the Senate Judiciary Committee, and I didn't want to be late.

I'd been thumbing through my notes, only half listening to the radio, but the note of anxiety in the voice of the young man from my office who was driving immediately focused me on the words coming out of the car's speakers: an airplane had flown into the World Trade Center.

I immediately called a friend in New York City, who told me it was a clear, gorgeous day in New York, just as it was in Washington. It wasn't pilot error caused by poor visibility. I said, "*Then you either have a suicide bomber or a terrorist act*," something I had worried about for years.

A couple of minutes after 9:00 a.m., I was inside the Supreme Court when we heard the news: a second plane had now struck the south tower of the World Trade Center. Judges were leaving the room, placing calls on their cell phones. Everyone knew someone in New York. I told Chief Justice Rehnquist that it must be terrorism.

We heard a muffled *boom* in the distance. Rumors flew of a car bomb detonated at the State Department. An ashen-faced aide rushed in and handed Chief Justice Rehnquist a note: a bomb had gone off at the Pentagon. "*We should let everyone go,*" said the chief justice.

I rushed across Constitution Avenue, where the streets were starting to fill with pedestrians. Staff was streaming steadily out of the Dirksen Building, headed for the surrounding neighborhoods and for the commuter trains at Union Station.

A Capitol Police officer recognized me and stopped me before I made it to the marble steps of the Russell Building: "*Senator, they're evacuating the Capitol; you can't go back.*"

I told him I had a rule about being the last one out; there was staff in the office who might not leave, and I would go in and make sure all of them were out before I left myself. He relented.

Staffers were coming down the staircases with shocked looks on their faces. Some were angry. There was something deeply enraging about being forced out of the people's house by thugs who had turned airplanes full of innocent people into weapons. It was so brazen. How could the United States of America, in the heart of our financial center, be so helpless?

As I walked into the office, Luke Albee rushed up to me with an update: a plane had hit the Pentagon. My God. The boom I'd heard wasn't a bomb, but a human projectile turned on our military establishment itself.

I walked through the office and told everybody to leave, get out, forget your computers and everything else, just go. I headed for my press secretary David Carle's house, about five or six blocks away, alongside my chief of staff, J. P. Dowd; my scheduler, Kevin McDonald; and Luke Albee.

Near the Library of Congress, I came face-to-face with Congressman John Lewis, almost a secular saint, the man who had faced down Bull Connor's police dogs in Birmingham and had his skull cracked open on Bloody Sunday leading peaceful protesters across the Edmund Pettus Bridge. We embraced. "*It's madness, Patrick,*" he said, his deep voice steady. John Lewis was unflappable. We clasped hands—the Baptist and the Catholic together—shared a quick prayer for all those in danger, and went on our way.

As I walked, I kept hitting "Send" on my flip phone—only to hear silence and then the grating recording: "All systems are busy. Please try your call later." I was desperately trying to reach Marcelle at the house in McLean. I'd never felt a greater distance from her so close to home.

It was almost impossible to get cell phone calls in and out. My children were trying to get calls through to me and Marcelle, and finally, I succeeded in getting a call through to her with an urgent plea: "Stay home, and no matter what, please don't go anywhere near our 'friends' nearby." She knew I meant the CIA.

At David Carle's house, CNN showed the evacuations in Washington before the news cut back to New York: the towers were swaying. Thousands were still inside. And then, just like that, in one horrific spasm as steel turned to jelly, they were all gone.

I was sick to my stomach. I sat on the couch with my head bowed.

"*Senator, they think the fourth plane was headed to hit the Capitol.*"

All the thoughts and emotions of the surreal morning flooded together as I closed my eyes: the terrified passengers, the crew dead in four airplanes, two into the World Trade Center towers, one into the Pentagon, and the fourth downed by heroic passengers in Shanksville, Pennsylvania, a plane targeting the US Capitol.

I walked back to the Capitol just in time to see F-16s, loaded with missiles, fly over low, and I went to the office, retrieved some things, and came back out.

The sense of déjà vu was overpowering: thirty-eight years before as a law student at Georgetown, I'd heard the news that President Kennedy had been assassinated and witnessed the pandemonium and then the stunned silence in these same city blocks, as everyone rushed home to mourn and to share in their collective shock.

And here we were now. The look on the faces of so many young staffers mirrored what Marcelle and I felt then and again now: anger, grief, shock, tears—everybody wondering how this could have happened.

In the coming days, it unfolded more, and a paralysis settled over the city.

Marcelle had headed to the Arlington hospital to see if she could volunteer as a nurse, assuming that many of the Pentagon victims were sent there. It didn't have a single patient: everyone from the Pentagon was either dead or ambulatory, nothing in between. She volunteered with the blood banks for the Red Cross. We all shared this desire to do something, anything, to avoid the helplessness of watching a country under siege.

Within a day, Attorney General John Ashcroft's Justice Department was proposing an immediate package of legislation—anti-terrorist legislation. The bandwagon effect was stronger than anything I'd seen before, so many screaming, "*Let's pass it, let's pass it.*"

I understood all too well the feeling of so many members of Congress: we'd all been helpless on 9/11. We were used to solving problems, and we'd been turned into spectators.

But there were many parts of what the Bush Justice Department was rushing to pass that would bend, if not break, the Constitution.

I wanted to believe them—but I wanted to make sure that we weren't merely depending on their good-faith assurances. Norms are imperfectly unreliable; they're why we insist on laws. Enormous new powers of wiretapping, surveillance, and detention went far beyond anything anyone could have imagined a few weeks before.

I thought of the panic that led to Japanese Americans being locked up on the West Coast during World War II and how a politically inclined Supreme Court upheld the detention. Even Earl Warren, then the liberal governor of California, had supported it. It did nothing to help the war effort, but instead terribly hurt the lives of loyal Americans. I simply wasn't willing to go back to the excesses of that era without a debate.

But it wasn't comfortable. On my own committee, many were pressing me to move forward, including Democrats like Chuck Schumer and Dianne Feinstein, and, of course, my Republican counterpart Orrin Hatch, who said there was nothing that created a problem for him in the legislation.

"*Orrin, have you read it?*"

He had not.

In bipartisan fashion, the House took up its version of the administration's legislation and announced that it would pass it the next day. It was a race for unity and comity, but it seemed also to be a race to the lowest common denominator: an emotional appeal ignoring the fact that we'd all live with the consequences for a long, long time after the legislation became law.

There was enormous pressure for me to move forward, and, to their credit, the members of my staff agreed with me in holding it up. A petition was signed by some of the most ultraconservative organizations in the country, along with some of the most ultraliberal, all opposed to it, and the slowdown suddenly worked.

It bought me time to meet repeatedly with the attorney general and others, where I reiterated that we would pass legislation, but not until we had something that would really help law enforcement instead of hollow constitutional hindrance conceived to make us feel good. Doing something wasn't the same as doing the right thing. Being scared and wanting revenge were thoroughly human emotions, but they weren't supposed to drive the Senate in moments of crisis.

I suggested we ought to find out why we had invested billions of dollars extra in recent years at the FBI, and yet it did not have up-to-date computers, did not have Arabic-speaking translators, was unable to find even some of its own files, and did not even know when law enforcement elsewhere was tracking a suspect already on a federal watch list. I wrote a series of reforms—sunsetting emergency powers so they didn't live in perpetuity, judicial review, tools for law enforcement—in a package called the "USA Act" to fix the administration's bill.

The words "PATRIOT ACT" couldn't erase history or the human failings behind it. But certainly, in my darker moments, I wondered: If there had been more attention to terrorism and less attention to political investigations in the years before the 9/11 attacks, would some lives have been saved?

But here we were. The stock market collapsed. Overnight, Congress injected a quick cash infusion to save the airlines. I refused to pass the

Judiciary Committee's component of the stopgap package of emergency spending until it included some compensation for victims. Children had gone to school in the morning with one or both parents and came home as orphans. One of Alicia's friends outside New York was on the phone in tears, sharing with her how the train station where she normally parks her car and takes the commuter train into the city, now, ever since 9/11, she sees cars in the lot each morning that were just getting dustier and dustier. Somebody drove to work that day and never came home—not just one person, but a dozen. Were there even family members left to pick the cars up? They called it the "ghost parking lot." I was immediately haunted by an image I would never erase.

After weeks of legislating, the Senate recessed for Columbus Day weekend. Finally, we could get home to Vermont, away from the smell of the smoldering ruins of an entire wing of the Pentagon, which we drove by each night on the way home.

We brought our grandson Roan home to Vermont with us. On Thursday, Marcelle and I walked through Dulles International Airport, which was nearly empty. National Airport remained shut down. Washington itself felt postapocalyptic.

As we made our way to the gate, we heard a familiar but subdued voice. Bill and Hillary Clinton were flying commercially to be home in New York. We sat together in the lounge near the nearly abandoned gates. President Clinton told me about a friend of his from Arkansas who runs a large mail-order business and who told Clinton that when he first heard that the FBI had been unable to find certain people of interest, he asked his systems manager if they had their names and addresses in their company's computer bank. Sure enough, their names were there, their addresses were there, something that he would have turned over to the FBI had it ever asked him.

"*Just what are they doing with those billions of dollars we gave them?*"

I could only imagine the former president was thinking about the US attorney for the Southern District of New York, who had spent the past year investigating the ex-president. How much time, comparatively, was being spent by the same US attorney and the same New York FBI office to investigate the threat of another terrorist attack?

At home in Middlesex, the frantic pace and pressures of the last weeks all fell into perspective.

Cable television was turned off. I heard the sounds of my grandson Roan out on the dirt road here on the farm, making echo noises as he walked with his grandmother. He and I had been down walking in the fields for about an hour, telling fairy tales on as beautiful of a fall day as I could remember in thirty years. The temperature was about seventy degrees; there was a light breeze and not a cloud in the sky. The flag was almost undulating in the breeze. There were no bugs, and the view was unsurpassed, a crystal-clear view of the mountains, a perfect sky.

I had stopped and closed my eyes, thinking about that sky—how hauntingly deceptive a sky just like this one was that awful morning when so many people boarded planes and walked into office suites for the very last time.

How the hell did we get here? And how do we get back to a time in America when beautiful mornings in Vermont can be taken for granted once again?

I felt a worry deep in my gut. I couldn't shake the feeling that we were headed somewhere dangerous as a country, even more dangerous than what we'd all just collectively endured.

We don't do complexity so well. Especially not in these moments. Of course, we'd have to fight terrorism, but what about the causes of terrorism, the breeding grounds for extremism in places where poverty is a generation upon generation matter, where dictators live in unbelievable luxury while their people live in squalor, and the disenchanted rise up against the symbol of affluence of the United States? And what were we really willing to confront about the contradictions of an Osama bin Laden coming from a wealthy Saudi family, or an Afghanistan that we'd provided with more food aid than any other country in the world and fought a covert war in, arming some of the people who now harbored the world's most wanted men?

I worried that we just didn't have the stomach to wrestle with any of these deepest, most painful contradictions.

I worried about stumbling toward something as debilitating as what we had just suffered.

I'd thought about our First Amendment more in the last four weeks than I had in fourteen years, about the remarkable language enshrined in our Constitution that allows diversity of speech without trying to crush it and allows us to practice any religion we want, or none if we want. What a balance we had struck that separated us from countries that inexorably slid toward theocracy, places where speech must follow just one pattern and where religious dictates promote intolerance of anyone who doesn't follow those same dictates.

Gazing at those pristine Green Mountains, I thought about the road traveled over the centuries after glaciers deposited these rock formations here, before there even was a Vermont or a Leahy family to live in it. Heretics had once been burned at the stake in the name of Christianity, and just years before I was born, the NO IRISH NEED APPLY signs in storefront windows in Montpelier made clear that not all had been forgotten. Here we were in 2001, with the Taliban insisting that non-Muslims must wear identifying insignia, similar to what the Nazis did to the Jews. Catholics killed Protestants and Protestants killed Catholics in the name of peace and democracy in Northern Ireland. Israelis killed Palestinians and Palestinians killed Israelis in a constant tit-for-tat, with terrorism and revenge and assassinations upping the unending ante.

Throughout it all, innocent people die.

I sat on the front porch and read the newspaper. The story of a young man leaving a message at the World Trade Center site left a lump in my throat: "*Dad, I came looking for you.*"

He would never find his father.

I thought about the legislative process I'd return to on Tuesday afternoon. I was the one person holding off the rush to jam through the Bush administration's new laws, even as I was certain there were extremists determined to hit us again. But I just didn't believe we could afford to lose who we were in a headlong and almost futile rush to confront something that'd been with us in all of recorded history.

The thought struck me: *Suppose I'm wrong.*

I heard Roan's laughter as he raced through the fields and as the sun started to go down.

A month from now, the mountains would be on fire with orange and red foliage, and the days would be shorter. Night would come early.

But nightfall for a democracy was something I simply could not risk. I could "*offer my industry*," but never could I betray my conscience. I was willing to get beat up by the partisans and the press for changes that protected who we were supposed to be as Americans.

— 44 —

The Target

That's a Justice Department phone number, I thought, as I looked down at the caller ID on my phone.

I knew I had to pick up, but I let the phone ring an extra beat as I indulged one last look out the window at the fading sun. A harvest moon would soon hover over the Washington vista tonight. The summer heat of the Potomac that lasts well into September had given way to the first feelings of fall. The drive back to McLean from Capitol Hill in the autumn evening had always been a relaxing one, the last chance to stretch, shrug off the workday, and absorb the sunset along the National Mall winding its way to the river. And this fall, after the terrorist attacks and the mad rush at home by too many who were willing to give President Bush all that he asked for without thinking first of the unintended ramifications, let alone our own responsibilities as a coequal branch of government—well, in this moment, any respite or refuge in my own thoughts was even more invaluable, however fleeting.

The phone buzzed again. I picked up.

"*Hello?*"

"*Senator Leahy, the director would like to speak with you as soon as possible.*"

The director. The FBI.

I had a sense of foreboding. This couldn't be good.

For the first moment of the Bush administration, I had a thought I'd probably never have again: I actually *wished* that it were Attorney General Ashcroft calling for me. Ashcroft was a former Senate colleague, albeit one from the Republican Party's social conservative movement, ideological and out of step with the majority of Americans, but I knew what to expect from him. One of his first decisions as attorney general was to spend thousands of taxpayer dollars draping the partially nude female statue *Spirit of Justice*, which had long stood uninhibited in the lobby of the Justice Department. But at least I knew that if it was a phone call I was receiving from John Ashcroft, it was most likely about policy or the lingering issues around the Patriot Act. John knew my views about civil liberties, and I knew his. We were on the opposite sides of the issue, but it was a collegial, if adversarial dance.

The FBI director? This could only be a more serious issue, and more immediate. The Bureau didn't make social calls.

Robert Swan Mueller was a respected, straitlaced Brahmin who had spent the better part of four decades inside the Department of Justice as a US attorney and, later, as head of the Criminal Division. A rock-jawed Marine combat veteran from Vietnam, Mueller looked every bit the part of a post-Hoover-era FBI director: the walking, breathing personification of rectitude and seriousness. The Senate had confirmed him 98–0 just weeks before September 11. Just eight weeks after prostate cancer surgery, Mueller was in command of a vastly complicated domestic law enforcement operation.

The phone connection was notoriously unreliable at a few points on the drive to McLean, so I suggested we speak on my landline as soon as I got to the house.

My premonition had been more prescient than I would have liked.

Less than a month after the terrorist attacks, we'd all been jolted by the news of media and journalism figures suffering from anthrax. Reporters and law enforcement knew right away it was no coincidence that first in Florida in the offices of the *National Enquirer* and soon thereafter at NBC News and ABC News in New York, this disease, which had largely been relegated to the dustbin of history, was resurfacing. Exactly who was behind it and wherever it was coming from were unknown, but one point was clear: we seemed to be witnessing the abuse of deadly, weaponized anthrax as a tool to attack other pillars of America's free press and popular culture. The first victim to die was an employee of American Media, the parent company of the *National Enquirer*. Days later, the FBI found the trace substances in the mailroom and the ventilation system of his office. But the trail of terror was only beginning.

In the Senate, earlier in October, Leader Daschle announced that anthrax had been found in the mailroom of his office. First, the employees who worked on the affected corridor were sent home. Soon, everyone who worked in the entire building did the same. The area and its ventilation system were sealed off. Thankfully no Senate staffers tested positive for the disease, but many were treated to a long swab up the nose and healthy doses of Cipro. Two post office employees on the outskirts of Washington, DC, weren't so lucky: at the Brentwood facility, which routed mail to the Capitol, inhalation anthrax killed two among their ranks. As they had for years, Joseph P. Curseen Jr. and Thomas L. Morris Jr. had gone to work one night loading piles of mail onto the barcode scanner for delivery. Enough of the lethal poison had found its way through the porous envelopes onto their hands, up to their mouths and noses when they wiped the sweat from their brows, and, from there, down their nasal passages or through their parched throats into their lungs.

They were dead in just days.

The FBI had gone on a mad scramble intercepting mail to the Capitol, trying to stem the chain of custody before yet another innocent person became a tragic statistic.

And that trail had led me to this Thursday evening conversation. Here I was on the phone with the director of the FBI.

"*Pat, you know those 280 drums of letters that we confiscated?*"

My heart sank in my chest.

"*We've always known that one of them probably contained another anthrax letter because it's so hot.*"

Hot. The word itself reminded me of the Geiger counters they waved over nuclear testing sites to measure the radioactive poisons lurking in the soil.

"Pat, the good news is that we have found the letter in there. It was unopened. It's isolated now. It's all locked down."

"Bob, I have a very sinking feeling about what the bad news is going to be."

"Yes, it was addressed to you."

I wasn't unfamiliar with threats since I'd been in public life. Life as a prosecutor meant the occasional "I'll get you, Leahy!" shouted across a courtroom or the rare—and sometimes amusing, other times slightly nerve-racking—campaign trail encounter with someone who would say, "Remember me, Pat? You sent me to jail for two years, and I've wanted to give you a piece of my mind ever since." Of course, election night 1974 would be the high-water mark. The police had received a death threat from someone promising to shoot me in the hotel ballroom during my speech. I'd looked out into the audience to see ten or more undercover police positioned throughout the crowd in a phalanx of impromptu security. The threat never materialized.

This was different.

"Have you opened it?"

"Yes. It's evidence, Pat, so I shouldn't get into all the details. But you should know it's similar to the letter Daschle received. Death to America, be afraid—not a lot else. We're doing all the forensics."

My mind was moving rapidly as my blood pressure elevated.

"Is it because I'm chairman of Judiciary?"

"We don't have a motive yet."

"Are there others?"

"We're still searching."

"Have you told my office? I don't want them opening mail—"

"I wanted to reach you first. We can—"

"I should call them. They should hear it from me."

"About that, Pat—another reason I'm calling—the Capitol Police are putting a security detail on you right away."

I'm not sure why the existence of a death threat letter full of deadly poison and addressed to me hadn't achieved the same result, but the imminent assignment of full-time security certainly focused my mind on the urgency.

"*Thanks, Bob. I can have them work with my office tomorrow—*"

"*Pat, if you look out your window, they're pulling up now.*"

I saw the lights of two big black sedans with multiple antennas roll up in front of the house.

"*And so they are.*"

"*We take this very seriously. Pat, it will be in the news shortly, with very little detail from us.*"

Mueller himself was a complete professional. But I knew what this meant: the Bureau itself leaked like a sieve.

"*I should talk to Marcelle now.*"

"*Thanks, Senator—and we can be back in touch.*"

I first dialed my chief of staff.

"*Luke, I have some bad news. Bob Mueller called. There was an anthrax letter intended for our office. They caught it, but I don't want any more of the mail opened—*"

"*Senator, I actually had us pause on opening the mail since the Daschle news—*"

I was relieved. We'd lived through weeks of innocent people placed in grave danger: the interns who opened Tom Daschle's mail in the Capitol, the postal workers, even the toddler child of a network producer exposed to anthrax. The thought of one of our interns or staff assistants exposed to a disease intended for me was sickening.

Marcelle was stoic, always at once more composed, more insightful, and more practical. She held my hand. "*Are you okay?*"

"*We're all going to be okay. But, Marcelle, there will be security with us until this is over.*"

"*Patrick, you should call the children. They shouldn't hear this on the news!*"

I didn't sleep well that night and awoke to the morning paper's latest reporting about the anthrax attack. The details of the forensic and scientific elements were both horrifying and awe-inspiring. The anthrax-laden letter intended for me contained enough anthrax to kill thousands upon thousands of people. It seemed at once diabolically sophisticated but also ham-handed. Why so much? If the intent was to kill, and kill many of us—why not be more discerning with less powder and increase the chances that the poison would go undetected until it was too late?

I was reading and learning more about the byzantine Senate ventilation systems than I'd ever wanted to know. The ventilation systems that had once carried Jim Eastland's wafting cigar smoke into every Capitol nook and cranny were now a pathway for pathogens.

My mind came back again and again to the postal employees. The handwritten letter intended for me was misread by the mail scanner, which mistook one number in the zip code and shuffled it off into a pile of mail bound for the State Department. A postal worker there became disabled for life by the fleeting contact with the paper and another died from it.

I couldn't help but think of the randomness, the accident that spared our office but endangered the postal workers who were just doing their jobs, their unprotected, ungloved hands in contact with a forgotten poison that literally hadn't killed a single American in more than a quarter of a century. How easily it could've been one of my staffers or interns. How easily the Senate air ducts could've conducted the tiny spores of deadly powder and killed dozens.

Not a happy thought.

I wanted to go into the office and reassure the staff. I walked out the front door, down the steps, and right away heard the unmarked vehicles warm up. A police officer spoke into his sleeve and said, "*Shamrock is moving.*" Hell of a circumstance to pick up a code name or nickname, but I could use a little Irish luck, I figured.

Marcelle and I valued our privacy and reveled at times in the sheer anonymity we often found in McLean or home in Vermont, where we were just part of the community. But now, Shamrock was my code name, and these police would go with me everywhere.

I wanted the case to be solved. I wanted our life back.

But when I got back to the house Friday night, Marcelle reminded me of our weekend plans.

"Patrick, we have dinner at Bill and Robin's on Saturday. Robin called to see whether we still wanted to go."

I had completely forgotten. All the media interviews since September 11, especially the questions about my committee's work on the civil liberties issues, had led me to spend a lot of time with CBS's bureau chief Bill Plante. He'd suggested getting our families together when the pace began returning to normal.

This was now hardly "normal" territory.

"*Patrick, we should go. They've planned this.*"

"*They know we'll be bringing some uninvited guests?*"

"*Patrick, everyone knows about the security.*"

"*I hope we can talk about something besides . . . this.*"

Marcelle had an idea.

Saturday evening, we arrived at Bill Plante's door with yellow rubber gloves on.

"*It's been a busy week—I haven't had a chance to answer all my mail. Could I borrow your kitchen table to open the rest of my mail?*"

The ice was broken wide open.

Bill's wife, Robin Smith, confided in us that *she'd* thought about possibly putting rubber gloves on to greet us, as all the news was hitting about this, but then thought that might be something that I would not find very funny, and so they did not.

"*We all need to keep our sense of humor—especially at times like these.*"

But at home, tossing and turning at night, it was I who needed convincing to keep my sense of perspective.

At times, it felt like someone else's life I was living. Poison powder sounded like something straight out of Batman, a diabolical plot conjured up by the Joker or Scarecrow. Surely, this didn't happen in the real world of 2001, in the twenty-first century.

I wondered who was really behind it all. I knew from Robert Mueller that the letter had been postmarked in New Jersey. Already, there was public speculation about an al-Qaeda sleeper cell. But I kept thinking: If it was al-Qaeda—why just target me and Tom Daschle and not others in Congress? Why just target two Democrats when so many others had been in the news?

I wondered whether the almost showy, ostentatious way the sophisticated weapon had been delivered in such an unsophisticated way tipped the attackers' hand: Were they looking for attention as much as results? Were they trying to make a political statement for headlines? Or had they methodically cased the Senate ventilation systems knowing that we could all be endangered before the news became public? Still, I thought, if they were in New Jersey all this time, couldn't they have more easily driven the weaponized poison down the highway in just four hours and delivered the attack with greater precision?

These unanswered questions haunted me. The bags under my eyes were the only "tell," but I was consumed by them. I was also fascinated by knowing that whoever was behind this plot must know by now that they'd caused millions upon millions—soon into the billions—of dollars to be spent on security in the Capitol, revamping ventilation systems and irradiating every piece of mail, delaying responses to urgent constituent letters and sending hundreds of terrified staffers to the doctor for precautionary treatment.

They had proven what almost any terrorist, foreign or domestic, loves to prove: that they can create mayhem and interrupt the way we live.

I was determined not to give them any more of that kind of psychic victory than I could allow. Adversaries are adaptive. I didn't think that they would be coming back after me next time with anthrax any more than terrorists would be taking box cutters to hijack large airplanes and run them into buildings.

After that, any time a story on the anthrax investigation came on the news, I started leaving the room. It was a convenient time to do the dishes or call our children and grandchildren. I didn't want this perpetual, low-volume stress to invade our home any more than it already had.

The months ticked by. The security detail remained. They became part of our daily lives. Marcelle brought them iced tea on warm days and freshly baked chocolate chip cookies hot out of the oven on cold days.

The media leaks intensified about the investigation. I tried hard to block out those that either smacked of sensational speculation or seemed manufactured by someone inside the FBI to show how hard they were working.

But one leak bothered me immensely. It was a wild theory that Iraq's Saddam Hussein may have weaponized anthrax and handed it off to a terrorist group to deploy against the United States. The Saddam Hussein theory did not come from the FBI but was clearly from someone in the neoconservative ranks of the administration. It was no secret that Hussein had a biochemical weapons program in the 1990s that he'd sworn to surrender after the Gulf War. But it was ludicrous to imagine that he had an operational relationship with al-Qaeda. In fact, the extremists hated Hussein and all the secular autocrats in the region. He was a bully and an adversary of the United States, but he was simultaneously an obstacle to al-Qaeda's jihadi dreams, to Osama bin Laden and other zealots who aimed to build a new caliphate in the Middle East. I could only deduce that the White House wanted Director Mueller to blame Hussein for the anthrax attack to bolster its growing campaign for action against Iraq.

Mueller, the by-the-books, law-and-order picture of reserve and rectitude, wasn't biting. President Bush and Vice President Cheney publicly speculated that it was al-Qaeda. Mueller didn't corroborate what they were saying, which, to a knowing audience, was a "tell" that the investigation may have been headed in other directions. But I worried that not every audience was as knowing.

After a Judiciary Committee hearing, I buttonholed Mueller.

"*Bob, I worry these leaks about Saddam Hussein and anthrax are for domestic political consumption.*"

He bristled.

"*I know they don't come from the FBI,*" I clarified.

"*Pat, you know we can't comment on investigations.*"

"*Yes, Bob, but clarifying when someone is saying things that are untrue—*"

"I will take that under advisement."

"That's all I can ask."

But the damage, I feared, was done. There were so many ways truth was being abused and distorted in the post-9/11 frenzy to find someone, blame someone, and apply old political grievances to a new national security reality.

As Marcelle and I were talking after dinner one evening, my mind flashed back to the conversations with the Justice Department about this personalized threat. It was almost exactly thirty-eight years since I first went to the Justice Department at a far more innocent time. It was 1963, and Attorney General Robert Kennedy had invited a handful of law students for a meeting in his office to encourage us to join the Department of Justice. I was a twenty-three-year-old with a young wife working as a registered nurse to put me through law school, living in a basement apartment, with absolutely no money, and in awe of everything in Washington. How on earth had such carefree, innocent times in America led all of us on this winding journey—airplanes and passengers turned into human weapons of mass destruction in our greatest metropolitan city, envelopes of poison aimed at US senators by anonymous killers?

But the oddest realization gave me a strange comfort. My twenty-three-year-old self never could've imagined peering into a future in which I'd be called "Mr. Chairman" and guarded twenty-four hours a day because of an assassination attempt. But neither at twenty-three could I have imagined that in seven months, President Kennedy would be killed in Dallas, Texas, or that his brother the attorney general, and one of my first political heroes, would be struck down in the kitchen of the Ambassador Hotel five years after that first meeting with the starry-eyed law students.

Life, it seemed, hadn't ever really been so innocent. The idea that we could predict the future had been an illusion I should've appreciated sooner. You just keep trying to live and use the time you have as best you can.

I looked out the window at a quarter moon in this lovely, pleasant, safe neighborhood. But I could also see the unmarked black police car parked in front of the house with two heavily armed officers. Maybe someday, I thought, I would have the time or the desire to put all this in context, but for now, I just had to keep moving in the one direction I knew how—forward.

I thought of the brave men and women in my office, who came to work under the same threat and did not have police officers walking them home. I knew how angry and frustrated they felt that anybody would attack us as they did on September 11 or threaten us directly as they did with the anthrax, but I also knew how loyal they were, and we'd all keep it going.

But most of all, I looked forward to the weekend and being able to have time to hold Marcelle. We'd been reminded of life's fragility. I thought of those postal workers, just a few years shy of retirement, how they must've known they were hitting milestones toward pensions and could almost reach out and touch a life of grandchildren and quiet. What a bitter reminder of how life could end too abruptly. I was determined it wouldn't, and that I wouldn't live in fear.

Besides, Marcelle wouldn't let me.

— 45 —

All We Have to Fear

I'd never seen America seem so frightened by the world in which we were living, or the conditions at home so ripe for political exploitation as they were in the two years after 9/11.

"*Some concede that Saddam is evil, power hungry, and a menace, but that until he crosses the threshold of actually possessing nuclear weapons, we should rule out any preemptive action. That logic seems to me to be deeply flawed.*"

I was sitting in the kitchen of our tree farm in Middlesex. The doors were open, and a wonderful little breeze blew in, the cross ventilation New Englanders prefer to air-conditioning—when you can find it. It was a perfect end of a summer day, and I felt a wistfulness knowing I'd be heading back to the humidity of Washington in a couple of days—a city built on a swamp. The sound of my grandson splashing in the pool, and Marcelle's laughter as she cheered him on, filled my ears. But these sounds of innocent contentment were competing with the bellicose chords reverberating from the little television set on the countertop.

C-SPAN was broadcasting Vice President Cheney's speech to the Veterans of Foreign Wars convention. I scanned the audience: a sea of older veterans, gray and weathered. I thought of Bob Dole and John Glenn and Danny Inouye—colleagues all who had distinguished themselves in war as they had in peace, men who had come home with both a determination always to defend America and a hard-earned sense of reality about the horrors of battle. Cheney didn't seem to be speaking to them. His audience was the editorial boards of the *Washington Post* and *Wall Street Journal*, and the case he was making wasn't for peace or diplomacy but war—a war of choice. In that sense, the VFW seemed an appropriate setting for Cheney's neoconservative saber-rattling: with one war now well under way in Afghanistan against those who had protected the al-Qaeda terrorists who had actually attacked the United States, the vice president seemed to be not a statesman reluctantly preparing a nation for the last-resort possibility of a war, but rather a cheerleader hell-bent on creating another generation of combat veterans.

I remembered the Dick Cheney I'd first met. He stood out in my memory for many reasons, many seemingly innocuous coincidences. My first year serving in the Senate, I'd met President Ford's wunderkind deputy chief of staff: he too was in his thirties, new to Washington, from a rural state, with a hairline that perhaps made him seem a little older and less boyish. By November, he had moved up the ranks—the youngest White House chief of staff in history. Cheney was shrewd, and he seemed to know everyone inside the Ford administration, an early master of understanding the vast power that comes from being able to navigate the intricacies of a bureaucracy. One a Democrat, one a Republican, we were friendly and cordial, forever connected in those days by the surprise our age and relative political accomplishment created in many we met. He moved home to Wyoming after President Ford's defeat, but he wasn't in Casper for long: by 1979, Cheney was back in DC as Wyoming's lone congressman.

Something had changed in him over the years, something that none of us who had known him back then had seen coming. Cheney had served as President George H. W. Bush's defense secretary. He'd been part of the successful military intervention to expel Iraqi president Saddam Hussein from Kuwait, and he had supported the smart decision not to invade Iraq and bring down the regime in Baghdad. Bush, James Baker, Joint Chiefs of Staff chairman Colin Powell, and National Security Advisor Brent Scowcroft had all shown a deft adroitness in deciding to punish and effectively contain Hussein rather than occupy Iraq. It reflected a maturity in their foreign policy. To those who said the United States should have toppled the regime in Baghdad, Cheney said, "It doesn't work that way in the Middle East; it never has and isn't likely to in my lifetime."

But here he was a decade later, his famously inscrutable poker face long gone. Now, no one could doubt what Vice President Cheney was campaigning for: a hasty invasion of Iraq. Maybe it was the three heart attacks he'd suffered and the confrontation with his own mortality. A brush with death can change a person. Maybe it was the impact of 9/11. But the careful, calibrated, steady hand added to provide seasoning on the Republican ticket in 2000 was gone.

"*Wars are never won on the defensive. We must take the battle to the enemy. We must take every step necessary to make sure our country is secure, and we will prevail,*" Cheney stated plainly. The audience erupted in applause. It wasn't clear whether the vice president was talking about the war in Afghanistan or the next war he was promoting in Iraq—or the increasingly vague catchall for every action by the Bush administration: the "global war on terror."

9/11 had struck a deep chord in all of us. I'd studied the Middle East for years. I knew the extremism that could be unleashed in the region; much more than jet fuel propelled the two airliners into the World Trade Center buildings. If anything, I thought the Bush administration had been too hesitant to get the truth about September 11 from the partner country from which so many of the terrorists came: Saudi Arabia. We faced a moment of reckoning about terror and how to prevent it.

But Cheney seemed hell-bent on a different goal. He wanted to transform the Middle East by force and settle a score against Saddam Hussein. He lacked patience for diplomacy. He ignored its value.

Saddam Hussein had been left in power after Operation Desert Storm with a promise that he would allow unfettered inspections of his weapons programs to prove he wasn't building chemical, biological, or nuclear weapons. Saddam had kicked out the inspectors in 1998. Getting inspectors back into Iraq seemed imperative—but not to Cheney.

"*The return of inspectors would provide no assurance whatsoever of his compliance with UN resolutions. On the contrary, there is a great danger that it would provide false comfort that Saddam was somehow back in his box.*"

No, this was a clear public relations offensive launched to validate war.

What worried me most was that I knew Bush had a strong hand to play with the country. This administration, inaugurated without a proper mandate, had shared in a national shock on September 11, 2001, and the president had rallied the country as President Clinton had after the Oklahoma City bombing and as President Reagan had after the *Challenger* shuttle explosion. The president's popularity remained sky-high. Now, they seemed to believe that they could test its limits.

I flipped the channel. CNN was discussing new polls that claimed strong support for an attack on Iraq. I worried the administration was so caught up in its own hubris, trapped in its own bubble, misreading history and inflated polls that reflected America's unity in a time of crisis. They seemed determined to crash right into a war of preemption—without even talking to Congress.

After all, it had become the rule, not the exception, in the last year. The unilateral actions of a few in the White House had empowered an attorney general to propose a "*spy on your neighbor*" program—until he was reined in by members of Congress, ranging from Dick Armey, the conservative Republican majority leader of the House, to myself. If we had not spoken up, I'm sure that program would be in place by now.

Who would speak up now?

The political calculations inside the White House, far from a brake on Cheney's ideological fervor, must have been an accelerant. George W. Bush did not want to be the one-term president that his father was. They would continue with an agenda addressed to the Christian Right and to those who want powerless government, especially business executives who no longer wanted anyone to ask embarrassing questions, as we did of Enron, and tax cuts for the wealthy piled on top of tax cuts for the powerful. When the president spoke of sacrifice in the "war on terrorism," it never seemed to include those with the highest level of income, and ignored the hundreds of thousands out of work as the economy collapsed.

I thought of my father's stories of the days of World War II, when shared sacrifice in Vermont actually meant everyone going without, to support the cause. But it was also an abuse of reality around us. The president argued we were in a "state of war," but really, we were in a state of plenty of comfort and almost exclusion from the rest of the world. Would we one day face further terrorist attacks? Of course, as would all other countries. We would also face them from people like Timothy McVeigh within our own borders. The answer was not the simplistic political narrative the administration promoted; the answer was the international efforts needed to lower the power and the ignorance of those who militantly wanted to strike out at us.

I felt compelled to say something, to remind the Senate, at least, that before the Bush administration went to war in Iraq, it had to come to us first. For two hundred years, the Constitution had come in pretty handy. This moment wasn't the time to toss it aside out of political convenience.

In our caucus luncheon, the administration's Iraq campaign was the only topic. Our majority leader, Tom Daschle, encouraged a number of us to speak, starting with the chairman of the Foreign Relations Committee, Joe Biden.

Joe laid out a complex picture. Saddam Hussein was indeed flouting the world's insistence that he allow weapons inspectors into the country, which made the United Nations appear feckless. Biden said the White House was confident that Hussein was rebuilding his chemical weapons program, no small matter since Hussein had used mustard gas in the past, even against his own people. Was the White House determined to go to war? Biden wasn't sure. Some were firmly in the Cheney camp, obviously, he said, but he'd spoken with Colin Powell and believed that still others, including the president, were instead open to using an authorization of military force as a threat—as leverage to compel Hussein to allow weapons inspectors back into the country and avoid war. What the White House *wasn't* willing to do, Biden said, was wait forever.

Biden said he had talked with Dick Lugar, my friend from those many years on the Agriculture Committee, and Lugar similarly thought there might be a way to temper the administration's enthusiasm to run headlong into a war of choice and instead build a coalition to confront Hussein one way or another.

Others spoke up. Joe Lieberman made a full-throated case to do whatever it took to disarm Hussein, including acting unilaterally. I disagreed with Joe, but it was clear that he believed what he believed. John Edwards, the hard-charging star senator from North Carolina, argued that he was absolutely certain that the case about Hussein's drive for nuclear weapons was strong. But on balance, the caucus consensus was about finding ways to stand in the way of a rush to war—to force the White House to come to us and to work with allies, against its own instincts. Max Cleland, a triple amputee from the Vietnam War, became choked up as he talked about the horrors of war. Paul Wellstone talked about our duty to oppose a reckless war, even if it cost us at the polls in November. He had put his finger on the unspoken issue lingering in the air: we were sixty days from an election, with a fifty-one-vote majority hanging in the balance, and the Bush administration was determined to ride 9/11 every inch of the way toward winning a Senate majority.

As I thought about John Edwards's comment, I decided to go see the intelligence for myself. Given my role on the Foreign Operations Subcommittee, I'd always stayed in close touch with the CIA. I wanted to understand what it believed about the Middle East, rather than accepting at face value what leaders told us about these countries. I headed to a secure room in the Capitol to read the intelligence community's best analysis of what was happening in the authoritarian police state in Baghdad.

The solitude of the secure room was a grounding experience: no staff, no phones, just an individual senator and classified documents, to consider the unbiased, unvarnished findings of the intelligence community. Sometimes, we used to joke that the front page of the *Washington Post* was a better place to find out what was really happening in the intelligence community. Under Reagan, the CIA had been frustratingly porous, spouting media leaks long before the intelligence ever made its way to Congress. But since 9/11, the community had gone out of its way to be solicitous of Congress, to forge a sense that we were all wrestling with hard decisions together and deserved a common set of facts. My former staffer on the Intelligence Committee, George Tenet, a career intelligence staffer, had performed admirably in this respect.

Thumbing my way through the material, which was similar to the public record, what jumped out was the conclusion that Saddam Hussein *coveted* weapons of mass destruction, but the reality was that little had really changed over the years. I wondered whether the eyes of any freshman senator saw the same things that I did with five terms under my belt. Sure, Hussein had pursued weapons of mass destruction since the 1970s, and in the 1980s, we'd been his biggest benefactor as he barreled into an ill-advised war against Iran. This wasn't new behavior for this master of miscalculation in Baghdad. Where was the smoking gun of a newly revived threat?

Many in the administration seemed to draw tenuous connections between Hussein and al-Qaeda, but I remembered just how much he—a largely secular autocrat—had long been the target, not the patron, of al-Qaeda zealots who dreamed of restoring a religious caliphate and kicking out the existing order. I read the details: the conclusion was thin; if an al-Qaeda terrorist had found safe passage through Iraq en route to Iran, it was hardly a sign of Saddam's cooperation with al-Qaeda and more likely proof of Iraq's porous border, or the old saying "the enemy of my enemy is my friend." If a terrorist thug was on his way to create chaos in Iran, the regime would happily turn a blind eye to his safe passage.

My conclusion was caution: I simply didn't see proof of an imminent threat or a new rush by a madman to obtain weapons of mass destruction. I saw the status quo as it had been for a long time. "*Looks like the Middle East,*" I said to the intelligence officer sitting at the desk.

The following Sunday, Marcelle and I went for our usual early-morning walk in the neighborhood. It was a warm September day, and we walked hand in hand.

Two fit joggers trailed behind us. They stopped and asked what I thought of the intelligence briefings I'd been getting. Marcelle realized this was a conversation that normally she would not be involved in and kept on walking ahead.

I went through a requisite disclaimer that if I was in briefings and if they were classified, I could not acknowledge that they even occurred and could not talk about them if they had. They told me they understood that, but asked whether the briefers had showed me File Eight.

It was obvious from the look on my face that I had not seen such a file. They suggested I should and that I might find it interesting. Quickly thereafter I arranged to see File Eight, and it contradicted much of what I had heard from the Bush administration.

Days later, Marcelle and I were out walking again when the two joggers reappeared. After the opening greetings, they told me they understood I had seen File Eight and asked what did I think about it?

It was the eeriest conversation I'd experienced in Washington. I felt like a senatorial version of Bob Woodward meeting Deep Throat—only in broad daylight.

I went through the usual disclaimers that I could not talk about any file and if such a file was available and so on. They said of course they understood, but they wondered if I had also been shown File Twelve, using a code word.

Again, I think the look on my face gave them the answer. They apologized for interrupting our walk and jogged off. The next day, I was back in the secure room in the Capitol to read File Twelve, and it again contradicted the statements that the administration, and especially Vice President Cheney, seemed to be relying on, and I told my staff and others that for a number of reasons I absolutely intended to vote against the war in Iraq.

I'd been around too long to do differently. It is hard to think of any vote that is taken by the Senate that is more important than voting to go to war or not. While we never had a declaration of war in Vietnam, the falsehoods and misleading information regarding the Gulf of Tonkin episode brought about a vote in the Senate that guaranteed the continuation of the war. Only one senator voted no. Had the Senate asked more questions—had it drilled down into the facts—who knows how history could've been different? Instead, that war went on for years and thousands of deaths later, until it was officially ended by a one-vote margin in the Armed Services Committee of the US Senate in 1975.

I wasn't alone in questioning the intelligence about Iraq. A conservative Democrat from Florida, Bob Graham, was the vice chairman of the Intelligence Committee and urged everyone to read the intelligence, which he could not talk about on the floor or in open meetings. His warnings and those of Senator Carl Levin, the lead Democrat on the Armed Services Committee, were a contrast to the administration's cheerleaders urging senators to meet with a man named Ahmed Chalabi, source of many of the stories that the *New York Times* and others had printed claiming that Saddam Hussein had weapons of mass destruction. I refused to meet with him, as I knew his reputation for falsehoods was high and that the press who had backed him were being fooled. The intelligence community referred to him as "Curveball" for a reason.

That Sunday after church, Marcelle and I were out walking through McLean, going by Hickory Hill, the former Robert Kennedy estate, as black cars with multiple antennas and darkened windows passed us by. That was not unusual because of various officials in the administration who lived out in that area. As we reached Georgetown Pike, right by the Quaker meetinghouse, one of the vehicles pulled up. A member of the presidential inner circle leaned out from the back window, greeting both myself and Marcelle, and asked if he could talk with me. We were about a half mile from home, and she continued on walking. I got in the car with him while the security people got out of the car. We sat there and talked, and he said, "I understand you've seen File Eight and Twelve." I said I had, and I knew of course that he'd seen them. He said, "I also understand you're going to vote against going to war."

I said, "I am, because we all know there are no weapons of mass destruction and the reasons for going to war are just not there."

He asked if he could talk me out of that, and I said no, and we ended the conversation. I started to get out of the car, and he said they would give me a ride home.

"Thanks—let me tell you where I live."

"*We know where you live.*"

In caucus on Tuesday, the debate continued. The administration was grudgingly coming to Congress to negotiate a use of force resolution, something that many senators believed could actually be a tool to prevent a war. But I suspected the die was cast.

"*I heard James Baker convinced William Safire to write that skeptical column to convince the president to tread carefully,*" said one of my earnest colleagues.

Washington's latest parlor game was fixated on whether the people around the president's father were using third parties to persuade this President Bush not to rush into war. Secretary of State Colin Powell had become the vessel into which they'd poured all their hopes that diplomacy would prevail, that together, we'd be "tough" on Saddam Hussein without an invasion. I feared it was an elusive unicorn they were hunting for—it would've been great to find it, but ultimately it was a fiction.

"*I spoke to Colin Powell. He said that if we have a smart resolution, if we force Bush to go to the UN, we empower the diplomacy so they come our way,*" said another colleague.

It was a glass-half-full way of looking at the situation. They believed they could shape the White House's trajectory.

"*Well, I can't tell you what's going on in President Bush's head,*" I said. "*So, I'll just have to trust my own eyes. I don't think they're making the case for why they need this authorization now if they don't intend to use it. Why the hurry? I watch the vice president's speeches. I don't think he's freelancing. And if he is—well, that's a whole other problem. I think they're telling us they want to go to war in the worst way. And I'm afraid they really will go to war in the worst way.*"

Days later, I spoke in opposition to the Iraq War authorization.

It passed 77–23.

My colleagues who made up the overwhelming majority did so for various reasons. I remembered Mike Mansfield's argument to never question anyone's motives, just their position. Some probably did fear Bush's commanding poll numbers and his ability to weaponize national security against them. Others believed the intelligence, and still others genuinely believed that they were empowering diplomacy, that this vote didn't mean what it said it meant, which was that the president could go to war with our blessing. But I'd been there long enough to have seen life come full circle: I'd cast that first hard vote to end the Vietnam War, and I didn't intend to cast this one on a new Gulf of Tonkin for the Middle East.

Two weeks later, we lost the Senate. The 2002 midterm elections were as painful as any since 1994 and 1980. Max Cleland lost his race in Georgia, attacked for being "*weak*" on terrorism, excoriated by an opponent who hadn't, as Max had, proved his courage on the battlefield. Paul Wellstone had been killed in a plane crash shortly before the election, and Vice President Mondale had stepped in to run on his behalf. He lost too. We lost incumbents from Missouri and open seats in South Carolina.

The Bush administration had waved the flag of war to win the Senate. Now they were going to make a push for the real thing.

After the Bush administration went to war in Iraq, trust was badly broken in the Senate. Lawmakers felt burned by the vote. The spectacle of the White House effort to turn the war into a political weapon compounded the feeling inside our caucus that all the talk of diplomacy had been a ruse to win a lopsided vote for a blank check for war. Inside the administration, Colin Powell felt betrayed.

I went to work focused on the things I could control in the minority—demanding oversight and accountability of the war, of White House ethics, and of judicial nominees. I didn't have a gavel, but I did have a bully pulpit, and I could assert my position on the Judiciary Committee and through the FOIA process to ask tough questions, including about Vice President Cheney's contacts with his old company, Halliburton, which looked to profit in what one administration official foolishly called a "gold rush" in liberated Iraq.

One day, the vice president was in the Senate presiding over votes in expectation of close margins where his vote could break a tie. I thought vice presidents should always be in a good mood when they were on the Senate floor—as Al Gore used to joke, "every time I vote, we win." I also remembered what an opportunity it was to curry goodwill, remembering

Vice President Bush and his note card writing down requests from senators, talking to members of both parties. Cheney was huddling only with the Republicans.

"*Mr. Vice President, I know there are some Democrats who would like to see you today, if you want to come over*," I said with a smile. Cheney looked straight ahead at me and said, clearly and loudly, "*Go fuck yourself*."

Well okay then, I thought. The word spread quickly. It became a feature of entire segments on late night television. We quickly capitalized on the attention. I was on the ballot for reelection. Garry Trudeau had drawn a hilarious cartoon about the incident. We asked for his permission to put it on a T-shirt for the campaign. "Patrick, with the intellectual property laws, I'd have to be compensated," he replied.

"How much, Garry?"

"How about five T-shirts? Two for me and Jane, and three for our kids." It was a deal. The cartoon was on one side of the shirts, and the other read: "*Annoy Cheney. Vote Leahy*."

They sold out in a few hours.

My reelection wasn't close. But Cheney would be smiling on election night as the votes trickled in nationally: a narrow reelection decided by half a football stadium in Ohio.

— 46 —

Rebuilding

"*Hey, Patrick—hi—no, I'm fine here . . .*" The words trailed off in a whisper, the sound of someone trying to slip into the caucus meeting a minute or two late, hoping to go unnoticed, as if hunting for a seat in a darkened movie theater after the lights are down and the projector has started rolling.

John Kerry seemed to be trying in vain to will himself invisible—a hard task on the best of days for the lantern-jawed, lanky senator from Massachusetts trying to camouflage his six-foot-five frame into the furniture of the Old Senate Chamber.

And for John, this couldn't have felt like the best of days.

Thirteen days before, he had stood up at Faneuil Hall in his hometown of Boston and conceded Ohio and, with it, the presidential race to the incumbent George W. Bush—almost a day after exit polls had incorrectly indicated Kerry might well become the forty-fourth president of the United States.

Now he was back here in the Senate, hounded by television cameras, once again the junior senator from Massachusetts, among the walking wounded in our caucus.

Our minority leader, Tom Daschle, had lost his reelection. His counterpart, Majority Leader Bill Frist, had shattered years of Senate protocol by campaigning against Tom in person. It was a line that a previous

Republican leader like Bob Dole would never have crossed. It had been an ugly campaign. The Democratic whip Dick Durbin whispered to me about the dirt that the Republicans had thrown during the Daschle campaign, even attacking him for being divorced. Republicans suggested Daschle had abandoned his family, even as his first wife and children were going door-to-door throughout South Dakota, pleading with voters to support Tom. The money flooding South Dakota with lies took him down after thirty years in Congress. A mere 4,500 votes were the difference between remaining Senate leader and leaving elected life. It had to sting, especially in a state where politics was intimate and personal. Majority Leader Frist must've felt lucky. Had Daschle been narrowly reelected, how awkward it would've been to run the Senate together, let alone rebuild trust.

Some other familiar faces around the room were soon to be gone as well. Fritz Hollings had retired, and in his place, South Carolina had elected a neo-populist, right-wing conservative in former congressman Jim DeMint, who had promised to move South Carolina to the right and shake up the institution. It was an abrupt break with the decades of at least on-the-surface comity, which had defined Hollings and even his ability to find some common ground on the interests of the Palmetto State with Strom Thurmond. Bob Graham, who had been so wise warning his colleagues about the coming war in Iraq, had also called it quits after three terms in the Senate, and he had been replaced by a somewhat anonymous member of President Bush's cabinet. John Edwards, the vice presidential nominee, had chosen not to run for reelection, and in addition to not carrying his home state on the presidential ticket, he suffered the indignity of watching his Senate seat go Republican. Edwards's Senate career had been like a shooting star—burning fast and bright before disappearing in the clouds. Now he was gone. He didn't come back to say goodbye in what would've been one of his final caucus gatherings.

The Senate itself seemed to be getting smaller. Legends of the old Senate were being replaced by partisan cookie-cutter replacements, like Russian nesting dolls, the next one smaller than the one before. I kept wondering, Where were the new John Glenns? Where were the new

Howell Heflins? What did it say about the Senate that we were no longer a place extraordinary citizens dreamed of serving?

55–45 would be the new Republican margin come January, but even worse was the *feeling* hanging over the caucus. In politics, "hope" isn't just a word thrown around in elections to excite voters. It matters to the public servants in government themselves who work long hours, who came to Washington to do things, not just to be there. This day, there wasn't a lot of hope floating around in that room. President Bush's chief political advisor, Karl Rove, had been on television the weekend before our caucus meeting. He clearly saw himself in sweeping historic terms. He had long argued that Republicans were poised to seize the ascendancy for a long time to come and that Bush's presidency was the harbinger of tectonic shifts. Rove had already beaten the midterm curse and won back the Senate a year after 9/11, riding the wartime president's popularity to victory. Now he'd done it again: Bush had been reelected in a rough and tough campaign, by the skin of his teeth but reelected nonetheless. Close, I remembered, only counted in horseshoes and hand grenades. "*The victory in 1896 was similarly narrow,*" Rove crowed to Fox's analysts. "*It was an election that realigned American politics for years afterward. And I think the same thing will be true here.*" Republicans were gleeful about the prospects of a permanent Senate supermajority. There was a miasmic pessimism hanging over the room.

It wasn't just the defeat in 2004 of two of our own. It was the way we'd lost the election. That was what I suspected weighed on John Kerry as he sat ramrod straight, his crossed left leg bouncing up and down tensely over his right leg, releasing waves of nervous energy. He'd seen his war record scurrilously slandered. He'd been up in the polls until seventy-two hours before the election, when Osama bin Laden released a propaganda tape savaging Bush, and suddenly the election was again a referendum on Bush's stoicism and determination on 9/11. Kerry looked like a man who wanted so much to be in the back row, even as so many of the caucus speakers brought the discussion back to him. I felt nothing but empathy for him.

When Kerry was first recognized, there was a long-standing ovation for him, and Barbara Mikulski read a generous tribute to him on behalf of the caucus. John thanked all of us for all we'd done to support him, but his eyes communicated just how hard it was to process the loss.

But then the caucus meeting turned to our current conundrum.

Robert Byrd got up to speak, leaning on his cane, looking very, very frail. Byrd's hair had grown longer and wispier in his most senior years. His skin was ghostly white, almost translucent, matching his mane. I realized how few of my colleagues had known Byrd at the height of his command, those years in the 1970s when he had internalized every arcane procedure and personally managed the Senate schedule. Now, more than a quarter century later, even before he began speaking, he had trouble getting his composure and seemed almost in tears. Byrd spoke first about how proud he was of John Kerry. Byrd said he'd watched all the debates and was very proud of how John had represented us, and he apologized for his own state voting once again for Bush. It was in West Virginia where scurrilous leaflets had appeared on car windshields outside of churches, warning that if Kerry-Edwards won, gay couples would be getting married everywhere. Byrd, himself an evangelical Christian who hosted old-style revivals across Appalachia, was stunned by people's willingness to ignore even trusted voices like his and instead believe a big lie.

Byrd then spoke about how he grew up in a mining town and was the first one in his family to go to college. It was a journey many of us could relate to; certainly I could, as the first Leahy to go to college. Byrd mentioned that now we'd have another Senate Democratic leader who had come up from such roots: Tom Daschle's successor, our soon-to-be leader Harry Reid, grew up poor and scrappy in the tiny mining town of Searchlight, Nevada, and Byrd believed he would provide the leadership we all needed to navigate a difficult passage with cohesion.

But then the old leader, the man who literally wrote the history of the Senate and published it for his colleagues, grew emotional—and almost apocalyptic in the dystopic vision he shared with us. The room was quiet. Byrd said that there were great battles coming that could undermine the power of the Senate and undermine the constitutional balance among people, and that above all we had to hold together. He said he knew that Harry Reid would hold us together.

I looked around the room. I knew what Byrd meant. He saw Social Security on the chopping block, a packing of the courts with ideologues, efforts to jam through Republican wish-list nominees and legislative hobbyhorses with fifty votes, outcomes decided by Vice President Cheney's tiebreaker. The purging of moderates.

I wondered how many of my more recent colleagues were processing what Byrd really meant, the weight of his words. He was contemplating a Senate in which a president and his party rode roughshod not just over the minority, but over the institution itself. My younger colleagues had never really known a particularly functional Senate. They had never known the halcyon days of Mike Mansfield's back room, where differences were worked out collegially. They had never known the Senate of Dole and Baker, Byrd and Mitchell, where the leaders and their whips wore out the carpet walking back and forth to each other's offices all day, making the Senate function. If they'd been elected since 1995, they'd seen how Daschle and Lott worked out the calendar and the schedules in good spirits, but they'd also seen Leader Lott increasingly held hostage by the endless anti-Clinton crusade of some of the newer members of his caucus and by the tail in the House too often wagging the dog. Newt Gingrich had been audacious enough to think of himself not just as Speaker of the House but as Speaker of the Senate. And if these senators had been elected after 2000, they'd seen Lott himself deposed and replaced with a handpicked Bush acolyte the White House believed would be a reliable partner. They'd all seen 9/11 weaponized to brutally paint our candidates in 2002 and 2004 as weak, despite the way Democrats had reached out to the other side after the terrorist attacks.

I suppose that if you never really knew how extraordinary the institution could be at its best, it was harder to appreciate what we still had to lose—and what a true threat to the Senate might look like. But surely, Robert C. Byrd saw one coming.

This was the first time in the thirty years I had been here that I had to admit I may have felt old. I thought back to the thrill I felt during my first organizing caucus as Hubert Humphrey and Scoop Jackson joked about the reasons this kid from Vermont might be hiding out in the back row.

Seeing John Kerry sitting there for entirely different reasons, and seeing Bob Byrd evoking one era while clinging to this one, brought back the full sweep of what I'd witnessed.

Harry Reid got up to speak. He spoke first of Tom Daschle and was emotional when he said that he came here with him in 1986. He said that while no one denied that Bush had won, we shouldn't be chastened by our defeat: no wartime president had ever lost reelection. Reid said, "We faced a wartime president, but with a war brought on by his own hubris." He gave an excellent speech about our values. Searchlight, Nevada, and Montpelier, Vermont, had little in common, but we'd learned some of the same life lessons. Reid pointed out that more people voted for Democrats in the Senate races than Republicans, and that while Republicans controlled the Senate 55–45, we had a constituency to fight for across the country.

I tried to take the long view. As I walked out of caucus, reporters barked at me, asking whether I cared to comment on the rumors that the White House hoped to replace pro-choice Republican Judiciary Committee chairman Arlen Specter with a social conservative who might ram through its nominees more quickly. I smiled.

"*I don't think the Republican Party is calling me for advice on their purity tests,*" I replied.

It reminded me that their party would face a challenge as well. Victory itself could leave a White House or a caucus feeling like the dog that caught the car. I was amazed by just how much the Republican senators seemed willing to allow the White House to openly and flagrantly take their independence away from them. I cannot imagine why anybody would want to run for an office where they were supposed to be independent and then cede their independence to the staff at the other end of Pennsylvania Avenue who was really calling the shots.

I heard footsteps behind me, hard shoe leather slapping the marble floor, and then the *click-click-click* of cameras.

"Senator Leahy, is it always like this? Is it always this much of a downer? I am beginning to wonder why I ran."

I laughed.

Trotting up behind me was the newly elected junior senator from Illinois, Barack Obama. I'd met him in Boston the summer before on the eve of the convention speech that launched his star into the political stratosphere.

"Well, Senator Obama, hello there—"

"Barack, please."

"Well, Barack, today was sort of like it was in 1980, after we went into the minority for the first time in decades. We were all down, but then we got unified and came roaring back. And I'm just hoping the same thing happens now."

I remembered how we spent the first four years after President Reagan was elected doing everything possible to protect him from himself and protect the Senate Republicans from themselves. Well, when we stopped doing that after four years, we took the majority back.

"I hope you're right. It'll be good to work with you."

I smiled, staring into the sunshine as we walked outside the Senate. Barack climbed into a waiting car, as I stretched my legs and headed across Constitution Avenue back to the Russell Building.

It seemed so incongruous that it was such a sobering time on such a gorgeous fall day. It was hard to think of the troubling things that were happening while it was so nice outside, but Robert Byrd was right about the coming storms.

1

My mother, Alba, took this picture of my brother, John; my father, Howard; my sister, Mary; and myself celebrating the steamship *Ticonderoga* soon after it made its last trip on Lake Champlain in 1953. The "Ti" was fortunately saved from the scrapyard, moved two miles overland, restored, and is now located at Shelburne Museum, where thousands visit it every year.

2

Dressed up for a college dance with Marcelle. We were already very serious.

3

Dad at work at the Leahy Press. The printing plant was at the back of our house. I often fell asleep to the humming of presses running below.

When Governor Hoff tapped me to be state's attorney for Chittenden County in 1968, the office had a huge backlog of cases that had not been tried. I would argue cases during the day, hustle home for dinner with Marcelle and the kids, and then spend well into the night/morning writing briefs for the next day. As a recent Georgetown law graduate, I felt like I was on trial myself, but I relished the opportunity, and the experience was invaluable.

4

5

To Patrick J. Leahy
Best wishes
J. Edgar Hoover
6.8.71

National District Attorneys Association meeting with FBI Director Hoover. We all noted how he wore platform shoes and that the legs on our chairs around the conference table had been lowered, whereas the legs on the director's chair had been raised to compensate for his physically diminutive statute. The director was not amused by the national headlines I had generated from a memo I had written advising Vermont police departments about skinny-dipping.

6

Marcelle had a genuine touch as we started our campaign in 1974. Her parents, Phil and Cecile, immigrated from Quebec, and French was her first language. That allowed her to have a special connection on the campaign trail with the many Vermonters of French Canadian descent. Here she is introducing us in French to a voter in Winooski.

7

Going over campaign information in 1974 with Marcelle and campaign manager Paul Bruhn.

8

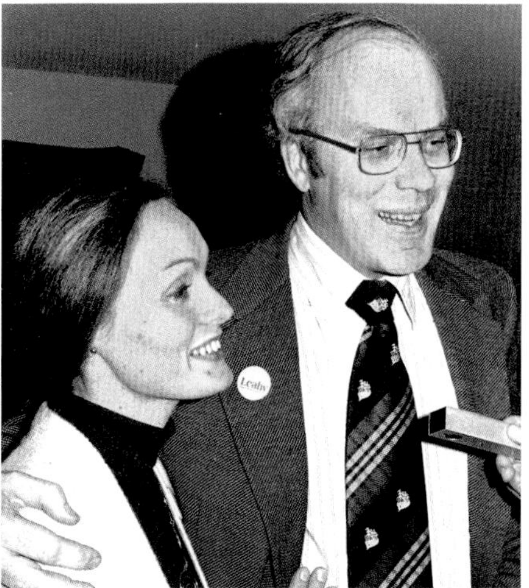

Getting some good news on a close election night in 1974. We campaigned up until the last poll closed, and that was a good thing because I won by a tiny margin.

 9

Conferring with Chairman Stennis. While having completely different political views, we had a good personal relationship.

 10

With Senator Barry Goldwater on a visit to Vermont in 1976. Vermont Adjutant General Reginald Cram is in the background. Goldwater made the trip to see the Vulcan weapons system that was made by General Electric in Burlington.

 11

When I was the junior-most member of the Senate, Hubert Humphrey invited me to join him on a CODEL to the USSR. I snapped this picture of him and Senator Hugh Scott when we met with Soviet leader Leonid Brezhnev. When Humphrey was heading out for a jog one morning, he quipped: "Patrick, bring your camera—this is the only time you will see Hubert Humphrey jogging in Red Square." He was stopped with applause so many times as soon as he went out the door that he never got in that jog.

12

13

Left: Marcelle took this photo of me at the Great Wall of China on a CODEL in 1978 during the Carter administration and prior to normalization. The delegation was led by Budget Committee chairman Ed Muskie, whose young staffer Madeleine Albright was also on the trip. *Above:* With Ted Kennedy, a dear friend and mentor. Our offices were one floor apart and we often walked over together to the Capitol for votes. I will always remember our conversations and his wonderful laugh.

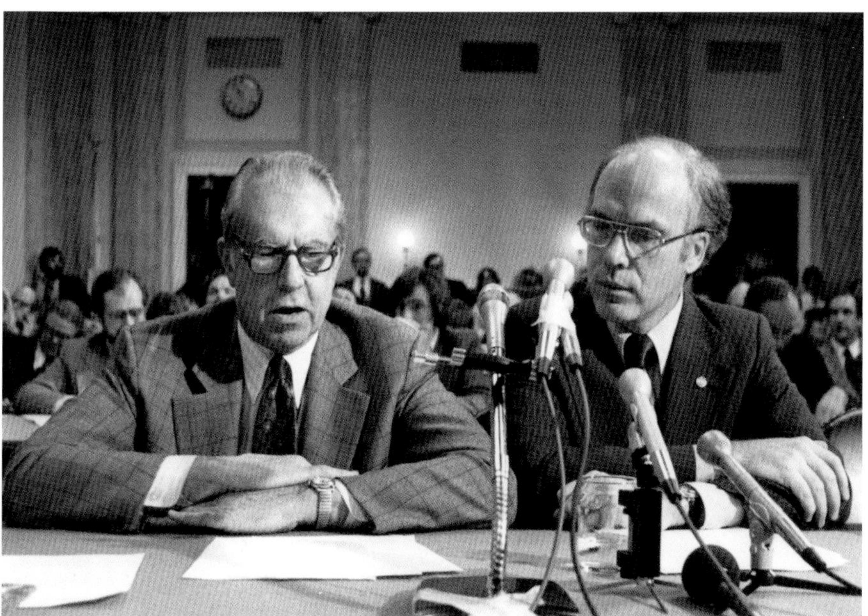

14

Testifying with my friend and partner Vermont Republican senator Bob Stafford. We were in different political parties, but we always worked together on legislation to benefit Vermont.

15 

 16

Left: Meeting with President Carter at the White House. He always made me feel at home. We would often laugh and talk about family before or after official meetings.

Right: I call this my "conscience" photo. I snapped it during a visit to a refugee camp in Central America in 1982. When it was developed, I was forever struck by this man's eyes and expression, as if he were saying: "So what have you done for poor and powerless people today?!" This hangs on my office wall to this day.

 17

Conferring with senators Alan Simpson, Bob Dole, Joe Biden, and "Mac" Mathias at the nomination hearing of Sandra Day O'Connor. A historic nomination that was approved 99-0.

18

In August 1983, I took this picture of USSR General Secretary Yuri Andropov. When it was developed, I realized it showed he had a stent inside his sleeve. He died months later after serving only fifteen months in office. I was the last westerner to photograph him.

19

To Pat Leahy - With Very Best Wishes & Regards Ronald Reagan

President Reagan said this photo I took of his second inauguration was his favorite and happily told people it was taken by a Democrat!

20

Family outing at our home in Vermont.

21

Standing with dairy farmers Bob Howrigan and Albert Tetreault while filming a political commercial in 1986, where we suggested that Vermont farmers should put Leahy campaign bumper stickers on their cows (look for the stickers on the cows behind us) as I was next in line to be chair of the Senate Agriculture Committee.

22

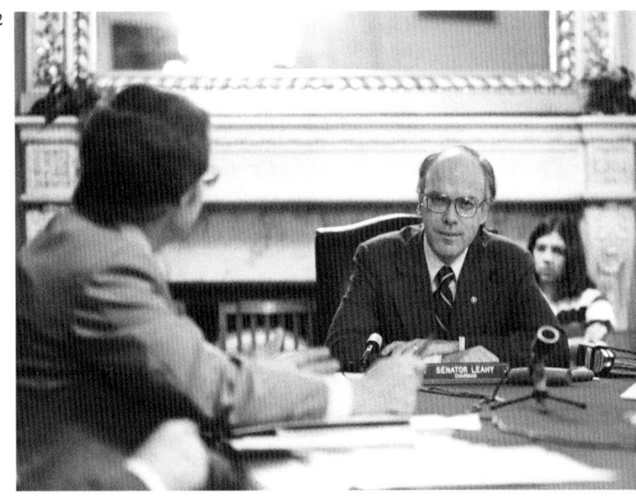

After being reelected in 1986, I became chair of the Ag Committee, which we renamed the Committee on Agriculture, Nutrition, and Forestry. New chairman, broader priorities.

23

In 1988, I led the first Senate CODEL to Tibet. While I was walking through the streets of Lhasa, this man insisted I take a picture of him and the photo he held of the Dalai Lama—risking everything, as Chinese authorities considered that a crime. When asked why he took such a risk, he told the translator: "Because they have to know." When I later showed this picture to the Dalai Lama, he was brought to tears.

24

With President Bush enjoying a Congressional picnic at the White House. He made Republicans and Democrats feel at home, and it was appreciated.

25

President Bush signing the 1990 Farm Bill, my first as chairman of the Senate Committee on Agriculture, Nutrition, and Forestry. The bill included the first-ever title on standards for organic foods, which became the foundation of the soon-to-blossom organic foods industry.

26

President Bush in a light moment in the White House family quarters with Senator Don Riegle and Senator Bennett Johnston looking on. President Bush insisted that I take the picture.

27

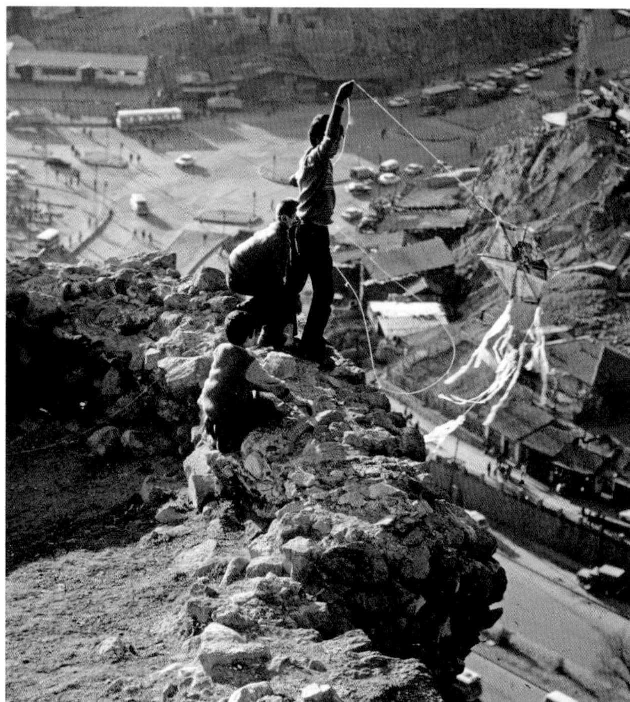

On an official trip to Turkey, I snapped this picture of children perched precariously, trying to get air under a kite on top of ancient Roman ruins that were hundreds of feet above busy Ankara traffic below.

28

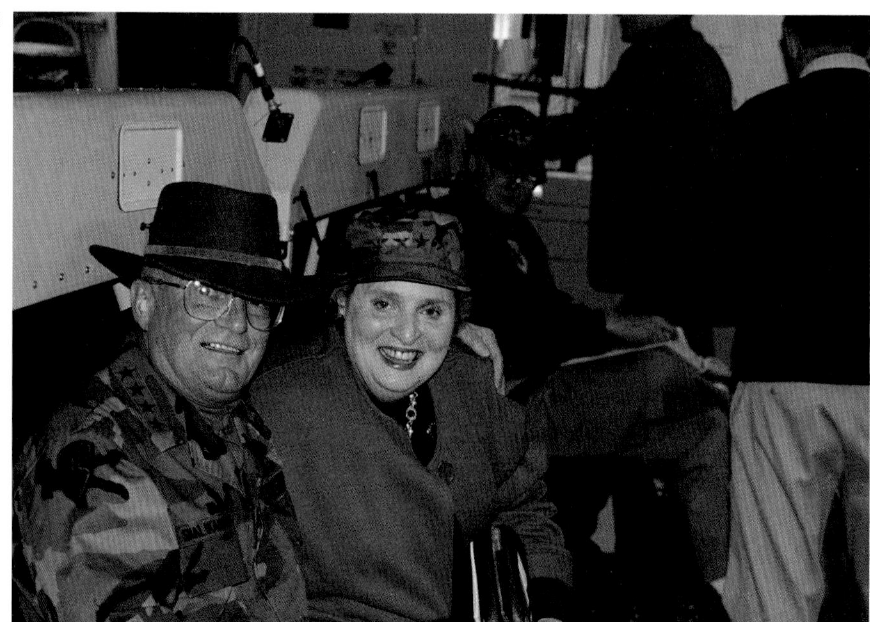

Flying a cargo plane into Bosnia with General Shalikashvili and UN Ambassador Albright, who swapped hats. The plane's call sign was actually Air Force One—note President Clinton, in the background, watching the hat swap.

29

When I attend bill signings at the White House, I have a unique vantage point as a photographer.

30

Access to affordable prosthetics offers those maimed by landmines an ability to walk and work again.

31

On a visit to Havana in 1999, Senator Jack Reed and I had a dinner with President Fidel Castro that lasted for hours, with serious discussions about moving forward toward a more open relationship between our two countries. Marcelle photographed a light moment as Castro signed baseballs.

 32

The light was perfect on the Havana skyline one evening,
so I went on a rooftop to take this photo.

 33

In 1999, I joined former presidents Clinton, Carter, Ford, and Bush at King Hussein's funeral in Amman, Jordan. The King was a remarkable leader for his country and in the Middle East. The attendance by three former presidents and the current one spoke volumes of our strong ties with him and Jordan. I enjoyed sharing stories and talking policy with all four of them during the long flight on Air Force One.

I had the only camera in the Mansfield Room when Barack Obama returned to the Senate for the first time as President Obama, addressing the Democratic caucus beneath the portrait of George Washington—our first president.

34

Marcelle has been my constant partner on the road taken.

35

My office in the Capitol shares a balcony with the House Speaker's. A great vantage point for capturing the Mall at different times of light and weather. I took this at dawn, after the Senate had been in session all night to pass the Affordable Care Act/Obamacare.

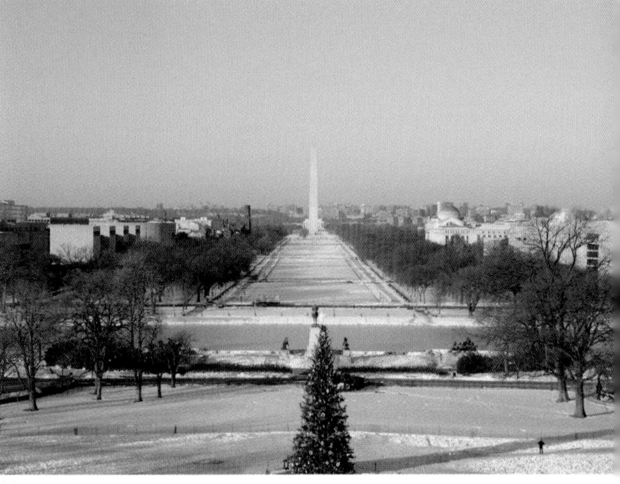

36

Marcelle photographed me cutting a birthday cake that President Obama presented to me on Air Force One en route to Burlington.

37

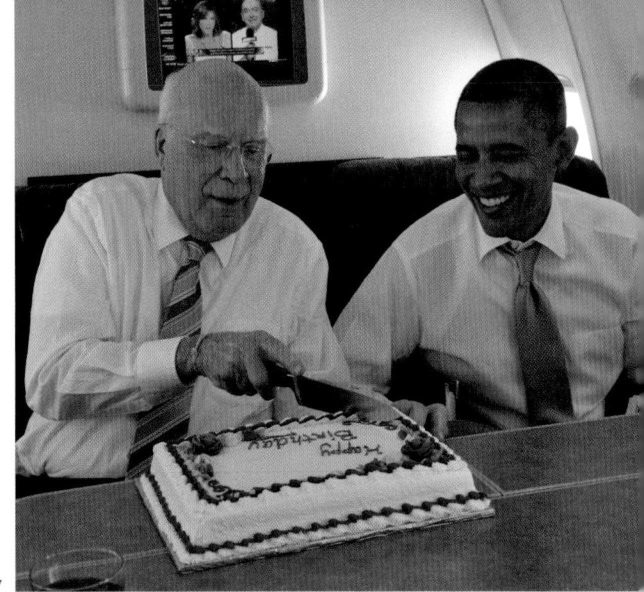

President Obama pointing and giving me his vintage warm smile on Air Force One as he sees me raise my camera in his direction.

38

Campaign parade in 2010 in my hometown, Montpelier, Vermont. Lawrence of Montpelier and Roger of Richmond are the standard bearers.

39

Patrick Leahy
United States Senator
Paid for by: Leahy for U.S. Senator

Congressman and future senator Chris Van Hollen and I visiting Alan Gross during a CODEL to Cuba. When I took a picture of Alan to take back to his wife, he made sure his Cuban handlers were not looking and cracked a wide smile. He knew he was a political prisoner and was not going to give his jailers a photo they could use for propaganda.

40

Freedom! Alan Gross reunited with his wife, Judy, after we took off from Havana. As I took the picture, I knew their hands told the story.

41

At the reopening of the US embassy in Havana, three former Marines who lowered the last US flag there more than fifty years ago returned with the same flag and presented it to the new Marine embassy unit to raise again.

42

43

44

Left: The Dalai Lama showing me the watch that President Roosevelt sent him when he was a young boy.

Right: "Never before in these chairs . . ." Vice President Harris and Speaker Pelosi at the State of the Union. Inspiring.

45

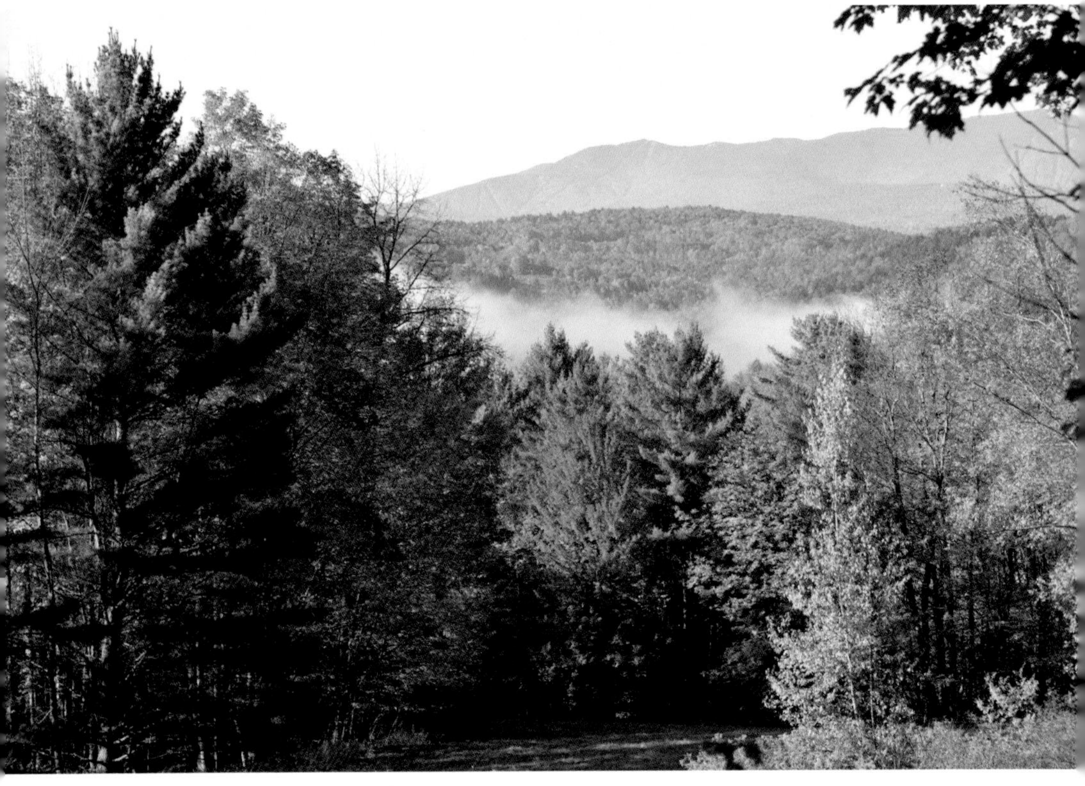

View from our farm in Vermont. Home.

— 47 —

I'll Call You Patrick

"*Pat, the eighties called, they want their sneakers back.*"

I looked down at my scuffed white sneakers. They were certainly broken in and comfortable, with more than their share of miles on the odometer, but never before had they attracted any notice in the Senate gym.

The colleague on the StairMaster next to me knew how to joke and jab like an old pro, a seasoned veteran. He was well versed in talking smack.

"*You're late to the gym today—did you get stuck in front of a camera, Barack?*"

The freshman senator from Illinois let out a big laugh. He could dish it out and take it just as easily.

"*Not bad, Leahy.*"

He kept one hand on the handle of the StairMaster and reached for the remote control to the television set beaming CNN overhead. *Crossfire*, the cable network's long-running flagship debate show, was on the screen, and I could see Barack Obama's eyes narrow disapprovingly. The contrived disagreements, the made-for-television small controversies—something about cable's frenzied furor over too little of substance seemed to irritate him, or at least he deemed it unworthy of his attention.

"*Enough of this,*" he said to no one in particular.

He switched the channel to the NCAA basketball tournament—March Madness.

"Now we're talking. The Fighting Illini!"

Barack Obama grinned, reset the timer on the StairMaster, and started climbing again, as he affixed both eyes on the game. Indeed, his home-state team was making a deep run in the tournament, coming off a great run in the Big Ten Conference, and he had reasons both parochial and impassioned to watch the game.

"Pat, do they play basketball in Vermont?"

"I'll have you know, Barack, you can thank the University of Vermont when you don't have to play Syracuse in the next—"

"I know, Pat. And I appreciate the first-round upset. How did they do in the second round? What was the final score then?"

"Barack, why don't you just watch the game?" I tried to forget that the Catamounts' Cinderella story had turned into a second-round pumpkin, an 11-point loss to Michigan State. We'd all been so proud of Coach Tom Brennan, it was sad to see the ride end.

Obama chuckled.

Most afternoons, he seemed to escape to the Senate gym around the same time I tried to—but while other senators beat a quick path for the steam room or the massage table for their aches and pains, and long conversations, Obama preferred the solitude of a StairMaster or stationary bike.

He wasn't one for idle chitchat, not one of the Senate's revered storytellers, like Ted Kennedy or Chris Dodd. It took a little while to know him, and his flashes of unguarded interior were ephemeral, but they were there.

"Did you grow up in Chicago?"

"No, I mean—where didn't I grow up?" he said with a light self-deprecating laugh.

In an instant, I flashed back to the Democratic National Convention the summer before and the keynote address that had launched this then little-known state senator's sudden and seemingly improbable rise. He'd referenced then his mother from Kansas, his father from Kenya, and a grandfather who "marched in Patton's army." What hadn't fit so neatly into this origin story was a father who left the family and moved back to Africa, a mother who, eager to see and experience the world, uprooted her son and headed for Indonesia, and later years growing up mainly with his grandparents in Hawaii.

"*Michelle's the one from Chicago. We met there.*"

I knew Michelle Obama a little bit through Marcelle, who had been matched with her in the Senate spouses' "big sisters" program, a well-intentioned effort to welcome Senate spouses to Washington and to ease the transition that was hard on so many families. Marcelle took to the role eagerly, remembering always the way Helen Stafford and Colleen Nunn had gone out of their way in 1975 to ease our own transition.

Barack and Michelle were just a few years older than we were when we came to the Senate, but Michelle kindly made it clear that, with two young daughters and her mother living with them, there was only so much up-rooting they were going to manage at once. They weren't putting down new roots in Washington. The family would remain in Hyde Park. Barack was commuting each weekend back to Illinois. Although the endless cycle of flights often left bags under his eyes, he acknowledged it was best for the family: his girls loved their school, their friends, their time with their grandmother, and the neighborhood. I wondered if having experienced so much change himself as a kid was why he was willing to go out of his way to ensure his own children were comforted by a regular routine, familiar places, and a home they could count on.

I couldn't help but wonder whether Barack had ever longed for that kind of tight-knit family as a little boy. John Kerry had once told me about his nomadic childhood, moving from country to country as a foreign service brat, a string of boarding schools, missing out on having a paper route. It was always interesting to me how every colleague had their own unique story, their own individual path that shaped who they were and who they'd become as US senators. There's a lot you can learn about a person if you listen, and particularly if you're not too eager to fill in the silences and actually let someone share with you.

"*Pat—did your family always live in Vermont?*"

As I huffed and puffed on the stationary bike, I told Barack about growing up in Montpelier—my Italian American grandparents just thirty miles away, the stone carvers from Italy who immigrated to Vermont and the quarry workers who emigrated from Ireland, and the modest house that was both home and the print shop for my parents.

"*That's a Norman Rockwell painting,*" he commented, and smiled.

"*If Rockwell was Irish-Italian Catholic in a country club Republican state.*" I shared the story of the unsolicited advice my father had received from the local chamber of commerce: that he might be advised to change his religion from Catholic or his party loyalty from Democratic, or both.

Obama laughed. "*Pat, as the guy who ran after 9/11 and during the Iraq War with the middle name Hussein and a last name that sounds like Osama—I can relate.*"

There was always a shyness with Barack. It wasn't an aloofness, but a reserve, a sense of privacy. I could relate to it myself. Maybe it was growing up with my eyesight a challenge, or coming to the Senate with people twice my age, or a press corps that saw my presence in Washington as altogether "*accidental*"—but you sometimes hold something back for yourself, remain a little private, and protect yourself from being overly familiar. Perhaps because we didn't try to bowl each other over with bromides, Barack and I found a comfortable rapport from the start, and not just in the schoolyard give-and-take and gentle ribbing of two friends sweating out the day's ups and downs on the treadmill.

The following week, we were back together again in the gym.

"*Pat, I noticed something. Your wife calls you Patrick.*"

"*Yes, she does,*" I said, curious as to where this was going.

"*Michelle calls you Patrick too, because she got that from Marcelle.*"

"*Okay.*"

"*What do you prefer?*"

"*Well, in my family, people who know me best do call me Patrick.*"

"*Not Pat.*"

"*As an elected official, Barack, people could call me a lot worse than Pat, but yes, my friends call me Patrick.*"

"*Well, Patrick—we still need to get rid of those ugly sneakers.*"

It was Barack and Patrick from that day forward. But I wasn't relenting on my footwear.

As the summer progressed, we'd have more weighty matters to discuss.

Barack was a onetime editor of the *Harvard Law Review* turned constitutional law professor, and he was fascinated by Judiciary issues even though it was not among his committee assignments. I was the second most senior member of the Judiciary Committee, the committee's ranking member, as Joe Biden had decided to serve as senior Democrat on the Foreign Relations Committee, and I'd experienced nine confirmation debates for the Supreme Court.

My tenth was fast approaching, sooner than I'd hoped.

Confirming Sandra Day O'Connor had been one of my proudest votes as a sophomore senator. I could still hear Barry Goldwater's voice on the Senate subway: "*Keep an open mind, Patrick.*"

For twenty-three years since, she'd been a swing vote on the Supreme Court, where she'd guarded her brand of Goldwater-esque libertarian-leaning conservatism against the Left and the Right, protecting the right to privacy, about which she felt especially strongly. I didn't always agree with her decisions or her dissents, but always I knew she was applying the law with her best judgment and her common sense, honed in a life outside the judicial monastery.

And now, when we least expected it, Justice O'Connor was retiring to spend more time as a loving caretaker to her husband of fifty-three years, John Jay. His Alzheimer's was not a particular secret in Washington, DC, but less well known was the fact that it was getting worse. They'd been together since law school. Sandra was clearly one of those public figures who, when they say they're stepping down to "*spend more time with family,*" really meant it, in the saddest, sweetest way imaginable.

The news of her decision to retire hit me hard, not only because I respected her, but because I feared what would come next.

I didn't have especially high confidence that President Bush would use the first Supreme Court appointment of his presidency to bring the court or the country together. I'd watched four years of a political strategy aimed at sharpening divisions rather than dulling them, and the wounds were fresh among Senate Democrats who had suffered at the pointy end of that Republican wedge.

We'd seen our colleagues lose ugly, blistering races in 2002 and '04. Republicans' take-no-prisoners approach had lasted through the presidential campaign, and John Kerry was back as the junior senator from Massachusetts rather than sitting at the other end of Pennsylvania Avenue.

The president's chief political strategist, Karl Rove, seemed to be a Rasputin-like figure: he was reviled by Democrats, he was known for years as a tough and mean operative, and yet his tactics had worked for the Republicans ever since George W. Bush came into office with the thinnest of Electoral College margins. If there was one issue over which Rove hungered, it was control of the courts—and a chance to deepen the administration's ties with religious conservatives. The year before, his weapon of choice had been gay marriage. Now, I feared, it would be the fight over the O'Connor seat that would take center stage.

Two days after the O'Connor bombshell, the president stood in the Rose Garden and announced that Judge John Roberts of the US Court of Appeals for the DC Circuit would be his choice to replace O'Connor. He was fifty years old and a trusted conservative choice.

Roberts wasn't a stranger to any of us. We'd first faced his nomination for the circuit court four years before, when I was still chairman, and in the larger dispute over judgeships, his nomination had been stuck in limbo and then he was quickly confirmed, with bipartisan support, when control of the Senate switched hands. Two years into his service on the bench, he'd authored forty-nine opinions, mostly unanimous, and three dissents of his own. None of them revealed him to be either a fire-breathing ideologue or a closeted liberal.

I believed the president was choosing to elevate him now to the court because he'd be a conservative jurist—and his nomination a boon to Catholic conservatives whom Rove hoped to pull closer into the GOP fold.

But I didn't believe these were reasons to reject his nomination out of hand. The president had not chosen a firebrand like Samuel Alito, nicknamed "Scalito" as an ideological facsimile to Antonin Scalia.

I'd let the hearings shape my views, not a rush to judgment by interest groups. I remembered how so many of them, on both sides, had been wrong about O'Connor, and were left to eat crow as her confirmation process unfolded.

I was immediately frustrated by the screaming from the activist groups on both sides. Fundraising emails bring out the worst in our politics. If I wasn't ready to roar into a filibuster, I was being too soft on the nominee, was the message from the Left. It chafed. I'd fought against nominees I believed were ill-suited for the court before, from Bork to Thomas. But always—always—I had insisted on the prerogative to keep my own counsel and make my own judgments, the words of Edmund Burke ringing in my head.

The Right, on the other hand, was desperate to label any hesitancy to support Roberts as thoroughly anti-Catholic. An activist in a red shirt, a banner of the pro-life movement, walked by me in the Russell Senate Office Building.

"*Senator Leahy—will you stand up to anti-Catholic bigotry and support John Roberts?*"

"*You know, I was just thinking about that at Mass this Sunday. Thank you for your opinion,*" I replied, and walked along. There was something patronizing in the convenient, sudden interest from so many non-Catholics in defending the faith I'd been baptized in and lived my whole life from Sunday to Sunday.

The hearings were slated for September after the long, hot summer recess. Then another bombshell. Just as we were preparing for one Supreme Court vacancy, a news flash: Chief Justice Rehnquist had died.

In many ways, this was the news we'd all girded ourselves for in the last year. The chief justice had been battling an aggressive thyroid cancer for over a year. He had missed dozens of oral arguments and hadn't looked well at President Bush's inauguration, wan and gray and moving weakly aided by a cane. We'd all worried about the gaunt justice that day.

Now Bill Rehnquist, our summer neighbor from Vermont, was gone too.

President Bush moved quickly and withdrew Roberts's nomination for O'Connor's seat. The question now before the Senate was simple: Would we accept or reject not just a Roberts nomination, but a Roberts court? A fifty-year-old chief justice could leave a forty-year legacy.

The hearings were revealing—for what they revealed and for what they failed to reveal.

Roberts, the former Rehnquist clerk, presented a steadiness and a public commitment to following precedent. He described the role of a jurist as something akin to an umpire in baseball. "*My job is to call balls and strikes and not to pitch or bat,*" he said.

Of course, that's not to say he didn't demonstrate also that he'd be pretty shrewdly discerning standing at the plate with a bat in his hand—carefully avoiding ever swinging at any senator's curveball questions, reserving judgment on policy matters.

But after hours upon hours of thoughtful and intelligent answers, I found myself torn about my own judgment. I didn't doubt Roberts was a conservative. I suspected he may have concealed an affinity for, if not an affiliation with, the conservative movement's post-Souter Federalist Society, although Roberts himself had successfully forced retractions from newspapers that he said wrongly identified him that way. But I didn't come away with a reason to oppose him.

This wasn't Bork.

This wasn't Thomas.

And I personally was pained at the prospect of another Judiciary Committee party-line vote on chief justice.

I announced I'd support Roberts. I knew my staff would've voted the other way. I told my chief of staff Ed Pagano and Bruce Cohen, my brilliant staff director on the Judiciary Committee, that they and the rest of the team didn't have to be with me on the floor when I spoke, but they insisted. My eyes misted over at their loyalty. If Stennis knew something about "Senators" with a capital S, these were all "Staff" with a capital S and an underline. They were the people who made it possible for me to be a senator.

It was a lonely position. There was some solace in the fact that two

Judiciary Committee colleagues, Russ Feingold and Herb Kohl, also followed suit, but both were generally known for approving most nominees of presidents of both parties.

The ire was saved for me, the committee's most senior Democrat. It stung. Some even called for me to relinquish my spot on the committee.

"*You can tell them they're welcome to their opinions,*" I told my Judiciary Committee counsel. "*It's my name on the ballot every six years, not theirs, and I think Vermont knows me.*"

I thought of Abe Ribicoff's warnings in 1979 about the power of interest groups. I'd worked too hard, too long, to govern in fear of my own friends among liberals.

I was sitting in my office a week later, watching the Senate floor on the little television set behind my desk.

"*Mr. President, I'd ask for ten minutes to address the Senate as if in morning business,*" said Barack Obama. He paused, looked down at his notes, and proceeded to deliver an eloquent analysis of why he would be opposing the Roberts nomination.

It was reasoned, it was careful, it was calibrated. We'd come to different conclusions, but both were tough judgment calls. Having heard how Barack would be voting, I turned back to my reading. But then I heard a familiar name in his remarks: my own.

"*I was deeply disturbed by some statements that were made by largely Democratic advocacy groups when ranking member Senator Leahy announced that he would support Judge Roberts,*" said Barack. "*Although the scales have tipped in a different direction for me, I am deeply admiring of the work and the thought that Senator Leahy has put into making his decision. The knee-jerk unbending and what I consider to be unfair attacks on Senator Leahy's motives were unjustified. Unfortunately, both parties have fallen victim to this kind of pressure.*"

I was stunned.

In a Senate where, too often, very few senators even really knew each other anymore, Barack had done something no one had asked him to do—without any imaginable reward whatsoever. He had defended a colleague's judgment and integrity against pressure groups that would have surely otherwise applauded every word coming out of his mouth. And he hadn't even told me he was doing it, let alone asked for anything in return. I thought of my freshman conversation with an astonished Russell Long: "*But I never promised you or gave you anything . . .*"

Thirty years later, I was the one whose turn had come to be pleasantly taken by the kindness and thoughtfulness of a colleague committed to defending my judgment and prerogatives as a US senator.

I pulled Barack aside on the floor that evening. "*Barack, that meant a lot—*"

He cut me off and patted my arm. Barack didn't do emotional conversations. "*Patrick, I said what I believed. If I didn't, I wouldn't.*"

My eyes watered.

"*But, Leahy, we still have to do something about your sneakers.*"

— 48 —

Encouragement

Soon enough, I was having a different quiet conversation with Barack Obama.

"*I think you* should *think about it, Barack. Actually, I think you should do more than think about it. I think you ought to run.*"

We sat in my Capitol office, facing each other from opposing wing-back chairs.

A long night of votes at the end of this Congress was almost through, and we'd both be heading home the next morning.

Just weeks before, the 2006 elections had changed the entire political outlook in Washington. Ever since 2002, we'd been on the outside looking in: Democrats hadn't controlled the White House, the House, or the Senate.

After 2004, Karl Rove, whom the president had described as "*the architect*" of his presidency, had even predicted that "*structural issues*" in the United States could keep the Senate and White House in Republican hands for a generation. We'd been through an awkward political adolescence, with pundits hypothesizing whether Democrats had to change on core issues of belief and conviction—civil rights, human rights, the right to privacy—in order to even have a fighting chance at the ballot box. It felt reminiscent of the endless political autopsies after the Reagan revolution of 1980.

But on November 7, Democrats had run the table, winning back the House and the Senate—and the pessimism that had accompanied the two bitter Bush victories had been replaced by a giddy optimism that in 2008 we could win the White House again. The most in-demand surrogate for the party this election cycle, one of the few liberals invited to campaign from Virginia to Montana to little Rhode Island, was Barack Obama. He'd been greeted everywhere by swelling crowds.

Now, Obama said, opinion leaders were calling him from around the country, urging him to run.

"*I'm not surprised. Barack, you've touched a chord with people.*"

"*I'd ruled this out, on television and with the press.*"

"*What does your family think?*"

"*Michelle isn't there yet. She's also skeptical of all these new friends.*"

"*She's smart. When you ran for Senate in that primary, you did it without these new friends—*"

"*They were all with the other guys.*"

"*Barack, when I first ran in Vermont, no one thought I had a chance, besides me and Marcelle. That's what counts—the two of you. What do you think? Do you want to run for president? And do you want to be president?*"

"*Those are two different questions.*"

"*They're very different questions.*" I shared with Barack lessons learned from some of the good friends I'd seen run for president from the Senate—Fritz Mondale, Ted Kennedy, and John Glenn among them. "*I've known people who ran because they thought it was their time or their turn. I've seen some people who would've been very good presidents who weren't very good candidates. But I've never seen someone win who didn't want to run and who didn't want to do the job.*"

"*Like Teddy Kennedy.*"

"*Ted found out he loved the Senate. Is this where you see yourself?*"

Obama paused. "*Patrick, I get frustrated here sometimes. I think you probably do too. There's a lot of talk for talk's sake—this isn't exactly a golden age of legislating, Patrick. Washington is so balkanized . . .*"

We talked about the changes I'd seen here: how the Senate had, regrettably, become more like the House; how the very definition of the word "senator" itself seemed to be shrinking with each successive election. How politics had come to feel like a blood sport in some quarters. How voting percentages seemed to go down year after year, as Americans threw up their hands about the political process.

It was an interesting and an unexpected commonality we discovered in our conversation: in our own ways, Barack and I had both come here as outsiders. The Watergate Class of 1974 was determined to fix Washington. And we had. We'd forced open government to sunshine, the best disinfectant. We'd been mentored by an old guard of institutionalists whose faith in the ability of institutions to respond when it mattered had been redeemed again and again. And I'm convinced that the reforms we passed—from oversight of the FBI, the CIA, and campaign finance—had stanched the bleeding of Watergate.

But exactly thirty years later, Barack arrived at a Senate in paralysis. Mike Mansfield would never have allowed a partisan White House to set the agenda in the Senate. Barack as a freshman senator in 2005 did not find a Mike Mansfield occupying the majority leader's office. Instead, he saw an extension of the Bush White House, and it left him skeptical that the Senate could ever again be what I had known it to be. It reminded me of an old saying: "Where you stand is where you sit." From where he sat as the junior senator from Illinois, Barack thought change could come only from the outside, and clearly that his opportunity to shape it was from the bottom up, not the inside out.

"I was thinking of running for governor. Be closer to the kids, be home, executive decision-making—get something done . . . but for one of those same reasons, I'm thinking about doing this now. Hillary has got a big head start. But this feels—"

"Barack, moments come along. Waves, really. They wash away the best-laid plans. Think about Lyndon Johnson. Incredibly successful Senate leader, piles of endorsements—Hubert Humphrey had been a star since the 1948 convention—and none of them could stop what John F. Kennedy tapped into."

Barack let the comment hang in the air for a minute.

"And for the record, Barack, I know you think I've been here forever, but

among the three of them, I only served with Hubert, and that was long after he ran . . ."

Obama laughed. "*Noted!*"

"*Of course, Barack, I won't talk about this with anyone while you're running. Besides, I'm the only senator not thinking of running for president in 2008. Who else would you be able to talk to?*"

"*The Clinton folks are running on her inevitability—the inevitability of her nomination, the inevitability that only they know how to win presidential elections.*"

"*I don't think our party usually works that way. No one wins a nomination a year before Iowa,*" I said. And I believed it. "*Barack, you know, the first presidential candidate I ever sat down with face-to-face was Jimmy Carter. 1974. We met at the Hanover Inn just over the border in New Hampshire. Nobody thought I had a chance for Senate or that he had a shot for president. Humphrey was probably going to run, maybe Teddy; Birch Bayh was running, Mo Udall, Scoop Jackson, all the big names. But I walked away from that breakfast, and I knew Jimmy Carter wasn't there for the pancakes. He was running because he believed in his candidacy. Carter tapped into something.*"

"*If I do this, will you be with me?*"

"*Barack, I'm here to talk any time. And I'll be there if you need me in Vermont or nationally. But I learned a long time ago, you don't win the presidency on endorsements, and it's better not to hurt a relationship with a colleague when other senators are running. A lot of senators have Irish amnesia, you know.*"

"*What's that?*"

"*They only remember the names of the people who endorsed their opponents.*"

"*That's pretty good, Leahy.*"

We shook hands, I walked him out, and Barack Obama went on his way down the Capitol corridor. His lanky aide stood nearby, wearily weighed down by a stack of binders for Obama to bring home to Chicago. I suspected I knew what decision Barack would make, even if he hadn't fully arrived there himself.

One quality I found refreshing about Barack was his candor, his instinct that there was a certain currency in sharing the truth, even if it was inconvenient. Armies of pollsters counseled that candidates must never "flip-flop," and this was certainly the popular conventional wisdom after George Bush had made the 2004 election a referendum on his certitude, whether right or wrong, versus the alleged indecision of his opponent. Obama wasn't cowed into twisting himself into knots in order to preserve some artificial version of the truth. Shortly after our conversation, he appeared on *Meet the Press*. He had unequivocally ruled out running for president, said Tim Russert—would he reconsider? Yes, Obama replied. He was reconsidering. *He had changed his mind,* he said succinctly. No artifice, no contortion. How refreshing, I thought.

Marcelle and I, together with the family, spent a blissful Christmas week at home in Vermont, steering clear of cable news and the chatter of the Sunday political talk shows. But by New Year's Day, word was leaking out: Barack Obama, just forty-six and three years removed from the state senate in Springfield, was soon announcing that he'd be running for president of the United States.

True to my conversation with Barack, I held back on any endorsements and watched the race with interest. The field was quickly crowded. My two old friends and colleagues since 1975 and 1981, Joe Biden and Chris Dodd, were running on the basis of their experience and time-tested credentials. They both reported how difficult it was to earn media attention in a field dominated by Barack—and by the perceived front-runner, just entering her second term in the Senate, my colleague from New York Hillary Clinton.

I liked Hillary. She had been unfairly vilified by the right wing during eight years in the White House as First Lady, and it left her understandably mistrustful of the media and at times suspicious of the political process. But she was smart and funny, and it was no small irony that both Hillary and Barack, in private, defied all the public stereotypes of them and their candidacies. Barack was seen publicly as a great orator, exuding charisma; but behind closed doors, he could be quiet, reserved, and even shy. Hillary was portrayed by many as calculated and scripted; in private, she was loose and witty. I could have pictured her holding court in Mike Mansfield's back room, more sure-footedly than many of the men.

Hillary had grown up in suburban Illinois, but she'd spent the better part of her life since in two states that proudly considered large swaths of their constituencies rural: Arkansas and New York, the latter with its upstate apple orchards and farming communities. She was fluent in the political language spoken outside big cities. We could talk agriculture, we could talk about the patches of red in our very blue states, and always I found her earnest. I often wished her critics could get to know *that* side of Hillary.

Still, my political thermometer told me that this year, on the Democratic side at least, would be defined by one word: "change." America had been through the wringer. The Bush years had begun with a divided election, escalated with rampant partisanship, the traumas of 9/11, the hubris of Iraq, the screeching of cable news. Theories had been punctured; the best and brightest of the Republican Party had led America into a quagmire overseas and a financial collapse at home that left Americans with a deep sense of unfairness. They were tired of being divided, tired of ideology, and tired of being told that the experts and elites had all the answers. The stage was set for something different.

Both Barack and Hillary represented change—the first African American and the first woman to mount big leads in a highly competitive field. But I suspected that the biggest change wasn't actually demographic, it was directional. I'd seen this movie before. Gary Hart had nearly upended Fritz Mondale's march to the nomination in 1984 with his promise of "new ideas." Gary had run out of steam and money, when the unions and African American voters in the South decided that, between two popular choices, one known and one less defined, they trusted Fritz Mondale more.

This time, it was the same but different. Barack and Hillary were both good, popular Democrats. Many of their policy differences were magnified in the fun-house mirrors of primary politics, the "instinct for the capillary" that Ted Kennedy used to joke about—how pundits and press strained to make any nuanced disagreement grow in importance.

But the biggest difference in this choice was real, and it was becoming symbolic of other differences, including generational ones, and was simple: Barack had opposed the Iraq War from the start, as I had, while Hillary had supported the invasion. No explaining or parsing could change it. For Democratic voters, it was the original sin of politics, and the ultimate break from George W. Bush was to nominate someone who had foreseen his deadly blunder from the start.

The Iraq vote followed Hillary everywhere. Chris Dodd told me it was the issue that came up at every political pit stop along the snowy roads of Iowa. "*How is it that every presidential candidate who got an intelligence briefing voted for it?*" Chris said wearily. It didn't matter that on every Iraq policy issue since 2002, they were all in concordance—agreed that Bush had managed the war dreadfully, opposed Abu Ghraib, opposed de-Baathification of the Iraqi military—it was the one disagreement that counted to voters. Barack was the only one who could tell the voters that he had opposed the misjudgment from the start.

By Thanksgiving, the days in Senate session grew shorter along with the disappearing daylight. On the Senate floor, those of us who were spectators to the presidential process swapped gossip. We could feel the field narrowing to just three: Barack, Hillary, and John Edwards, our former colleague who had left the Senate in 2004 and had been picked to serve as John Kerry's running mate. We swapped tidbits and political intelligence from the trail.

Ted Kennedy felt torn among five friends all running for the prize. He saw in Barack Obama shades of his brother Jack. He told me that he saw in John Edwards the passion of his brother Bobby and thought Edwards was tapping into something potent in Iowa. His family had long ties to the Clintons, but he clearly felt slightly put off by the lobbying he'd received for an early endorsement. Ted also felt conflicted about his close friend Chris Dodd's underdog campaign, and felt that both Chris and Joe Biden deserved to play out their own races in Iowa without endorsements of the front-runners potentially adding another burden to their already formidable load.

Marcelle and I watched eagerly as the Iowa caucuses quickly approached. On January 3, just three days into the new year, the news that evening was a record turnout. More than 239,000 Iowans came out to deliberate and discuss whom they would want to slingshot on to New Hampshire as their preferred potential standard-bearer for the Democrats. It was as if Democrats had organized their own papal conclave, and the winner would be greeted not with white smoke, but with a first-class ticket to the Granite State and a bevy of positive headlines. Political momentum was Iowa's chief export as much as corn or soybeans.

The results were a political earthquake. Barack Obama bested John Edwards by 8 points, Hillary running a close and disappointing third. Chris and Joe officially suspended their campaigns. I felt the sting for Chris and Joe, but knew that both were institutions within the institution, and they could return to the Senate with chairmanships that were the best imaginable consolation prizes.

Barack soared to double-digit polling leads in New Hampshire, and conventional wisdom shifted yet again: his momentum appeared unstoppable.

"Appeared," of course, is the key word. Hillary's grit and resilience were unmistakable. She'd built an impressive organization in New Hampshire, where her ties went back to Bill Clinton's 1992 "*comeback kid*" finish, which resuscitated his own presidential bid. Something I'd learned in 1974 in Vermont proved true again: voters don't like being told that an outcome is "*inevitable*." They didn't like it when the press proclaimed that Richard Mallary was a shoe-in to succeed George Aiken. They didn't cotton to it when Hillary's campaign appeared built on a foundation of "inevitability." They didn't like it when the roles were reversed and the pundits were prematurely declaring Barack the *inevitable* winner and the certain momentum-driven nominee in New Hampshire. I suspected the results in New Hampshire would be closer than expected.

Marcelle and I escaped the cold of Vermont and Washington, DC, to the Caribbean for a week and a long-delayed scuba-diving trip, but we were glued to the television at night to watch the news of the coming primary. Television showed a powerful clip of Hillary talking about the reasons she persisted in the campaign, her determination not to let down a generation of women who had struggled. It was raw and real; she choked up, and in that flash of emotion, you could see the real person her colleagues knew from behind the scenes in the Senate. "*That's going to hit home with a lot of women,*" said Marcelle. I nodded. Marcelle's sixth sense for politics had kicked in once again, her PhD in people still my best guide after forty-two years in public service.

Watching the primary results trickle in on Tuesday evening, I could feel the uncertainty. The cable news programs were clearly influenced by the polls and by the results in Iowa just one week before: their entire frame of reference was whether Barack could achieve a knockout punch. Exit polls were showing a race that was in the low single digits, I heard from John Podesta, who was working closely with Hillary.

The evening grew later and later. Barack's big victory was not coming to pass. When Manchester's working-class wards came in, Hillary had climbed into a lead of almost eight thousand votes and declared victory. This race wasn't going to end quickly—or neatly. Barack delivered a concession speech that only reminded me why I had invested such hopes in his ability to unite the party and the country. It was an optimistic speech about a struggle that would continue.

I didn't sleep well that night. I'd always been up front with Barack that I hoped the politics could work themselves out, that I'd be a private consigliere and sounding board.

But I didn't feel I could stay on the sidelines any longer and be true to my grandkids. Besides, after thirty-three years in the Senate, I'd earned the right to make the case for a friend—not against another friend, but in support of a colleague.

Marcelle and I scuba dived in the morning.

I emailed Barack afterward. He called my BlackBerry. He had already landed in South Carolina.

"*That was the best concession speech I've ever heard, Barack.*"

"*Well, Patrick, I hope I don't have to make too many more of those.*"

"*Barack, I want to endorse you and help any way I can.*"

There was a pause at the end of the line. Obama seemed to process the news.

"Patrick, that would mean a lot to me."

It's not loyalty or friendship if you're only there when it's easy, I told myself.

"Let's work out the details with our staffs."

"Thanks, Patrick. And, Marcelle—will you please be sure to put some sunscreen on that bald head of his? We can't have him blistered when he's out stumping for me."

Marcelle laughed.

"Hold on, Barack, I think I have John McCain on the other line—I may need to talk to John about supporting him instead," I joked.

"Leahy—you're a good man."

Speaking to reporters gathered on a telephone line shortly before the South Carolina primary, I shared my conviction about what Barack alone was best suited to do for the United States.

"We need a president who can reintroduce America to the world and reintroduce America to ourselves," I said. I meant it.

Barack won the South Carolina primary by 150,000 votes and was on his way to the Democratic nomination for president.

— 49 —

They Got Their Man

"*The FBI is calling, Patrick. They have Director Mueller for you.*"

It had been seven years since the anthrax attacks killed two postal workers in Washington, a publisher in Florida, a Vietnamese immigrant living in the Bronx, and a ninety-four-year-old woman in Connecticut and upended all the action in Congress for one disrupted autumn. The law enforcement process that followed was punctuated by frequent stops and starts, breakthroughs followed by dead ends, and leaks. It had been a drawn-out, interminable investigation. It was now four full years since my security detail went away, not because we'd learned anything new, but because we hadn't. The absence of urgency, I realized, is very different from the presence of closure.

Until now, perhaps.

The rumors from the FBI had indicated that it might be zeroing in on a culprit. I had steeled myself to dismiss the chatter, especially after a 2002 search of the home of a Fort Detrick scientist named Steven Hatfill seemingly led to little more than a multimillion-dollar suit against the government.

As I took the phone from Marcelle, peering out at a beautiful August morning in Middlesex, I had a twinge of phantom pain from those sleepless nights in 2001, when it always felt as if I were one phone call, one siren, one pair of flashing lights away from knowing more about why I'd been targeted and by whom. But the answers had never come, and over time the feeling of anxiousness, the immediacy of the threat, had faded some. Anniversaries resurfaced it. News stories brought it raging back, with all the complex emotions and memories of that time.

I'd almost given up hope that I'd ever learn what had really happened.

"Senator Leahy—it's Bob Mueller. I have some news to share with you about the investigation."

"The investigation?"

"Senator, we were about to make an arrest of the perpetrator behind the anthrax letters. We've built the case over two years. The evidence is very strong. I'd say definitive. Unfortunately, I'm sorry to report to you that the suspect has expired."

"*Expired?*" I shook my head in disbelief.

"Chairman Leahy, the decedent knew that we were about to make the arrest. He overdosed on pills. He couldn't be revived."

I thought back to my days as a prosecutor. One of the hardest phone calls to make was to share with a family the long-sought resolution of a cold case. The hardest ones were kidnapping cases. It was never good news being shared. There were no happy endings. But the hardest and heaviest phone calls were to share the conclusion with a family that a kidnapper or killer had been identified—but that the offender was deceased. Those phone calls or meetings were marked by an unforgettably painful flicker of cognition, the very moment when a family realizes that not only would there never be justice, there wouldn't even be answers. They were denied the chance to look a killer in the eye and ask him "Why?"

For seven years, Marcelle and I hoped for closure, but answers never arrived. Now I doubted they ever would. That hope was extinguished in a handful of twenty codeine-filled pills swallowed by a killer.

"Bob—can you at least share something—I mean, who was it?"

Mueller paused.

"Senator—Pat—we can get you a full briefing. But he was local. A microbiologist at Fort Detrick . . ."

"So, it was Hatfill after all?"

"No, Senator—it was someone else. A fellow by the name of Bruce Ivins. He was actually one of the scientists involved in the investigation."

I searched for the right words. They weren't forthcoming. The arsonist had been helping to investigate the fire he set?

"Was he part of a cell?"

"Senator—we will do a full write-up of how we got here. But we don't have any information suggesting he was anything but a lone operator."

"And what's the motive?"

"There was some evidence from the search that he was fixated on you and other Catholic pro-choice politicians—Tom Daschle too obviously—but we can't say for sure. You know we don't get to shoot from the hip. You wouldn't want us to. There will be a more comprehensive investigation."

I thanked the FBI director for the call and sat down on the couch. The range of emotions—relief, frustration, anger, and then a hollow emptiness—all surged through me one after another like little pulses of electricity.

Seven years. I'd been reading a biography of Winston Churchill, who had described the years of appeasement in the run-up to World War II as "the years the locusts ate." The phrase seemed apt right now. Seven long years and millions of dollars in an FBI investigation consuming thousands of hours and travel to a number of countries searching for terrorist biochemical cells, and now I was told the killer was inside our own laboratory less than an hour from the Capitol?

I thought about Steven Hatfill. Attorney General Ashcroft and his office had pointed to him, ultimately named him a "person of interest," and carefully leaked investigators' surmisals to reporters so that the reporters would know they were focused on the right target. They kept releasing more theories about Hatfill, always to the press, not to Congress, and ultimately Hatfill lost his job. Now I was supposed to believe that one of his coworkers a few offices away was the domestic terrorist all along, hiding in plain sight?

Bruce Ivins.

I struggled to feel convinced that he acted alone. How did he have the capability to weaponize anthrax? Did he have help in weaponizing it from someone? I considered a darker thought. I'd been in the Senate when the Church Report came out. I remembered the long line of secretive and extralegal activities carried out by the CIA during the sixties and seventies, without oversight. Did Ivins somehow have access to already weaponized anthrax, made illegally by the government or held in some classified area left over from the Cold War when it should've been long ago destroyed? If that were the case, it wasn't hard to imagine that to avoid scandal, someone would want to misdirect the FBI to believe he had been a lone operator.

But now we'd never really know.

Previously, the FBI had been accused of a rush to judgment with Hatfill; now, it had gone out of its way to be cautious before arresting Ivins. So cautious, in fact, that it tipped its hand to him and gave him an escape hatch to avoid the death penalty—and that option was suicide—and before he'd ever be forced to answer for his crimes in court. Now, we would only be left with a pile of questions a dead man wasn't going to be able to answer.

Mountains of circumstantial evidence would be interesting. But I mourned the lost chance to be a prosecutor again, to ask questions directly of someone whose actions or his role in a series of actions had thrown so many lives into chaos. Why were my name, Senator Daschle's, and Tom Brokaw's chosen as targets?

Where was any semblance of justice for the elderly woman whose mail might have just brushed up against an anthrax letter, or for the newsperson in Florida, or for the Vietnamese immigrant in New York who somehow came in contact with another stray lethal letter—why did five innocent people have to die?

Some questions only God could answer.

But others deserved better responses from the FBI. I rubbed my palms against my forehead. I would have to live without answers. But unlike five others who hadn't been so lucky, I had a sunny, beautiful day waiting for me to spend with my family, with Marcelle by my side.

— 50 —

A Weight Lifted

After the anthrax chapter receded more and more into the background, I found that a weight had been lifted. Instead of returning to and dwelling on the sense of security that had been lost, I was able to appreciate more the experiences I *did* have because of my service and my seniority in the Senate, especially the experiences and relationships with friends and colleagues that I could only have dreamed of in my earlier years.

One of those relationships that deepened was with the now senior senator from Delaware, Joe Biden. So much had changed since he'd swung through Vermont in 1974 to support the Vermont Democratic Party. After I joined him, however improbably, in 1975, we were the two youngest members of the Senate. We could laugh about that first event where we'd seen each other in action. Biden still wasn't quite sure how he had been roped into attending a state party function, which he said you could've fit inside a phone booth. But we had a lot in common—tall, Irish, Catholic, with young families, even similar hairlines—and similar interests. We quickly became friendly, even though we both gravitated toward deeper mentor-mentee relationships with older senators.

While I was getting to know those titans tending bar for them at night in Leader Mansfield's back room, Biden got to know them in the gym, where the frazzled father snuck in to lift weights, shower and shave, and sometimes sneak a quick nap. Biden wasn't around the Capitol most evenings, when he rushed to catch the last Amtrak up to Wilmington, where his boys awaited his return each night. Senator John McClellan, chairman of the Appropriations Committee when Biden arrived in the Senate, had told him that the only way to move on from the loss of his wife and daughter was to "work, work, work," but Biden had been determined to be both a good father and a good senator at the same time.

As we grew older, sometimes our common interests and longevity in the Democratic caucus created not tension, but question marks. When we were in the majority, Biden had a slight lead over me in time invested on the Judiciary Committee, but, like me, he had a love of foreign policy and could also claim the top perch on the Foreign Relations Committee. Which would we choose? We never knew. I didn't let it worry me too much. Biden seemed genuinely committed to sticking with the Foreign Relations Committee, which I could relate to, given how much I loved the Foreign Operations Subcommittee chairmanship on Appropriations. I urged the staff to relax and not look over their shoulders.

Besides, I was confident Biden and I could work out any turf issues if they arose. We were both happily old school about the institution. In the spring, after he'd run for president and dropped out, and as Senators Obama and Clinton pushed on in a marathon race for the nomination, Biden and I ended up in Europe together for a conference. It had become commonplace during the George W. Bush years for Democratic senators to travel overseas just to communicate by our presence that there were still Americans who believed very deeply in working with our traditional allies. It didn't repair all that Iraq had torn apart in the transatlantic relationship, but it helped underscore at least that all wasn't lost at home. Biden and I found ourselves on that same circuit now and again.

At the end of a long day of government meetings and conference appearances in Paris, Joe and I were both feeling a little "conferenced out." His wife, Jill, whom he had married in 1977, and Marcelle were both back at the CODEL hotel. Joe and I agreed we had earned a "dispensation" from the embassy's "official dinner," and we decided instead to go out, just the four of us, to a place where we could quietly catch up outside the glare of a working dinner.

Marcelle and I remembered a small bistro that we had been to before, very informal with superb food. It was the perfect spot to loosen our ties, relax, and talk about something besides all that was breaking or broken in the world. Biden had moved on from his presidential campaign, and he confided that for the first time in a long time, he was enjoying that he wasn't running for something or gearing up to run for something. It was a feeling as disorienting as it was liberating. He was in a good position in Delaware as I was in Vermont. If there was a future he was focused on, it was his son Beau's. As the attorney general of Delaware, many saw Beau as a successor when Biden hung up his Senate spikes. Joe's pride in Beau was palpable.

"Pat, remember when we were the young upstart liberals the Republicans had on their list to come after every six years?" He laughed. We both remembered those days, and just how many friends disappeared from the Senate in 1978 and '80 thanks to the sophisticated Republican targeting. Joe and I were among a tiny number left who remembered those days.

We talked about the giants of the Senate we'd both learned from. Stennis had been a friend to both of us. Joe had a different relationship with Strom Thurmond, who defended him in 1987, and even Jesse Helms, with whom he had worked on the Senate Foreign Relations Committee, from the one I did. We talked about it. We had both heard Mike Mansfield's advice to remember that in the case of every senator "*someone's state had found a good reason to send them here.*" Biden believed it was entirely true; I believed that every rule has its exception.

"*I'm still looking for that good reason with Helms,*" I joked. Joe laughed.

Mostly, we discussed two topics: the breakdown of the Senate and the joy of our families.

Joe brought the conversation back to something Chris Dodd had shared with him: that a Senate where no one really knew each other wasn't a Senate that could work very well for very long. We both felt a responsibility to bring the institution a step or two back toward what it had once been. But Joe and I were two of the only ones who remembered it that way; others, like John Warner of Virginia—whom we jokingly called "the Squire"—were retiring, while still others, like Howell Heflin, were in the grave.

The other topic was family. We talked about becoming grandparents, how transformative it was. Marcelle and Jill had been friends for a long time. They loved to laugh together. But it was wonderful to hear Jill talk about their grandchildren—Beau's and Hunter's children. I remembered both boys as little kids coming to the Senate on spring break to see their dad, the doting, dedicated single father. Jill had come along and made them one seamless, loving family. Hunter and Beau were her children too, before they added a daughter named Ashley. She brought out the best in Joe.

"Beau's going to be deployed this summer," Joe said. Attorney General Biden was in the Delaware National Guard. He was bound for Iraq. His father had been pressing for the Pentagon to buy more up-armored Humvees for years. Now, he and Jill would soon worry about having that young father himself in a war zone. "*He's just so good, Patrick—you know, he didn't have to go to Iraq. He didn't want special treatment.*"

It was one of the most enjoyable nights Marcelle and I had shared in the Senate in a long, long time.

As we walked back to the hotel afterward, it was almost the top of the hour, and I mentioned that the Eiffel Tower lights up with twinkling lights for a few minutes every hour on the hour every night. It was almost ten o'clock and there was an empty park bench. I said to Joe, "Why don't you and Jill stand on the park bench, and I'll get a picture of the two of you with the Eiffel Tower behind you twinkling away?"

Click, click, click—I handed the camera to Jill and took one with Marcelle in the same pose. What Joe didn't know was that Jill and Marcelle conspired that I would pretend the picture didn't come out, because Jill already had plans for it. Back in the Senate, Joe kept asking me about the picture. I told him I had problems with the camera, but I sent it back to the factory and they were trying to retrieve the information and get the picture. He was honestly disappointed, and he said, "Well, we had a great evening and that's what counts."

Joe and Jill had an anniversary coming up, and she took the picture of them with the Eiffel Tower behind them fully illuminated and had it matted in a silver frame engraved to read JOE YOU LIGHT UP MY LIFE. HAPPY ANNIVERSARY!

I got a call very early the next morning from Joe.

"Patrick, you're a terrible liar—but I forgive you."

Joe and Jill, Patrick and Marcelle, these moments really were a kind of glue that holds the Senate together.

Months later, Barack Obama would add Joe Biden to the presidential ticket as vice president—and another friend would move on to the White House, where, like Walter Mondale, he too would be a bridge back to the Senate, and the Senate of old.

Life in the majority was rewarding. The opportunity to make good things happen instead of just stopping bad things from happening was what made being a legislator energizing, and I hoped that some of my younger colleagues were drinking it in, savoring it, remembering it, so they'd understand always what the institution could be. Sure, we had only fifty-one votes in the Senate, and yes, we were in a transitional period, the last year of an administration of the opposite political party. There were limits on what we could achieve, but we could achieve something. Hope was on the way for a Democrat in the White House again, as Barack Obama steamed ahead, or, even the alternative of a President John McCain. John had taken some odd twists and turns to become the Republican nominee; his trademarked "straight talk" had given way to some compromises he wasn't especially proud to have made to become the nominee of an ideologically orthodox political party. But he was a senator at his core, and if he were president, he would find a way to work with us. But I was energized by the thought of having Barack in the White House next year. We were three weeks from a convention in August that would officially make him our party standard-bearer for the fall campaign.

Shortly after the Fourth of July, we were poised to vote for a second time on a measure to help doctors who treated Medicare patients. In a Senate where the average age was north of seventy, this should've been an issue close to home, if not for everyone's older constituents, then at least for their own families. We were going to vote to prevent a coming 10 percent cut to the reimbursement rate for those physicians. The only real opponents of the measure were the big insurance companies, and yet, in a surprise, we'd lost on this almost exact measure weeks before. We'd lost by a single vote, with one of our senators out sick, Ted Kennedy, who was battling brain cancer. We were trying again; there was hope that a Republican or two would break our way.

I heard a stirring on the Senate floor. Senators who had been milling about or talking among themselves craned their necks to see what the buzz was all about. A crowd parted and revealed a familiar thick shock of white hair. It was Ted Kennedy. We all knew Ted had been trying to spend the summer at home in Massachusetts to preserve his health and strength with chemotherapy weakening his body. But here he was, unexpectedly.

Stooped a bit, slowed by his perpetually bad back, Ted walked toward the well of the Senate and raised his thumb high in the air so the clerk could record his "yes" vote, and the gallery upstairs burst into cheers.

More than a few senators had tears in their eyes.

Ted was quick to leave, surrounded by aides and by John Kerry and Chris Dodd, who escorted him back out. A plane waited to whisk him back home.

After Ted left, the roll call vote ticked down. To everyone's surprise, instead of winning by one vote as expected, sixty-nine senators backed Medicare and seemed to stand with Teddy. It was enough votes to override a Bush veto, which suddenly looked unadvisable to the White House, I suspected.

My mind flashed back to Hubert Humphrey battling bladder cancer from his home in Waverly, returning to the Senate less and less often, and how much it meant to us those times when we saw him, always fearing it might be the last. A colleague came up to me and remarked that this was a beautiful moment, one that said everything about who Senator Kennedy was. I didn't disagree, of course. It was Ted to a tee. He wouldn't have allowed one of his signature issues to be hurt by his absence.

But even in this beautiful moment, something didn't sit right with me. Ted had many friends across the aisle. Surely, they knew his immune system was compromised. Surely, they knew that no measure should lose by a single vote because one of us was battling terminal cancer. I thought of John Stennis pairing his vote so that Hubert Humphrey didn't have to come back and vote during his battle with cancer, even though it meant that Stennis's position lost. I'd paired my vote for my friend Dick Shelby years later when he was hooked up to an IV enduring a bout with norovirus, to save him an unnecessary ride back into the Senate. Sure, there was at most a momentary partisan advantage to be gained by the other side missing a senator. But so much was lost when you operated the institution that way. While so many celebrated Ted, rightfully so, I wondered what had happened to the Senate that ever made his risky flight to Washington necessary in the first place. Where were all those senators who voted with Ted and with Medicare this second time, when, if they really wanted to pay tribute to him, they would've voted that way the first time when Ted was home in a hospital bed watching on C-SPAN?

— 51 —

Fresh Start

The election of Barack Obama as president of the United States was a moment of elation I couldn't have ever imagined. He was the third Democratic president I'd known in some personal way before being elected, but far and away the one I'd known best. Michelle Obama had meant so much to Marcelle as her assigned "little sister" in the Senate. But more than the personal dimension, I felt as though part of my own journey and the country's journey had come full circle.

Seared in my memory were the images of my childhood on the issue of race in America. I remembered President Eisenhower sending those National Guard troops into Arkansas to stand up to Governor Orval Faubus and desegregate classrooms after *Brown v. Board of Education.* I remembered asking my dad to explain to me what was happening in front of our eyes on that tiny black-and-white television. Dad could relate to it in some ways because of his own experience in Vermont, where we Irish and Italians looked like everyone else, but there were lines his generation had been told not to cross. But race—race was the dividing line, the barrier that couldn't be wished or washed away. It was stubbornly resistant to change. It was incomprehensible to me. As a senator, when the Oval Office tapes first of President Kennedy and then of Lyndon Johnson became publicly available, I studied them. I was fascinated to hear how Kennedy, this charismatic New Englander, and later Johnson, this former master of the Senate, tried to hold the southern wing of the Democratic Party together as they pushed to pass progressive legislation. On those tapes, I heard the voices of Jim Eastland and John Stennis as I'd never experienced them; they were southerners talking about preserving a way of life that depended on discrimination and even violence, while swearing that they couldn't control what might happen in a place like Mississippi or Alabama. They weren't the Eastland or Stennis whom I'd known in the 1970s. The echoes of that past haunted me. I thought of all the hours I'd spent with Hubert Humphrey, whose 1948 speech at the Democratic National Convention started the party's march toward a complete breakup with a segregationist wing and, ultimately, an opportunistic Republican Party's inroads in the South by embracing its dog whistles.

At least for a few glorious months after November 2008, with the election of Barack Obama, it seemed as if we were reaching a pinnacle past generations could never have predicted. There was poetic justice in his victory; Barack became the first Democrat since Lyndon Johnson to carry Virginia, the cradle of the old Confederacy. Marcelle and I both cried on election night.

The pride we felt in Barack's election would endure. But the heady euphoria of that moment and of his inauguration dissipated quickly. It became sadly obvious that an ugliness didn't just remain in American politics, but that it felt emboldened to rear its ugly head in ways that were more public than it had been in decades. The Tea Party marches against the Obama administration's agenda had an overt racist tinge that stunned us. I turned off CNN as I saw a protester's sign: THE ZOO IN WASHINGTON HAS AN AFRICAN LION, AND THE WHITE HOUSE HAS A LYING AFRICAN. It was brazen, raw, vulgar bile.

The president seemed remarkably serene and poised, and in a dignified way he never seemed to acknowledge how much of the opposition bubbling up outside was based on race. But he certainly bristled, rightfully so, at the way in which the Republican Party clearly saw its own political fortunes rise with the advent of the Tea Party. He knew that the Republican Party was going to treat him as an illegitimate president.

Early and immediately in the Obama administration, we Democrats felt besieged by a Republican blockade of all we had worked to accomplish, even in cases where they'd previously supported our position. It was frustrating, even, and maybe especially, for an eternal optimist like me.

After all, Barack Obama had earned a mandate. Whether Senate Republicans liked it or not, he'd won red states like Indiana that hadn't gone Democratic since LBJ. While previous nominees had fought to win either Ohio or Florida, Barack and Joe carried them both. It was a landslide against John McCain that helped to build a majority of fifty-nine, soon to be sixty, Democratic senators. Certainly, it was time to govern, but I had big hopes that it would also be time to unite the country.

My optimism couldn't have been proved more wrong, sadly. Barack and Joe had not been 2008's only winners. Out of the ashes of the John McCain campaign emerged Sarah Palin and the Tea Party. Palin had been the governor of Alaska and an absolute, unmitigated disaster as McCain's running mate. She evinced not a shred of curiosity, let alone mastery, of the core issues, but she put her finger on the pulse of a new populism that eschewed facts and sought only wedge issues. When the ticket went down in flames, many hoped this would be the end of her brand of politics, that John McCain, not Sarah, would chart their party's return to a more familiar, civil politics. The opposite emerged almost immediately.

Oh, sure, Barack as president didn't particularly enjoy the art of ingratiating himself to Congress. Much like President Carter's team, many of his advisors believed his brand and the secret of his success was as an outsider. But by the same token, it's awfully hard to try to work with an opposition party whose Senate minority leader declares his top priority is to make sure "Barack Obama is a one-term president."

Mitch McConnell had proven to be a different person as minority leader from the one I'd known as my counterpart on the Appropriations Committee. The suit of partisan leader fit him differently from the wardrobe of an appropriator whose job is to make the process work so everyone wins. "The job of the minority is to become the majority," he declared.

Barack and Joe were not going to win over Republican votes for much of anything.

That, in part, was what brought me on a mission of inquiry with a very discerning audience.

Two months shy of seventy years old, I felt like a young lawyer going into court for the first time—and not just any court.

The court.

"*Justice Stevens is waiting for you, please go in,*" said the receptionist, as she politely hung my hat and coat on the hook.

John Paul Stevens was in shirtsleeves, but his bow tie was crisply knotted.

"*Just sit wherever you're comfortable,*" he said as he moved a pile of memoranda from the coffee table to his dark mahogany desk.

I was nervous, but the justice quickly put me at ease.

"*This was Sandra's office.*"

With his long arms, the eighty-nine-year-old justice motioned toward the view outside his window: the Capitol.

"*I took it temporarily because they're doing so much construction and mine was all torn up, but once I got here, I decided to stay for the view of the Capitol.*"

The Capitol was on both of our minds—and not just for the view.

"*I know you're very friendly with David Souter,*" said Stevens with a smile.

"*Well, we are—and we had talked a lot about when he was going to leave and all.*"

A knowing smile crossed the justice's face.

I asked him how Justice Souter was enjoying retirement in New Hampshire.

"*Very much—he's now moved into his new house.*"

We chuckled at the shared knowledge of our friend: Souter had to buy a new home to fit decades of accumulated, well-worn books.

"*Oh gosh, did he have a lot of books in his chambers. I really miss him. He spent a lot of time with me when he first came here, almost like I was a mentor.*" The self-effacing justice paused a beat, caught himself, raised a hand, and added, "*Of course, with his brilliance, he didn't need any mentoring.*"

The justice was feeling nostalgic today, clearly. He had an interview scheduled later that day about the legacy of Chuck Percy—the legendary Illinois senator who had championed Stevens's appointment to the Seventh Circuit Court of Appeals by President Nixon. Five years later, Stevens would become a fifty-five-year-old Supreme Court justice, nominated by Gerald Ford.

"*I was a kid then,*" Stevens said, and laughed.

"*Oh, I know—I voted on your nomination.*"

"*But you didn't go on the Judiciary Committee until a year later.*" His memory and attention to detail were as sharp as could be, if they needed any proving. If this was a tennis match of trivia, he was sending the ball whizzing right back into my court every time.

"*Well, that's right. I only got to vote for you the one time, on the floor. You know, I've had the opportunity to vote on every member of the Supreme Court, including some who've left, and Bill Rehnquist as chief justice.*"

Stevens brought up a memory that seemed particularly on his mind.

He'd been newly appointed by Nixon to the court of appeals, and former Supreme Court justice Tom Clark, who had retired to pave the way for his son Ramsey to become Lyndon Johnson's attorney general, volunteered as a sitting judge on the court of appeals in Chicago—picking up the slack and helping to reduce the backlog left by the indictment of a number of justices in Illinois.

"*I liked Justice Clark right away for his bow tie,*" said Stevens. "*But—I thought—what does it say that he'll take all the tedious cases and do the job, just because he misses what he's been doing the last eighteen years? It was like an old soldier who reaches down to itch a leg amputated long ago.*"

It was obvious where the conversation was going, as lunch arrived, adding to the suspense. We both stopped while the justice's personal aide put the sandwiches and the glistening coffeepot and the tiny carafe of milk on the coffee table amid the silverware. Stevens looked at me. "*Now, where were we, Patrick?*"

He bit into his sandwich, swallowed, and looked up, exhaled deeply, and continued.

"I'm sure you've noticed I've only hired one law clerk, and of course some speculation in the paper on that."

"Yes, I have."

"There comes a time when you have to decide what you're going to do with life."

"With life." It was such an interesting choice of words. I couldn't possibly imagine how an eighty-nine-year-old associate justice of the Supreme Court of the United States thinks about the runway left in front of him, and how it compares to the decades trailing out behind him like the wake of some massive destroyer, a fitting analogy for Stevens, who had volunteered for the Navy one day before Pearl Harbor. I flashed back to Hubert Humphrey calling and confiding that he had only "*a short time left.*" Like Humphrey, Stevens didn't need to say more: he knew that he had a set of choices about how to spend the time left and how to write his legacy while it was still under his control.

"*We all have to think about when we're going to leave,*" he said, and he kind of left it in the air, waiting for what I was going to say next.

I didn't know quite what to say.

"Well, you must have to do that in the Senate, but you have to make a commitment for six years, not just for one more term of the court."

"Well, you know, I went through all that this year—I'm going to be seventy in March."

"I'm going to be ninety in April."

"Sure, but you look a hell of a lot younger than that—you've got a big head of hair."

"Well, how did you decide that you were going to run again? I mean, you don't have any problem running, you've got to be there. You're one of the senators we need."

"Well, I appreciate that. I had debated it—I think the president heard I was debating it. He called me up—he said, 'It's Barack, uh, Obama . . .'"

Stevens smiled.

"I said, 'Mr. President, how many Baracks do you think I know?'"

The justice roared. "*Especially in Vermont.*"

So, I said, "*Well, now that you brought it up—though we kind of both brought it up, haven't we?*"

"*Yeah.*"

"*First, you have got to know you're one of the justices I've always admired. I've admired you the entire time you've been here. I'd be happy to have you here for the rest of my life.*"

He replied, "*That means a lot to me, but you know, I'm a realist. I feel great now, but at some point, you have to make that decision.*" He paused. "*What happens if I do make that decision?*"

"*Well, John, that's what I want to talk to you about.*"

The clock seemed to stop for a few seconds. I could hear my pulse ringing in my ears.

"*Oh, good!*"

I breathed easier.

"*John, this conversation is between the two of us, but if you're going to leave, let me tell you how the time frame works, because it's complicated.*"

I unburdened myself about how terribly polarized the Senate had become.

"*John, it's not the Senate of just a few years ago. It's sure as hell not the Senate that Chuck Percy knew. It's not the Senate I first knew.*"

I told Stevens about the days when I would walk Humphrey over to votes in the Capitol and pretend to be one of his staff members to get him there without interference from the tourists.

"*Nobody knew who I was,*" I said with a laugh.

"*Well, they know who you are today.*"

"*Well, John, we'd all be better off if senators weren't in such a rush to be seen and known.*" He knew where I was headed. "*Let's really talk about this, because if the show horses see an opportunity to make it political—*"

"*Does the president have people in mind?*"

"*Well, they had some names, of course, when Sonia Sotomayor came up.*"

He interjected. "*Pat, I've got to tell you how happy I am with her. There's no learning curve. She just plunged in knowing exactly what she was doing—and she is doing a great job.*"

"*I'm going to tell you in total confidence, if you were to retire, the president will do the usual thing he has to. He'll call in the majority and minority leader, myself, and the ranking member, and we'll sit and discuss it. But I had a long talk last month with the president, just the two of us, about judicial things. Everybody thought we were talking about health care and Afghanistan, and we were talking about judges. I will go down and privately meet with him ahead of time, and we'll go over the names. I will have a pretty good idea of who they're thinking about. He was ready to give me names then, but I told him that the less people that have those names the better. But I will make recommendations."*

"*Well, what would the timing be? When would I have to resign?*"

We were getting down to reality.

"*If you wait until the end of the term, we don't have the time to do it until late September. If it's going to be late, in past years I would say we'd still just do it on this schedule, but they are being so partisan and so antagonistic to Obama, they would hold it up until after the congressional elections, hoping they might be in the majority or at best would cut back our majority enough that they could filibuster.*"

"*It's really that bad?*"

"*It's worse.*"

Stevens digested every word, every example of the bitter partisanship. He knew I wasn't exaggerating.

"*John, you could announce that you'll be retiring only after your successor was confirmed.*"

We were no longer even dancing around the theoretical retirement but speaking about practicalities.

"*But if I did that, wouldn't that give them an excuse to hold it up? Saying there's no vacancy?*"

"*You're right, and what David Souter did was to announce that he was leaving and would resign after the last day of the session, which is toward the end of June. But because he did that in May, it gave us time.*"

I said that because of that date, we could begin the process even though Souter was still on the bench, and that's when I could do the "*if it was good enough for Roberts, it would be good enough for Sotomayor.*"

Stevens took it in. He was internalizing details of the political back-

and-forth that he hadn't ever rationalized: he may have grilled the sausages, but he'd never had reason to ask how they were made.

"Even then, we are so polarized, but Arlen Specter and I were trying to make the Roberts hearing a model of what the Senate could and should be. I wanted to do the same thing with Sotomayor.

"You know, this is why I voted for John Roberts—I did not want the chief justice of the United States to be there on a party-line vote. And because of my vote it wasn't. I wanted to have my credibility to call everyone on the carpet to do the same."

"For the sake of the country you did the right thing, and it's just one of the many reasons why I admire you."

I told him about how I used to hang around the court and the Senate when I was in law school at Georgetown. I told him about my long-ago meeting at the law review luncheon with Justice Hugo Black, and how I'd been riveted by that former Klansman's story of how and why he and the eight other justices came to concur in Chief Justice Warren's unanimous ruling in *Brown v. Board of Education*: some issues were so vital, the entire country needed to hear that the highest court in the land spoke with one voice as an institution about the meaning of our foundational documents.

"Pat, isn't it amazing how things happen that set us on these paths?"

He didn't say the words *"I'm ready to retire."* He simply speculated about what might happen if he did—and asked how one knows the right moment to cross that threshold.

I shared a memory that had haunted me—a memory that helped me visualize in my mind when it was time for any of us to go. I told him what it had been like sitting in the hallway off the Senate floor with John Warner, talking about whether he should retire, in 2007.

John was still at the top of his game, his mind sharp, his humor quick as ever. But he felt the years more with each step he took. He revered the Senate. He couldn't imagine life anywhere else. But Warner told me that he didn't ever want to end up like Strom Thurmond had, essentially living out of Walter Reed hospital, unaware sometimes of what was happening in the institution where he'd served for decades.

"The institution shouldn't be your institution, if you know what I mean,"

he said. I told John what Russell Long had told me in 1985: "*Try to leave with some snap in your garters.*"

We watched Robert Byrd go by in a wheelchair pushed by an aide.

I touched John's forearm. We were both thinking the same thing.

"*I know,*" he said. "*I know.*"

Warner's decision crystallized: he was going to step down while he was still in a position to say goodbye on his terms—as the statesman he'd been—not as a memory, not as a relic, not as a shell of who he'd been for so long. And John Warner knew how quickly the Senate could become an anesthetizing nursing home for those who didn't see the days getting shorter and dusk coming earlier with each passing night.

I had prepared to show Stevens charts of how we might ensure a smooth process to confirm his successor. But I didn't need to bring them out of my briefcase and risk adding a clinical component to a heartfelt conversation.

I hadn't come over here to try to push him out. But I wanted him to understand that it was well within his power as a decision-maker to help us keep an ever-corrosive contagion of politics out of the process if he decided, of his own volition, to set the confirmation timetable ahead of the political season. It was a chance to protect at least some of the best of the institution to which he'd dedicated nearly half of his life.

"*Who do you think the president will appoint? Will he do the right thing?*"

"*I think he will. I know some of the names that were bandied about before, and it's not like I have to explain to this president how the Supreme Court works.*"

"*Oh, I know that.*"

"*John, if the president comes up with a bad name, I'm going to tell him so. And I'm going to say I'm really opposed to that.*"

"*Maybe my birthday in April would be a good time to announce I'm going to step down.*"

We'd been John and Pat up to that point.

"*Mr. Justice, that's going to have to be your decision, you know, and I'm going to support you either way. I thought about whether to come over here like this, because I don't want to look like I'm coming over and handing you a pink slip. That's not my place."*

He smiled. "*No, of course not—but I knew why you wanted to see me. Thank you for doing this. I understand it better. Now, I've got to think about it—I've got to reach a conclusion. At ninety years old, at some point you've got to make a decision, but you're going to have to make sure he gets a good person."*

He looked around the room—it was almost like he was looking around thinking, *I'm going to have to leave this.*

My heart pounded again. The wistfulness, the nostalgia, the attachment—those feelings were something I understood walking around the Capitol, thinking, *Someday I'm going to have to leave this.*

We stood up to shake hands.

"*Pat, come here,*" he said. Stevens didn't have a vanity wall of framed pictures from adoring devotees. His walls were not spartan, but neither were they stacked floor to ceiling with framed tributes, just a few photos of family and friends.

But there was one framed letter. It was one former president Gerry Ford had written to a historian about how proud he was of nominating Justice Stevens, of his integrity. Next to it was a picture of Vice President Biden being sworn in by Stevens in 2009, including a handwritten thank-you note on a card with the letterhead marked simply THE VICE PRESIDENT. Biden and I had both voted to confirm the Republican Stevens in 1975. Now all of our lives were coming full circle—we each had a job to do to protect the kind of court Stevens had believed in for nearly four decades. Stevens's secretary came in as we were saying goodbye.

"*Senator, the press saw you coming into the Supreme Court and they're asking why."*

"*You know, it's not even on my schedule I'm here—I come over here all the time. I could say I just wanted to see the renovations."*

Stevens put his hand on my forearm. "*No, if they ask—because they're coming over to interview me about Chuck Percy this afternoon—if they ask, I'll say you were here, but it was a private conversation between us.*"

"Well, that's exactly what I'll say too, and this is a private conversation between the two of us."

Stevens interrupted: "*But it means a lot to have a conversation like this between friends.*"

As I walked out, I thought how difficult it must've been for Justice Stevens. I thought of Chief Justice Bill Rehnquist, who was ill and suffering from adverse reactions to his medication, but had held on because he couldn't contemplate life without the court. Now here was John Stevens, in great physical and mental shape, but almost ninety years old—pondering whether to leave of his own volition and shape his succession while the politics was ripe or stay in an institution where he mattered, potentially putting at risk its future. What an unenviable choice.

Eleven days later, Justice Stevens announced that he would be retiring at the end of the court's term. There would be time to confirm a Supreme Court justice while we knew a majority still existed to do the right thing by these two institutions, the Senate and the court.

As the Russell Building elevator door closed, a feeling somewhere between déjà vu and phantom pain hit me suddenly. It was eerie and I struggled to explain it. There are moments we all feel when our subconscious tells us something's missing, left unfinished; it felt a little like the pedantic, everyday worry that you left the garage door open or the water running, or that your keys were still in the car. But there was nothing small or ordinary about this void. In the office building that had felt like home away from home for so long, I couldn't quite put my finger on it, until, just as quickly, I realized the source of the emptiness I was feeling.

It was Ted Kennedy. Our offices were just a floor apart in the Russell Building, and we would often walk over to the Capitol for votes together, either through the tunnel or outdoors, and I realized I hadn't heard his roars of laughter in months. Ted's laugh was especially contagious. When we were in the tunnel, it would echo off the ceiling. It was a physical manifestation of his personality: a spasm, an impulse, a larger-than-life reflection of a person who was so good at bringing people together.

Ted's diagnosis of a vicious brain tumor the summer before had stunned us all, but for the longest time, he'd been responding well to treatment and remained a presence in Washington. Marcelle and I had been over to his home months before, and Ted and his wife, Vicki, shared that he was trying to work from his library office as much as possible, heading into the Senate mainly to vote at the beginning of the week to limit his chemo-weakened immune system's exposure to germs.

Now, I realized, he'd quietly stopped coming in at all. My hallmate, the senior senator from Connecticut and Ted's best friend, Chris Dodd, told me Teddy was spending more time up in Hyannis Port, at the iconic family home on Cape Cod. Ted felt stronger being by the ocean. It was in his blood, just as Vermont's mountains and maples ran through ours. Chris had gone up to visit him and go sailing on Ted's boat, the *Mya*. Kennedy instantly transformed into a captain again, ordering Dodd to go faster and faster. The wind was very strong and it was very stormy, and Chris pointed out that he was the one who still had a very long life ahead of him and maybe they should be more careful. Ted loved it; he howled with laughter, the laugh booming out of his weakened body. It was obvious that he would keep living life on his terms right until the end, even if the physical distance between him and the Senate had grown.

I realized how much Ted's presence was inseparable from the Senate as I'd known it; being near the ocean may have made Ted feel strong, but it was Ted whose presence in the Senate so often strengthened the institution and showed his colleagues the art of the possible. He could bring people of differing views together, often on technical issues where work was done quietly and in a bipartisan fashion.

As the years pass, particularly in the Senate, you slowly accept that change and churn are the yin to the yang of tradition and consistency. But certain changes hit you harder than others. I'd always tried to savor the moment and live in what I was doing now. Perhaps I owed that mindset to the difficult early races that had first made me and then kept me a senator and the sense of liberation that came with those elections. But knowing that Ted wouldn't be with us much longer made me take a longer view about what I might leave behind in this special institution. Ted had been a teacher to so many, as Humphrey had been to me; as we started losing people who had been such leaders, it was time for me to work even harder to be a mentor and to share with younger senators what people like Ted had shared with me: that you could enjoy the prestige of being one of a hundred, or you could accomplish something by helping that one hundred come together as one institution. It was important to be a bridge in time back to a very different Senate where remarkable breakthroughs happened remarkably often and routine progress was the norm, not the exception; I felt a responsibility to help people stop at times and, without being grandiose, think about what we should do for history.

As the August recess drew to a close, the inevitable moment arrived. We awoke to the news that for the first time in his life, Ted, who was larger than life in every way, had marked a big moment quietly; he'd gone to sleep peacefully, surrounded by his family, and never awakened. The outpouring at his funeral was profoundly real, a celebration of life that joined equal measures of tears and laughter. Senators traveled to Boston together, and we climbed into a bus reserved for the occasion to head to the church. I wondered whether, for many, this was the first time they'd sat with their colleagues from the other party at all. Marcelle and I remembered the first Kennedy funeral we'd watched as a young couple, saying farewell to President Kennedy. This moment was different—Ted had lived a full life; his passing was sad but not tragic—but the feeling in Massachusetts was not so different. From the window of the bus, we could see people holding up copies of magazines they had saved over the decades, some with Ted's face on the cover, others with Robert Kennedy's, and still others with John Kennedy's. It was a truly American moment, a shared experience. I wondered whether we could all take something from this time and hold on to it as senators.

— 52 —

Forcing the Lock

Harry Reid told me President Pro Tempore Inouye had died. Would I be sworn in immediately as his successor? "No," I replied. I went home. The next morning, Danny's long town car pulled up. I sat in the cavernous back seat. A Senate giant, Danny was diminutive but must've thought, *This is the car for a president pro tempore.*

His passing also affected committee leadership. I was next in line to be Appropriations Committee chairman, but President Obama had been reelected. Since my work on Judiciary could have consequences for decades, I decided to stick with it, making Barbara Mikulski the first woman to lead Appropriations. I asked her to keep Vermont in mind.

I set my mind on unfinished business elsewhere.

I had experienced now seven presidencies, one in which I believed, ultimately in vain, that there might be a meaningful opportunity to change America's policy with respect to Cuba. Now, as President Obama started a second term, I was not going to see a second Democratic presidency go by without trying my best to persuade both sides that some kind of rapprochement was possible.

Over President's Day weekend in February, a lot of people from New England go south for the sun and the warmth—most of them to Florida. Fifteen years after I'd first visited Fidel Castro, I had a different southern destination that weekend to escape the cold and a more serious mission in mind. I was headed back to Cuba. Fidel Castro's younger, quieter brother, Raúl, had been reelected as president, a position that had been transferred to him by the National Assembly five years before while his enigmatic and charismatic brother nursed failing health and lived a more reclusive life. Fidel wasn't coming back, and the world knew it. But what kind of leader Raúl might be, I wasn't prepared to assume. He was a revolutionary like his brother. He was the last surviving public figure of the generation that had lived by its wits in the Sierra Maestra mountains and won a guerrilla war. But he was also the person Fidel charged with overseeing the show trials and firing squad executions of scores of Batista sympathizers purged from the remaining Cuban national army. He saluted and carried out the orders that sent many to their deaths for war crimes. Raúl's hands were no cleaner than his brother's. I had no illusion that there was a Jeffersonian democrat hiding beneath his well-worn fatigues. But I believed in engagement; certainly, the alternative had gotten America nowhere in our own neighborhood other than isolation, as now a second President Castro reign could attest.

Castro had made it a point not to meet with any government officials since his inauguration, but I still believed it was important for me to see for myself what was happening on the ground in Cuba for two compelling reasons.

I hoped that President Obama, now freed from the burden of running for reelection and beginning his second term, when many presidents focus on securing their foreign policy legacies, would see the wisdom of ending the unmitigated disaster of our Cuba policy. The year before, I'd been to Cuba, and Raúl Castro took me aside and asked to speak with me privately. He had the same translator with him that his brother Fidel had used when we had dinner with him those many years before. Castro said he had been reviewing the polls and was concerned that Obama could lose. I said, "I read the same polls, but I also talk to people in the various states, and I am convinced Obama will win." There was obvious relief in his face, and he said, "That's good, because I think he's a good man, an honest man, and somebody I can work with." Then he chuckled: "*Of course I won't say that publicly before the election, because I don't think it would help him.*" We both agreed. Now, in 2013, I wondered whether that promise of some kind of cooperation might come true. Political capital in a president's second term runs out quickly before he becomes a lame duck. Change on Cuba had to begin now.

But I knew it couldn't and wouldn't while an American USAID worker named Alan Gross was wasting away in a Cuban prison going on four years. He had been arrested and convicted on trumped-up espionage charges for working to enable Cubans to communicate without fear of government surveillance under a USAID-funded initiative. He was on the ground in Cuba trying to connect Cubans to the rest of the world, the kind of work we'd funded in other closed societies during and since the Cold War. But to the Cubans, its purpose was to bring about regime change. In their minds, it was subversive. In my mind, it wasn't effective—it wasn't going to unlock Castro's grip on the country—and more important, now we faced a humanitarian crisis: Alan Gross, this idealistic father of two daughters who was in his sixties and had been sentenced to fifteen years, was losing hope with each passing month that he'd ever see the United States and know freedom again. I had to talk face-to-face with the Cubans about his safety and his future.

While having lunch with the foreign minister, I received a call from Raúl Castro himself, inviting me over for the evening. I asked to bring Marcelle. There was a bit of a pause, and he said that was okay. I said, "There are other senators here with me." He said, "Well, I'm not inviting your delegation." I said, "Well, I'd like to bring the senior Republican," to show that we were bipartisan. There was some hesitation, but it was agreed to.

I was traveling with the ranking Republican on the Appropriations Committee, Senator Richard Shelby of Alabama, a former conservative Democrat who switched parties in 1994 after the Gingrich revolution because he saw the handwriting on the wall in a state trending from pink to ruby red. Shelby was an old-school southern politician who measured his success by what he could bring home for Alabama. He agreed to come to Cuba with me because there might be a market there one day for agricultural exports from his state. Now I was asking Dick to please bring his wife, Annette, to meet Fidel Castro's brother. Dick's a friend through thick and thin—he relented.

Raúl was in no mood for pleasantries.

I tried to steer the conversation toward hope for the future.

"People our age may remember the history of our two countries—"

Raúl cut me off. "I'm older than you are," he said emphatically.

I thought, *Well, this could be going better.*

I picked up where I'd left off.

"We all think of things you did wrong, and of course you will think of the things we did wrong—"

Cutting me off again, Castro interjected: "*You are a bigger country and did more things wrong.*"

Strike two.

I felt a little like the teenage Cuban batter I'd watched fourteen years before, a kid with a homemade bat trying to fend off the pitcher's nastiest curveballs. Except Raúl was throwing fastballs high and inside.

I tried one last time, and swung hard. "*Wouldn't it be nice for our children and our grandchildren to grow up in a different world?*"

Raúl's face changed. The ice melted. "*I have a great-granddaughter.*"

At which point Marcelle said, "*Do you have a picture of her?*"

Castro replied, "*Why yes, I do!*" He ran to his desk, got the picture, and said, "*Isn't she beautiful?*"

Marcelle asked, "*How old?*"

Castro asked, "*Do you have grandchildren? How many?*"

"*Five.*"

"*Do you have pictures?*"

We didn't, because all of our communication gear and electronics were locked up in lead bags in our military airplane.

He asked that "*next time*" we remember to bring pictures.

Before I left, I pulled Castro aside and reminded him of our conversation the year before about President Obama and about Alan Gross's safety. "*There will be time to talk,*" he replied.

— 53 —

The Young President

"*It all flies by,*" President Obama said wearily. "*Every minute of every day is scheduled—you have to fight to protect time to step back and reflect a little bit.*"

His hair was grayer than I'd remembered even from our last long meeting the year before, the furrowed creases around his mouth more visible. The presidency ages everyone, but in a person elected so young, let alone one I'd known as an even younger Senate freshman, the impact of four long years in the White House was even more pronounced.

"*You can do more of that now that you don't have to worry about reelection,*" I replied. "*And you know how this time will race by too.*"

"*Malia will be going off to college in three and a half years—as soon as we're done here,*" he added.

"*Marcelle and I are reliving our children in our grandchildren now.*"

The president brightened at the mention of the family. "*I've met your grandchildren with Lawrence—and they are beautiful.*"

The president opened up in a way I'd never heard him do before.

"*Lawrence really is the kind of father I'd have liked to have had as a young kid growing up.*"

I could feel a lump in my throat. It's a proud feeling to know that your children have found good, strong partners to share their lives and raise a family. But the president was saying something deeper than that, and it didn't have to be said out loud. It was a wistfulness in seeing in my son-in-law, Lawrence—another strong, nurturing African American man—what he had missed out on growing up in Hawaii with his mother and his grandparents.

"*It's been a long time since you emailed me after I lost New Hampshire,*" added the president. "*We've been through a lot since then.*"

The president seemed nostalgic. For someone often described as overly intellectual, when he was at ease with a friend it was clear how contemplative he really was, and how much he did internalize the personal moments that marked the journey. He was a shy person, not an aloof one, if you really got to know him.

But his mood shifted immediately when he got down to talking business. He was worried everything was getting bogged down in the Senate, and he could feel the days ticking away.

"*The gun hearings went well—but are the votes possibly there to at least close the loopholes, do background checks?*" The president sighed. He'd been moved by the images of Gabby Giffords testifying in front of the Judiciary Committee, her brave words somehow more stirring because of her labored speech. You could feel the impact of all the energy she had invested in her rehabilitation and speech therapy.

Every front page of every newspaper in the country had covered her powerful appeal to common sense and conscience. But had anything changed in the votes of our colleagues?

"*I suppose it's possible, Mr. President. A lot of the Republicans say in private they'd like us to do something. But they go back home and—*"

"*Yeah, and then the NRA—*"

"*That's right. It's a tight grip. But, Mr. President—there are things you can do without Congress—that create a very big legacy. Land mines—*"

The president smiled, knowing that I was going to arrive at my pitch and I'd found the right opening.

"*Patrick, my main issue is immigration—and we have to keep that on the front burner.*"

I said that I understood, but explained that I'd lived through President Clinton's eight years and knew how many regrets he had that when he finally tried to turn to the international landmine issue, the time had gotten away from him—it was too late. This president should not let that happen.

We got very serious. "*Patrick—we hit the military with a whole lot of things from benefits for gay partners, women in the military, repealing Don't Ask, Don't Tell. I need to pressure test this one. I don't know what the market will bear.*"

He was being candid about the politics of working with the Pentagon.

"*But I want to get there,*" he said, and leaned forward for emphasis. "*I do want to try and get there.*"

I raised with him the specter that if the policy remained the same when he left, I knew he'd be disappointed when history wrote that he left behind the same policy that George W. Bush did.

"*If you do this, it has got to be done in a way that you don't give them any way to drag it out. You have a short window. The way to do it is to tell them you are going to be in compliance with the landmines convention and you want them to bring you back a plan for Korea. In the meantime, start destroying the ordnances we have.*"

"*That's right, Pat—and it is going to cost a couple billion or* more *to destroy the land mines, but we cannot use them. None of NATO allies can, and we are not going to use them.*"

"*Right—and you cannot export them,*" I added as an aside.

"*I know—because of something they call the Leahy Law—I wonder who wrote that.*" He chuckled. "*Look, give me a couple of weeks or as much as a couple months, and let me try to do this.*"

I could always tell when the president had said all he could say at the moment and was ready for the conversation to move on to the next topic.

"*I want you to succeed, Mr. President.*"

"*Oh, I know it. Pat, I don't think there's anyone I feel closer to in Washington.*"

"*And Cuba—it's such an opportunity to break with the past.*"

The weary Obama half-smile reappeared.

"*I feel the same way about Cuba as you do. But every time we try to make a play, somebody screws things up. You know, Bill Clinton told me how much he wanted to make the opening to Cuba—how much he wanted to be the Cold War kid who said the Cold War's over, we need to try a different future. But then Cuba shot down the Brothers to the Rescue, and it just stopped things cold. Fifteen years later, here we are, and they've created a new hurdle.*"

The hurdle was Alan Gross, the USAID worker wasting away in a Havana jail cell. The president was worried about his failing health. He'd lost eighty pounds, and he was sounding increasingly despondent, worried he'd never again see his elderly mother who was fighting cancer.

I told the president I'd suggested to Raúl Castro that I bring him back with me on the plane, and Castro replied, "*Nice try*," and patted me on the arm. I did the same to the president, who laughed.

"*Some of the Cuban diplomats, when they're being frank, they wish they had just said about Gross—'You did a horrible and terrible thing, and we are kicking you out of the country and you can never come back again.' Holding him this long has complicated everything, but they don't know how to get out of this predicament.*"

"*Well, Pat, it would have been a lot easier. They never miss an opportunity to miss an opportunity.*"

"*They want the Cuban Five issue addressed. It's not just their side that thinks there was an overeager prosecution,*" I added.

"*I've had that sense myself.*"

I could feel the president becoming more careful with his words.

"*Barack—I just worry that if everything gets into baby steps, it's like in Northern Ireland with the Catholics and the Protestants. Any one thing can derail it. Little steps forward won't give people on either side the chance to see the big possibilities of changing this relationship. That's how you get to something unstoppable.*"

At this comment, the president brightened. "*I don't disagree—you have to rip off the Band-Aid.*" It was the right summation.

The Cubans could be constructive when they wanted to, I reminded the president. They had been helpful to Colombian president Juan Manuel Santos in his peace negotiations with the FARC guerrillas, trying to end the world's longest continuous conflict.

"*You could lift their terrorist designation, easily, because they don't really pose a threat to us, and I don't see any reason why you can't allow their diplomats to travel around this country. Create a little breathing room and see where things can go. It wouldn't be a quid pro quo, but I can guarantee they will do the same for us because we both have something to gain from that."*

"*Some of those are easy things and those should be done,*" he responded. "*But we've got to resolve Alan Gross. Tell them you have talked with me and that I am interested in things being better.*"

"*I will, Mr. President. You know they're paranoid about some things. Even though I have a good rapport with them, and Raúl Castro loves Marcelle, he is not going to forget what he knows, having been part of the revolution—and where he has grudges against us. He isn't quick to let go of history.*"

"*Well, we don't want to be imprisoned by history either.*"

It was Obama at his most eloquent, the best of his ability to distill a political situation into a strategic imperative. I knew he wanted to find a path that could work on Cuba.

He leaned forward again and put his hands on his knees.

"*Pat, something else I want to bring up. You were the first person that told me Souter and Stevens were going to leave—what do you think is going to happen now?*"

"*We could have two go.*"

"*I worry about Ruth.*"

"*Mr. President, I am friendly with Ruth, but I don't have the kind of personal relationship that I did with David Souter and John Paul Stevens. But I would like to know what she is going to do. I am trying to figure out who can talk to her about that. I worry that if she waits too long, and God forbid we are in the minority in two years, we're screwed.*"

He nodded. "*If it gets too close to the election, you know they will stall anyone I send up. Not that you don't have enough else to do in your committee, but I can't tell you how happy I am that you kept Judiciary.*"

But he came back to immigration quickly. "*But, Patrick—tell me how we get immigration done. We need it complete.*"

"*I wish you would send up a bill that I would be glad to introduce by request.*"

"*I have held off because Schumer and Durbin have asked me to hold off, and I get it: they want to start with something bipartisan. But McCain hasn't come back to the table since his primary. Graham's scared.*"

Primaries had become the death knell of progress. John McCain had gone from being a brave figure on immigration to running television ads saying, "*Just build the dang fence*," a sad surrender to the forces in his party that made immigration reform heresy. His heart wasn't in any of it, but John McCain couldn't fathom life without the Senate. He was frozen by his own politics. Sadly, he'd boxed himself in.

"*If you even have John McCain insisting we have total border security before anything can be done—we've never had total border security*," I said. "*You can spend hundreds of billions of dollars, and you will never totally secure the border.*"

"*I know that, and we cannot be held hostage to that. One way or another, I am going to start marking up something in the next few weeks.*"

We stood up to leave.

"*How are you liking being president pro tempore?*"

"*I pray now more than ever for your health and safety.*"

He flashed that dazzling smile.

"*Well, the job must have some benefits.*"

"*Yeah, I have the security detail driving me around.*" I pointed out the window to where his helicopter Marine One had just landed and added, "*I don't quite get anything that fancy, but you know, I am not sure I would land that at my farm.*"

"*You know, they really can land it anywhere.*

"*So, Pat—immigration.*" He put his hand on my shoulder and tightened his grip.

"*And landmines, Mr. President. And Cuba.*"

"*You never give up.*"

I walked out of the Oval Office more aware than ever of just how many different priorities crowded the inbox on the Resolute Desk. Immigration. The Supreme Court. Foreign policy issues that left us falling short of our ideals. Time was short.

— 54 —

Raúl, Again

The next time we headed to Cuba, in the winter, we did remember to bring pictures of our grandchildren. Raúl saw the pictures of the "*Real Patrick*" and said immediately and affectionately, without pretense, "He's like my great-granddaughter."

Castro's grandson, his head of security, is white, and his wife is Afro-Cuban. Raúl looked at our Patrick and saw his great-granddaughter, the mere mention of whom had broken through the formality and fighting posture of that testy meeting after his inauguration.

But we were not breaking through on the most difficult, pressing issue between us: the fate of Alan Gross. I'd appealed to Raúl's humanity in private, reminding him how much he loved his deceased wife, Vilma Espín, and how painful still her passing was six years later. I told him that I'd feel the same way if ever I was without Marcelle. He nodded. I told him that Alan Gross loved Judy the same way and that they belonged together. He replied, uncomfortably, that we would find time to talk later.

I insisted on my trips to Cuba that I be able to visit Alan in prison. I wanted to do something to keep up his spirits. Alan's lawyer warned us that Alan might do something to harm himself. Four years without freedom will break a human being. I always snapped pictures of Alan to give to his wife, Judy, who lived in the Washington suburbs and would come to my office to debrief after my trips to Havana. Alan's cell had a computer and books, but it was a cell nonetheless, and he was a prisoner, a prisoner who resented the mockery of one particular guard who Alan said seemed to revel in his suffering.

When the official photographers from Cuba were in there, Alan would put on a stern face. He wasn't going to give his captors a propaganda photo that pretended all was great. But when I stepped in front of the photographer, blocking his view, Alan smiled for my camera, and those would be the pictures that would go home to his wife and daughters.

I was back in Havana in January 2014, accompanied by Congressman Chris Van Hollen, for whom Alan and Judy Gross were constituents from the district. Alan held up a homemade sign proclaiming that he was still a political prisoner, four years into a virtual death sentence. I took pictures, to the horror of the Cubans. As we were preparing to leave the prison, the Cuban guards ordered me to surrender the chip from my camera.

I stood up to my full six feet two inches, puffed out my chest, and looked down at the much shorter Cuban and declared, in a stentorian voice I didn't fully realize I could summon until I needed it at that exact moment, "*I* am the president pro tempore of the United States Senate. I am third in line to the presidency of the United States. I am the highest-ranking American official to visit this country since the revolution. I will *not* be told what to do. Congressman, we are leaving."

I was delighted that Chris was able to keep a straight face, but once we were alone, we both collapsed in laughter.

"I have never seen you do anything pompous like that; how did you keep a straight face?"

"If you had even smiled the tiniest bit, I would have lost it, so thank you for keeping a straight face," I replied. We both laughed and continued on with our meetings.

Later that evening, Raúl Castro drew close to me and in a stage whisper announced, "*I heard about the photograph.*"

I said, "*Yes, and I knew I was there as a guest of your country, and I am not about to show that photo to anyone else, that's for my private collection.*"

He said, "*Well, my staff told me I should cancel the meeting with you because of that photograph—but I knew you well enough to know that you wouldn't embarrass me.*"

But Castro had a request for me that was as personal to him as Alan's predicament had become to me.

The Cubans asked me to squeeze in another meeting before I left the island. I didn't recognize the name Adriana Pérez, but I had every reason to know the name of her husband, the Cuban spy Gerardo Hernández, one of the so-called Cuban Five still serving two life sentences for his role in the shoot-down of airplanes belonging to the anti-Castro group the Brothers to the Rescue. But here was Adriana, her eyes full of tears, appealing to me and Marcelle, but especially to Marcelle, with a deeply personal plea. She said she'd been in love with her husband since she was a teenager, and she wanted to have his baby, even though he was locked up for life, and begged us to try to arrange that.

I didn't know what to say, and I had to leave soon for another meeting. Marcelle tried to throw me a lifeline. "*My husband has no authority to do such a thing,*" she said sympathetically.

Adriana responded, "*I've seen the two of you walking hand in hand, I know he loves you, and that if you ask him to do this, he'll find a way.*"

Her heartfelt appeal, and my surmisal that by helping Adriana we might also gain ground in our push to free Alan Gross as a humanitarian gesture, was the origin of one of the strangest conspiracies in the history of the US Senate, and after all, I could never say no to Marcelle.

My long-serving staffer on the Foreign Ops Subcommittee was a wiry, tenacious activist at heart named Tim Rieser. When he was on a mission, he was a dog with a bone. He would not stop until every last drop of marrow and morsel of sinew had been licked clean. Only Tim would make the many phone calls it took to learn that in the entire history of the Federal Bureau of Prisons, there had been one and only one instance anyone could recall of allowing for artificial insemination. But that's the good part of a precedent—it takes only one.

We knew that there was no way the attorney general could allow Adriana to come to the United States for a conjugal visit, which is prohibited in the federal system, and artificial insemination was not allowed in Cuba, a Catholic country. I told the Cubans they would have to pay for it. They arranged to send her to Panama, where the first attempt failed, to her great dismay. The second time worked. She was carrying her miracle baby.

As for me, I'd begun my own form of senatorial shuttle diplomacy, bringing unsigned messages back and forth between the Obama White House and Raúl Castro, trying to get the two sides "pregnant" with the possibility of change in the long-frozen conflict between the two countries.

Sometimes it was easier than others. In late September 2014, I'd had a fall hiking at Sugarbush in Vermont and injured my leg. The pain was omnipresent. But I'd promised the Cubans I'd come to New York to see their foreign minister, Bruno Rodríguez, who would be there for the UN General Assembly. I had to get on and off the airplane in a wheelchair, and hobbled on crutches up to the Cuban residence in New York. Bruno was a formal man, a diplomat who rarely veered from his brief. He was stunned to see me there on crutches. We had a long and serious discussion that evening. Bruno acknowledged, as we said our goodbyes, that the fact that I kept the meeting when I had such a reasonable excuse to cancel proved to them that I was serious. I looked at him and thought that this hardened bureaucrat himself was perhaps wondering for the very first time whether some real change was at last possible.

But there were still skeptical audiences in Washington about how to get there, not whether it was a good idea to try to get there. I'd spent years in Washington arguing that our Cuba policy was a mistake. Now we had a president who agreed. Obama, after all, had been born in the summer of 1961, years after we'd broken diplomatic ties with Cuba. He knew we weren't winning the argument in our hemisphere. He had run for president in 2008 promising to meet with adversaries and pursue engagement, reminding the country that conversation isn't a reward, it's a means to an end. He knew it was time to try something else with Cuba. But he also knew that he couldn't lift the embargo without Congress, and the votes weren't there. Even more so, he knew that he couldn't normalize relations while Alan Gross sat in a prison cell, and the Cubans were unflappably clear that Gross would not be released while, in their minds, Cubans sat unjustly in American prisons.

Gerardo Hernández wasn't alone. There were two other Cuban spies who made up the remaining three of the original Cuban Five. Their story is a frustrating one. I'm convinced that President Clinton was determined in his second term to make a fresh start with Cuba. But the anti-Castro operatives in the Miami area, despite warnings from our own government, had been flying planes over Havana dropping anti-Castro leaflets. It was dangerous. With tips from the Cuban Five, Cuba's MiG fighters shot them out of the sky. At that very moment, any hope of a Cuban rapprochement under Clinton ended in an instant. The Cuban Five were arrested and, in 2001, convicted after a Miami trial that had seemed unfair from start to finish.

But what could we do now? I went over the trial record page by page. I was convinced it had been an unfair trial. I talked with Attorney General Eric Holder, who didn't disagree and said he wouldn't stand in the way if the president came to the same judgment.

Majority Whip Dick Durbin and I asked to meet with the president. The Cubans wouldn't sign off on a quid pro quo prisoner exchange, and neither should we, we argued. Alan Gross wasn't a spy. The Cuban Five were. But I was convinced that if we did something about the three Cubans left, they would respond in kind. I also reminded President Obama that Cuba had held a CIA agent for years and that we could seek his release too. I think the president was surprised that I knew about that agent. I leaned in and pointed out that Raúl Castro had once told me that if they wanted to prosecute somebody for the shoot-down of the planes, that they should prosecute him, because he's the one who ordered the shooting down of the American planes. The president was noncommittal. I leaned in and pushed again. I knew he didn't like to be pushed. "*Patrick,*

I'm thinking, and you've given me more to think about," he said mysteriously.

I knew from the president's national security advisor, Susan Rice, that Cubans had been meeting with the administration's designated people in Canada on a regular basis that year. The Canadians knew what was going on, but not a word leaked out. But time wasn't on our side.

— 55 —

Please Hold for the President

The caller ID on my cell phone flashed 202—the White House.

"*Is this a good time to talk with the president?*"

I laughed. "*When the president calls and wants to talk with you, it is always a good time.*"

I asked if they would call me back on the direct line in the office.

The phone rang immediately: "*Please hold for the president.*"

"*Hey, Patrick, how are you doing, buddy?*"

"*You must be exhausted after that trip to South Africa.*"

The president had just returned from Nelson Mandela's funeral. It had been a gathering of world leaders like nothing I'd ever seen—democrats, royal families, strongmen, and all those in between, united in celebrating the life of the man who had broken the back of apartheid and taught all of us how to forgive for the sake of nationalism.

"*Pat, well, you know the way it is. It is easy on the plane I have, and it beats doing photo lines at the White House Christmas parties.*"

I can't say that I was surprised that the challenge of eulogizing a giant in South Africa seemed to him less daunting than running the gauntlet of holiday parties, the endless backslapping and small talk.

"*It's hard work for Lawrence too. All those folks want pictures.*"

We chitchatted a little more, and I told him how Marcelle and I thought so highly of his speech. I said it was well done, and I could see a lot of it he wrote himself.

"I wanted to do it right, but I was also so pleased that Bill Clinton and George Bush were there. That demonstrates something to the rest of the world."

I told him I was pleased he shook hands with Raúl Castro and how ridiculous it was that some had criticized him for returning a handshake at a funeral, when, after all, Nelson Mandela certainly would have shaken hands with world leaders, no matter their ideologies or disagreements.

President Obama turned to business.

He thanked me for all I had done in getting his judges through, but I had a feeling I knew what he was building toward—the real point of this conversation. It took him only a short while before he started to talk about places like Wisconsin, where we couldn't get judges because Republican senators wouldn't return "*blue slips*" signifying their comfort with their home-state nominees. He mentioned Arizona and Texas.

"*Mr. President, I talked with Jeff Flake yesterday to point out McCain had returned his blue slips and it looked silly for Flake not to, and he is supposed to get back to me.*"

"*Patrick, well, in Texas we are never going to get a single judge with the two senators we have there, Cruz and Cornyn.*"

I was well aware of the fact that the White House Counsel's Office had been putting out the suggestion to a lot of people that if only I would dispense with the blue-slip tradition, they could get more judges through, which ignored how slow they were in getting judges up to the Senate in the first place.

"*Mr. President—I am a traditionalist on these things, but I know what you're saying. I just think we have to exhaust our remedies first.*"

Obama sighed. "*Patrick, we may just have to ignore them.*"

"*Well, you might be willing to, but I am not prepared to do that yet and I will think about it. But, Mr. President—with Texas, we have got both senators who are on the committee, which makes it even more difficult to just roll over them. Why don't you and I and the two senators from Texas sit down and at least have a come-to-Jesus kind of talk after the first of the year? We can script it out a little bit ahead of time, and we can decide what to say to them. I certainly wouldn't do anything without first making one more try, especially with two senators who are on the Judiciary Committee who could block a lot of the judges Democratic senators want. . . .*"

Obama sighed again. I think he imagined a sit-down with the two Texas Republicans with about the same joy as he did the White House holiday parties.

We each had a role to play in this dance. He was doing his due diligence in trying to get me to change things, but I was pushing back to let him know that it was my decision as chairman of the Judiciary Committee, not the White House's decision.

We changed subjects to one where our hopes were aligned—as were our worries.

"*I'm getting nowhere with Ginsburg.*"

I explained the smoke signals I'd tried to send her way, and the briefing I'd done with Justice Breyer about the good chance that we very well could be in the minority after the next elections and there would be no way the president would get any judges through.

The president said he had been optimistic that we would stay in the majority, but he was less optimistic now.

He said to give his best to Marcelle. I told him that she had just been here in my office and threw him a kiss as she went out the door. He seemed to enjoy that.

"*You're a lucky man, Leahy.*"

— 56 —

Decisions

Justice Breyer stretched out comfortably in the wingback chair facing me in the president pro tem's office.

What an amazing journey we'd shared. I'd first known him as Steve Breyer—counsel to the Judiciary Committee, my partner as we had worked on the uncomfortable Winberry nomination and subsequent investigation. Now, thirty-four years later, I was in what had been Bob Byrd's office, and Breyer was an associate justice of the Supreme Court. The Capitol no longer contained Eastland's reserves of Chivas Regal, and gone was some of the hair both Breyer and I enjoyed back then. But decades later, we were still friends.

Justice Breyer asked to see the photos of our grandchildren Patrick and Sophia. He clearly thought often of the country his grandkids were living in. It was personal to him, as it was to us—personal in a different way from how it was in 1979. Breyer mentioned that he spent time each summer in Vermont and it would be wonderful if all of our grandchildren could get together with us.

Breyer joked about just how different the previous presidents pro tempore had been: rough-around-the-edges Eastland with his cigars and his liquor; Robert Byrd, who had his own famous quotations painted in calligraphy on the wall; stoic Dan Inouye with the warm colors and art from Hawaii; and now me.

I told Breyer that the real beauty of it was that I'd found that sometimes inviting Democrats and Republicans in here invoked a certain sense of tradition in the Senate, something beyond the daily partisan back-and-forth. I mentioned that with the bipartisan senators-only dining room long gone, there weren't many places like that left in the Senate.

He nodded.

We talked about the hideaway and the balcony and the Leahy prayer meetings, where you had your choice of twelve-year-old or eighteen-year-old single-malt holy water.

"*I wish I could be invited. I'm Jewish, but I would happily be the altar boy for that kind of prayer hour,*" he joked.

Breyer and I recalled my vote for John Roberts and the reason: it had been important to me that Roberts knew he had not been installed on the court by just one side.

We talked more about my conversations with David Souter and John Paul Stevens about retiring.

He looked at me, wondering if I was about to ask him.

"By the way, Steve—you're seventy-three—and I just turned seventy-three on Easter Sunday. I went scuba diving on my birthday. Neither of us are going anywhere."

But I said I wanted to talk about Ruth Ginsburg.

His brow furrowed.

"Ah, have you talked to Ruth?"

"No, I know Ruth well, but not that well."

Steve stared ahead.

I told Breyer my concern about losing the majority and how difficult it might be for the president to get a nominee through.

"*Well—wouldn't Hillary easily get elected president?*"

I wasn't so convinced.

"Steve—I want the president to have as much flexibility as possible, and I can guarantee you that if we are within a year of a presidential election, these people are irresponsible enough to hold up the nomination just as they have held up so many judges for such a long time."

Breyer seemed surprised, but he listened, and he understood how worried I was.

"Pat, I am not going to barge into Ruth's chambers and say, 'When are you going?' But we have conversations all the time and something will trigger a way to do it gently.

"By the way, Pat—Ruth is sharper than heck. She has a first-rate legal mind."

I walked from my office toward the Russell Building, strolling outside for a change of pace.

The Capitol complex had changed so much since I'd first come here—back in the days before the security barriers and the heavy concrete pots installed to prevent tourist cars from driving up to the Capitol steps. At the corner of Constitution and Delaware Avenues, I spotted a man in a wheelchair with oxygen to his nose.

The voice croaked out a greeting—a familiar voice, however labored.

"*Who is that?*" I asked as I squinted through the sunlight.

It was eighty-five-year-old Jim Schlesinger—formerly President Nixon's young wunderkind secretary of defense, President Ford's CIA director, and President Carter's secretary of energy.

"*Mr. Secretary, Mr. Director—how are you?*"

"*Well, right now I am enjoying the fresh air almost as much as I would Scotch. Although Scotch is probably better, this one will keep you alive.*"

He asked how Marcelle was, I said we still talk about the time we sat on the front lawn of our Middlesex home and he identified birds by their sounds and shared their ornithological names in Latin. That got a good smile out of him.

Minutes later, he was gone—his friend helping pull his wheelchair and oxygen tank into an awaiting black sedan.

I was reminded right away how fleeting life in public service can be.

I was also reminded that in this life, the one resource you must protect above all else is your word. Bernie Sanders came to see me. Forty-one years had passed since we were young candidates and young dads running against each other in that first race for Senate. We'd both turned out okay! Senate colleagues, older and grayer, but just as passionate as we'd been back then, if stylistically different. Bernie told me he was going to announce for president and asked for my support. I paused. Years before, I had encouraged Hillary Clinton to run in 2016, and she was building a campaign. I explained it to Bernie. "*You know I can never go back on my word*," I explained. He knew me, and we knew each other. He understood where I was coming from. I hadn't seen his candidacy coming, but I wasn't surprised as he lit a grassroots prairie fire around the country, drawing big crowds and enthusiasm for full-throated appeals running on the same themes that had animated him in 1974.

On Marcelle's birthday, December 16, I knew the Senate was going to be in session late, and I knew I was sitting on a big secret. The White House earlier that day had asked me, Senator Jeff Flake, and Congressman Van Hollen to be ready to fly the next morning to Cuba to bring Alan Gross home at last, in advance of a joint announcement by President Obama and President Castro of a new chapter in our two countries' relationship.

Our daughter, Alicia, and our son-in-law, Lawrence, took Marcelle out to dinner for her birthday while I was at the Senate with late votes. Lawrence got a phone call from the White House, asking him to be at Andrews Air Force Base around 4:00 a.m. for a secret mission. The White House couldn't tell him the details. Marcelle took him aside and said she knew what it was about. "*Patrick will be on the plane, and you can have breakfast together.*"

Just a few hours after the Senate finished voting that night, Lawrence and I were aloft in the big blue-and-white plane belonging to the president of the United States, on our way to Havana for a quick stop. We were on the ground for all of thirty-eight minutes, all before the sun was high in the sky. In the hangar, we were face-to-face with Alan Gross. He wasn't entirely sure what was happening at that point. "Alan, do you want to go home today?" I asked. Tears were in his eyes.

Over the ocean, it was reported that anonymous sources had told CNN that Gross had been freed. "*I can confirm that*," he joked. A phone call came in from the president. "I'll leave you to take that call," I whispered.

Back at Andrews Air Force Base, I sat with Alan, his wife, Judy, and my old Senate colleague turned secretary of state John Kerry, and we watched on a television set as a president of a new generation delivered a speech wiping away the failed Cuba policy. I thought back to those anxious October days in 1962, when Marcelle and I had fixed our gaze on a television set in our tiny apartment, wondering if the world was going to come to an end over Cuba. Life had come full circle.

— 57 —

Breaking the Senate

The news alert on my phone popped up like a seven-word exclamation point, just a few minutes before each and every phone in the house began ringing simultaneously.

"Supreme Court Justice Antonin Scalia Has Died," read the *Washington Post.*

The staff from the Judiciary Committee, the minority leader's office, and former staff—all flashed on my phone as missed calls while I processed what I was reading.

Soon that familiar caller ID came through: simply 202—the White House.

I hadn't been ready for this moment. Justice Antonin "Nino" Scalia was dead at age seventy-nine, his body found in his bed in West Texas at a hunting lodge where he'd spent the day hunting for blue quail.

It was a fitting end for the brilliant jurist who loved hunting. Now there'd be no bigger game in town than the fight over a Supreme Court vacancy, and no bigger hunt than the search for someone who might fill Scalia's giant shoes but also stand a chance of Senate confirmation in a divided government.

My first thought was about Scalia himself. I knew his wife, Maureen. I'd met his nine children. I'd known Scalia since the early eighties when we first confirmed him to a seat on the court of appeals, and I liked him personally, even if our ideologies diverged considerably—and even that was an understatement, particularly in recent years.

Scalia was as smart as they come, a fact that never escaped him, but somehow his unyielding confidence made him even more likable. He loved to joust and debate—both from the bench and over dinner at Nina Totenberg and David Reines's, often with Ruth Bader Ginsburg and me and our families all together. He was charming and witty, a storyteller and a gifted mimic—and all those traits were on display at Nina's, where both Scalia and Ginsburg knew they could trust that never a word would be repeated. We would invoke our shared Italian heritage and talk about the old world of Italy that our families had left long ago in search of opportunity.

Scalia had grown more and more conservative over the decades since the Senate confirmed him unanimously. We'd always known he was an archconservative. Reagan apparently had only two candidates in mind in 1986 when he tapped Scalia—either Antonin or Bork. Reagan's determination to put the first Italian American on the court was a factor, but so too was Scalia's youth and ideology. I suspect Reagan, the master image maker, also appreciated that Scalia would not just fill up the television screen but devour the cameras with charm and charisma.

We'd confirmed him unanimously because his fitness for the bench was undeniable. That fall of 1986, just two months before we won back our Democratic majority in the Senate, even with the political winds at our backs, Scalia's confirmation was never in doubt.

I was sorry to see he'd become a less attractive figure on the court in recent years. Some of his comments about gay Americans had seemed biting and bullying, small for an intellect so large.

He became tribal, but I never stopped admiring his friendship with Ruth Bader Ginsburg. They were the best kind of odd couple—at the opera, which they both loved, and on the court, which had become their shared workshop. And now not only was Scalia gone, but the Senate that had thirty-one years before given him its advice and consent had proven itself long since weakened.

An hour after Scalia's death was confirmed, Mitch McConnell sent out a statement that weakened even further the foundations of the world's greatest deliberative body. He pledged that the Senate would not consider or confirm a replacement for Scalia—the next president would choose the next justice, well over a year from this new vacancy.

It was a body blow to everything the Senate had stood for, including history and precedent. It was a rebuke Leader Mansfield would never have dared inflict upon Nixon or Ford. It wasn't something any majority leader had done in all of our history, and there was a reason this was a precedent that had never been breached: it damaged the Constitution. We're a nation of laws, but we're also a nation of norms. If senators were willing to bend the Constitution and shred centuries of norms to do so, it only weakened both institutions in the process.

The most upsetting part of it to me was that I'd been there through fifteen confirmation processes, including some that came apart at the seams: Bork and Douglas Ginsburg and Harriet Miers. But none had ever been denied consideration.

I knew the history. I knew that this was without precedent. And I knew that Mitch had been there long enough to know better. He'd seen a Democratic Senate confirm Anthony Kennedy unanimously in 1988, well into a presidential election cycle under a Republican lame-duck president named Ronald Reagan. He'd been a freshman himself when we confirmed Scalia, rather than Democrats waiting until we were back in the majority to squeeze Reagan for a more liberal nominee. But this was the new politics. The Tea Party and the Far Right were taking over the Senate.

I can't imagine that Scalia himself, a conservative but a caretaker of the court, had much appetite for this body blow to an institution that would be deadlocked for over a year if McConnell got his way.

A week after McConnell rolled his hand grenade into the aftermath of Scalia's passing, after the funeral and the tributes, the president invited McConnell, Leader Harry Reid, me, and Chuck Grassley, the Republican chairman of the Judiciary Committee, down to the Oval Office to try to reason together.

I hitched a ride with Leader Reid. One of the things I learned when I was president pro tempore was it is a lot easier to get onto the White

House campus when you arrive with an armed security detail from the Capitol and an armored SUV. We were met on West Executive Avenue outside the West Wing by McConnell and Grassley.

President Obama asked Joe Biden to join us. He was the first former chairman of the Judiciary Committee to serve as vice president of the United States. He was also the only living former senator to have voted on almost as many Supreme Court nominees as I had. Joe was first elected at age twenty-nine in 1972, an upset in tiny Delaware that mirrored what was to come for me in equally cozy Vermont two years later.

The president laid out specifically why he intended to follow the Constitution and fulfill his duties and nominate somebody to the Supreme Court. He went through the laws and the Constitution and past practice. Ever the constitutional law professor, Obama had memorized the history, the number of nominees, and all the precedents. McConnell's face was expressionless.

McConnell spoke up and tried to say the last time that anything like this had happened was during the time of Grover Cleveland.

The president interrupted him and said, "*No, you know that's not so, Mitch.*"

I'd observed before that President Obama bristled sometimes when colleagues made statements that were simply untrue, particularly when the facts were known to us. His voice became flat.

The Oval Office was tense.

Obama repeated the numbers again, calmly.

McConnell didn't respond. He simply went on to say he understood why the president wanted to put a nominee forward, but he'd seen times—like Alito—when Obama had tried to stop judges.

The president calmly but directly responded.

"*Mitch, Alito was a vote that expressed people's opinion, but he still got a vote and he got seventy-two votes to proceed to a confirmation vote. Then he got confirmed. That's how the process works.*"

They went back and forth for a while.

McConnell was listening but did not intend to budge.

McConnell asked Grassley if he had any thoughts.

Grassley muttered a version of McConnell's position: the president could send up a nomination, but they had the right to do nothing about it.

Harry Reid turned it over to me.

I didn't want to merely repeat the case the president had made. I felt a responsibility to provide some personal perspective.

"The president is correct. We've done this a dozen times in presidential years. I was there—and Mitch and Joe were there—for Tony Kennedy. This shouldn't be partisan."

The president turned to the vice president and said, "Joe, what about your experience?"

Biden flashed his bright white grin. "Well, we always meet with the president to have this discussion, don't we?"

He was locked in on me, Mitch, and Chuck.

"We've sat here before. I remember coming down here when Ronald Reagan was president."

He paused again.

"Remember Reagan inviting us down, going through a list of names: 'What do you think of this one? What do you think of that one? Guys, he even did that after Bork had failed and Ginsburg had been withdrawn, so he went down through different names, and Byrd and I would say, 'Yeah, Mr. President, that name would probably get good support,' or 'That one would,' and Reagan went down through several.

"And, Mitch—I remember Reagan said—he said, 'What about Tony Kennedy?' and I said, 'Well, I don't really know him, but I think he'd probably get bipartisan support.' Reagan said, 'That means you'd support him?' And I said, 'I think he'd get bipartisan support; I'm not going to commit one way or the other until we have the hearing.'"

Biden paused a beat.

"*And then—swear to God*"—Biden made the sign of the cross—"*I mean it, right then Reagan said to somebody in the office, 'Open the door.' They open the door, there's Judge Kennedy standing there, and Reagan goes, 'Senator Biden said he'd support you, come on in.'*"

I jumped in. "*And of course, he did get confirmed unanimously, and we still held the hearings.*"

Harry Reid chuckled. "Mr. President, are you hiding a nominee behind that door?"

Obama was direct. "We have one president at a time. I've sent the Senate two nominees who got bipartisan support. A broken Supreme Court is bad for the country. I'm going to nominate someone. Before I do, I'd welcome your ideas."

The meeting ended. Harry and I headed back together. *"Mitch didn't listen to a word he said,"* said Harry.

"If we'd asked Mansfield to just pocket Ford's nominee—he'd have thrown us out of the Capitol."

"Pat, the inmates run Mitch's asylum."

More than a month after Scalia died, Barack Obama introduced his nominee, Merrick Garland. Orrin Hatch had even called him a "consensus nominee" for the Court. But McConnell was true to his pledge, if not the institution. There would be no hearing or vote. The next president would fill the vacancy, and the next Senate would be a smaller place.

After celebrating my reelection, I sat up on election night disgusted: that next President would be Donald Trump.

The morning after, Marcelle and I flew to Chile for a ceremony honoring her brother Claude. A tourist recognized me and joked "Are you fleeing the country?"

I had decisions to make. Four years before, I'd deferred Chairing the Appropriations Committee. The role was again open. I sent word to Washington that I would take it. I hungered to lead a more bipartisan committee.

It triggered an unexpected campaign to have me reconsider. President Obama called from Air Force One. I was barraged with gentle-but-not-subtle calls arguing that with my experience during previous Republican administrations, I should lead Judiciary.

But I was committed. Appropriations would be contentious but collegial. I'd remain active on Judiciary, but on Appropriations, I could help defeat Trump budget proposals that would gut everything I cared about. Republican colleagues there would be pressured to support Trump, but those budget cuts also hurt people they represented. We'd have our work cut out for us.

— 58 —

A Cult of Personality

"*I heard you're staying here in Washington, Mr. President*."

"*I think it's time you call me Barack again*." He flashed a quick smile.

"*Patrick—we wanted Sasha to finish school here with her friends, and we just didn't want to uproot everyone in the middle of so much change*," said the forty-fourth president of the United States, as he waited in the narrow corridor inside the Capitol, just off the steps that would lead outside to the inaugural stand where, at noon, the forty-fifth president would be sworn in to succeed him.

A phalanx of Secret Service and Capitol Police made the small space feel even more cramped. This was no safe space for the claustrophobic—but with the sheer amount of artillery around, if ever there was a moment to feel completely safe in Washington, DC, this was it.

"*That's so important, Barack. Those were some of the hardest decisions that Marcelle and I ever made with our children. It's great to have that time as a family when they want to be close to home*."

"*You mean, before they really* don't *want to be so close to home*," replied the president.

I smiled.

Obama always had a dignified reserve, ever an interior figure. But the moments when he invited you in were revealing. They usually involved candid admissions about his kids, with a wistfulness that harkened back to his own youth, and the sense, I gathered, of never quite feeling fully rooted anywhere. We had long ago bonded over family and parenting, and they were the familiar subjects we typically returned to in these quiet moments when the president, who could be soft-spoken, would find a little corner of an area and almost will himself into the background in a way the most famous person on Earth could only dream of doing. I got the distinct sense that small talk in a big group tired him out, depleted him of his energy. His pensive, introverted side came to the surface, and he seemed most comfortable just making quiet conversation with me instead of glad-handing.

Feet away from us, a different president was, conversely, absorbing the energy from the gathering crowd. President Clinton's right hand was working the air, in mid-illustration, finishing a story. His hair had gone completely white. What a journey from that fresh-faced governor at the rally in Vermont in 1992. While one arm waved in the air, his other was protectively, lovingly, around his wife.

President Clinton and Hillary were surrounded by Senate friends, including the Democratic leader Chuck Schumer, who was animatedly holding court.

A phalanx of associates had formed almost a protective cocoon around them, and I wondered what it was like to stand in their shoes.

I'd seen it happen in 2001 for Vice President Al Gore, and I'd watched it again with Senator John Kerry: I couldn't imagine what it was like to have to attend the inauguration of the person you'd run against in such a close, fiercely contested, bitter contest.

Now Hillary Clinton was girding herself for the same experience—only so much harder.

Al Gore, I'm sure, was convinced he'd carried Florida in 2000, if only all the votes had been counted. But he'd been so magnanimous in accepting a Supreme Court decision so bizarre it was specifically written not to establish precedent. John Kerry had lost his race weighed down by savage lies about his military record and by the shadows of 9/11, which had lifted up President Bush to a sliver of a reelection.

I'd known all three of them—Al, John, and Hillary—as colleagues.

They were, all three, perhaps a little harder to get to know than some other senators. But they were, all three, once you got to know them, once you pierced that protective layer that they relied on to protect themselves, good people—and real people.

I think both Al and John believed they'd lost the presidency to a lesser intellect and to a badly flawed president. But I don't think either one believed he'd lost to a bad person. Neither one had been denied the prize of the presidency by a person who had run such a disgraceful, divisive, and demagogic race as Donald Trump. I couldn't imagine how Hillary felt, having come so unbelievably close to breaking the glass ceiling and becoming our first woman president, only to lose to someone who was sexist, willfully ignorant, and hateful.

Now here I was at a moment none of them—not the Obamas, not the Clintons—had ever imagined would come to pass. I had agreed as dean of the Senate to walk the new vice president, Mike Pence, to the inaugural stand, because he would be the president of the Senate, and maybe, just maybe, that would be a gesture that could help really start to restore some sense of bipartisanship.

Pence was generally regarded as something Trump never was: a person of unwavering, deeply held principle. An ideologue, but a sincere one, I thought. His Evangelism was genuine, even if his sugary midwestern radio broadcaster voice could, at times, sound rehearsed, almost theatrical. But by all accounts, he had not changed much over the years: the former foot soldier in the Reagan army was on hand now as an unlikely vice president to reassure conservatives that the wild card they'd nominated in Donald J. Trump would toe the party line on social issues and judges. How he would find working with his unlikely dance partner and boss—the thrice-married, philandering, formerly pro-choice, nightclub-frequenting president-elect—was one of Washington's most speculated about subjects.

Now, Pence and his wife, Karen, were deep in conversation with Speaker Paul Ryan and Leader McConnell, his counterparts in what was the Republican establishment until Trump turned it all on its head. I didn't want to butt into their conversation, and honestly, I was happier to speak with the outgoing president and, for a moment, stop thinking about the incoming one.

But then a small, almost dainty manicured white hand at the end of a long arm landed on President Obama's shoulder.

"*Barack—it's a beautiful day. Beautiful day.*"

It was the president-elect.

I hadn't been up close to Donald Trump in years. I'd been a table or two away from him in the 1990s, when he was a guest of New York senator Al D'Amato's at the Radio and Television Correspondents' Association Dinner, in Trump's New York tycoon phase, and I'd turned down Al's offer to introduce us. The glad-handing at those black-tie galas had just never been my favorite use of time. Little did I know our paths would cross again under such different circumstances.

And now, here he was in front of me. The years had changed Trump. His bright red tie dangled well lower than his belt. It was odd. From what I'd read about him, I knew he'd grown up around extraordinary privilege and been wearing a jacket and tie most of his life—by his own boasting I knew he'd gone to private boarding schools—and yet, he didn't have that effortless physical grace of a Robert Mueller, a Jay Rockefeller, or others who had grown up in similar settings. He didn't seem to know how to tie a tie properly, or else he was making some kind of fashion statement. His face was heavily made up, maybe for the cameras. Beneath the powder, his face was tanned beyond anything a Vermonter could recognize: not a skier's tan, but a tanning booth tan, and around his eyes were tiny white patches where tiny goggles had protected his eyes from the rays. His hair was a multicolored nest—reddish brown and almost blond in places—and it was stiffly sprayed with I don't know how much hairspray to stay in place. I spotted a bobby pin behind his hair. All in all, his presentation threw off kind of a *What Ever Happened to Baby Jane?* effect.

So much effort, I thought. It was interesting. Trust me, no one particularly likes to lose his hair. No one likes to go gray when you feel otherwise young. But Trump didn't just seem to be fighting the aging process; he seemed to have convinced himself that all this effort was successfully convincing the rest of us that he alone had discovered Ponce de León's Fountain of Youth hidden at Mar-a-Lago.

He hadn't.

Barack Obama seemed momentarily flummoxed by his successor.

"*Donald—you know Pat Leahy, don't you?*"

Trump replied, "*Oh yes, of course, my neighbor! Just a wonderful man, a wonderful senator.*"

I opened my mouth to reply. "*Mr. Presi—*"

"*One of the best senators,*" Trump interjected, apropos of nothing.

Trump clapped me on the shoulder, but it was as if he was looking right through me toward someone else. Only there was no one else. We couldn't tell whom Trump was looking at or whether he had even heard President Obama correctly.

Or whom he was really talking to.

Or whether he had actually listened for any kind of response.

And before we figured any of it out, Trump moved past us quickly.

Obama gave me a quizzical look. "*Neighbor?*"

"*Maybe he thinks Vermont is one of the outer boroughs? He must have me mixed up with somebody else.*"

Less than an hour later, as we all sat outside on the western front of the Capitol, the sunlight streaming down, listening as Trump gave his inaugural address, the feeling was the same: Did he know whom he was addressing?

"*American carnage stops right here and stops right now.*"

"*It's going to be only America first. America first.*"

The president who had lost the popular vote and was entering office with the lowest approval ratings of inaugurated presidents kept saying "we" when, clearly, he meant "I." I'd sat here for Carter in 1977, Reagan twice, Bush in 1989, Clinton in 1993 and 1997, Bush's son twice, and then Barack Obama twice. Never before had I felt the tone—the bellicosity—of an inaugural address fail to even attempt to create healing and unity. Other presidents had inherited divided times. Others had run as outsiders. But never before had any of them tried so mightily to bring that sense of division and disruption to their inaugural address.

Interspersed between the campaign slogans were what I had by now come to accept as simply Trumpian asides.

"*Winning.*" "*Totally unstoppable.*" "*Big.*" "*Bigger.*"

It was as if someone had taken what they thought an inaugural address should sound like, riddled with clichés and efforts to hit familiar high notes, and then the speaker himself had jotted down in the margins his own greatest hits. Not just "unstoppable," but "*totally unstoppable.*"

"Make America great again."

I thought about the poem I'd read by Langston Hughes, of the dreams of a different kind of forgotten American, of an African American speaking for the poor, the immigrants, the Native Americans, the young people without hope. "*Let America be America again,*" Hughes had written. It was a humble appeal.

There was nothing humble in Trump's address.

As we processed out, Senator Tim Kaine of Virginia, who just weeks before had been Hillary Clinton's running mate, whispered to me, "*We're not in Kansas anymore.*"

I wondered whether there was a wizard behind this curtain.

It's going to be a long four years, I told myself.

At the traditional lunch in the Capitol afterward, Senator Lindsey Graham sidled up next to me. Lindsey had been vociferous in his criticism of Trump during the primaries, when Lindsey himself ran a somewhat quixotic and short-lived attempt to win the nomination. He was quick with a quip and always glib. Lindsey was my counterpart now on the Foreign Operations Subcommittee, and we got along well because Lindsey believed in the State Department and was an internationalist in every way. We parted ways on issues of military adventurism, but on the notion that the United States needed to invest in allies and alliances, there we were simpatico.

"*What did you think of 'America first'?*"

"*Oh, Pat—I think it's like anything—what he says isn't what we're going to get. You can't take it at face value.*"

I looked at Lindsey, perplexed.

"*I opposed this guy on every television show, from* Meet the Press *to the Food Channel. But he's picked Rex Tillerson [for secretary of state], he's going to have Jim Mattis [as defense secretary], he's surrounding himself with the right people. He's going to listen. You get in the Situation Room, are you gonna listen to General Mattis or are you gonna listen to some guy who looks like a space alien?"*

Lindsey had a way with words, although I was tempted to ask him to be more specific about which member of the Trump inner sanctum he had in mind as appearing extraterrestrial in nature: Was it Steve Bannon, the long-haired Breitbart provocateur who looked like he was perpetually unshowered, or Stephen Miller, the anti-immigrant bomb thrower off of Senator Jeff Sessions's staff, whom most of us believed had penned the inaugural screed?

But Lindsey wasn't alone in his argumentation. Indeed, the latest Washington parlor game had been devoted to decoding Trump's appointments to his cabinet. Many believed that between Rex Tillerson, the former ExxonMobil CEO heading the State Department at James Baker's urging, and the "warrior monk" General Mattis at the Pentagon, and various Bush administration reruns installed in senior positions, Trump would be tamed.

I didn't buy it.

"*Lindsey, you're assuming he knows how to listen at all.*"

Lindsey smiled. My mind flashed back to the encounter just a couple of hours before and the distinct feeling that Trump's communications went in only one direction.

"*But for everyone's sake, I hope you're right, Lindsey.*"

Listening. It was the secret to governing. I'd seen colleagues struggle to really listen, struggle to hear what their colleagues were really saying, and end up disappointed, inserting hope where reality should've safely resided. I'd seen this movie before as well, but never as extreme. I could still remember that look on Vice President Mondale's face from time to time, although he would never complain, but it left me with the sneaking suspicion that the Georgia outsiders didn't heed his Washington-tested wisdom. More recently, I'd heard my friends convince themselves that George W. Bush would somehow be persuaded by Brent Scowcroft and

James Baker and Colin Powell—his father's wise men—and proceed cautiously on Iraq.

I decided instead that there's a lot of truth in the phrase "*when somebody tells you what they are going to do, believe them.*"

Trump was telling us what he was going to do.

Maybe it was a lesson I'd learned as a child in Vermont: leave the feral cats in the barn, they'll never do anything but scratch up your house; they *can't* be domesticated.

About two months later, I was back in the Capitol for the annual St. Patrick's Day luncheon put on by the Speaker.

The event's roots were with President Reagan and Speaker Tip O'Neill, two Irishmen proud of their heritage. A bipartisan cadre of both House and Senate members come to it, and the president, the Speaker, and often the vice president are all there. I was standing there talking with Enda Kenny, the taoiseach of Ireland.

President Trump began making the rounds. His hair appeared a bit redder than the last time, or maybe that was just the spirit of the day.

He threw an arm around Enda Kenny. "You know my good friend Senator Leahy—well, we call him *Patrick* today especially—a great senator!"

Hmm, they call me Patrick *every day,* it's my name, I thought.

All the time the president was clapping me on the back of my arm: "*Great senator! Wonderful leader! One of the best, totally great senators in the country!*"

On and on he went, just praising the hell out of me, with me not getting a word in edgewise.

As Yogi Berra said, "*Déjà vu all over again.*"

Trump walked off, at which point the prime minister turned to me and, in his thick Irish brogue, said, "*Well now, Pat, do you suppose he has any idea at all who you are?*"

"*I don't think he was listening.*"

That, of course, would be a theme of the Trump presidency: not listening. He wasn't listening to anyone who did anything but prop up his formidable ego. It was different from anything I'd ever witnessed in

Washington. Every president must learn to resist the "bubble" that can separate them from reality. Trump, it seemed, had never been in anything but a bubble in his life—almost a cocoon.

He was the ultimate extreme outsider. He had little patience for Congress, which wasn't so different from some of his predecessors, though he did defer to Mitch McConnell on the strategy to confirm conservative judges and justices. I don't think Trump had conviction on any of it, but he loved the fawning praise that came along with pulling the federal judiciary to the right for generations to come. I think Mitch McConnell saw him as an empty vessel into which he could at least pour the Federalist Society agenda.

Meanwhile, I saw colleagues on both sides of the aisle dispirited. "You can't attach amendments or legislation to judges, can you?" quipped one who was heading for the exits and an early retirement. His observation was correct. We simply didn't legislate anymore.

I bent down and kneeled next to the wheelchair of the man I'd met in 1975 as a freshman senator. "*Mr. Leader.*" I smiled and leaned in. "*How are you doing today?*"

"*Doing better than the alternative.*"

Bob Dole had just turned ninety-five. His hearing was fading, but his wit was as sharp as ever, and, amazingly, he was still going into the office at the law firm of Alston and Bird, representing a few lobbying clients, keeping busy when others would have long ago retired. Dole had successfully engineered an early Trump phone call to the president of Taiwan. He seemed determined to stay in perpetual motion. Work kept him going.

Dole had endorsed Donald Trump after Trump became the apparent nominee and urged his fellow Republicans to fall in line. Bob was a loyal party leader down the line.

But he was also my friend. In half an hour, he'd head into the Capitol Rotunda to receive the Congressional Gold Medal. I hoped his example—demonstrating that even fierce partisans can be institutionalists—might not be lost on some of those in positions of responsibility who would gather for the ceremony. Bob Dole was Mr. Republican, but he also knew how to govern, he knew how to compromise, and he knew how to find a way forward to legislate.

But even if no one internalized that part of Bob's history, I hoped they appreciated the life he'd lived. Dole had left so much of himself on the battlefield in Europe, pushed himself back all the way from ninety-five pounds and a full body cast to walk, move, and work again. Nothing but grit and community had propelled him to the House and then to the Senate. He deserved every accolade. He'd trained himself to grip a pen in his unreliable right hand, so that it didn't splay outward uncontrollably. He tied a perfectly square knot with a dimple in his tie every single day and came to work with the joy and zeal of a person who knew how lucky he was to be alive. Dole, whom so many had caricatured as mean or dour, was an early lesson to me in just how wrong the mainstream representations of a person really could be.

The delegation prepared to process out to the Rotunda for the ceremony. Senator Pat Roberts of Kansas, who held Senator Dole's seat, and I were the designated Senate speakers.

I heard a bustle behind us, and Bob Dole's wife, Liddy, turned his wheelchair around to greet the late entrant into the room: President Trump.

Trump touched Dole on his shrunken, twisted right shoulder.

"*Bob Dole! Great American. My big supporter.*"

He paused a beat.

"*Is this a great American or what? Great American.*"

Trump bent down and said in a stage whisper, "*I see you have a Democrat speaking for you.*"

Bob responded that we served together in the Senate and that I always kept my word.

Trump didn't respond.

"*Great day for a great American.*"

I wondered if he really knew the meaning of two of the words in that sentence. I was confident he hadn't thought hard about either one of them.

I couldn't imagine two more different leaders of the Republican Party. Watching Trump and Dole together seemed to tell the story in two contrasting images of the entire metamorphosis of American politics.

"Great, great, great," he rattled off again, and then he was gone.

There weren't many great days in the Senate to come.

The Trump presidency had begun with a deeply depressing move to install a hard-right justice in the seat that had been held open when Merrick Garland was denied even a hearing for the last several months of Barack Obama's second term.

Knowing that the gut punch of seeing President Trump fill the seat was coming didn't make it any less painful. Senate Democrats had a choice: do nothing, mount no protest, roll over, and let Mitch McConnell install a conservative jurist without making our voices heard—or do so and have McConnell eliminate the filibuster for Supreme Court nominees. There was no satisfaction in either alternative. Neil Gorsuch was a Federalist Society conservative, and he was going on the Supreme Court through an ugly abuse of senatorial prerogatives.

The Senate became a miserable place for those who came to Washington to legislate. Once President Trump passed a massive tax cut for the wealthiest—the easiest feat in American politics—the legislative agenda withered. Leader McConnell focused on confirming more judges and more judges—and, after that, more judges.

I sat next to a colleague who was finishing her second term, a Republican. I asked her what her plans were this coming month. "Well, Patrick, I think I'll be voting on judges, after which I'm going to vote on judges some more." The look on her face of grim resignation said it all. Floor time had become a robotic exercise. It simply wasn't what hardly anyone in the Senate had signed up to do.

But that was the new politics of Washington during the Trump years. When Reagan appointee Anthony Kennedy stepped down, it seemed inevitable that Trump would ram through another conservative activist. Judge Brett Kavanaugh was no stranger to many of us on the Judiciary Committee. He'd been a partisan warrior during the Kenneth Starr investigation into President Clinton, an activist who saw politics as a no-holds-barred, win-at-all-costs proposition.

After the hearings began, credible charges of sexual harassment swirled around his nomination. It wasn't lost on me that a well-respected colleague, Al Franken, had been run out of the Senate without the benefit of a complete investigation, and months later it appeared he'd been a victim of a smear campaign from the Right. Now, conversely, Judge Kavanaugh was being rammed through by his party, which opposed even having a comprehensive background check—mind-boggling in the case of a lifetime appointment. I found Kavanaugh's accuser Christine Blasey Ford very credible. When she appeared before the committee, I asked her about her memories of the alleged incident when she and Kavanaugh were in high school. What did she remember?

"The laughter," she said, as her voice broke for a second. She was a research psychologist by training. She said that for decades since, Kavanaugh's laughter had remained fresh in her brain's hippocampus—the part of our brains where trauma lives on forever. She was haunted by what had happened, and had come forward reluctantly, willing to weather death threats and horrific accusations.

Her story was harrowing. But every bit as troubling to me was what Kavanaugh's tactics said about the new Senate.

Kavanaugh faced the committee. I will never forget his body language—watching him angrily flipping the plastic pages of his binder, threatening the Judiciary Committee that "what goes around comes around," and laying out a political enemies list.

When I'd first come to the Senate, any nominee of either party who behaved that way would've had their papers yanked away by any White House. I could imagine Hugh Scott or Howard Baker asking the White House to please send up a new nominee. No one would've rewarded that behavior—the politicization of the highest court—with a lifetime appointment.

But in the Washington, DC, of Donald Trump, all the old rules were gone out the window.

— 59 —

A Country, Not a War

With so little to celebrate in Washington legislatively under the Trump administration and a fully Republican Congress, I focused more and more on the places where one senator could make a difference regardless of control of the chamber or the White House. Vietnam was one of those places to which I returned again in my thoughts, my memories, and my work.

On a CODEL, I found myself talking with a young Vietnamese student who barely topped five feet tall, if that. Her long black hair was neatly braided, and she wore glasses that somehow made her appear even younger.

"*How old are you?*"

"*Nineteen.*"

"*Which part of Vietnam did you grow up in?*"

"*Ho Chi Minh City,*" she replied.

I did the math in my mind. She'd been born in 1997. A wave of nostalgia rushed over me. Here was a young woman who had never lived a day of her entire life when normal diplomatic relations between the United States and Vietnam weren't a fact—not an aspiration, not a controversy, not a goal. Just a fact. Her "*normal,*" her "*just the way it is,*" was so different from everything we'd struggled to achieve in all the years I'd been in public life.

I thought back to my first trips to Vietnam. It had been so controversial to even travel to Vietnam. We had an embargo. We had unresolved issues like the POW/MIA question, all subject to conspiracy theories and political exploitation. But there was a group of senators from both sides of the aisle who had taken it upon themselves to try to change the status quo. They were liberal and conservative. Sometimes they were friends, other times bitter adversaries, but on the issue of Vietnam they had each other's backs. It was Frank Murkowski from Alaska, who championed trade and an end to the embargo. It was the Vietnam vets—Bob Kerrey, John Kerry, John McCain, Chuck Robb, and, later, Chuck Hagel and Max Cleland—who formed a phalanx to defend each other for making peace if they were attacked for being "weak" on Vietnam. And it was my work with Bobby Muller on land mines and Agent Orange that resolved that issue. In all these overlapping efforts, many independent of one another, the Senate, more so than even the presidency, had been the active catalyst to make peace with a former enemy.

My first trips came flooding back. The streets were teeming then with young people dressed still in black revolutionary garb, mostly on bicycles. Back then, some, out of habit or out of courtesy to their American guests, still referred to Ho Chi Minh City as "*Saigon*," or they'd rush the words together into a verbal mishmash, blurting it out too quickly: "*Senatorhowwasyourtriptoo HoChiMinhCitytheoldSaigon . . .*"

But for this young student at Fulbright University, Saigon was at most a faded nomenclature in old history books that her parents may have read growing up. The streets were filled with motorbikes and cars. This student wasn't dressed in black revolutionary garb. Her shirt read IZOD LACOSTE. We knew that every student at the university had English as a second language, but this young woman had told us she didn't start speaking English until she was ten, and she apologized in advance if she got some of her words and pronunciation wrong. Then she began making her point: "*Well, when you stop to think of it, that would be indicative of . . .* " I looked at everybody's open mouths. Her English was flawless, and her big smile made it clear that she didn't think of the war as a memory—because for her, and even for her parents, it wasn't. She was living a life like any college student in which we were the visiting Americans, not occupying enemies.

I'd been to Vietnam several times. But this time was different. The arc of history is something you can lose track of when you're riding atop it. I've always loved history, but maybe I hadn't always paused enough to appreciate it.

I thought about the amputees I'd met on my first trip, the generation that had fought in the jungles and been maimed by land mines. I thought of the trips to the orphanages and the field hospitals to see the children living with birth defects from Agent Orange. I'd been to Da Nang, which had been poisoned at the airfield by Agent Orange, and met those still suffering because of it. We had worked with our Department of Defense, and the funding I secured helped the Vietnamese build a multistory, football-field-long device that would cook the soil until all the Agent Orange was out of it: not a microbe left alive in it. It was interesting to see the reaction of the Vietnamese who welcomed the American delegation with open arms. I told the senior commander of their military that John Tracy from my office in Vermont had last been in Da Nang when he was serving as a helicopter gunner in the Army. The senior commander, in full uniform, walked up to John and saluted him. What a journey. So much pain that had to be reconciled. I flashed back to the faces of the Amerasian orphans I'd met in the 1990s, young men and women who had largely been abandoned to raise themselves, often on the streets, left behind when our last helicopters left the embassy roof in 1975. The Vietnamese called them *bui doi*, "*dust of life*," such a tragic term for these sons and daughters of American GIs. The dust of history was finally settling.

In the Senate, we'd worked to "*fight the forgetting*," to resist the temptation to just turn away from a place where American troops had fought so long and sacrificed so much, and where the Vietnamese had sacrificed in numbers almost indescribable: almost three and a half million dead, five times the population of Vermont.

I remembered those early conversations with President George H. W. Bush and James Baker and Secretary of State Lawrence Eagleburger, first to help landmine victims and then to clean up the damage from Agent

Orange. I remembered telling President Bush about the amputees I'd met and the life-changing wheelchairs our partnership had delivered to those grizzled war veterans outside Ho Chi Minh City: the ordinarily reserved elder Bush just patted my arm and said, "*Patrick, we are on the right road.*" And we really were. The quiet, behind-the-scenes beauty of the Senate Appropriations Foreign Operations Subcommittee had always been that we could work with an administration and work with our colleagues to invest in a country like Vietnam, and few people really ever sifted through the line items to understand what we were doing was actually making American foreign policy.

By contrast, I thought about just what a raw, open wound Vietnam had been in our political dialogue at home: the editorials when I first voted in 1975 to end the war. The chastisement from the rock-ribbed American Legion and VFW after that vote, and their bewilderment when I turned up a couple of years later in Burlington with Mr. Conservative, Barry Goldwater, by my side to encourage the federal government's greater investment in GE's Vermont-made military manufacturing. It had been such a divisive time, when too few realized you could support the troops but oppose a war, let alone think that the best thing for those brave Americans was to bring them home. And Vietnam? I didn't like the Communist government's oppression or its devotion to a failed ideology. But I didn't much care for the similarly oppressive behavior of the nominally democratic government in the south, and I knew we couldn't prop up South Vietnam forever. But more important, I knew we didn't belong in the middle of their civil war any longer, if we ever had. It hadn't been easy, but it was a vote of conscience, and it was worth the scars that followed.

I wasn't alone on that score. I'd heard the stories of Barry Goldwater's successor, John McCain, being labeled the "*Manchurian Candidate*" by the right wing because he dared to help open a new chapter with a country in which he'd left so much of his youth and health behind. I remembered walking on Delaware Avenue, headed into the Russell Building one day with my colleague from Massachusetts John Kerry. John had volunteered and served on the Mekong Delta, and returned home, heavily decorated, to protest the war. "Hanoi John, we'll never forget," bellowed an angry voice from the park across the thoroughfare.

We were still fighting a war over the war.

Kerry's jaw tightened, but he pretended not to hear it, and we kept walking and talking. But I knew he'd heard it, and that he'd heard it many times over the years since he'd testified against the war in front of J. William Fulbright's Foreign Relations Committee in 1971.

And here I was, face-to-face with a young student from a new generation in Vietnam—at Vietnam's first independent American-style university, named after that US senator who had convened that anti-war hearing: J. William Fulbright the Arkansan.

The saying goes that history doesn't repeat itself, but it rhymes.

History was rhyming today.

We weren't fighting the war over the war anymore, certainly not here in Vietnam. I wondered how many of the students had ever had reason to think about the American for whom their university was named.

I remembered Bill Fulbright. I hadn't served with him: the same year that I was elected against all odds, Fulbright, an institution within an institution, had lost his Democratic primary to the charismatic young governor Dale Bumpers. It was Fulbright's opposition to the war in Vietnam and his globalism that had worn thin in Arkansas. For many, he was a cautionary tale. But to me, he was a reminder of why the Constitution gives senators six-year terms: to take positions of conscience worth losing the next election, if that's what it takes. Senate freshmen together, Dale Bumpers and I would become close friends. But I'd always remembered Fulbright's example, as both a warning about staying closely connected to your home state and an exemplar that some fights really were worth losing a Senate seat.

I'd met Fulbright years later when he practiced law and lobbied in Washington, DC. He missed the Senate deeply. It had become his life. Watching him reminisce wistfully reminded me to savor the time here, to cherish the privilege knowing it could be fleeting. He died in 1995, two years before full diplomatic relations were restored with Vietnam.

But I was still here, and I still had what Fulbright had cherished: a voice.

Another young Vietnamese student raised his hand with a question. What was the hardest part of public service?

I chuckled. I looked over at my Senate colleagues who had joined me on this trip to Asia: Lisa Murkowski from Alaska, Tom Udall from New Mexico, Sheldon Whitehouse from Rhode Island, Mazie Hirono from Hawaii, Wisconsin's Tammy Baldwin, Debbie Stabenow from Michigan, Tim Kaine, and Rob Portman from Ohio.

"*Well, in our country we have freedom of expression and freedom of the press. So, when you're the government, you're always criticized. And sometimes it isn't fair. You should see what our newspapers write about us.*"

More knowing chuckles from my colleagues.

"*But you know what? That's a strength of our society. We're very proud of that. We think people should always have the right to criticize their government. Even when we're the government. Because in a democracy, we work for the citizens, and they get to tell us how they think we're doing.*"

Our Vietnamese minder from the Foreign Affairs Ministry stood stoically in the corner. Vietnam had a way to go. But I believed that with students who went to a university where they could ask tough questions themselves, it wouldn't be another generation and it certainly wouldn't take another civil war before that government official would have to understand who he worked for too.

After meeting the students, we went to lunch with the leadership of Fulbright University, the Americans and Vietnamese who had been building this vision of a free and modern university in the middle of an authoritarian state. Their Pied Piper was an American: a Vietnam veteran, a marine who had spent years working first on normalization and later in academia. His name was Tommy Vallely. Tommy had two passions: Vietnam and American politics. He'd been a right-hand aide to Senator Joe Biden. Tommy was an incurably Irish storyteller. "*Senator Leahy, you know, when Joe Biden was elected, he told William Fulbright that he cared about foreign policy—so he wanted to be on the Foreign Relations Committee. You know what Fulbright told him?"*

I arched an eyebrow and waited for the punch line. Fulbright, Tommy continued, said, "*Oh, if you want to do that, you're in the wrong place. Go down the hall and see Senator McClellan—it's the Appropriations Committee that makes foreign policy.*"

We both laughed. We'd both been a part of healing Vietnam's past. But now the foreign assistance was being tested in a new way: Could it build Vietnam's future?

But first, and one of the driving purposes of this trip, we had to make sure we still knew how to build our own future, as senators working together. We had started the trip in Seoul, South Korea, and gone to the demilitarized zone, standing within inches of armed North Korean soldiers who photographed us as I photographed them through a window. We'd seen what a fifty-year frozen stalemate still looked like, and we knew that many thought the Congress of the United States was becoming a bit too much like that itself: a DMZ at best, a place where both sides knew each other only as adversaries, partitioned into bitterly warring camps.

On the flight to Vietnam, we'd done our best to find out more about each other. I asked the military aide to make sure that the assigned seating wasn't by political party or even by seniority. I thought of Mike Mansfield and Bob Stafford: no juniority, no seniority—just senators. We were flying to Ho Chi Minh City in the middle of Passover, and Senator Udall's wife, Jill, who was Jewish, had told Marcelle that she had hoped to find a place in Seoul where she could do a Seder but couldn't find one. For the flight, Jill arranged to have all the provisions needed, from a lamb shank to kosher wine, the prayers printed out and everything available for a six- or seven-mile-high Seder over the South China Sea. I talked with the pilot, who filed a new flight plan to avoid a storm on our flight path, and we held the Seder in the conference area of the military plane, with Protestants, Catholics, and Buddhists joining Mrs. Udall as we each said our prayer, took our sip of wine, and marked the occasion together.

When all was done, the pilot signaled that now we were going back into turbulent air and instructed us to put our seat belts on. Refreshed and recharged by a shared ritual, we headed back to our seats.

That Sunday in Ho Chi Minh City, all of us went to Easter Sunday Mass at the beautiful old French cathedral. Afterward, Sheldon Whitehouse shared his experience in Saigon, the son of a foreign service officer and an ambassador remembering how everyone was evacuated at the end of the war.

Rob Portman leaned forward: "Sheldon, I never knew that about you."

Afterward, Alaska's resolute senior senator, Republican Lisa Murkowski, looked at me and said, more aspirational than wistful, "*Why can't the Senate be like this all the time?*"

It was worth the journey of 8,756 miles to hear that observation.

I wish I could say that the spirit I found overseas with some remarkable colleagues had proven infectious. It did not.

The Senate remained in the grips of polarization and dysfunction, though many senators chafed against it. It was always interesting to me how often it was younger senators who were most interested in hearing about the distant times when the institution actually functioned. They longed for something so much better than what they'd found.

In the Senate, Democrats had their eyes and hopes pinned on 2020 and the possibility that the fever would break if Donald Trump was just a one-term president. Bernie Sanders came to me early this time and shared that he was going to run again for president. I reminded him that I didn't usually get involved in primaries among friends, but told him I would support his candidacy—not that he needed it. Bernie's political strength has never been built brick by brick on endorsements. But soon in Vermont, buttons appeared that proclaimed "*Sanders, Leahy, Welch—Vermont's 2020 Dream Team.*" We were united at home, but more important, Democrats, including Bernie, were determined to shape a united party for November, no matter who the nominee was. The Senate couldn't withstand the alternative.

But the Senate had not yet hit bottom. In the late winter of 2020, the news stories were suddenly everywhere: a virus that originated in China had spread to Europe. In the cloakroom, we watched images from Italy of hospitals that were running out of ventilators and of neighbors singing across their alleyways—locked down, but refusing to give in.

We sometimes in America think of ourselves as invincible. I don't know why. Certainly, no senator watching that television screen imagined what would come next: masks, virtual voting, quarantines, emergency rooms full, and schools closed.

But what I really never could've predicted was the reaction of so many elected officials in Washington to demonstrate such callous disregard for the people with whom they worked and shared the Capitol Building.

It was stunning to see senators refuse to wear masks, even as clerks and staffers endured chemotherapy and came to work with weakened immune systems. How little appreciation can you have for the way you're supposed to treat people? The political statement of refusing to protect your fellow citizens was surreal and offensive.

I couldn't help but think of how many elected leaders who talked about being pro-life, and who had railed against right-to-die laws in states where terminally ill elderly people believed they should be able to choose a peaceful end to their lives, were not even willing to suffer a minor inconvenience—a mask—to protect the elderly or the immunocompromised among them.

But that was, unfortunately, a microcosm of what was happening under the Capitol Dome. Words and statements of values were situational and could be erased from one day to the next like they were written upon a chalkboard. I watched as the Senate parliamentarian Elizabeth McDonough, wearing latex gloves and a face shield, came to work day in and day out, even as she battled through chemotherapy. How callous that some colleagues wouldn't wear a mask in deference to her fragile immune system.

We hoped so much that it would all start to end on November 6, 2020, that a presidential election would bring the United States a reset. I'd backed my colleague from Vermont, Bernie Sanders, in the primaries, and I was impressed by the way Bernie and the entire party threw their arms around Vice President Biden as the results of the nominating contests became clear. We had to win.

But 2020 wasn't done with any of us yet before tragedy struck again. The news we had all feared for years arrived like a jagged pill on September 18. Ruth Bader Ginsburg had passed away after battling health challenges for years.

With her passing, the Republicans who had once said that ten months was too soon in a presidential election year to confirm a nominee now thought it could and should and had to happen in the sixty days before an election, with their incumbent nominee trailing in poll after poll.

It was hypocrisy of a higher order than anything I'd ever witnessed, and above all, it was an exercise of brute political force without any regard for the consequences for the institution.

Lindsey Graham, chairman of the Judiciary Committee, embodied the complete whiplash of the Republican position. Graham had been a cheerleader of the ten-month stonewall of Merrick Garland.

"I want you to use my words against me," Graham said in 2016. "If there's a Republican president in [2020] and a vacancy occurs in the last year of the first term, you can say Lindsey Graham said, 'Let's let the next president, whoever it might be, make that nomination.'"

Indeed, here we were—and here was Lindsey rushing to confirm President Trump's nominee and create a 6–3 conservative, ideological majority.

President Trump chose Amy Coney Barrett, a young jurist embraced by all the very conservative lobbying groups. It was a circus. Some of the liberal groups who obviously had never studied the Senate rules were spouting all kinds of recommendations—like demanding that we boycott the hearings so that the nominee couldn't be voted on, even though that wouldn't have stopped anything, it would only have meant that she wouldn't face rigorous questioning. The Left, understandably upset, seemed hell-bent on proving how bad of a job they could do reaching the heart of the country and those on the fence; they sent people dressed up like handmaidens to shout at the Democratic members of the Judiciary Committee.

It was a reminder to me of how much we had to wrestle with cold, hard realities. This tragedy unfolding before our eyes wasn't a sign that we needed costumes or slogans, but it was proof of why elections matter. Anyone who had taken a pass on our nominees in 2000, '04, or '16 in protest, delighting in "purer" alternatives, needed to understand what we were up against now and what consequences it would have for a long time.

The lockstep machinations of the Republicans hid any question of whether their nominee was qualified or not, but they made it very clear they had one set of rules for Republicans and a different set for Democrats, and were willing to demean the Senate.

I particularly tangled with Senator Josh Hawley from Missouri. Any time anyone asked Barrett a probing question, Hawley volunteered, theatrically, that he was standing up for Catholics, in some of the most condescending, demeaning references to Catholics I'd ever heard. I told him I was sick of hearing his political baloney. I wanted to use a somewhat stronger word. After all, they were the ones breaking the rules and breaking their word, and I told him it made me think about all the lessons I'd actually learned in catechism, which started with "tell the truth." But here he was, a non-Catholic, self-appointed to lecture those of us who were.

Barrett was confirmed just days before America voted.

But at last, on the direction of our country, Americans would finally have a say.

Elections really did matter—and this one mattered more than any other. Joe Biden was going to be President of the United States.

— 60 —

The Breaking Point

"*I rise up, both for myself and sixty of my colleagues, to object to the counting of the electoral ballots from Arizona.*"

It was pure partisan theater, orchestrated by one of the House's most bombastic members, Paul Gosar, a former dentist representing western Arizona. Until this moment, his claim to fame was that his own siblings had run a television ad opposing his reelection.

Vice President Pence steeled himself and, without expression, read the words on the papers in front of him. I didn't envy Pence at this moment.

"Is the objection in writing and signed by a senator?"

"Yes, it is," replied Gosar.

A few feet away from Gosar, a stocky COVID-masked man in a bright blue suit rose.

"*It is,*" he announced dramatically.

Ted Cruz, the Texas Republican, had an uncanny ability to snatch any right-leaning, hyperpartisan political opportunity from the jaws of reality.

Four years before, Cruz was an anti-Trump presidential candidate whose own wife was mocked by the future president and whose father was falsely accused by Trump of being a Cuban accomplice to the Kennedy assassination. But years after his candidacy got stuck somewhere in the tuba section of the Republican presidential parade, Cruz had shape-shifted into an adoring more-MAGA-than-thou cheerleader. He was making his stand on behalf of the legions of red hats in 2021, but I suspected that 2024 was on his mind.

Groans echoed through the House chamber. It was a visceral reaction to the manifest preening and opportunism. Cruz reminded me of something Fritz Hollings had once leaned over and told me about Jesse Helms: "*Pat, do you know why people dislike Jesse Helms as soon as they meet him?*" Hollings paused. "*Because it saves time.*"

Sensing the waves of groans, the House MAGA boosters rose and applauded Cruz, who stared straight ahead admiringly, one hand in his pocket, the other stretched forward plaintively, as if he were about to launch into a soliloquy. His now-familiar pose reminded me of a college Lincoln-Douglas debater, always ready to make one more polished, practiced point.

Pence continued in his dusty baritone. "*The Senate will now retire to its chamber.*"

The senators lumbered back to the floor.

There was eye-rolling at the impending political theatrics orchestrated by a handful of our colleagues, and largely resignation that this momentary indignity was to be endured by the institution, one last spasm of the Trump years.

Still, as I sat down at my desk with a legal pad full of notes, I was haunted by what was happening to the institution. What possible spell did Donald Trump and his most fervent followers hold over the Republican caucus that the institution itself seemed an afterthought? What did that say about the state of our democracy?

Not a single senator doubted that Joe Biden was going to be sworn in as the forty-sixth president of the United States. Some who objected to the certification of the votes said as much, and some even acknowledged that he'd been duly elected and argued instead that Trump's supporters "*had to be heard.*" It was bizarre: if people believe a lie, you don't help them find the truth by echoing the lie. I expected little from Ted Cruz. I expected even less from Josh Hawley, having seen Hawley race to the cameras on issue after issue, a young man in a hurry with his own eyes on 2024. But more than a dozen Republican senators had pledged to object to the Electoral College vote count. Senator Cindy Hyde-Smith from Mississippi had once said that if Trump invited her to a public hanging, she'd "*be on the front row.*"

What I couldn't simply shrug off was the consequence of more than 10 percent of the US Senate giving voice to the big lie that an election was stolen after an exhaustive legal process overseen largely by Republican-appointed judges had overwhelmingly proved otherwise, conclusively. I wondered why they were comfortable proclaiming that our democracy was really that broken, particularly when many of them had been on the ballot in the same election themselves and when all of us counted on the currency of electoral integrity to do our jobs as senators. Did they really believe that if millions of citizens were allowed to believe that one election was stolen in several states in an invisible, undocumentable conspiracy, that future elections wouldn't be seen as just as illegitimate? It seemed like it would require an out-of-body experience for any senator to believe this moment wouldn't taint the institution and hurt their own ability to govern. If there's one thing the Senate teaches you, it's that precedents, even those created in regrettable it-felt-right-in-the-moment rash actions, have an uncanny way of confronting you in unforeseen future moments of consequence.

But here we were. We were all waiting for what we believed would be a made-for-television spectacle designed to raise money from the MAGA crowd for the most sycophantic heirs to the Trump throne. It was insulting to the institution, it was discourteous to colleagues, and it was horrifically condescending to the American people. These Republicans had so little regard for their own grass roots that they believed they'd buy any diction under the sun.

At least this step in the process would be over relatively swiftly, I concluded. Except it wouldn't be.

There was a sudden flurry around the well of the Senate. Whispering around the vice president. He looked puzzled and was quickly rushed out of the chamber by Secret Service. I wondered if he was taking a phone call from President Trump, who had been addressing the MAGA crowds on the Mall.

The chair of the presiding officer was vacant for a few seconds, a breach of protocol. Someone rushed the president pro tempore, Iowa's Chuck Grassley, into the chair to preside.

A man with a short-barreled submachine gun suddenly appeared a few feet away from me in the aisle. I looked up at him, and my expression must've been revealing. "It's okay, Senator," he said, and he pointed to the lanyard carrying his badge: he was law enforcement.

More police came in with drawn guns.

I'd been here forty-six years. Police and Secret Service never come onto the Senate floor. In fact, I'd witnessed for years the occasional frustration of the Secret Service that they couldn't accompany vice presidents and senatorial presidential candidates they were protecting. It was simply the way things were done here: the Senate belonged to the senators, and implicit in that covenant was that we trusted one another.

Was there a bomb scare? A gunman running loose nearby?

A familiar-looking Capitol Police officer scurried up to the chair and was talking worriedly with Grassley. I made the connection right away: he was Mark Gazelle, the jovial, big, burly officer with whom I used to talk about Jerry Garcia.

I'd never seen him look so shaken. He started pounding the desk for order, saying something over and over. But no one could hear him over the chatter and whispers on the floor.

"*Use the microphone!*"

"*We have to evacuate,*" he directed in his amped-up and amplified voice.

"*My wife texted me—the mob is in the Capitol,*" shared a bewildered colleague. "*They're trying to get onto the floor.*"

My adrenaline was up immediately as a line of senators moved through the lobby in the back of the Senate chamber near the president's room. A Capitol Police officer directing senatorial traffic shouted, "*We have to go down the back way.*"

I made my way toward the narrow stairs next to the ornate Senate Foreign Relations Committee meeting room. I'd spent hundreds of hours there meeting with heads of state, talking about the prospects of peace, sharing thoughts about democracy and free elections, encouraging leaders to take risks in the name of nation-building. Now here we were, escaping that hallowed space, our own democracy under assault by a mob.

I looked down at the shadows of the narrow nineteenth-century marble staircase. It would be an inopportune time for a tumble.

A police officer saw me pause.

"*I have bad depth perception,*" I explained.

"*That's why I'm here, Senator,*" said the officer, and he guided me by my arm as we moved down the steps together to begin the long trek toward the secure area in the Hart Senate Office Building. "*I will stick with you.*"

Down below in the bowels of the Capitol, the Senate trolleys weren't running. Accompanied by police wearing riot helmets and Kevlar vests and toting guns, we moved in a procession along the white walls next to the abandoned trolley tracks. A helmeted, uniformed police officer behind a COVID mask sidled up to me, winked, and said, "*Don't worry, Shamrock, we will keep you safe.*"

Shamrock. It had been the Capitol Police code name assigned to me after the anthrax attacks and during my years as president pro tempore after Danny Inouye died.

And now the surreal realization hit once again, and I felt my eyes water.

To think that twenty-four hours before, I'd been up late following the Senate run-off elections in Georgia, realizing that our upset twin victories would mean that I'd once again become the Senate's president pro tem. I'd thought of the spirit of reconciliation I'd hoped to bring to the Senate.

And here we were, not even a day later, forced out of the Senate chamber by a violence and a sickness in our politics that underscored just how wide the divide had become, not just in our politics, but in the shared experience of being an American.

The otherwise sterile underground path from the Capitol to the Hart Building is often dotted with framed works of art from schoolchildren around the nation representing each state, adding a touch of humanity to the otherwise stark whitewashed walls that evoke hospitals and industrial efficiency.

But up above, from the ceiling, hang the fifty flags of the Union—arranged in the order they adopted the Constitution.

I came to the fourteenth flag—Vermont's state emblem. I looked up at the familiar pine needles I'd been taught about in grade school. I thought of my father's love of history, how proudly he remembered that the flag's design commemorated the tiny pine branches worn by young Vermont militiamen at the Battle of Plattsburgh as a young nation vanquished the British for a second time in the War of 1812. They surrounded a sturdy and steadfast lone pine tree.

I whispered upward, "*I'm here—I'm still here, we're going to get through this.*"

Just thinking about the meaning and history of that flag energized and angered me.

Eight times I'd been sworn into the Senate. I thought again of those pine needles and the blood and bravery they signified: more than two hundred years before, Vermont patriots left fields and farms and quarries and volunteered to defend their young country in a war in which the Capitol Building in Washington, DC, was ransacked and invaded.

But today, teeming crowds in camouflage and red caps who misappropriated and bastardized that very word—"patriots"!—were turning democracy and the rule of law upside down, invading our Capitol just as violently as King George's redcoats ever had.

It was treason before our very eyes.

I was furious.

In our secure workspace, the rank and file of the Senate milled about. We knew that the Senate leadership had been brought to a different bunker and Vice President Pence was somewhere else. As the minutes ticked by in the windowless room, the nervous energy turned into banter.

Then someone turned on the television sets, and the mood became somber. If anyone hadn't processed what was happening outside and above us, there was suddenly no escaping it. It was anarchy. Footage of the crowd parading Trump flags and Confederate flags through the Capitol were stunning.

The buffoonery. The bellicosity. The bedlam.

But when the footage turned to the Senate floor, the gasps were audible. A Trump supporter scaled the wall of the Senate chamber. Others stood in the well. Still others dared sit at the antique desks that had once belonged to Henry Clay, Daniel Webster, Mike Mansfield, Howard Baker, and Bob Dole.

This was the home of American democracy, and this was an unthinkable home invasion.

My phone vibrated again and again: it was Marcelle texting me the images from television.

"We're watching."

"We are too. We're safe."

"I love you."

"Please stay safe."

I called my office in the Russell Building. "*Stay locked down. Stay safe. Barricade the doors if you need to.*"

I knew that those old dark oak doors would require an army to knock them inward.

But an army was exactly what appeared to have descended on the Capitol complex, an awful, angry army of haters and misfits who had been led down a path of lies to a course of violence.

I wondered, *Will my Capitol office be destroyed?*

I could picture every irreplaceable, sentimental item hung so carefully on the walls: the framed clip from the *Rutland Herald* in 1974—"Poll Dooms Leahy"—just above the clip five days later—"Leahy Unexpectedly Elected to Senate"; my "conscience" photo of the man I met at a refugee camp; the pictures of Marcelle and my parents standing with us on the eastern front of the Capitol; the photos of our children and grandchildren.

It was my inner sanctum: a stone's throw from that balcony view of the Washington Monument, the treasured landmark where my father had paid his final visit to look out from the observation deck and look down the Mall at the place where his son worked.

Were all those treasures of a life in the Senate now trampled upon, lying in a mess of broken glass? Security and Senate administrative staff jostled about in a corner of the bunker, trying to maneuver a pair of loudspeakers into place to deliver reports and instructions about the action in the Capitol—operational security reports.

Soon, they were bringing in chairs and bottled water and setting up microphones at a series of tables, cognizant that the Senate in emergency circumstances could pass a resolution to gather and meet wherever it needs to. My mind flashed back to a flight into Bosnia on a military cargo plane—battleship gray, not blue and white. It was too dangerous for President Clinton and his entourage to be as visible as what we all identify as Air Force One would make them. But lo and behold, I heard the pilot announce, "This is Air Force One." There was no announcement now, but right here in a fortified bunker—sadly, this was now the floor of the US Senate—the Senate chose to open session in this sterile, sequestered spot outside the Senate chamber for the first time since it convened in a special public session at Federal Hall in New York City after 9/11, as the World Trade Center still smoldered.

"We don't have to wait to certify the vote. We can do it right here," a colleague suggested.

Heads nodded in agreement. I admired his initiative and his spirit: he was thinking, if the thugs had driven us out of the Senate, we'd show them they couldn't stop us from doing our jobs. But my reaction was just as strong. I heard a voice from deep inside suddenly take over, and I was waving my arms to get the attention of my colleagues over the rush to leap back into session.

"*No, no, no—look, I hear what you're saying. But I'm the dean of the Senate—this is my forty-sixth year here—and I will be damned if we cower in here and hide the people's business for the first time in Senate history just because these bastards did this.*"

The room got quiet.

I rarely got so animated. No one needed a stem-winder. But this was all from the heart, every word of it, even those that were four letters.

"*After the bomb went off in 1983—my God, you could still smell it the next morning. Shards of wood were everywhere over by the chamber. The door to the Republican whip's office was blown in! Howard Baker had us sit—all one hundred senators—right there in our seats to open the Senate the next morning and show those bastards that no terrorist could shut us down.*

"*After 9/11—all one hundred of us were in our seats to say we don't cower, we are the conscience of a nation, and you don't change who we are.*"

Chuck Grassley and I were the only senators remaining who had been there for those two events.

"*So, look—so what if we have to sit here and wait a few hours before we go back in the Senate—hell, it's a six-year term, we've got the time.*"

Younger members of the Senate who had never experienced an institution like that—Republicans and Democrats—said they agreed.

On an encrypted text chain set up so we could communicate at all times, more senators weighed in and said they agreed that it was important that the country should be able to see democracy carry on.

"*Even if we stay all night long, we go back in as soon as we can,*" said one senator.

It was an inspiring aspiration, but one that would be tested by the extended presence of a roaming, maskless Senator Rand Paul, the ophthalmologist who thought he knew more about COVID-19 than did Dr. Anthony Fauci, the director of the National Institute of Allergy and Infectious Diseases. I watched as Rand Paul walked up to groups of colleagues, trying to make conversation. Senators moved back six feet to socially distance. Others shifted politely and turned their backs. No one was particularly interested in chitchat with a potential human super-spreader.

Likewise, Ted Cruz and Josh Hawley were deep in nervous conversation with each other. I wondered whether it was sinking in that their orchestrated stunt played a role in all too real consequences. They looked like the dogs who had caught the car, these two Ivy League–educated elites who had tried to reinvent themselves as Trump-era populist defenders against the stolen election.

The news that the Capitol had finally been secured broke the sense of claustrophobia and sent all one hundred of us off to check on our staffs and survey the damage.

The trains were running again, so I walked halfway underground and took the elevator back up to the Russell Building. The staff was shaken but focused intently on the televisions blaring everywhere.

Then I was off to confirm whether my vision of my Capitol office being destroyed had come true.

I walked up the stairs, stepped into the hallway, and my heart sank: the office door was wide open. I knew that just feet away, the Speaker's office had been violated, a goon with his feet on Nancy Pelosi's desk.

Amazingly, the office was untouched. In the cloakroom, the scene was much as it had been with the staff: everyone was staring at television sets in disbelief.

Delaware senator Chris Coons had studied abroad in apartheid-era South Africa and traveled as a freshman senator to post-revolution Libya and Ukraine. "*Looks like a scene out of a post-conflict state. It looks like the kind of place the State Department tells you not to travel to.*"

He didn't say it sarcastically, he said it sadly.

The images of lawlessness triggered in me another nagging question, as a former member of law enforcement and as a grandfather of five. The Capitol Police had been wonderful protecting me and ninety-nine other senators today, whisking us to safety. But why had the angry hordes been allowed to pass through the metal detectors? Why had the guardrails and Jersey barriers been pulled back to accommodate the mob? Why had they paraded through the Capitol seemingly uninhibited to wave Confederate flags and try to intimidate? And why, when they were all through with their rampage, had they been allowed to simply go home without being arrested? How would I ever explain to *my* grandkids how differently peaceful protesters of color had been treated just that previous summer in cities across America?

It was a reminder to call Alicia. She put the children on the phone. Their first question was whether I was safe. My eyes welled with tears, not for the first time today.

The entire mood had changed.

When President Trump appeared on our screens, telling the protesters that they were "special" but that they could "go home" now, senators screamed at the televisions. The blame was on Trump and it was universal.

Lindsey Graham looked ashen, sitting in a chair staring off in the distance. He'd traveled such a journey the last few years, from Trump critic joined at the hip to John McCain to top Trump ally. I had the sense that Lindsey was constantly improvising, making up the rules as he went along, always jostling to find some advantage. Now he looked like a man coming to terms with the inevitable, that anyone who rode the roller coaster of trying to rationalize the irrational would end up haunted by it.

Senator Portman was among a group of senators talking to one of the twelve who had planned to object, Senator James Lankford of Oklahoma. Lankford was a quiet, smart conservative, and one who was close to a younger generation of centrist Democrats. Senator Kelly Loeffler from Georgia soon joined their circle. Lankford looked stricken. He was looking for a way to climb down from the heights of polarization he'd climbed earlier.

The evening was getting late.

We needed to go back to work and finish what we'd all started.

Every senator was on the floor, all but a couple of us masked and somber. Chuck Grassley and I were the only ones left who had been here the morning after the bombing in 1983, both of us sent to Washington by very different electorates in 1974. Grassley gaveled us in as president pro tem, the act of which garnered a hopeful round of applause.

Chuck Schumer, the Democratic leader who would soon become majority leader, a long-sought and hard-fought destination, tried to stay above the political fray. He talked about the Senate's history, the difficulties in this chamber, and the many close elections in which bitter enmity had surrendered to the peaceful transfer of power. I looked around the chamber and was dismayed to see so many looking down at their phones. The 24-7 social media culture could reach into even a moment like this one. I thought back to 1977, to Gerry Ford and Jimmy Carter and a national election decided by 0.1 percent of the vote after all the division of Watergate. The Republican ticket had carried four more states than the Democrats. But I knew that if anything had happened then like what we'd just experienced, no one would've dared to do anything but pay full attention as Hugh Scott and Mike Mansfield addressed the Senate.

But this was not 1977. This was a time in America when so many centrifugal forces were pulling apart the institutions that had kept us strong for so long. Cable television and social media had become platforms for politicians to cultivate a cult following by saying outrageous and unfactual things, and to be rewarded for it. Local newspapers were dying. Political primaries had become races to the extremes, and often it was the primary that effectively sealed the general election in red states. In 2016, America had elected a celebrity president who spoke lie after lie—so why would insurgent, post-truth politicians listen to their leadership in Congress when it seemed to pay greater dividends to follow Trump's lead and spout off on Facebook or Twitter? They wanted to bottle Trump's magic elixir, not bury it.

Leader McConnell tried to walk a fine line, making clear it was time for this division to end but giving space to the twelve in his caucus who had carried President Trump's water on the election conspiracies. He couldn't help but invoke protests by the Left and the history of Democrats outraged by Florida in 2000, talking about a stolen election, as if the disenfranchisement of so many in Florida and a contested and controversial legal process in one state could be compared to the sixty court decisions against a flailing Trump campaign. I knew Mitch didn't believe it. He looked exhausted, a man who had seen Trump's insanity cost him his majority the night before and was now watching the place that had been his life since 1985 under assault by a mob of supporters his president had whipped up. This wasn't the Appropriations Committee, where Mitch was well suited to work things out and cut a deal; there was no negotiation with Trump that didn't empower and enhance the grip of a demagogue on the Republican Party.

I knew Mitch didn't like Trump. But he knew that Republican voters would've taken Trump over their incumbent senators any day. He reminded me a little of the leaders I'd gotten to know in the Middle East over many years. When you spoke to them in private and asked why they couldn't hold free elections, the answer was always the same: If we did, Osama bin Laden would win. These Middle Eastern autocrats were afraid of their own citizens. Senate Republicans lived in fear of their own voters.

I wondered whether this place could ever really be put back together.

I listened to the speeches reflectively. Mitt Romney excoriated Trump, the insurrectionists, and the false choice between certifying the election and disrespecting Trump voters: you respect voters, Mitt said, by telling them the truth. It was a brilliant line and a reminder of the journey Romney had traveled from former Republican presidential nominee to political apostate in his own caucus. I couldn't help but think of the later years of Barry Goldwater, warning of the rise of a so-called Moral Majority that was neither moral nor representative of the interests of a real majority. Sometimes in the Senate, there's a miraculous alchemy that occurs when senators give up the temptation to tailor every position to presidential aspirations and just speak their mind. I had watched it happen with Ted Kennedy, and now I wondered if Mitt might play such a role on the right. But there was one more lesson to follow about what one senator with courage can mean to the institution when we're listening to one another.

The junior senator from Illinois, Tammy Duckworth, whose helicopter was shot down in Iraq, was a double amputee and a Purple Heart awardee. She was as smart and well-liked as she was brave and resilient. She often addressed the Senate from a wheelchair. But today, wearing stainless steel prosthetic legs, she pulled herself to her feet, hunched over her podium, flexed her arms to keep her balance, and addressed her colleagues about the real meaning of patriotism. I flashed back to John Stennis rising from his wheelchair, standing on his solitary leg, sweating through his suit to pay tribute to Tom Eagleton: Tammy and John had nothing in common ideologically, but in this moment, they were both, as old Stennis would've said, *"SENATORS!"*

I slipped a note to the independent senator from Maine, Angus King: "*I'm glad I'm here.*"

In the early-morning hours after the Senate dispensed with the fraudulent challenges to the electoral certification, I walked through the Capitol to head home. I had to be careful where I walked because of the slippery residue of fire extinguishers on the marble floors.

The Capitol was still and hushed.

It felt much as it had the last eleven months of COVID quarantine, but doors were open to the outside to let the cold fresh air in and force the stench of chemicals and perspiration out. A mob leaves behind an awful odor. Fear has its own brand of sweat.

Glass crunched under my feet.

As I got to the door of the Capitol, my car waiting under the breezeway, I looked out through a smashed door pane and saw in the glass spiderweb the lit-up image of the Supreme Court.

I stood there speechless.

It was the only appropriate way to see America this awful, exhausted morning: smashed, but still standing. I felt as I did on 9/11, watching the F-16s screech up the Mall to protect Washington against any more suicide missions. This was another attack, but this time it wasn't plotted in another country, but in the White House. It was an insurrection begun by the president of the United States.

I inhaled and exhaled. *Whatever time I've got left in the Senate, I just want to help put us back together as who we are,* I thought.

Pulling out onto Constitution Avenue in the dark, trash and tents and bottles littering the streets, barricades being erected, I called Marcelle.

"*I'm coming home. I need to come home.*"

— 61 —

History Calls

We were hours away from the start of the second impeachment trial of President Donald J. Trump—this time as a former president. Trump had been impeached by the House in 2019 already for trying to extort Ukraine for dirt on his political rivals, serious charges the Senate Republicans had dismissed without even probing. Now, I had an unusual responsibility under Senate traditions and norms: the president pro tempore, regardless of political party, has historically presided over Senate impeachment trials of non-presidents, mainly the impeachment trials of federal judges. When presiding over an impeachment trial, the president pro tempore takes an additional special oath to do impartial justice according to the Constitution and the laws.

Until now, of course, there had never been an impeachment trial of a *former* president. Feelers had been extended to Chief Justice Roberts to ascertain whether he wanted to or was willing to preside over a second Trump impeachment trial.

The chief justice declined: just follow the precedent, he suggested.

And so we were: the precedent for impeachment trials of nonsitting presidents was unimpeachable. The president pro tempore was to preside, period. I figured I'd be in the political crosshairs.

"*Senator Leahy, there's a tweet you need to see,*" said my chief of staff, J. P. Dowd.

Oh, how many conversations in Washington had begun this way through four years of the Trump administration.

After all, so much of the public dialogue, and Twitter in particular, had become a cesspool for inflammatory statements, and too often it had been a mirror held up for all to observe the extent of our political polarization and dysfunction. In my mind, it was also an accelerant for those sad trends.

If Russell Long had been prescient thirty-seven years before that the installation of television cameras in the Senate debates would tempt the worst instincts for senatorial grandstanding, I could only imagine what Russell and the old bulls would've said about social media.

Only this day, it wasn't a tweet from an angry former president, who had already been banned from social media for spreading disinformation.

It was a tweet from another senator, a colleague—and not just any colleague but the former Senate Republican whip John Cornyn of Texas, a critical member of Mitch McConnell's leadership team.

"*He cannot be an impartial judge. No American, let alone a former President, should be tried before a juror who has already determined guilt or innocence, and who also serves as a judge.*"

The "*he*" that Cornyn referred to was me.

So much was wrong about Cornyn's accusation.

It started with the stunning, willful abandonment of facts in the first line of the tweet.

I wasn't the judge in Trump's trial. I was to preside. I was to preserve order. I was to serve as a neutral arbiter, issuing rulings where appropriate with guidance from the parliamentarian. One hundred senators were the judge and jury.

My job was to mind the procedure and look out for the integrity of the Senate, not of either side. John Cornyn had to know this. And if he didn't, he knew me—he had to know that I'd never have it any other way.

But his agenda wasn't the institution; it was protecting the former president.

I chuckled regrettably: I knew that this tweet was a fundraising ploy, not a reflection of how John really felt about me. But if we were to take it literally—where was Senator Cornyn's concern about impartiality in 2019, when the Republican majority declared that they didn't need to hear from any witnesses or see any evidence to declare Trump innocent well before Justice Roberts had gaveled the first impeachment trial to order?

And today, how could Cornyn criticize me for believing that Trump's incitement of insurrection was impeachable, when one of his main talking points was that no trial was needed because enough Republican senators had already announced their commitment to acquit the former president?

Of course, if they were so intent on having someone other than the president pro tempore preside over this trial, why hadn't they held this trial before January 20? It was a sad game of political Kabuki theater. The circular arguments frustrated the Georgetown-educated lawyer inside of me: Didn't logic matter? But most of all, what stung about Cornyn's tweet was what it said about where we found ourselves as an institution.

My mind flashed back to a very different US Senate. In 1975, senators didn't even travel to one another's states without the courtesy of a heads-up. Mike Mansfield instructed freshman Democrats, "*You can question a colleague's position, but you never question their motivation.*" Bob Dole was hardly a squeamish partisan; he'd gleefully chaired the Republican National Committee, and Bob enjoyed the political fray. But Dole refused to campaign against the Senate Democratic leader because he worried it might hurt his ability to reach across the aisle and govern with someone he had to sit down with every single day. Dole knew his first responsibility was to the Senate. And underscoring all these written and unwritten rules of the institution was a simple principle: senators first, and ideally only, raised in private any important disagreement that might spill into public view.

That Senate was long gone.

Left in its place was a Senate where the governing principle too often seemed to be: *Ready, aim, tweet.*

I'd been a prosecutor. For forty-six years, I'd sat on the Judiciary Committee and chaired it for a total of seven years. If anything, my belief that Supreme Court nominations should ideally not be decided by party-line votes, which had led me to support John Roberts's nomination in 2005, and my fidelity to the blue-slip process on judicial nominations had put me in the crosshairs of activists on the left from time to time.

But never had I been accused of anything but carrying out my duties in a fair and evenhanded way—particularly in the hundreds of hours I'd presided over the Senate.

Until now. And without even the courtesy of a conversation. My Irish was up, momentarily. Sensing that, someone asked, "*Should we send out a tweet replying?*"

I paused.

"*No—there's been too much tweeting here already. That's the problem.*"

"*You don't want to respond?*"

"*No—the proof will be in how I preside.*"

I'd learned by now that in the end, that's always the case: partisans can spin their version of events in the moment and conjure "*alternative facts*" to whip up a crowd, but the lens of history has a pretty reliable habit of telling the real story, especially about moments like this.

After all, I was about to become the only senator in the history of the country to preside over the trial of an impeached president: the eyes of history were on me, but really, they were on all of us.

On February 9, I swore in the entire Senate as jurors.

I asked my predecessor as president pro tempore, Iowa Republican Chuck Grassley, to swear me in so that I could preside. I could've asked the majority leader. But I thought the symbolism mattered. Chuck knew that we were both loyal to the institution—both the Senate and the special role of the president pro tem, which I didn't want to be associated with partisanship.

I took my place in the presiding officer's seat, gaveled us in, and looked out at the back of the chamber. A memory flooded back: I was a thirty-four-year-old senator-elect, and Frank Church had escorted me onto the floor after the momentary interruption of a clerk who warned that senators and senators alone were allowed through that doorway. Since that walk and talk with Frank Church, I'd served alongside 402 senators—more than a fifth of the 1,994 men and women who had been sworn to that office since 1789.

And here we were—this group of one hundred senators—about to do something no previous group of senators had ever been charged with undertaking.

I thought about the story Senator Symington had told me in 1975 about Harry Truman: this really was a "*how the hell did* I *get here?*" moment.

But I hoped it wouldn't become a "*how the hell did* they *get here?*" moment. The Senate itself, as it was in 1999 with the Clinton impeachment, was on trial: Could we break the ugly, polarized national fever of four years that had led to an assault on the Capitol itself? Could the Senate be part of the solution, not part of the problem? Could we still find that "conscience" for a nation in need of healing?

I wasn't ready to surrender those hopes to the political cynicism of the moment.

When I look back on the 402 senators I've known and the hundreds more I've read about, I suppose it's a bit like human nature: some very good people, some very bad people, all wonderfully human and imperfect, most committed to doing the right thing by their states and the Constitution, even if they disagreed about what that was.

I knew that on this matter, there would be senators who would look at the evidence and, irrespective of any political consequence, want to do what is best and reflect what the Senate is supposed to do, which is to put the facts and the analysis ahead of party or president, and render a decision you can explain whether you're a Democrat, Republican, or independent, but a senator first.

I also knew that there were some who would consider what the political response might be in their home state and would determine how to vote based on that.

And I knew, perhaps most of all, that many others seemed to just want it—all of it, all of Trump, all the memories of the insurrection—to be over. They wanted to "*move on.*"

But I'd been here long enough to know that there's no such thing: you can't put your head in the sand and will away something that's eaten away at the integrity of an institution. You have to confront it forthrightly. It's just common sense.

I thought about the custodians and Capitol architects I'd gotten to know these last forty-six years. Every day, they checked on the foundation and the walls of the Capitol. They spackled the holes; they made sure that the hairline cracks of aging plaster were puttied over. They did it in real time because they knew that, left unattended, the damage would only grow.

It reminded me of the walks I'd take on our tree farm in Vermont, near the old stone walls. I'd grown up reading Robert Frost's words about the Vermont farmers repairing their stone walls:

Something there is that doesn't love a wall,
That sends the frozen-ground-swell under it,
And spills the upper boulders in the sun;
And makes gaps even two can pass abreast.

Vermonters pass by hundreds of old stone walls; those that survive intact are those that are carefully protected and maintained by people who care enough to put in the labor. But in other places, you'll find only ruins. After years of neglect, a stone wall—worn down by weather, knocked over by deer and moose, toppled by frost heaves—just becomes a scattered and forgotten pile of rocks.

We were here to repair the cracks in the institution that was attacked on January 6. It wasn't just the glass windows or the furniture or the doors that had been targeted that day; it was democracy and the rule of law. We couldn't just "*move on*" and pretend it hadn't happened. There had to be accountability for the insurrection. There had to be consequences, and if those weren't available, there would at least be a confrontation with the truth.

The Senate I'd joined in 1975 was filled with people who knew that and had done that when history demanded it. Barry Goldwater and Minority Leader Hugh Scott had taken that longest drive a short distance to the White House to tell Richard Nixon that he couldn't be president anymore. A year later, Frank Church led a painful investigation that exposed the FBI and the CIA to the sunshine of oversight and unearthed abuses of administrations both Republican and Democratic. Both actions had been taken for the good of the country. Just retreating to partisan corners on Watergate, or just "moving on" with respect to oversight, had never been a palatable option for any of these Senate giants.

I wondered: Could we do anything to live up to that legacy? Could we reckon with what happened on January 6—and how we got there? I wrote and underlined three times in my notes: "I am ready."

We began with the adoption of the resolution that Chuck Schumer and Mitch McConnell had agreed to for the rules that would guide the trial, including the allotment of time for each side to present its case. I read the vote tally, and it was overwhelming: 89–11. "*The resolution is agreed to.*"

But that moment of consensus was quickly followed by an opportunity for politics and partisanship. Senator Rand Paul immediately offered a motion that the trial itself was unconstitutional because you couldn't impeach a former president, a motion to effectively end the proceedings.

Rand Paul's entry into this process reminded me of the old Carl Sandburg quote I'd first heard in law school: "*If the facts are against you, argue the law. If the law is against you, argue the facts. If the laws and the facts are against you, pound the table and yell like hell.*"

Rand Paul spoke with the passion of a lawyer without either the facts or the law on his side.

It was defeated 55–45.

Five Republicans—Susan Collins, Mitt Romney, Ben Sasse, Pat Toomey, and Lisa Murkowski—voted against it.

Still, I worried that this was the start of a game of evasion: from here forward, even senators who loathed President Trump's actions leading to January 6 could avoid the heart of the issue. If the process of accountability was moot in their eyes, it was so much easier to defer the hard reckoning the moment demanded.

But the House impeachment managers were not going to allow anyone to look away from their responsibilities so easily. Their opening presentation set the tone and tenor, a more succinct and powerful presentation than any I'd heard in the two previous presidential impeachment trials.

Congressman Jamie Raskin laid out his case like a prosecutor confident in the facts, by not making himself the center of the show: he let the events speak for themselves—literally—through the power of video. On the presiding senator's desk was a small monitor. I watched in rapt attention as we all revisited the president's words and speeches leading up to those horrific moments on January 6.

It all came flooding back. My adrenaline started to flow. I watched every detestable quote from the former president from election week forward, all the way through his remarks that morning about "*stopping the steal*," his exhortation to the protesters about "*showing strength*," and his lawyer Rudy Giuliani's phrase about what was needed that day: "*a trial by combat*."

Raskin stated simply: *If these actions aren't impeachable, what is?*

But it was the images in the video that spoke to us just as compellingly. For many senators, it was the first time they'd sat quietly to relive that day. To see the footage of the angry mob outside the Capitol while we had all been sitting in the House and Senate chambers. The violence. The vitriol. There was so much we hadn't known in real time, including the gallows erected on the Mall with a noose reserved for Vice President Pence. The screaming about "*getting the traitors*."

It hit my colleagues that we had been *the hunted* that day.

I looked out at the chamber and saw senators sitting in silence. They breathed heavily behind their masks. Someone gasped as we relived the footage of Officer Eugene Goodman tricking the mob into chasing him down another hallway so senators, the vice president, and his family could evacuate safely. Some protesters had been caught on camera saying they were looking for Mitt Romney. I looked at Mitt. His eyes were shut tightly, the tension clear on his face.

Raskin spoke of his daughter being there on January 6, just a day after their family had buried his son, her brother. He became emotional as he talked about telling his daughter that she'd be safe. "*Dad, I don't want to come back to the Capitol,*" she responded.

My heart sank. I made a note to myself. This was the Capitol I'd cherished walking through from the first time I visited as a teenager with my parents, the Capitol where Mark and Kevin and Alicia had roamed freely as children, the Capitol where I'd brought my grandchildren to ride the Senate subway. How sickening to think that a congressman's daughter had been made to feel unsafe at one of the hardest moments in her life.

The president's defense lawyer Bruce Castor seemed to grasp just how much Raskin's presentation had taken the air out of the chamber. He spoke about his background as a former prosecutor, but he did not really address the heart of the charges, merely the alleged motivation of those who brought the charges. His goal seemed to be to appeal to the foundation of Trump's support—on a partisan basis.

Shortly thereafter, news broke that President Trump didn't think he'd been strong enough in defending him. I imagined Trump in Mar-a-Lago, screaming at the television set, ever the counterpuncher like his mentor Roy Cohn.

The president got what he wanted from the second member of his defense team, David Schoen. Schoen was animated and fiery. He argued that the impeachment was very political, raw sport, party over country. I could feel my temperature rise. The irony of anyone suggesting that accountability for an insurrection was "party over country"! Raging partisans were the ones who had stormed the Capitol. Raging partisans were the ones who had interrupted the ultimate "*country over party*" process, the certification of votes that allows for the peaceful transfer of power in a democracy.

His theatrical performance was a marked departure from the previous presentations: the others had read from notes, whereas he was clearly reading a speech. Just a couple of minutes into it, he turned to me and said, "*With all due respect*"—the telltale sign that something less than respectful was coming—and then attacked my role of presiding senator, projecting a quote of mine on the screen a few feet away.

I looked around the room at a number of senators having difficulty staying awake.

During a break, I spotted Dick Shelby—even in a mask, at a towering six feet five inches tall, he stands out in a crowd. I had read a news story in which Dick had unabashedly told the reporter that I would live up to my responsibilities as judge, juror, and witness. He didn't ask me whether he should talk to the reporter or what to say; he had just gone ahead and done what he felt was right. It reminded me of the old Senate. I thanked him for his comments. "*Well, I believe it, you know that, Patrick,*" he said. "*Everyone does. Don't let the politics allow any doubt.*"

Still, I was touched: Dick was a seasoned survivor who knew that Alabama was Trump country—a place where Jeff Sessions had been Trump's first Senate endorser, and a state where newly elected Tommy Tuberville had objected to the certification of the vote—but he was always going to keep his own counsel and speak his mind.

The trial proceeded at a crisp pace. We jurors listened to Donald Trump's recorded phone calls to Georgia to pressure the secretary of state and others, and the impeachment managers laid out the fact that history had repeated itself on January 6: after Trump's previous interventions against state officials who were following the law, death threats from Trump supporters had followed. I was struck by how the targets of these threats weren't liberal Democrats but conservative Republicans: there really was a new "Trump Party" in the United States, hard partisans willing to follow him anywhere.

And they had.

We watched the gripping videos and listened to the radio calls from the police during the breach of the Capitol. There were a number of things I had not seen before. I felt again the shock of watching the rioters going into the Speaker's office, just feet from my own unlocked Capitol office. Much of the footage was from security cameras and showed images of senators fifty-eight steps away from the mob.

There was footage of the police officers trying a variety of techniques to deal with the crowds that awful day. I thought of Officer Howard Liebengood. Howard had for years manned a door in the Russell Building not far from my office. I'd known him since he was a teenager, the son of the Senate sergeant at arms. After January 6, he went home and committed suicide. The weight of his memory was heavy in the chamber. I thought, *My God, how can people not take this personally—this was an attack on our whole Senate family.*

The next presentation was perhaps the most chilling. Again, the House managers didn't gild the lily: they let the events speak for themselves, this time relying on the statements of the insurrectionists themselves. It was a hard thing to hear. Americans from across the country who said—publicly, unapologetically—that they weren't doing anything wrong because they were in the Capitol following Trump's orders. My mind flashed back to the Washington I'd known. I had been elected to the Senate amid a tide of public backlash because a president had behaved as if he was above the law. There had been moments of political courage in that era—a "*Saturday Night Massacre*" in which the president fired official after official at the Department of Justice because they refused to carry out his orders to fire the special prosecutor. Here we were nearly a half century later and the opposite was true: violent people had broken the law, and their defense was that they were *just following* the president's orders. Something had gone terribly wrong in our country.

But the House managers also presented reasons for hope. They showed Phil Scott, the Republican governor of Vermont, calling January 6 one of the darkest moments in our nation's history. They talked about all the people who had resigned in protest after January 6, including Secretary Elaine Chao, Mitch McConnell's wife. They read aloud her quote, describing "*a traumatic and entirely avoidable event as supporters of the President stormed the Capitol building following a rally he addressed*," which left her "*deeply troubled . . . in a way that I simply cannot set aside*." I looked down at Mitch McConnell sitting there, stoically, just listening. It was one of many times I've wondered what was going through Mitch's head.

Representative Diana DeGette returned to the lectern and quoted Trump saying, "*Our journey is just beginning*."

I thought about all we had heard: the deep belief among the president's most fervent base that threats should be made and action taken against members of Congress. *This has to be the end of that journey,* I thought. I looked over at the newly sworn-in senator from Arizona, Mark Kelly, whose wife, former congresswoman Gabby Giffords, had been critically injured when she was shot ten years before. How real all of this had to seem to him—all too real, all too awful. And all it would take would be one hundred senators standing up as the conscience of the nation to say that it had to end right here.

The closing arguments of the president's defense team were surreal.

Michael van der Veen, the criminal defense and personal injury lawyer from Philadelphia, came out swinging. I hadn't known his name until the trial. His claim to fame was that he'd once represented a plaintiff who alleged to have been served a fried rat at Kentucky Fried Chicken. I took this to be a coincidence and not anything prescient about his current client, the former president.

Clearly his target audience was at Mar-a-Lago. We had already heard that Trump was very angry at the conciliatory words made by Castor earlier. As I listened to Van der Veen, I jotted down a note to myself: "*Well, this is not conciliatory.*"

It reminded me first of the president's personal physician, who wrote that he'd never seen a healthier patient than Donald Trump, or then of Press Secretary Sean Spicer, early in the Trump presidency, racing out to the cameras to argue the inaugural crowd size was far greater than it was. This was a ventriloquist act—and, in absentia, the former president was pulling the strings.

A witch hunt!

The Democrat parties! (This strange habit of the most partisan Republicans to deliberately mispronounce the words "Democratic Party" always struck me as particularly juvenile.)

I wondered whether Van der Veen thought he was playing to the senators as jurors, giving Republican senators cover for voting for Trump even if they felt he had broken the law, or just playing to Trump's ear. I assumed it was the latter, though I knew that the Trump legal team had met with Ted Cruz, Lindsey Graham, and other Trump defenders the night before.

Schoen was next, his bottom-line summation being that President Trump did nothing wrong, it was all about the Democrats, and making arguments tailored to help those who needed a reason to vote for Trump.

I got up and stretched my back, taking the advice of Chief Justice Roberts. Schoen saw me stand up and, panicked, thought I was about to make a ruling. He glanced back at me with a worried look, and I whispered loud enough for him to hear, "*I'm just stretching!*" He looked relieved that I wasn't about to rule him out of order.

If I could've ruled him out of order for audacity, I would have. He wove into his argument video clips of Democrats using the word "fight" in our own speeches, including one from me. Schoen just kept repeating the words out of context. One clip was even of Majority Leader Schumer saying, "*We must fight*"—but it ignored the rest of his sentence: "*to save the lives of people who are facing COVID.*" It was almost comical. As if Donald Trump was on trial for speaking figuratively; he was on trial for speaking as literally as one ever could, and he had gotten exactly what he wanted.

Time for questions followed, and the process seemed to devolve into a shouting match. Van der Veen grew heated with Senator Bernie Sanders, and I had to interrupt and require them both to follow Senate procedure.

As the afternoon turned into evening, there were a number of empty Republican seats on the floor, but after the questions ended and Schumer moved to award the Congressional Gold Medal to Officer Goodman, which McConnell agreed to, all one hundred senators took their seats. Goodman's eyes filled with tears as we all stood and gave him a standing ovation.

I thought of a conversation I'd had with him earlier. He always went out of his way to tell me how much my grandchildren had grown, and we talked about how racism was still an everyday fact in the country. He spoke about even having a police officer question why he was in his car waiting somewhere.

I wondered whether the Senate would be there for him in helping to right the wrongs of racism the same way it had in awarding him a medal. Standing ovations are easier than facing hard truths. It was time to bring this process to an end.

As Van der Veen engaged in a final stem-winder, he saw me suddenly start to lift the gavel and he acknowledged, "*I've got to calm down.*" I quoted Chief Justice Roberts about the need for decorum.

With a last-minute back-and-forth over subpoenas, we went into a very long quorum call. Senator Dan Sullivan moved to interrupt the quorum call, and I had to rule that he couldn't. He and John Barrasso came over to talk to me, and I pointed out that I tried to just follow the rules and I had to actually cut off Bernie Sanders yesterday. I told him I tried to be fair to both sides. Both Sullivan and Barrasso said, "*You've been totally fair, Pat*," which pleased me more than they might know.

We were soon in a protracted dispute over calling witnesses. Eleven Republican seats were empty, and all the Democratic seats were filled except for mine, and that's because I was in the presiding officer's chair.

President Trump's defense counsel objected several times, and I had to find the right diplomatic verbiage for "sit down and wait your turn." A squabble began again with Trump's attorneys getting out of line. I had to restore order and there was a long discussion at the bench.

Nerves were frayed.

Congressman Joe Neguse of Colorado spoke from the heart. He described contacting his wife and children when the mob was coming through just in case he did not see them again. He also talked about how the Senate could be bipartisan at critical moments. He said that when Congress passed the anti-apartheid legislation, Ronald Reagan vetoed it, and in a rare occasion the Congress overrode President Reagan's veto. He said there were two people sitting in the Senate today who voted to override—one Democrat and one Republican.

The Democrat was me and the Republican was Mitch McConnell. I flashed back to the memory of sitting on a couch facing Nelson Mandela. He thanked me for my vote. I asked him how he stayed so positive when he suffered years upon years in prison. Why wasn't he bitter? I'll never forget the answer. He said, "*Patrick, because I was in prison, I was able to lead my country out of apartheid. I am not bitter, I rejoice.*"

I had to think of all the history I'd seen over these years and how the Senate had evolved, in many ways not for the best. As I presided over this trial, I wished I could wave a magic wand and restore just a little bit of the Senate of old, the place where one hundred senators sat in awe to hear Mandela speak all those years before. That kind of Senate wouldn't have had a hard time deciding what to do with former president Trump.

But I also knew that if Nelson Mandela could spend all those years imprisoned and never get bitter—always continue the struggle—then it wasn't time to give up on the Senate yet either. I thought of Mandela's great expression: "*It always seems impossible until it is done.*"

It was time to vote.

Senators' names were called, and they were asked to stand when their name was called.

Among the votes to convict were Richard Burr of North Carolina, Bill Cassidy of Louisiana, Mitt Romney of Utah, Susan Collins of Maine, Pat Toomey of Pennsylvania, Lisa Murkowski of Alaska, and Ben Sasse of Nebraska.

More senators of the president's own party had cast a guilty vote than ever before.

Donald Trump was the first president in history to be impeached twice. And now I was the only senator in history to preside over the trial of someone who had been impeached while president. It wasn't a place in history that I had sought or ever imagined occupying, but I knew I had done my job to the best of my ability.

I sat with my discouraged staff, who had been counseling me throughout the trial, led by my extraordinary chief counsel Dave Pendle. They couldn't believe that only seven Republicans had done the right thing about the insurrection.

"*You can be pessimistic or optimistic,*" I said. "*I choose to be optimistic. You see forty-three who didn't stand up. I see fifty-seven who did. I see seven Republicans willing to be . . .*"

I stopped for dramatic effect, stood up, and channeled John Stennis's emphasis on the word: "*SENATORS!*"

I thought about the old saying "*One person with courage makes a majority.*"

"*If there are still SENATORS here, that means that there can be more of them. And that's what we need.*"

I thought, *Forty-seven years after I first walked onto the Senate floor—that's why I'm here, now: to remind the Senate that our job—all of us—is to be the conscience of our nation.*

And as Mike Mansfield told me, a senator always keeps his word.

EPILOGUE

"*What a life this has been.*" I write those words in the margin of my legal pad as I ride back to our house late one evening after a full day in the late winter, March 12, 2021.

What a life this is still.

Oh, what this eighty-year-old president pro tempore of the US Senate would love to say to the thirty-four-year-old version of myself nervously walking for the first time onto the Senate floor.

"*Don't lose that sense of awe, kid. Hold on to it. Treasure it. Don't even for a minute forget what a privilege and a responsibility it is to serve here.*"

I never have forgotten.

As I drive back to Virginia, this familiar commute the days and nights we're in session, I think about a day of exceptional privilege. The chance to sit in the Oval Office and hear the president and vice president of the United States speak with empathy for families suffering from COVID, with urgency about their efforts to bring the country back from the brink of economic and health disaster, with none of the braggadocio suffered at similar events just weeks before. And the chance, most of all, to think, *Now I get to go back to the Capitol and try to find the votes needed to make us a Senate again, to make this place work.* The chance to help in the healing. How blessed I am to have been doing that for close to half a century in the Senate.

We drive down the Mall, passing the Ellipse. I see children out in the dimming light kicking a soccer ball, willing the spring to come early. I think of our granddaughter playing field hockey. Now *there is life*, and I hope that life is coming back and that the things that have brought us joy all these years will be there again, so close that we can touch them and hold them again.

My car nears the Jefferson Memorial, the Capitol Dome peeking above the skyline, silhouetted in the distance. I know it's there because I know every yard of this drive by heart. I look at Jefferson in his marble Rotunda, as much a reminder as any imaginable of the tension that was and is America: imperfect people struggling to make reality out of ideals that they fail themselves to meet, but always, always, keep on trying. I think of my father, the self-taught historian: he loved to share with me the twists and turns of times gone by, not to lift up heroes as idols or to point out their feet of clay, but to find meaning and purpose in the journey. Only first-generation immigrants whose parents had fled homes where such journeys of change and redemption were not possible could have such a gleeful appreciation for the fact that America wasn't a place but an idea, an idea of unmatched possibilities ever in search of its own perfection, for new and next generations to write.

I have so loved the privilege of being even a small part of this story—America's story.

We cross the Fourteenth Street bridge and turn onto the George Washington Parkway. I put down what I was reading and just look out the window at the Washington skyline in the glow of the sunset. The Washington Monument. I think of my dad coming there as a young man, a young father determined to raise his children with opportunities he never had, and returning as an old man at the end of his days, content that he had given life his all, with pride in his three children and with resignation about the future, as if he'd absorbed the words of 2 Timothy 4:7: "*I have done* my *best in the* race, *I have* run *the full distance, and I have kept the faith*." What a gift to have had a mother and father who passed down to their children and grandchildren not privilege, but a powerful example.

We pass the Kennedy Center and the Watergate Hotel in the distance, forever two unmatched bookends in the American history that I've lived: President Kennedy and his brother Robert who inspired me, as a young man in Vermont, to dream of public service, and Richard Nixon whose abuse of the rule of law created a wave that helped lift me all the way to Washington, the first and only Democrat Vermont ever elected to serve in the Senate.

We ride along the Potomac River. I've loved the view since my days as a law student at Georgetown, even earlier when I was a tourist in Washington with my family. I've cherished the family times at Theodore Roosevelt Island with our three children, amid the pine trees that remind us always of the warmth of late summer in Vermont. And I've never forgotten the "pinch me" moments, boating with John Glenn and his wife, Annie, getting to know the man and the colleague, beyond the myth and the hero.

I think of John Glenn often on these drives. I think of who he was and the generation and the Senate he represented. I wonder what he would think of how we carried the baton he passed to the next generation. But then my mind flashes back to John's interment at Arlington National Cemetery. In the chapel, the Marine bugler played taps, paused, and then, completing a request John himself had made but long kept as a surprise, burst into reveille. That was John Glenn: there was a time to mourn and remember what was lost, but there was always another mission—another call to serve—another day.

And that's how it has to be. For all of us.

Yes, the Senate is a broken place. No, our institutions are not what Mike Mansfield and Hugh Scott and Gerry Ford and Hubert Humphrey and Ted Kennedy and John Stennis and Barry Goldwater knew them to be.

Some of that change is good, a lot of it is tragic, and all of it simply is what it is: you can point fingers, or you can point the way forward to something better. That's America, again, isn't it?

I haven't written a requiem for the Senate. I've shared a recipe for its renewal. Not *taps*, but *reveille*. Always reaching, always repairing, never retreating, never retiring from the journey.

A year ago, I was presiding for the first time in history as president pro tempore in an impeachment trial of a former president, and days after that I was announcing the results of legislation designed to bring relief to Americans after a pandemic cost half a million lives; and just months ago, I was back where it all began, in Vermont, sharing the news that it was time for a new generation to make its mark in a Senate in need of their idealism and impatience.

America doesn't stop. Our country just keeps turning. There are no permanent victories or defeats. And we—if we're lucky—all of us get a chance to help tilt the trajectory toward progress.

I arrive home. I see the security detail outside our house, the permanent fixture that I never got used to after an attempt on my life with anthrax poison and during my first time as president pro tempore, but now I understand the reason for it.

The light is on downstairs. Marcelle is waiting. What a long trip this has been from our days as a young nurse and a Georgetown University law student living in a basement apartment, to a state's attorney investigating murder scenes at 3:00 a.m., to a life with three growing children and now grandchildren.

I'm taking my "conscience" photo home with me, but I know that man's eyes will keep watching all of us. What a life.

What a journey.

What an abiding hope that someday after I've gone, the Senate will come back together to be the conscience of the nation.

And what a nation it is: a very rich and diverse history, diminished if we ever accept a destiny as something less than we can be, not a country defined by sound bites and polls, but one strengthened when women and men with a sense of history insist that our republic move forward.

What a prayer that, for the sake of all those children and their children, and all children and all Americans, it not only can be done, it has to be done.

I enter our house and hug Marcelle. We stand together in the silence, rocking back and forth as our own internal orchestra performs "Moon River."

I think of the miles and the milestones.

Of family, service, and country.

For me, the words of a Vermont poet apply equally to all three.

Robert Frost really was right: it's the road taken that's made all the difference.

ACKNOWLEDGMENTS

There aren't adequate words to express the kind of extraordinary people who have been by my side to write the real-life story of this road taken—let alone this look back at the road, so far.

The challenge of thanking those who made both the journey and its retelling possible is a daunting one; in a life that has been marked by so many friends, mentors, and colleagues, it is too easy to inadvertently leave someone out.

The many, many people whom I have met, worked with, been inspired by, and come to respect are a part of me and a part of this book forever.

But I'll start with the person who makes the journey a happy one, every day. My closest friend, confidante, and inspiration from college and law school days to decades of Senate service is my wife, Marcelle. She knows our life story together because she cowrote it from the moment we met. Her name could just as easily be on the cover of this book as mine. She also has urged me for years, along with our children, Kevin, Alicia, and Mark; Mark's wife, Chase; and my sister, Mary, to write my experience of public life. Of course, after Alicia's talented husband, Lawrence Jackson, published his book about his years as one of Barack Obama's photographers, he and Alicia pushed me even harder to write it. Pat Robins and his wife, Lisa, reminded me of Vermont stories, and Marcelle's cousin Ernie Pomerleau; his wife, Dee; and the myriad Pomerleau cousins filled in with family anecdotes.

I am forever grateful to Simon & Schuster for believing this was a life story worth publishing and an example of what public service and institutions like the Senate might one day mean again for our country.

Stuart Roberts, my patient and superb editor, believed in this book from the very beginning. He weighed in every step of the way with brilliant advice and an ability to separate the extraneous from the essential. I am grateful for his knowledgeable guidance. Simon & Schuster is blessed with a talented team, including Brittany Adames, whose work was critical to bringing this project in for a landing; Larry Hughes, who devised a strategy for marketing; and Jonathan Evans, a masterful copy editor. Of course, all of this benefits from my day-to-day collaboration over two years with David Eckels Wade. Bob Barnett introduced me to David, who had worked with Simon & Schuster on a previous memoir. David is a gifted writer and serious student of American history. His role was absolutely essential, enjoyable, and deeply appreciated, and I am proud to say that his young sons, Robert and Alec, became devotees of Vermont maple syrup in the process.

My friend, the extraordinary lawyer Bob Barnett, brought me to Simon & Schuster, and, just as important, he shared the gift of his experience of bringing hundreds of books to life.

I can't say enough about two people who oversaw the big and small tasks of ensuring *The Road Taken* didn't end in a cul-de-sac. Week after week for two-plus years, JP Dowd and Cabelle St. John pushed me to carve out time on nights, weekends, and early mornings to reflect and write. Their constructive feedback was unflinching. They also became frighteningly adept at bringing order to my sometimes chaotic notetaking, as did the talented archivist Keri Myers, assisted by Vik Kulkarni, who provided essential support. The chore of organizing thousands of pages of notes, journals, schedules, and photographs is formidable; I couldn't have done it without them. And JP, as chief of staff, had the added chore of flawlessly running my Senate office, all during a pandemic to boot.

I sometimes joke that senators are merely constitutional impediments to their staff. The hundreds of staffers who have been a part of this journey, in Vermont and Washington, are remarkable public servants. They chose this life for all the right reasons. And while there wasn't room to share every story in the pages of this book, I can tell you that behind every piece of legislation there is a senator—but there are also dedicated, creative, and innovative staffers who bring good ideas to life in ways that help people.

It isn't always the legislation that gets the biggest headlines or leaves the biggest mark. Toiling behind the scenes, you really can make a difference, and there is no better example of that than my foreign policy advisor, Tim Rieser. Because of my long tenure in the Senate, we have had the ability to work on issues for decades, such as landmines and human rights, and gotten remarkable results. Perhaps I am proudest of something that became known as the Leahy Law, which holds our defense and foreign aid spending up to the light of our values. How incredible it was to hear the chairman of the Joint Chiefs of Staff General Joseph Dunford speak at St. Michael's College and describe the difference that law has made overseas.

There are other stories that remind me that even for all the dysfunction of Washington we still make good things happen. Ed Barron authored nutrition bills over decades that have helped millions of poor and needy children. I could not have reauthorized VAWA to include protection for Native Americans and the LGBTQ community and to combat sex trafficking were it not for Kristine Lucius. I could not have passed the first reform of patent laws in fifty years were it not for Susan Davies and Aaron Cooper. And I have been fortunate to have a team of legislative assistants and committee staff, too numerous to list, that on issue after issue has made Vermont and our nation proud.

They were all led by my chiefs of staff, Paul Bruhn, Marty Franks, Sam Kinzer, John Podesta, Ellen Lovell, Luke Albee, Ed Pagano, and JP Dowd, and talented legislative directors like Janet Breslin, Eric Newsom, Theresa Alberghini, and Erica Chabot.

My long-serving deputy chief of staff, Ann Berry, is one of the finest managers and people Marcelle and I have ever met. Having served for multiple senators before coming to my office, she has a wealth of knowledge about the Senate and has helped countless young staffers throughout her career with her caring, no-nonsense advice. She has now risen to be the Secretary of the Senate, and I could not be prouder of her. She passed the torch to Annette Gillis, who has been an immense help running the office.

When I assumed the helm of the Agriculture Committee, I focused on revitalizing nutrition and conservation programs under its jurisdiction. Chuck Riemenschneider, John Podesta, Janet Breslin, Jim Cubie, and

Ed Barron led a team of staff that delved into those issues and have all left their legislative marks on nutrition, conservation, and dairy support programs in Vermont and the entire nation for many years to come.

I have been the beneficiary of incredible staff work on the Judiciary Committee over the years, from John Podesta and Ann Harkins to lawyers like Todd Stern, who went on to negotiate the Paris Climate Accords, and Cathy Russell, who later became Ambassador for Global Women's Issues and now is head of UNICEF. Bruce Cohen assembled and led the best team of legal minds and dedicated public servants for most of the twenty years that I served as chair or ranking member on Judiciary. Much of what I accomplished on Judiciary is due to the strategic and legal advice Bruce provided me. After the 9/11 attacks, Beryl Howell and Julie Katzman led a team of lawyers that crafted the Patriot Act, providing not only legal brilliance but also bringing to the table important law-enforcement prosecutorial experience. Later, Chan Park was an essential advisor on national security and privacy as we worked on reauthorizations of the Patriot Act. Jeremy Paris and Noah Bookbinder were a dynamic duo during these years. Tris Coffin toiled tirelessly on the committee and went on to be US attorney for Vermont, where he set off early alarm bells about the opioid crisis. Lisa Graves and Helaine Greenfeld managed a nominations group that remains a template for the committee today. Helaine's subsequent work guiding nominees through the nomination process is legendary. Ed Pagano, before rising to be my chief of staff, cut his teeth on the committee and was the force behind what is now known as the Leahy Bulletproof Vest grant program. Tara Magner and, subsequently, Anya McMurray knew the immigration code down to the last subsection. Kristine Lucius, one of the smartest and most dedicated public servants I have served with, led the staff for several years. After I had moved over to the Appropriations Committee, my chief counsel, David Pendle, led a smaller staff on Judiciary that was equally as impactful as a ranking member's full staff throughout the Trump administration and two impeachment trials. His insight and support from Raj Venkataramanan guided me as the presiding officer in that second trial in my capacity as president pro tempore of the Senate.

As vice chairman and now Chairman of Appropriations, these last six years have been some of the most enjoyable and substantive during my time in the Senate, in large part due to the excellent professional staff of the Appropriations Committee, led by Charles Kieffer and Chanda Betourney. Charles, following in his father's footsteps, is the consummate public servant. He is an institution of knowledge about federal programs, solving problems and getting to "yes" in negotiations on completing appropriations bills. Chanda, my deputy staff director and chief counsel on the committee, is one of the most talented legal minds I have met, and her calm demeanor and leadership matches her nickname from law school: the " Betourney General." I am also thankful to Jessica Berry, who returned to the committee, bringing a wealth of knowledge about federal programs and Vermont.

In Vermont, I had an office led by Tom Davis, Chuck Ross, and John Tracy, assisted throughout the years by staffers such as Bob Paquin, Liz Slayton, Ted Brady, Chris Saunders, Maggie Gendron, Tom Berry, Lisa Brighenti, and dozens of others. Joe Jamele and David Carle craftily managed my communications and press operation in Washington for most of my tenure. David is renowned among the press corps for the exhaustive background he provides reporters, and he is a masterful speechwriter. John Goodrow served faithfully as my press secretary and scheduler in Vermont over the span of three decades, and nobody had a better sense of what was important to the average Vermonter than John. And my Vermont casework team over the years has been second to none. Thousands and thousands of Vermonters, regardless of their political affiliation, were helped by dedicated case workers such as Kathy Martin, Kathy Bolduc, Katherine Long, and Graham Forward. Jack Rouille was there from the start, moving from the state's attorney's office to my Senate operation. We likely put over 100,000 miles on the road driving around Vermont together to events. His commonsense Vermont values were a guidepost, and I consider him more of a friend than a staffer.

I think of political campaigns, from the first and seemingly impossible race run with total perfection by Paul Bruhn, to 1986 when Bill Gray and Mary Beth Cahill joined the team. They all helped me to run and win what many considered to be the best campaigns of some of those election cycles. Carolyn Dwyer is the best political mind in Vermont. I am still in awe of my good fortune when she came to run my political operation in Vermont in 1998, and she has been with me since. Her passion, wit, and instincts have been invaluable to me and Marcelle. And Tina Stoll, the best fundraiser in Washington, provided us with the support we needed to win time after time. I am forever grateful to the many hours she has toiled with me over the past four decades.

In writing this book, I was lucky to rely on loyal alumni. Matt Gerson first demonstrated how I could lay out a chapter. Luke Albee, Ann Berry, Bruce Cohen, John Tracy, Ellen Lovell, John Goodrow, and so many others shared their memories of events over the years. Kevin McDonald, who has been present for decades of events at home and abroad and has been with us for so many family times, was indispensable. Erica Chabot, who has juggled my legislative accomplishments for years and is now my deputy chief of staff, brought many highlights together. Leah Gluskoter and Clara Kircher, who were with my office for many years, are an important part of this book. Patricia McLaughlin Smith, a close friend and staffer who started her career with me, also shared her memories to bring this book to life.

In the final weeks, I asked a few of my oldest friends to read through key chapters and a couple of folks to read from start to finish. My profound thanks to Luke Albee, Carolyn Dwyer, and Ed Pagano.

To my friends in the Senate and House who continue the fight, thank you for your service and your friendship. To my Senate colleagues, many who are no longer with us, I thank you for your mentorship and your countless contributions to our country.

To everyone in my native state of Vermont—there are no words. Thank you for trusting a thirty-four-year-old with the gift of representing you, and for keeping that gift alive through seven more elections. Thank you for allowing this Vermonter to represent you across six different decades in the US Senate.

To the road ahead,
Patrick Leahy

INDEX

ABOUT THE AUTHOR

PATRICK LEAHY was elected to the United States Senate in 1974 and is currently President Pro Tempore and Chairman of the Senate Appropriations Committee. He served for twenty years as chair or ranking member of the Senate Judiciary Committee, where he remains as the most senior Democrat. He is also the most senior Democrat on the Senate Agriculture Committee, where he previously served as chair for seven years. Senator Leahy has been married to Marcelle Pomerleau Leahy since 1962. They have a daughter, two sons, and five grandchildren. The Leahys live on a tree farm in Middlesex, Vermont.